⪻ CATO ⪼
SUPREME COURT
REVIEW

2010 — 2011

⟜ CATO ⟞
SUPREME COURT
REVIEW

2010—2011

ROGER PILON
Publisher

ILYA SHAPIRO
Editor in Chief

ROBERT A. LEVY
Associate Editor

TIMOTHY LYNCH
Associate Editor

WALTER OLSON
Associate Editor

DAVID H. RITTGERS
Associate Editor

WITHDRAWN

CENTER FOR CONSTITUTIONAL STUDIES

CATO
INSTITUTE

Washington, D.C.

THE CATO SUPREME COURT REVIEW (ISBN 978-1-935308-50-8) is published annually at the close of each Supreme Court term by the Cato Institute, 1000 Massachusetts Ave., N.W.,Washington, D.C. 20001-5403.

CORRESPONDENCE. Correspondence regarding subscriptions, changes of address, procurement of back issues, advertising and marketing matters, and so forth, should be addressed to:

Publications Department
The Cato Institute
1000 Massachusetts Ave., N.W.
Washington, D.C. 20001

All other correspondence, including requests to quote or reproduce material, should be addressed to the editor.

CITATIONS: Citation to this volume of the Review should conform to the following style: 2010-2011 Cato Sup. Ct. Rev. (2011).

DISCLAIMER. The views expressed by the authors of the articles are their own and are not attributable to the editor, the editorial board, or the Cato Institute.

INTERNET ADDRESS. Articles from past editions are available to the general public, free of charge, at www.cato.org/pubs/scr.

Cato Institute
1000 Massachusetts Ave., N.W.
Washington, D.C. 20001
www.cato.org

Contents

CONTENTS

THE OUTER BOUNDS OF CRIMINAL LAW

FEDERALISM, CIVIL PROCEDURE, AND THE PROPER JUDICIAL ROLE

THE YEAR TO COME

FOREWORD

Ten Years in Perspective

*Roger Pilon**

The Cato Institute's Center for Constitutional Studies is pleased to publish this tenth volume of the *Cato Supreme Court Review*, an annual critique of the Court's most important decisions from the term just ended, plus a look at the cases ahead—all from a classical Madisonian perspective, grounded in the nation's first principles, liberty and limited government. We release this volume each year at Cato's annual Constitution Day conference. And each year in this space I discuss briefly a theme that seemed to emerge from the Court's term or from the larger setting in which the term unfolded.

Although the Court heard several important cases over the past year, the term was not marked by high-profile, landmark decisions—which is just as well for us, because for reasons only a numerologist would understand, when you reach the ten-year mark of an undertaking, you want to pause, step back, and take stock, if only to try to gain a little perspective. And so I shall do so, forgoing the more focused discussion that is the usual fare in this space in favor of a more wide-ranging review. And where better to begin than with our inaugural volume's foreword, entitled "Restoring Constitutional Government." Audacious as that title might have seemed, it captured what we at Cato's Center for Constitutional Studies have taken as our mission—long-range, to be sure—since the center was founded in 1989. More modestly, but precisely, we have sought to play a part in changing the climate of ideas to one more conducive to that aim, since we take it as axiomatic that ideas matter: they have consequences.

* Roger Pilon is vice president for legal affairs at the Cato Institute, director of Cato's Center for Constitutional Studies, and publisher of the *Cato Supreme Court Review*.

Thus, in that inaugural volume I wrote that what distinguishes Cato's from other reviews, apart from its appearance soon after the term ends, is its perspective: "We will examine [the Court's] decisions and [upcoming] cases in the light cast by the nation's first principles—liberty and limited government—as articulated in the Declaration of Independence and secured by the Constitution, as amended. We take those principles seriously. Our concern is that the Court do the same." That it had not, for the better part of a century, was no better evidenced, we believed, than by noticing the Leviathan about us and then recurring, by way of contrast, to the Constitution's principal author, James Madison, who had promised in *Federalist* 45 that the powers of the new government would be "few and defined." Since the Court had long sanctioned and even abetted the transformation from limited to largely unlimited government, a sustained critique of its work from the perspective of classical liberalism was in order, we concluded, and we intended to provide it.

So how have we done—and how has the Court done—over the ensuing decade? As for us, not bad, if I may. As a benchmark, in the balance of that inaugural essay I outlined a general critique and agenda, beginning with the principles underpinning the Declaration, as incorporated at last in the structure of the Constitution through the Civil War Amendments, then turned to the social engineering schemes of the Progressives. In time those schemes were "constitutionalized" by the New Deal Court, not by amendment, as constitutionally required, but by legerdemain, following Franklin Roosevelt's infamous Court-packing threat. The evisceration of the doctrine of enumerated powers, the very foundation of constitutional legitimacy; the bifurcation of the Bill of Rights, combined with varying levels of judicial scrutiny; and the demise of the non-delegation doctrine all conspired to give us modern "constitutional law"—not to be confused with the Constitution. Thus emerged the modern executive state, dedicated far less to securing our rights and doing the few other things we'd authorized our government to do than to providing us with all manner of goods and services, reducing so many of us to government dependents.

It was a supine Court that emerged from the New Deal constitutional revolution, deferring to the political branches, federal and state alike. Over time, however, two schools of thought about the proper role of the Court took shape. Modern liberals urged continued judicial deference, except when "fundamental" rights were at issue—defined quite often not as the Framers would have defined them, drawing on the common law, but as reflections of egalitarian aspirations. In reaction, conservatives too urged judicial deference to the political branches, partly from resignation, but also, for many, from deep-seated antipathy to what they saw as liberal judicial "activism" on the rights side of things. Thus, they urged judicial "restraint," calling on the Court to secure only those rights that were expressly "in" the Constitution, thereby ignoring the vast body of unenumerated rights the Framers surely meant to be protected.

Since neither camp could be said to have grasped the Framers' essential vision, it fell to those of us in the reemerging school of classical liberals to chart a different course, one in which the Court would extricate itself from the mistaken strictures of *stare decisis* and return to the Constitution's first principles. That would mean, above all else, reviving the doctrine of enumerated powers, which the Framers understood as the very foundation of the Constitution, the method, by way of ratification, through which "We the People" authorized, instituted, *empowered*, and then *limited* the government that ratification brought into being. So fundamental was the doctrine that the Framers believed a bill of rights was not only unnecessary but dangerous: unnecessary because where there is no power there is, by implication, a right; and dangerous because the failure to enumerate all of our rights, which would be impossible, would be taken, by ordinary principles of legal construction, as implying that only those that were enumerated were to be protected.

And so we went for two years without a bill of rights, protected simply by the doctrine of enumerated powers. As a condition for ratification, however, several states insisted that a bill of rights be added. Madison drafted one during the first Congress; it was passed and sent to the states, ratified, and added to the Constitution in 1791. In it, of crucial importance, were the Ninth and Tenth Amendments, which summarized the Framers' philosophy of government. The Ninth made it clear that the enumeration in the Constitution of *certain* rights was not meant to be construed *to deny or disparage others retained by the people*—and a right can be "retained" only if it is first held, as clear an allusion to the natural rights foundation of the Constitution as one could hope to find. The Tenth made it equally clear, by contrast, that the federal government had only those powers that had been delegated to it by the people, as enumerated in the document, the rest being reserved to the states or the people. Thus, the doctrine of enumerated powers was reaffirmed. But of equal importance, the implication—that where there is no power there is a right, *whether enumerated or not*—was made explicitly clear by the Ninth Amendment. And with the ratification of the Civil War Amendments, that vision of individual liberty secured by limited government was at last imposed upon the states as well.

Thus, with that explication of the Constitution's first principles in view, we called upon the Court not only to revive the doctrine of enumerated powers but to abandon the spurious New Deal distinction between "fundamental" and "nonfundamental" rights and begin protecting both enumerated and unenumerated rights against federal and state actions alike. There, in a nutshell, was the classical liberal agenda.

Obviously, however, the Court could not pursue that agenda oblivious to the fact that it does not operate in a political vacuum. The Court may be the non-political branch, but its members are cognizant, of course, of their having neither sword nor purse but merely judgment, as Alexander Hamilton put it in *Federalist* 78. Yet judgment has a force all its own, to influence and change the climate of ideas, which in time constrains the political forces that brought us Leviathan, forces that in turn and in the end must free us from those shackles. In short, the Court cannot roll back Leviathan on its own, but it can put a brake on it and, by controlling its docket, chip away at its substance, all the while laying the intellectual and legal foundations for a revival of liberty through limited constitutional government.

*   *   *

In our pages, then, we have sought, insofar as we might, to encourage movement along those lines, as a few examples will illustrate. These examples are of two closely connected kinds. First, there are the general discussions, as in these forewords, which have covered a variety of subjects: "Substance and Method at the Court," "Politics and Law," "Facial vs. As-Applied Challenges," and the like. More important have been the annual B. Kenneth Simon Lectures in Constitutional Thought, which conclude the annual Constitution Day conferences at which this volume is released. Appearing in the next year's volume, these lectures afford a distinguished legal authority an opportunity to step back from the cases and issues of the day to reflect more broadly and deeply on the larger themes just discussed.

A perfect example was our inaugural Simon Lecture, "On Constitutionalism," delivered by Douglas H. Ginsburg, then the chief judge of the United States Court of Appeals for the District of Columbia Circuit. In his lecture Judge Ginsburg—noted for having coined the phrase, "the Constitution in exile"—developed many of the issues discussed above, from the evisceration of the doctrine of enumerated powers to the demise of the non-delegation doctrine, and more. The stage was thus set for the move from powers to rights, as discussed above, and for the next year's lecture by Professor Walter Dellinger, acting solicitor general under President Clinton, "The Indivisibility of Economic Rights and Personal Liberty." And a year after that, Professor Richard A. Epstein, whose seminal writings over the years have been so important for the revival of classical liberalism, took us to the great watershed in constitutional history with a lecture on "The Monopolistic Vices of Progressive Constitutionalism."

I would be remiss, of course, if I did not mention each of our Simon lecturers, since each has made a distinct and important contribution to this series: Professor Nadine Strossen, Judge Danny J. Boggs, Judge Janice Rogers Brown, Professor Randy E. Barnett (speaking of someone whose writings have been seminal in reviving classical liberalism), Professor Michael W. McConnell, and, in this volume, Professor William Van Alstyne. And this year we will hear from Judge Alex Kozinski, chief judge of the United States Court of Appeals for the Ninth Circuit, whose topic, "On Privacy and Technology," could not be more timely, even if the principles he will doubtless invoke in the course of discussing his subject are timeless.

The second way we have sought to encourage movement along the lines discussed above is of course through the bread-and-butter of the *Review*, the articles on specific cases the Court has handed down during the term just ended, and the annual "Looking Ahead" articles about cases coming up. Here the examples are so numerous that I can mention only a few by way of illustrating our aim, which is to both praise the Court when it gets it right and criticize it when it gets it wrong—our normative judgments grounded in the principles discussed above. Not that we always agree, even among ourselves. In fact, in cases where we think it useful to offer more than one view, we do. Thus, in the case of *Hamdan v. Rumsfeld*, we offered contrasting essays by Professors Martin S. Flaherty and John Yoo. And with *Boumediene v. Bush* we did likewise, featuring essay's by Professors Eric A. Posner and David D. Cole.

That is not an issue in the great range of cases, however, and especially so when the Court gets it quite wrong, as Professor Epstein demonstrated in the first essay of our very first volume when he made short work of the Court's egregious decision in the *Lake Tahoe* case, which once again butchered the Fifth Amendment's Takings Clause. Nor was it the case in the next essay in that volume, where Robert A. Levy, now Cato's chairman, tackled difficult sovereign immunity issues under the Eleventh Amendment to show how the Court got it wrong in *Federal Maritime Commission v. South Carolina State Ports Authority*. In fact, in those cases, as in a good many we've covered, the Court comes in for criticism in substantial part because it feels compelled to square its decision with a raft of precedents that ought really to be overturned, or else clearly distinguished. What better example than Professor Douglas W. Kmiec's essay, "*Gonzales v. Raich*: *Wickard v. Filburn* Displaced," unless it is Erik S. Jaffe's essay upbraiding the Court for its decision in *McConnell v. FEC*, which upheld the McCain-Feingold Act's restrictions on political speech in the name of campaign finance reform.

But we've praised the Court too, and increasingly so, I'm pleased to say. An early example, again from our inaugural volume, was Clint Bolick's essay, "School Choice: Sunshine Replaces the Cloud," the title of which speaks for itself. In our second volume, Professor Barnett's essay, "Justice Kennedy's Libertarian Revolution: *Lawrence v. Texas*," nicely captured how the *Lawrence* Court had abandoned its *Carolene Products* footnote-four distinction between "fundamental" and "nonfundamental" rights and its related "scrutiny theory" and instead spoke simply of liberty. It was a breath of fresh air in an unenumerated rights case. More recently, Clark Neily of the Institute for Justice had good reason to praise the Court in his essay, "*District of Columbia v. Heller*: The Second Amendment Is Back, Baby," as did Kenneth L. Marcus, in "The War between Disparate Impact and Equal Protection," a discussion of the Court's decision in *Ricci v. DeStefano* to uphold the claims of New Haven firefighters that the city had discriminated against them on the basis of race when it threw out the results of their officer advancement exams. And a final example of our giving the Court praise when praise is due—yet criticizing it at the same time—is the essay in last year's volume by James Bopp Jr. and Richard E. Coleson, "*Citizens United v. Federal Election Commission*: 'Precisely What *WRTL* Sought to Avoid,'" discussing another breath of fresh air, albeit mixed, coming in the extraordinarily and unnecessarily complex area of modern campaign finance law.

*   *   *

Turning then to our second question above—How has the Court done over the decade since we began?—as this brief survey suggests, the record, not surprisingly, has been mixed. And of course it is not "the same" Court it was when we began. In fact, mid-way it changed markedly, with the resignation of Justice Sandra Day O'Connor in 2005 and, shortly thereafter, the death of Chief Justice William Rehnquist, followed by the nominations and confirmations of Chief Justice John Roberts and Justice Samuel Alito and then, in successive years, the ascensions of Justices Sonia Sotomayor and Elena Kagan. Whereas the Rehnquist Court, in its final iteration, had been "the same" Court for eleven years, the Roberts Court, in its short life so far, has already changed twice. Such changes are said to make a difference, even if, in principle, they should not.

That issue aside, looking at specific areas of our law, the Court's protection of religious liberty has been quite good—a conspicuous exception being last year's decision in *Christian Legal Society v. Martinez*. And, for the most part, it has protected speech, not only traditional speech rights in "controversial" cases but, in recent years, as just noted, the political speech that campaign finance regulations threatened. On that front there is far more to be done, but we are hopeful that a majority of the current Court will continue to see that political speech and campaign finance law are intimately connected.

Several critics have noted the Roberts Court's "business friendly" rulings, the implication being that the Court has ruled on a basis other than the law. Yet as I point out in my essay in the present *Review*, ranging over the Court's five preemption decisions this past term, in three the Court found for the business interests, in two against them. (And I found one on each side to have been wrongly decided.) The Roberts Court may not always get the law right, but I see no evidence that it has a bias toward business interests—except insofar as it is recognizing that such interests are no less important than "personal" interests, which would be a welcomed shift from some recent Courts.

Another specific area in which the charge of political bias arises in some quarters is civil rights and, in particular, affirmative action. Here, the Roberts Court appears to be doing rather better than its predecessor at applying the Constitution's Equal Protection Clause. The 2007 Seattle and Louisville public school "diversity" decisions come to mind here—a welcomed shift from the University of Michigan rulings of 2003—as does the New Haven firefighters case mentioned above. By contrast, the Court's criminal law decisions remain quite mixed, in part because the Court is insufficiently critical of the legal underpinnings of the war on drugs. But we can be thankful, at least, that our right to have a gun for self-defense is now clearly protected under the Second Amendment, even against the states.

At a more general level, however, regarding how the Court is doing at reviving the doctrine of enumerated powers and securing both enumerated and unenumerated rights, as discussed above, the assessment is more difficult. Taking the rights side of things first, and unenumerated rights in particular, a decision like *Lawrence v. Texas*—in which the Court cut through the *Carolene Products* footnote-four nonsense in order to reach the essence of the matter, as any layman would—gives hope that the distinction between enumerated and unenumerated rights might be fading and that the Court might at last be grasping the theory of rights that underpins our entire constitutional order. But the decision and its methodology were something of an anomaly, and we haven't seen anything quite like it since the Court handed it down in 2003.

Regarding those *enumerated* rights that are treated like "poor relations" in the Bill of Rights—the apt description Chief Justice Rehnquist used for property rights in 1994—after a period in the '90s during which the Court better protected the rights of owners, things started to fall to pieces. The *Lake Tahoe* decision mentioned above was but a precursor for the three property rights disasters of 2005, culminating in the infamous *Kelo* decision, all of which Professor James W. Ely Jr. analyzed for us that year. And two years later, Professor Laurence H. Tribe examined a complex decision for us,

Wilkie v. Robbins, showing in exquisite detail how the Court again failed to protect property rights or afford *Bivens* remedies for an owner the federal government had harassed for nearly a decade as it sought an easement over his property, all the while ignoring the Fifth Amendment's compensation requirement.

Turning at last to that most fundamental of constitutional concerns, the demise of the doctrine of enumerated powers, a bit of context is required. In 1995, in *United States v. Lopez*, the Rehnquist Court, for the first time in 58 years, revived enumerated powers federalism, holding that Congress had exceeded its power under the Commerce Clause. Five years later the Court reinforced that decision in *United States v. Morrison*. Although neither decision went to the heart of the matter—indeed, they changed little on the ground since they both held that the power at issue belonged to the states rather than to the federal government—many of us hoped nonetheless that the process of reviving the doctrine of enumerated powers had at least begun, as some of the language from those opinions suggested.

Alas, it was not to be. As mentioned above, in 2005 in *Gonzales v. Raich* the Court went the other way, holding that Congress, under its power to regulate interstate commerce, could prohibit Angel Raich from growing marijuana on her own property for medicinal purposes, consistent with California state law, even though the marijuana was no part of commerce, much less interstate commerce. It was a breathtaking decision, but perfectly consistent with the rationale behind the modern regulatory state.

The Court's decision did not end the debate, however. In fact, if anything it only enlivened it, making it stronger for the next thing to come along, and come along it did—Obamacare, followed soon thereafter by federal deficits and debt as far as the eye could see. And so, with the rise of the Tea Party and more, the debate spread far beyond the confines of Court watchers, to the media and the population in general. Does Congress, under its power to regulate interstate commerce, really have the power to order us to buy a product from a private vendor—any product? A Congress whose powers are "few and defined"? Is this how we got these massive deficits and debt—our modern Leviathan? At this writing, two appellate courts are split on the Obamacare question. But the debate is already well beyond the courts. It is not the debate of 20 years ago, or even a decade ago. The climate of ideas is changing, in the direction of liberty through constitutionally limited government. And that is good.

*   *   *

I would be remiss, once again, if I did not pay tribute to four men who, more than any others, have been responsible for the character and quality of this *Review*. Our first editor in chief, James Swanson, who organized, packaged, and promoted the first and second volumes of the *Review*, as well as the first two Constitution Day conferences, was responsible for everything from selecting the authors and speakers, editing their essays, and contributing essays himself, to choosing the format and color schemes for the series. He is a scholar and a bookman of the first order, who left us, in fact, to pursue his first love, the life of Abraham Lincoln (they share the same birthday), and to complete his magnificent *Manhunt: The 12-Day Chase for Lincoln's Killer*, which went on to be a national bestseller. I treasure James, because he was there at the beginning.

He was followed by another University of Chicago man—law, not the college, as with James—Mark Moller, who came to us from a distinguished appellate practice at Gibson, Dunn & Crutcher. A common law scholar who had studied at Cambridge under the noted English legal historian J.H. Baker, Mark was for four years the consummate detail man, whose judgment in the most complicated of cases I came to rely on. Indeed, so good was he—developing a specialty in class-action litigation while he was with us—that we lost him to academia, where he holds forth now at the DePaul University College of Law back in Chicago.

Speaking of Chicago, the law school at the university named after that great city rescued us once again in the form of our third editor-in-chief, Ilya Shapiro, the impressiveness of whose credentials—Princeton, London School of Economics, Chicago Law—is exceeded only by his boundless energy and ability. Not only has he done all the administrative work that has been necessary to turn out a first-class review barely two months after the Court's term ends, contributing to it himself, but he has overseen our ever-growing amicus brief docket as well, all the while publishing beyond Cato's presses, appearing regularly in the media, and delivering over 50 law school speeches in the past year alone. And there's more, but his modesty precludes me from delivering it!

Finally, beyond the confines of Cato is a man who has been with us year in and year out, Tom Goldstein, the impresario of SCOTUSblog and so much more. One of Washington's leading Supreme Court litigators, Tom is the go-to man if you want to know something—anything—about the Court, from its history to its docket to—you name it. He has been exceedingly generous with us, his specialty being our "Looking Ahead" essays and Constitution Day conference panels. Tom's expertise and insights have been invaluable.

I have been fortunate to have had at my side these four extraordinary men, a sense of whose work I hope to have conveyed in this all-too-brief foreword. Now please enjoy the rest of this tenth annual *Cato Supreme Court Review.*

Introduction

Ilya Shapiro*

This is the tenth volume of the *Cato Supreme Court Review*, the nation's first in-depth critique of the Supreme Court term just ended. We release this journal every year in conjunction with our annual Constitution Day symposium, about two and a half months after the previous term ends and two weeks before the next one begins. We are proud of the speed with which we publish this tome—authors of articles about the last-decided cases have no more than a month to provide us full drafts—and of its accessibility, at least insofar as the Court's opinions allow. This is not a typical law review, after all, whose prolix submissions use more space for obscure footnotes than for article text. Instead, this is a book of articles about law intended for everyone from lawyers and judges to educated laymen and interested citizens—and even Chief Justice John Roberts, who this past summer questioned law reviews' utility and relevance.[1]

And we are happy to confess our biases: We approach our subject matter from a classical Madisonian perspective, with a focus on individual liberty, property rights, and federalism, and a vision of a government of delegated, enumerated, and thus limited powers. We also try to maintain a strict separation of politics (and policy) and law; just because something is good policy doesn't mean it's legal, and vice versa. Similarly, certain decisions must necessarily be left to the political process: We aim to be governed by laws, not

* Senior Fellow in Constitutional Studies, Cato Institute, and Editor-in-Chief, *Cato Supreme Court Review*.

[1] Chief Justice John G. Roberts, Remarks at the Fourth Circuit Court of Appeals Conference (Jun. 25, 2011) (video available at http://www.c-span.org/Events/Annual-Fourth-Circuit-Court-of-Appeals-Conference/10737422476-1/). I happen to agree with this critique generally but, of course, don't consider our *Review* to be in the class of publications the Chief Justice was criticizing: the traditional law-school-based, student-run academic journals.

lawyers, so just as a good lawyer will present all plausibly legal options to his client, a good public official will recognize that the ultimate buck stops with him.

*   *   *

October Term 2010 produced a striking amount of unanimity and near-unanimity, a phenomenon possibly related to the relatively low-key nature of the term but also perhaps to Chief Justice Roberts's long-expressed desire for the Court to speak with more of one voice. Of the 80 cases with decisions on the merits—75 after argument and five summary reversals—38 had no dissenters (48 percent, about the same as last year), 10 had only one dissenter (13 percent), and 12 more had but two (15 percent). That means that three-quarters of the opinions went 7-2 or better, which is higher than any term in recent memory (OT09 was the previous high at 71 percent, but OT08 was 54 percent).[2] While some commentators tried to create controversy by accusing the Court's "conservatives" of a pro-business bias, such entreaties fell flat given that so many allegedly anti-little-guy cases (including the main holding of *Wal-Mart v. Dukes*) were unanimously decided.

Indeed, only 16 cases went 5-4 (20 percent, about the same as last year), but of course these included most of the highest-profile ones like the Grand Canyon State trio of *Arizona Christian School Tuition Organization v. Winn*, *Chamber of Commerce v. Whiting*, and *Arizona Free Enterprise v. Bennett*. Equally interestingly, the total number of dissenting votes was notably low, with an average decision producing only 1.34 justices in dissent, about the same as last year but down from 1.70 over the preceding decade. Neither Chief Justice Roberts nor Justice Elena Kagan wrote a solo dissent—nor, curiously, any concurrences—and after six full terms on the Court, the Chief Justice has still never been on the short end of an 8-1 (or 7-1) ruling.

Justice Anthony Kennedy was, unsurprisingly, the justice most often on the winning side of a case (94 percent), just ahead of the Chief Justice (91 percent). Even more notably, Kennedy was in the

---

[2] This includes five 6-2 cases, four 7-1 cases, and 18 8-0 cases. All statistics taken from SCOTUSblog, Stat Pack for October Term 2010, available at http://www.scotusblog.com/2011/06/final-october-term-2010-stat-pack-available (Jun. 27, 2011).

majority in 14 of the 16 5-4 decisions—all those that divided on "ideological" lines (ten times with the "conservatives," four with the "liberals," but none in "unconventional" alignments). Justice Ruth Bader Ginsburg took over from retired Justice John Paul Stevens as most likely to dissent (26 percent of all cases and 50 percent of cases with dissenters). The justices most likely to agree were the pairs most recently appointed, by Presidents George W. Bush and Barack Obama, respectively: The Chief Justice and Justice Samuel Alito voted together, at least in judgment, in 76 of 79 merits cases (96 percent), while Justices Sonia Sotomayor and Kagan were together at least in part in 47 of 50 cases (94 percent). Justices Ginsburg and Alito found themselves on opposite sides most often, voting together in only 50 of 80 cases (62.5 percent). What's more, the four pairings who were least likely to agree all include Justice Ginsburg.

Looking beyond the statistics, this was of course the first term for Justice Kagan. After a somewhat tumultuous confirmation process—the 37 votes against her were the most ever for a successful Democratic nominee—Kagan quickly settled in to the Court's routines. Not unexpectedly for a rookie justice—and one who was recused from 26 cases—Kagan wrote the fewest opinions of anyone, just seven for the majority (all in relatively low-profile cases) and three dissents. She also asked the fewest questions of any justice save, of course, the always-silent Justice Clarence Thomas. The most notable of her writings came on the last day of the term, when she issued—and read from the bench—the dissent for four justices in *Arizona Free Enterprise* (the matching-public-campaign-funds case). Accusing the petitioners of "chutzpah," Kagan continued an unbroken line of left-wing support for all sorts of election campaign regulations. As Kagan further gains her judicial legs, we can expect more of the wit with which she approaches her work and, agree with the result or not, a clear and concise writing style.

Justice Sotomayor too, in her sophomore year, is starting to find her own voice. Not only did she ask the third-most number of questions (after Justices Antonin Scalia and Stephen Breyer), but she had the second-most number of concurrences (after Scalia). Clearly, she's not holding back like Justice Alito did his first couple of years. Perhaps showing her background as a prosecutor and district court judge, she wrote the Court's opinion in two Fourth Amendment cases, *Michigan v. Bryant* and *JDB v. North Carolina*, as well as the dissents in three preemption cases, *Bruesewitz v. Wyeth*, *PLIVA v. Mensing*, and *Chamber of Commerce v. Whiting*. Curiously, Justice Sotomayor joined the "conservative" majority in *Sorrell v. IMS Health*, the prescription-related commercial speech case—one of the few times she and Kagan were on opposite sides.

Turning to the *Review*, the volume begins, as always, with the text of the previous year's B. Kenneth Simon Lecture in Constitutional Thought, which in 2010 was delivered by Professor William Van Alstyne of William and Mary Law School. Having observed the four recent Supreme Court confirmation hearings, Van Alstyne analyzes "Clashing Visions of the 'Living' Constitution" to determine "the proper scope of judicial review of constitutional questions." Reducing the multifarious theories on judicial review to two—"opportunists" and "obligationists"—Van Alstyne assails both liberals and conservatives to describe how our constitutional discourse has detoured from interpreting the text of our Founding document and, when necessary, amending it via Article V. "My concern," he says, "is that we may have gotten so accustomed to the 'exogenous' constitution that the amendment process has itself begun to recede as down a rabbit hole, as in *Alice in Wonderland*, and the country, frankly, is significantly less well off on that account."

We move then to the 2010 term, with five articles on the constitutional provision that had the highest profile at the Court over the past year, the First Amendment. Temple University Law School's David Post, also a member of the *Cato Supreme Court Review*'s editorial board, provides a provocative essay on the "violent videogames case," *Brown v. Entertainment Merchants Association*. In *Brown*, the Court struck down a California statute that prohibited the sale of so-called violent videogames to minors because it was overbroad and tried to remove a new type of speech from First Amendment protection. After on overview of the Court's convoluted obscenity jurisprudence, Post evaluates the four very different views on the case provided by Justice Scalia's majority opinion, Justice Alito's concurrence, and the respective dissents of Justices Thomas and Breyer. Pronouncing himself somewhat of an outsider to the field—he specializes in internet and intellectual property law, with which this case obviously overlaps—Post teases out the "peculiarities" and "doctrinal oddities" in our First Amendment doctrine. After trying to reconcile what often seems contradictory, he gives the Court "two cheers" for its ruling.

University of Kentucky law professor Paul Salamanca then examines the "offensive funeral protest case," *Snyder v. Phelps*. In *Snyder*, the Court affirmed the lower court's ruling that the bizarre and often hurtful protesting techniques of a particular religious sect still constituted protected speech. Salamanca argues that the case was not particularly difficult doctrinally—even if the uniquely disturbing facts put pressure on the Court to reach the opposite result—especially once the Court found that the subject of the protests (homosexuality and America's wars) was a matter of public concern. That the demonstrations, which accorded with all municipal regulations, took place surrounding a private military funeral was simply of no moment for First Amendment purposes. "The Court therefore deserves credit," Salamanca concludes, "for adhering to previously recognized principles and for not constructing an artificial category to sustain an otherwise desirable result." Still, the decision was fairly "minimalist" and "left it to future cases to clarify the law in the area between the categories of protected and unprotected speech."

Professor Joel Gora of Brooklyn Law School, who has had a long involvement in campaign-finance litigation while in high-ranking positions with the ACLU and NYCLU, has contributed a detailed yet engaging piece on *Arizona Free Enterprise v. Bennett*. Known as the "Arizona public financing case," *Arizona Free Enterprise* involved a challenge to that state's "clean elections" scheme, whereby qualifying candidates could choose to have their campaigns funded by the government, rather than relying on their own or contributed funds. The problem was that every dollar raised or spent by that candidate's opponent *or independent groups supporting that opponent* triggered an equal amount of public funding for the "clean" candidate. Such a program would seem to be foreclosed, however, by the Court's 2009 decision in *Davis v. FEC*, the Millionaire's Amendment case, and indeed that's how the Court ruled (by the same 5-4 margin). Gora notes that "most 'triggers' are now presumptively unconstitutional, whether they result in more public funding or higher private-funding limits," but identifies a host of intriguing legal and political questions that remain open.

A less predictable First Amendment case was *Sorrell v. IMS Health*, wherein the Court grappled with its commercial speech doctrine in light of a Vermont statute—and, implicitly, several others like it—

that restricted the access of pharmaceutical companies to information about doctors' prescribing habits. (The companies use this information for marketing purposes, a practice known as "detailing.") The Washington Legal Foundation's chief counsel, Richard Samp, begins his treatment of *Sorrell* by noting a "remarkable trend" in First Amendment jurisprudence: conservative justices are now much more likely to strike down government speech restrictions than liberal ones—while these roles were largely reversed a few decades ago. And so it went here, as the Court struck down the Vermont speech regulations for being impermissibly viewpoint- and speaker-based—although, as I noted above, Justice Sotomayor joined the "conservative" majority (in one of only three cases where she and Justice Kagan differed). "While conservatives appear to be contemplating expanded commercial speech rights," Samp concludes, "liberals . . . appear ready to abolish the entire commercial speech doctrine."

Next, in a case that ended up not quite reaching its central First Amendment issue, Tim Keller, who directs the Institute for Justice's Arizona chapter, covers *Arizona Christian Scholarship Trust Organization v. Winn.* IJ represented one of the parties here, in a long-running legal saga involving an Establishment Clause challenge to the tax credit Arizona gives to those who donate to specially created charities that provide scholarships to a wide variety of K-12 schools. The Court ultimately ruled 5-4 that the plaintiffs lacked standing because no state funds actually went to religious institutions. Keller's article weaves together personal perspectives, policy perspectives, and legal doctrine to contextualize this latest battle over school choice. While the larger war will continue in other arenas, Keller generally approves of the Court's disposition here—particularly Justice Kennedy's distinction between state subsidies and tax credits. To hold otherwise, after all, would be to concede that the government owns all income in the first instance but allows taxpayers to retain some of it. "Fortunately," Keller concludes, "the money in your wallet still belongs to you and not the government."

From a First Amendment case that barely grazed the First Amendment, we go to a criminal law case that wasn't really about criminal law. *Bond v. United States* is your typical sordid tale of adultery, toxic chemicals, and federalism—or, as author John Eastman writes, "Don't mess with the husband of someone who works in a chemical lab!" The unique feature here is that instead of being prosecuted for assault or attempted murder, the defendant—who used the aforementioned toxins to injure her husband's paramour (her own erstwhile best friend)—was brought up on federal charges of violating the law implementing an international chemical weapons treaty. The Supreme Court wisely and unanimously held that Mrs. Bond does indeed have standing to challenge the constitutionality of the statute under which she was convicted. That is, she can raise a Tenth Amendment challenge even though she is not a state—because, as Justice Kennedy describes at some length (in a passage that should hearten those challenging Obamacare, among others), federalism is ultimately a means of protecting individual liberty. Eastman, law professor and former dean at Chapman University, says the case is an opportunity "for a further restoration of the principles of federalism that underlie our constitutional system." He also introduces a fascinating discussion about the scope of the treaty power that will likely heat up in future.

Cato's own David Rittgers makes his inaugural contribution to our house legal journal, writing about *Connick v. Thompson*. This case presents the unfortunate situation of a man who was wrongly convicted of murder and served 18 years in jail (14 on death row)—all due to prosecutorial misconduct. To add grievous insult to that nonremediable injury, the Supreme Court held 5-4 that John Thompson could not recover his jury-awarded $14 million dollars because the district attorney's office that framed him could not be liable for failing to train its prosecutors based solely on this one instance of not disclosing exculpatory evidence to defense counsel. Rittgers characterizes both the Court's ruling and the "current regime of immunity for constitutional violations" as an "injustice" resulting from the unfortunate convergence of a warped concept of prosecutorial immunity and a similarly flawed doctrine of municipal liability—which treats public officials' tortious actions differently than those of private entities. He suggests that legislative reform may be the best avenue by which to fix a criminal justice system that "locks up not just too many people, but too often the wrong people."

Orin Kerr of the George Washington University Law School presents a fascinating article on the law's development through the prism of two of this year's Fourth Amendment cases, *Davis v. United States* (which Kerr himself argued before the Court) and *Camreta v. Greene*.

Davis concerned the scope of the exclusionary rule in criminal cases, while *Camreta* involved standing and mootness issues in civil litigation. Kerr argues that both cases "deal with the basic tension between the costs of Fourth Amendment remedies and the needs of law-developing litigation" and finds a common theme: The Court is now "more focused on limiting short-term remedial costs than the long-term needs of elaborating Fourth Amendment law." That is, the Court is marginally more concerned about getting a particular case right and not imposing the short-term social cost of freeing guilty people than setting administrable rules for the future or establishing robust protections for civil liberties. "Such concerns may seem abstract," Kerr summarizes, "But today's decisions on remedies will have a major impact on tomorrow's decisions about Fourth Amendment substance."

Switching gears, the publisher of this august journal, Roger Pilon, ventures "Into the Preemption Thicket Again," continuing a theme he started in these pages two years ago. Pilon's essay begins with an overview of "preemption as federal supremacy": Article I, Section 8 of the Constitution grants Congress certain limited powers that, under Article VI's Supreme Clause, trump state action to the contrary. "To better protect liberty," Pilon explains, "the Constitution institutes federalism, a system of dual sovereignty between the federal and state governments, sometimes pitting power against power, other times allowing overlapping power." The rub, of course, is identifying when it is that state law conflicts with federal law—particularly when it is alleged to have done so *implicitly* rather than *explicitly*. The Court grappled with that problem five times this term—in areas of law ranging from immigration to arbitration, drug labeling and vaccines to seatbelt design—but, according to Pilon, only solved it correctly three times. But "even if the Court does 'get it right' in a preemption case," he observes, "that does not mean, of course, that the decision necessarily secures or advances the liberty the Constitution was written, at bottom, to secure."

Case Western's Jonathan Adler, another member of the *Review*'s editorial board and the third "Volokh Conspirator" in these pages (the others are Post and Kerr—while Randy Barnett and Ilya Somin have also contributed in recent years), takes a look at the term's "global warming case." In *American Electric Power v. Connecticut*, a number of states, New York City, and three conservation organizations sued several electricity companies, alleging that the power producers' greenhouse gas emissions constituted a public nuisance. While similar suits had been dismissed around the country, the Second Circuit allowed this case to proceed—until the Supreme Court unanimously reversed, on the narrow ground that Congress's environmental legislation (such as the Clean Air Act) "displaced" claims under the federal common law of nuisance. As Adler puts it, the Court rejected "an ambitious effort to turn the federal common law of nuisance into a judicially administered environmental regulatory regime." While the Court's reasoning didn't go as far as Cato would have liked—we argued that the plaintiffs' claims constituted a non-justiciable political question asking courts to resolve competing economic, environmental, and ethical concerns—global warming defendants are safe unless Congress withdraws EPA authority over greenhouse gases. Because the question of the degree to which human influence on climate is desirable or acceptable—and what remedial measures are needed—lie "far beyond the capability of common-law courts," Adler concludes, "we have to leave climate change in the hands of the political process."

In our final article about the 2010-11 term, McGuire Woods partner Andrew Trask examines *Wal-Mart v. Dukes*, the latest case that has driven left-wing activists to apoplexy over the Roberts Court's alleged pro-business bias. In *Dukes*, the Court rejected an attempt to certify a class of 1.5 million women because their alleged claims of sex discrimination failed the "commonality" prong of the applicable federal rule of civil procedure. That is, they failed to prove that Wal-Mart was engaging in some common practice that was harming all women. Dissenting from the Ninth Circuit ruling that the Court ended up reversing, Chief Judge Alex Kozinski—whose B. Kenneth Simon Lecture you'll get to read in these pages next year—remarked that the putative class members "have little in common but their sex and this lawsuit." Trask, who literally wrote the book on class actions (*The Class Action Playbook*, with Brian Anderson), calls *Dukes* "an important decision"—not least because of the size of the claimed class and large sums of money at issue—but predicts that it won't really change litigation strategy. "All it has done is make the game of certification a little fiercer."

Our volume concludes with a look ahead to October Term 2011 by former solicitor general Greg Garre, now head of Supreme Court practice at Latham & Watkins, and Roman Martinez, fresh off a

9

clerkship with Chief Justice Roberts and now a Latham associate. The Court's docket as of this writing already presents a more interesting mix of legal issues than we saw this past term, including broadcast indecency (the return of the "fleeting expletives" saga), the use of mandatory union fees on political activities, and religious institutions' "ministerial exception" to employment discrimination laws—and that's just the First Amendment docket. The Court will also take up cutting-edge criminal procedure questions involving warrantless GPS surveillance, jailhouse strip searches, and ineffective legal assistance relating to plea bargains, as well as its usual diet of regulatory preemption, sovereign immunity, arbitration, and intellectual property cases. There's even a quirky yet diplomatically significant case about whether judges can require the State Department to identify the birth country of someone born in Jerusalem to be Israel. And all that is before we even get to what Garre and Martinez call the "elephant in the room," the constitutional challenges to the Patient Protection and Affordable Care Act (Obamacare). Indeed, the room contains a veritable herd of elephants, with cases involving affirmative action, gay marriage, and Arizona's S.B. 1070 all on the horizon. It could turn out to be the term of the century!

*   *   *

This is the fourth volume of the *Cato Supreme Court Review* that I have edited—matching the output of my longest-tenured predecessor. While the learning curve keeps flattening, the amount of work has increased in parallel with the constitutional issues raised by various government actions. There are thus many people to thank for their contributions to this endeavor. I first need to thank our authors, without whom there obviously would not be anything to edit or read. My gratitude also goes to my colleagues at Cato's Center for Constitutional Studies, Bob Levy, Tim Lynch, Walter Olson, and David Rittgers, who continue to provide valuable counsel in areas of law with which I'm less familiar. A big thanks to research assistant Jonathan Blanks for making the trains run on time and keeping me honest, as well as to legal associates Trevor Burrus, Chaim Gordon, Paul Jossey, Anna Mackin, and Nicholas Mosvick, and to legal interns Matthew Carter, Mario Cerame, and A.K. Shauku, for doing the more thankless (except here) tasks. Neither the *Review* nor our Constitution Day symposium would be what they are without them.

Finally, thanks to Roger Pilon, the indefatigable founder of Cato's legal policy shop and of this now well-established journal. I don't know how Roger envisioned the *Review*'s content or reputation in its tenth year—or indeed how likely he thought it would be that we'd reach this milestone—but I'd like to think that his decade-younger self would be pleased. (You can read his reflections in the foreword to this volume.) I was incredibly fortunate that Roger plucked me off the Big Law treadmill when he did—as he reminds me each time we hear the latest discouraging news about the legal market—and much appreciate the opportunities he and Cato have given me.

I reiterate our hope that this collection of essays will secure and advance the Madisonian first principles of our Constitution, giving renewed voice to the Framers' fervent wish that we have a government of laws and not of men. In so doing, we hope also to do justice to a rich legal tradition in which judges, politicians, and ordinary citizens alike understood that the Constitution reflects and protects the natural rights of life, liberty, and property, and serves as a bulwark against the abuse of government power. In these uncertain times when it seems so difficult to rein in (largely unconstitutional) federal spending and reform our unsustainable entitlement programs, it is more important than ever to remember our proud roots in the Enlightenment tradition.

We hope you enjoy this tenth volume of the *Cato Supreme Court Review*.

Clashing Visions of a "Living" Constitution: Of Opportunists and Obligationists

by William Van Alstyne*

I

I am honored to have been invited to give the Cato Institute's ninth annual B. Kenneth Simon Lecture in Constitutional Thought and to join the distinguished judges and scholars who have preceded me in this series. Because this is an opportunity to step back and reflect on more timeless constitutional questions, I've chosen as my subject clashing visions of a "living" Constitution. And yet, however timeless, the subject is especially timely now since we've been privy recently to no fewer than four Senate confirmation proceedings in as many years respecting who should be sitting on our Supreme Court.[1] Those hearings have produced a broad range of views about whether we have a "living" constitution and, in particular, about the proper scope of judicial review of constitutional questions.

* Lee Professor of Law, William & Mary Law School. This is an edited version of remarks delivered as the ninth annual B. Kenneth Simon Lecture in Constitutional Thought at the Cato Institute on September 16, 2010.

[1] See, for a fair sample, the following references for the four most recent confirmation hearings of Supreme Court nominees: 1. The Nomination of Elena Kagan to be an Associate Justice of the Supreme Court of the United States, Before the S. Comm. on the Judiciary, 111th Cong. (2010); 2. The Nomination of Sonia Sotomayor to be an Associate Justice of the Supreme Court of the United States, Before the S. Comm. on the Judiciary, 111th Cong. (2009); 3. The Nomination of Samuel A. Alito, Jr. to be an Associate Justice of the Supreme Court of the United States, Before the S. Comm. on the Judiciary, 109th Cong. (2006); 4. The Nomination of John G. Roberts, Jr. to be Chief Justice of the United States, Before the S. Comm. on the Judiciary, 109th Cong. (2005). Moreover, there are a number of observers who also regard it as entirely appropriate for senators to vote "for" or "against" a Supreme Court nominee for political or ideological reasons. See, e.g., David Greenberg, "Admit the Obvious: It's a Political Process—Ideology Governs Judicial Confirmation. Let's Say So." Wash. Post, July 18, 2004, at B3.

Upward of 20 "schools of thought" on the "right" role for justices have emerged in recent decades, mostly from the legal academy, although shortly I will reduce that number to two—opportunists and obligationists. Before I do, however, I will treat very briefly just two or three of the main strains of constitutional interpretation, simply to give a flavor of the recent debate.

One such school goes by the ungainly but revealing name of "noninterpretivism." This innovative neologism emerged a few decades ago, originally in a well-noted essay by Stanford law professor Thomas Grey, and then again in some additional spirited writing by Michael Perry at the Northwestern Law School, who developed the theory in several lengthy articles.[2] As the name suggests, noninterpretivism is best understood as opposed to, well, interpretivism— the idea that a judge should interpret and apply the text before him, the text of *this* Constitution, not least because the oath he takes is an oath to support *this*—not even "the"—but *this* Constitution. But to do that, to interpret and apply the actual text, when you want with all your heart to make it a "living" constitution, is to be ruled by that dreaded "dead hand of the past." And so if the actual Constitution is to come alive, the literal text has to be treated as an altogether subordinate matter, which is precisely what the noninterpretivists prescribe.

Reduced to its essence, this is a strange doctrine, is it not? We do not purport even to be "interpreting" the particular text we mean to render in some *non*interpretive fashion. To be sure, we *are* presuming to deliver ourselves a statement about the supreme law of the land, pertaining to what governments and we may and may not do. But at the same time, we are *liberated* from the despair of textual uncertainty and, likewise, from the tyranny of endlessly contestable history. We're *free* to invent our "living" constitution.

Fortunately, noninterpretivism, as such, did not long endure. And I claim at least some modest share of credit for its decline insofar as I wrote to Tom Grey and to Michael Perry and put into each of those letters a mischievous footnote—a question asking merely

---

[2] See, e.g., Thomas Grey, Do We Have an Unwritten Constitution? 27 Stan. L. Rev. 703 (1975); Thomas Grey, Symposium on Interpreting the Ninth Amendment: The Uses of an Unwritten Constitution, 64 Chi.-Kent L. Rev. 211 (1988); Michael Perry, Noninterpretive Review in Human Rights Cases: A Functional Justification, 56 N.Y.U. L. Rev. 278 (1981).

which part of the Constitution was it that they were "*non*-interpreting" that day, insofar as they did not purport to be interpreting anything at all in the *actual* Constitution.

But no sooner had noninterpretivism declined than it was replaced by a school calling itself "nonoriginal interpretivism." Old wine in new bottles, it defined itself, like its predecessor, by what it was not—*originalism*;[3] the idea, as it eventually emerged, that the Constitution should be interpreted according to the original public meaning of its terms. It is called "nonoriginal interpretivism" because one is purporting to use the particular clauses as they actually appear in the document, at least as a forensic point of departure, if scarcely little more. But one is then proudly not to be ruled by the unreliable, possibly irresponsible, and almost always difficult-to-recover material of the original drafters or ratifiers in rendering *the* "interpretation" that appears to be the better or the "best." And so we're "freed," once again, to reimagine our "living" Constitution.

Beyond those two closely related schools is a third that warrants notice before we take up our main project. Less an interpretive doctrine than a frank acknowledgment of modern constitutional reality, it is a theory about how the Supreme Court has come to "amend" the Constitution outside the amendment process prescribed in Article V. It was formulated by Bruce Ackerman, a distinguished and exceedingly well-published member of the Yale law faculty.[4] And it begins by admitting, candidly, that much of modern "constitutional law" bears little correspondence to the Constitution itself as originally understood. Those changes, moreover, have come about without any *formal* change in the document—including any subsequent amendments, pursuant to the express formal provisions of Article V—to account for and document the decisions that produced the actual changes.

---

[3] See Originalism: A Quarter-Century of Debate (Stephen G. Calabresi ed., 2007). For what may be the most recent work deriding a different but not unrelated doctrine, "formalism," and belittling "formalists" (i.e., those who foolishly think that the text, and what was said of it by its contemporary drafters and ratifiers, are the proper focus for adjudicating constitutional disputes), see Brian Tamanaha, Beyond the Formalist-Realist Divide: The Role of Politics in Judging (2010).

[4] See Bruce Ackerman, The Storrs Lecture: Discovering the Constitution, 93 Yale L.J. 1013 (1984); Bruce Ackerman, 2006 Oliver Wendell Holmes Lecture: The Living Constitution, 120 Harv. L. Rev. 1737, 1794–98, 1809–12 (2007). Bruce Ackerman, We the People: Transformations 403–08 (1998).

But Ackerman's is not simply a descriptive account of constitutional history over the past century. No, he went on to declare forcefully that the Court's decisions could *rightly* be seen as solid "nontextual amendments"—"Ackerman amendments," one might say. His idea was, essentially, that if, through sustained elections like those that returned President Franklin Delano Roosevelt to office three consecutive times, the country's attention is riveted to certain crises of a constitutional sort, then by repeatedly returning to office a president who has made a political point of wanting a change in constitutional law *through the judicial appointment process,* if it meets with sufficient political approval (as evidenced by presidential and senatorial elections), the "changes" eventually effected by a Supreme Court thus created serve as "real" amendments. As such, it would be inappropriate for a later Court to revisit those changes, he added. Moreover, that such "amendments" are neither in the text nor brought about like real amendments is irrelevant because this is the way—or at least one equally valid way—in which you keep the Constitution "alive."[5] Indeed, one could say that it's the ultimate "politicization" of the Constitution.

Rather than continue, however, with yet more misbegotten recent efforts to keep our Constitution "alive," let me suggest that the field of constitutionalists may be divided usefully into two main generic groups: opportunists and obligationists. And opportunists, to be clear, are not of a single ideological hue; some are on the left, others on the right. Yet those two "opposing" camps share a common bond: they both "find" things in the Constitution that they *want* to find and ignore things that are inconvenient.

Opportunists "on the left" are hardly difficult to notice.[6] In fact, proponents of the noninterpretivist and nonoriginal interpretivist schools just discussed have been almost entirely self-identified with the left, especially in their promotion in recent decades of the Court's equal protection jurisprudence. But their opportunism goes much further back, as the Ackerman thesis indicates, focused as it is on

---

[5] Even now I can scarcely see this word in print without at once also "seeing" it in the original, namely, with Boris Karloff starring in his most famous role, exclaiming "It's alive!" as he jolted several thousand volts of electricity into the intimidating carcass of a soon-to-be-animated corpse, "the Frankenstein monster." Perhaps the reader might be spared this gruesome thought—then again, perhaps he ought not be!

[6] See, e.g., Ronald Dworkin, Law's Empire (1986).

the New Deal constitutional revolution as a "constitutional moment" amounting to a constitutional "amendment." Ackerman finds such politically driven, judicially crafted "amendments" perfectly acceptable, notwithstanding that this one "found" vast new congressional powers that restricted long-standing liberties—powers and restrictions that hadn't been found in the Constitution for some 150 years, but now suddenly appeared plain as day to those who looked long and hard enough.[7] Having "discovered" those powers (and ignored those rights), the political forces behind them were able at last to implement the New Deal programs the left had been promoting since the dawn of the Progressive Era.[8] In short, in finding the powers and restrictions they wanted to find, opportunists of the left emptied the Constitution of the limits the Framers had deliberately fashioned, thus bringing the document, to their mind, "alive."

Opportunists "on the right" seem at first blush more difficult to find, not least because they ordinarily count themselves interpretivists, originalists, and textualists. But a closer look reveals that many of them, too, are guilty of seeing what they want to see and ignoring what they want to ignore. Perhaps Judge Robert Bork, at a general level, best illustrates the opportunism on the right. Speaking of our "Madisonian dilemma," he wrote that our "first principle" as a nation is that "*in wide areas of life,* majorities are entitled to rule, if they wish, simply because they are majorities," whereas our "second principle" is "that there are nonetheless *some things* majorities must not do to minorities, *some areas of life* in which the individual must be free of majority rule."[9] That gets Madison exactly backwards. Madison stood for the principle that in *wide areas of life* individuals are entitled to be free simply because they are born free. Nonetheless, in *some areas* majorities are entitled to rule, not because they are inherently entitled to, but because we *authorized* them to, under the Constitution Madison himself drafted.[10] Ironically, opportunists of

---

[7] See Rexford G. Tugwell, "A Center Report: Rewriting the Constitution," The Center Magazine, March 1968, at 20: "To the extent that these new social virtues [i.e., New Deal policies] developed, they were tortured interpretations of a document [i.e., the Constitution] intended to prevent them."

[8] See Richard A. Epstein, How Progressives Rewrote the Constitution (2006).

[9] Robert H. Bork, The Tempting of America 139 (1990) (emphasis added).

[10] Recall Madison's promise in Federalist No. 45, that the powers of the federal government would be "few and defined."

the right generally reject Ackerman's claim that the New Deal constitutional revolution amounted to a "constitutional moment" that "amended" the document; but they subscribe to the vast majoritarianism the revolution unleashed when it eviscerated the doctrine of enumerated powers, a majoritarianism that not only is nowhere to be found in the actual—in *this*—Constitution—indeed, was assiduously guarded against—but one that gives us, practically, a "living" Constitution, an empty vessel to be filled by constantly shifting, "living" majorities.[11]

By contrast, obligationists, although not always in agreement among themselves, are identified by a singular common accord: they take their oath of office seriously, and that oath is to support and defend *this* Constitution, not some other. In so doing, they commit themselves neither to misread the document knowingly or carelessly nor to *over*read or *under*read it by reading their own preferences into it. In particular, in taking the Constitution *as is*, obligationists are committed not to make it "living" by imposing upon it a theory other than the theory on which the document itself rests. Rather, for obligationists the Constitution, from its inception, has been very much "alive" *in its ordinary operations*—and alive further, let me add, in that it remains subject to change through the processes reserved for determining change, namely, the amendment processes, neither more nor less.

II

Remember our title: "Clashing Visions of a 'Living' Constitution." I have given you alternative processes of growth and change: opportunists willing, even anxious, to implement constitutional change through judicially crafted, nontextual "amendments;" obligationists sworn to see constitutional change brought about through the constitutionally prescribed Article V amendment process. I am not inclined to impugn the motives of the opportunists. What I think instead is that they and their jurisprudence may simply proceed from a heartfelt effort to try to keep the Constitution from becoming disappointingly "out of date," even "ossified" and "petrified"; but that even in the interviews of Supreme Court nominees before the Senate

[11] See Roger Pilon, Lawless Judging: Refocusing the Issue for Conservatives, 2 Geo. J. L. & Pub. Pol'y. 5 (2001).

Judiciary Committee there is an unexamined premise, namely, that it is part of the task of Supreme Court justices thus to *update* the Constitution and to do so *by appropriate judicial "art"*: that is, by construction—by misreading, or *"rereading,"* or, if you prefer, "differently" reading various clauses of authorization and restriction, reading them such as they *ought* to be, whether or not they are.

But how do we know whether our Constitution is *truly* living? One way is by looking to see whether there have been any amendments and, if so, when they were made, by whom, and, indeed, just what their content may be—that is, what do they register, what do they tell us about some change that may have taken place in this society to such an extent as to have become embedded in some new text, as part of *this* Constitution. Let me try to shed light on those questions with a pair of comparisons, and then two actual examples from our recent history that I hope will illuminate these issues.

In my original home state of California, one of our ancient giant redwood trees will occasionally fall, and if we cut across its massive face we see its cambium rings, tracing the tree's natural history back to antiquity. When still alive, the tree's rings go on and on, recording changes year by year. Once a tree falls and dies, however, it cannot of course add any rings, so the tree begins nearly at once to petrify. These trees and their rings are rather like the Dead Sea Scrolls, to cite a different metaphor, which rely on learned rabbis to keep their meaning "alive" and pertinent by some kind of sublime interpretive art—at least until God returns to "explain" himself anew. So too a petrified tree is dead. It cannot add anything new.

And that furnishes a segue to a second comparison, between our "living" Constitution and Hans Christian Andersen's famous fable, *The Emperor's New Clothes*. The Constitution, in this likeness, does not on its face reflect *any* change—that is, any *actual* amendment—but the judges and the people nonetheless *say* that change is there! And so, by this congenial consensus of collaborative fabrication, they manage to find what they *wanted* to find to be authorized—indeed, *thus to be* authorized—and, likewise, they manage to find what they *wanted* to find prohibited is (behold!) prohibited!

But every once in a while, just as in the original endearing Andersen fable, a small child will look, ponder a bit, and then quite spontaneously declare: "Where? I don't see it! Actually, all *I* see is the emperor in his barely adequate underwear! I don't see any of that 'splendid raiment' you have all ascribed to the emperor!"

However charming, it is a very disarming, yet most telling comparison. And as I've reflected on these comparisons, it has occurred to me that *real* "cambium rings" have become increasingly difficult to add to *this, our* Constitution. They have, at least in part, as I hope soon to show, because people now far more greatly mistrust the addition of virtually *any* new language concerning anything but nominal "technical" amendments.

Indeed, it is doubtful that anything like the 10 amendments that eventually became our Bill of Rights could even be successfully proposed today by the requisite supermajorities in Congress, much less ratified by the requisite number of states. Far more than in 1789 (or even 1866), there is a greater collective suspicion of "new" amendments because, I believe, it is feared today that enactment of additional text may just give judges and others still greater license to use that language as one more springboard for reshaping our constitutional regime—which may then prove pleasing to new majorities, yet conform little if at all to the original proposal as presented, approved, submitted, and actually ratified by the states.

This phenomenon of a *diminished* Article V has in fact affected my own thinking on these matters. It is a *deadening* phenomenon, producing a kind of "negative synergy," clogging our Constitution. "Synergy" is usually defined as the operation of forces *cooperatively* producing *new* elements—*that is*, elements incapable of being produced by either original force in isolation. "Negative" synergy, in turn, and in the context of our "living" Constitution, operates like this: The more courts transform constitutional clauses without needing actual amendments to do so—*that is,* the more they do not require new text—the less necessary new text seems to be. But then exactly to the extent that courts do not require new text, neither may it be safe to provide it, for to the extent such text is provided to record a *definite* change, one may rightly be wary—merely reacting in tutored fear of the administration of that new text, given what the Court has previously presumed *already* to do.

From this "negative" synergy, then, both Congress and the public grow less willing to make changes through the normal Article V processes. But exactly in such measure as that becomes true, then even the more conscientious judges in turn will inexorably feel stressed to be forthcoming with "transformative" constructions of extant clauses—and "wisely" to do so because they understandably despair of the amendment process. So it continues, an endless cycle feeding on itself. And if Article V effectively dies, the Constitution itself dies with it, becoming simply a vehicle for either judges or majorities to implement their will, despite what the actual Constitution may say.

III

Two examples, not unrelated, may shed further light on the questions I raised above. Nearly 40 years ago, in 1972, large congressional majorities proposed a twenty-seventh amendment—not the "technical" Twenty-Seventh Amendment we have today, dealing with congressional compensation, which was finally ratified in 1992 after languishing in the states since 1789, but a far more substantive "Equal Rights Amendment." Section 1 of the proposed ERA provided simply that "Equality of rights under the law shall not be denied or abridged by the United States or by any State on account of sex." Section 2 provided for congressional enforcement. That was pretty much it.

Again, far more than the required two-thirds majority in both houses embraced the ERA in 1972. And over the next two and a half years the proposal was ratified by 34 of the 38 states required for ratification. But then progress ground to a halt, largely because of determined opposition from a variety of circles, led by a very capable woman, Phyllis Schlafly, of the Eagle Forum. And even after Congress extended the deadline for ratification by another seven years, the proposal expired, falling three states short.

Now on the merits it is clear to me that after you have accounted for everything else regarding the pros and cons of the ERA—the possibility of unisex restrooms, women in combat, same-sex marriage, and the like—an irreducible number of no votes stemmed from Schlafly's convincing observations that in similar circumstances in the past, the Supreme Court had taken the language of an amendment or of a constitutional clause, along with the original understanding about the provision, and had just ignored that text and understanding and gone merrily on its progressive way to fulfill its *own* vision of what the Constitution "ought" to provide. Thus, we now surely know that amendments are no longer trustworthy. "Vote for this amendment, and the next thing you know there will be women in foxholes, unisex bathrooms, and gay and lesbian marriages!" And that was it—the proposed twenty-seventh amendment simply lapsed.

To be sure, you may ask whether it matters. Are we actually worse off on that account? Well I for one care a lot. The ERA would have recorded a rite of passage for this country. In a mature country that had come to think differently about gender equality and "gender roles," it would have recorded on the face of our aging document a *real* change. Exactly what we ought well to want, but frankly altogether lack. What we have instead is but a quarrelsome series of brokered Supreme Court cases,[12] accomplishing most of what the ERA would have enacted, to be sure, but you cannot find *anything* in the Constitution that expressly attests to equal rights regardless of sex or gender—real text. *It's simply not there.*

Indeed, and in fact, the sole provision that speaks to the general issue most relevantly goes quite the other way. It is the provision in Section 2 of the Fourteenth Amendment that declares that insofar as a state denies the right to vote to "males" over the age of 21 and not previously convicted of a crime, then that state's representation in the House of Representatives shall be reduced proportionately. But the clause itself is an express textual recognition that the perpetual disenfranchisement of *women* not only is not to be regarded as inconsistent with the amendment's Equal Protection Clause, but also does not even require some downward adjustment of a state's allotment of representatives in the House. Indeed, it took the Nineteenth Amendment to change that constitutional fact.

That amendment, the Nineteenth, will further illustrate my larger thesis. In his recent book, *Active Liberty,* Justice Stephen Breyer suggested in passing that women in America did not have the right to vote until the Nineteenth Amendment was ratified in 1920.[13] The

---

[12] See, e.g., Tuan Anh Nguyen v. INS, 533 U.S. 53 (2001); United States v. Virginia, 518 U.S. 515 (1996); Califano v. Goldfarb, 430 U.S. 199 (1977); Rostker v. Goldberg, 453 U.S. 57 (1981); Michael M. v. Superior Court, 450 U.S. 464 (1981); Craig v. Boren, 429 U.S. 190 (1976); Reed v. Reed, 404 U.S. 71 (1971). See also Kathleen M. Sullivan and Gerald Gunther, Constitutional Law 591 (2010) ("Justice Brennan never did get his elusive fifth vote for his proposed strict scrutiny standard") and *id.* at 587 ("The U.S. Constitution is the only major written constitution with a bill of rights that lacks a provision explicitly declaring the equality of the sexes.").

[13] Stephen Breyer,, Active Liberty 32 (2005) ("Nor did women receive the right to vote until 1920.").

suggestion annoyed me even when I saw it there. It was not just careless; it was flat out incorrect. Indeed, if you thought about it, it could not plausibly be true. If women were denied the right to vote prior to 1920, then how could the Nineteenth Amendment have become ratified that very year? After all, since it takes two-thirds of both houses and three-fourths of all the states to do the job, and *no* state allowed women to vote as of that date, how many states would you expect to go on with this proposal *within a single year?*

In truth, of course, by the time the Nineteenth Amendment came up for a vote, a majority of the states had already fully enfranchised women. What is most interesting, however, is how this expansion of the right to vote can be seen as a significant cultural, political, and *real* prologue to the "cambium ring" that is our Nineteenth Amendment. These cultural changes were first reflected in the "lesser" cambium rings of state legislation and state constitutions. They report an evolution actively reflecting the cultural changes within each relevant polity. In time those changes are recorded in the Nineteenth Amendment and (behold!) there it is. *Now* we no longer need worry about whether the next Supreme Court justice would overrule the decision that enfranchised women. Their rights are right there, in the text, for all to see. It is otherwise with the ERA, of course, even though "the law" is today about the same as it would be if that amendment had been adopted.[14] But I do not think we are nearly as well off for having done it that way.

IV

Yet even with a "living" constitution, one that sees change made according to its own terms rather than through judicial or majoritarian machinations inconsistent with those terms, there will be issues that make it difficult to separate opportunists from obligationists. Suppose, for example, that a question were before the Supreme Court

---

[14] To be sure, by a combination of legislative grace (both state and federal) (e.g., Titles VI (42 U.S.C. § 2000d et seq.) and VII (42 U.S.C. § 2000e et seq.) of the Civil Rights Act of 1964), plus some mild displays of judicial hubris in the case law, we have experienced a "translation" of the Fourteenth and Fifteenth Amendments—albeit in a way that would have dumbfounded the women's suffrage movement itself—and so, by those means, have arrived closely to where we would be had the ERA passed. (See, e.g., cases and references *supra,* note 12).

concerning whether Congress could mandate that federal juries be composed of fewer than their traditional 12 members.

Well it turns out that the constitutional text on that question and the understanding surrounding the text are less than clear or helpful. Article III says simply that "The Trial of all Crimes . . . shall be by Jury." The Sixth Amendment says more, but nothing on point: "In all criminal prosecutions, the accused shall enjoy the right to a speedy and public trial, by an impartial jury. . . ." Nor was the question seriously debated in the Constitutional Convention or in the state ratifying conventions. It *was* debated in the Virginia convention, briefly, with people like George Mason and Patrick Henry generally and deeply skeptical about the proposed new constitution. But James Madison countered their skepticism on the jury question by saying that the term "jury," as provided in Article III, "is a technical term" that draws in its wake all its appurtenances so well and long established even as they are reflected in that book that "every member has," namely, Blackstone's *Commentaries on the Common Law*.[15] The 12-person jury, Madison continued, had been in existence for something like two centuries. No one contradicted Madison's statements explicating the relevant provision of Article III.

If opportunists are able to ignore clearer evidence in order to reach their desired ends, they are not likely to refrain from doing the same when the evidence is thinner, as in a case like this or like so many others that come before the Supreme Court. But even obligationists may be inclined to "impose their own vision" in such cases, thus appearing indistinguishable from opportunists. Here the evidence, thin as it is, fairly clearly favors the 12-person jury. But suppose it were still thinner. What might one look for? For starters, what was the then contemporary practice? Was it nearly universal to have 12-person juries (at least in federal, if not in state courts, as it was), or were they somewhat exceptional? How far back did the "tradition" of the 12-person jury go? Is there something said in the Blackstone *Commentaries* that may tend to inform us? Those are just a few of the questions that would concern an obligationist.

---

[15] Speech by James Madison at Virginia's Convention on the Adoption of the Constitution (June 20, 1788), in 3 Elliot's Debates in the Several State Conventions on the Adoption of the Federal Constitution, at 541 (1836).

In general, however, before a judge decides that the issue before him really is an open question—that is, that there really is nothing to tilt the balance—he should pause before "defaulting" and yielding the "difference" to Congress because, frankly, there is little evidence that Congress ever did this kind of research, or that its products are principally driven by this kind of genuine constitutional preoccupation. After all, Congress is mainly concerned with social policy (and of course with reelection), while the foremost concern of our courts is, or at least should be, constitutional integrity. It appears, moreover, that there is a correlation between the Supreme Court's taking constitutional questions seriously and Congress's doing so as well. Likewise, when the Court tends to abdicate and defer, Congress hardly even discusses constitutional points of law with any gravity. Witness the Court's recent "rediscovery" of enumerated powers federalism,[16] which has prompted many in Congress to again ask, for the first time in ages, "Do we have the power to enact this bill?"[17] That is a refreshing change.

Thus, whether members of Congress take their oaths seriously may depend to a very considerable extent on whether justices on the Court take *their* oaths seriously. And so, as a last word, as between the two groups I have juxtaposed, I have no doubt in saying that it is the obligationists who care about the *living* Constitution—*this* Constitution—the document that, if it is to remain alive, should be interpreted and applied *as is* and changed, when needed, not by judicial circumlocution or ungrounded majoritarian assertion but by the processes provided for in the document itself.[18] My concern

[16] Roger Pilon, "Congress Rediscovers the Constitution," Wall. St. J., Jan. 4, 2011, at A17.

[17] That, of course, is precisely the question before the five different federal district courts that have issued conflicting rulings on large parts of the recently enacted "Patient Protection and Affordable Health Care Act" (informally known as the "ObamaCare" Act), Pub. L. No. 111-148, 124 Stat. 119 (2010), amended by the Health Care and Education Reconciliation Act of 2010, Pub. L. No. 111-152, 124 Stat. 1029. Two have struck down certain sections (district courts in Virginia and Florida); three have ruled the other way (Michigan, Ohio, Virginia). These cases are currently on appeal and the Supreme Court will almost certainly decide this question, whether it comes in the 2011 term or a year hence, likely by a closely divided vote.

[18] I am, in this regard, at once reminded of Carl Shurz's sharp, well taken riposte to Stephen Decatur's overly celebrated patriotic toast. While Decatur famously exclaimed, "My country, right or wrong," Shurz observed, "My country, may it always be in the right, and, when in the wrong, *may it be put to the right.*" (emphasis added). So, too, with this, *our* Constitution, that is, insofar as it may be defective, let

is that we may have gotten so accustomed to the "exogenous" Constitution that the amendment process has itself begun to recede as down a rabbit hole, as in *Alice in Wonderland*, and the country, frankly, is significantly less well off on that account.

I am most grateful for this opportunity to share these thoughts and I do, genuinely, thank you for your time and thought in considering them for whatever worth they may hold in musing about this aging Constitution of ours, the oldest and still among the best in all the world.

---

us—by amendment—remove those defects but let us not just "paper them over" (in the manner of Hans Christian Andersen's clever tailors of Copenhagen, weaving invisible judicial patches to cover naked places obvious to any unspoiled child).

Sex, Lies, and Videogames: *Brown v. Entertainment Merchants Association*

David G. Post*

In *Brown v. Entertainment Merchants Association*, a decision that veteran Supreme Court watcher Linda Greenhouse called "the most surprising decision"[1] of the term (and the one that also received Greenhouse's "most unusual judicial performance" award, for Justice Stephen Breyer's dissenting opinion), the Supreme Court (7-2) struck down California's prohibition on the sale of violent videogames to minors on the grounds that it offended First Amendment protections for the freedom of speech.[2] Whether or not Greenhouse is correct—I think she's on to something, a point to which I'll return below—the case presents a fascinating snapshot of the state of First Amendment doctrine in the early years of the 21st century, and contains enough peculiarities and doctrinal oddities to keep law professors and their students busy for years to come.

To place the decision in its correct context, I'll begin with a brief review of "the somewhat tortured history of the Court's obscenity decisions";[3] though *Brown* is not explicitly about "obscenity," the decision rests entirely on, and is inexplicable without reference to, those decisions. Next, I'll examine each of the four opinions issued by the Court—Justice Antonin Scalia for the majority (joined by Justices Anthony Kennedy, Ruth Bader Ginsburg, Sonia Sotomayor, and Elena Kagan), Justice Samuel Alito (joined by Chief Justice John

* Professor of Law, Beasley School of Law, Temple University. David.Post@temple.edu. Many thanks to Joe Coleman for invaluable research assistance in putting together this article, and to Abner Greene for comments on an earlier draft.

[1] Linda Greenhouse, A Supreme Court Scoreboard, N.Y. Times Opinionator, July 13, 2011, http://opinionator.blogs.nytimes.com/2011/07/13/a-supreme-court-scorecard/.

[2] Brown v. Entm't Merch. Ass'n, 131 S. Ct. 2729 (2011).

[3] Miller v. California, 413 U.S. 15, 19 (1973).

Roberts) concurring in the judgment, and the two dissenting opinions by Justices Clarence Thomas and Stephen Breyer—in some detail, for they constitute a rather remarkable collection. In the final section I'll discuss some of the potential implications of the Court's decision for First Amendment doctrine and for future battles about the regulation of speech.

I. The Law of the Obscene

As something of an outsider to the study of the First Amendment,[4] it has always struck me as not a little odd that obscenity doctrine plays such a large role in our First Amendment jurisprudence. I will leave for future historians and sociologists to ponder the fact that a significant segment of our First Amendment doctrine has developed in the context of attempts to regulate and suppress sexually themed speech: the "obscene," the "indecent," the "pornographic." My strong suspicion (though I have not, I admit, confirmed this) is that other developed legal systems around the world do not spend as much time as ours limning the boundaries separating these categories, or considering these questions.

But be that as it may, the general contours of obscenity doctrine are well-known, well-established, and fairly straightforward. As a general matter, as every first-year law student dutifully learns, "the government['s] power to restrict expression because of its message, its ideas, its subject matter, or its content"[5] is severely limited by

---

[4] I should note at the outset that questions about the First Amendment, and constitutional law generally, are at the margins of my own scholarly interests. In the fields in which I'm most comfortable—Internet and intellectual property law—one does, of course, come across a fair number of hard constitutional (especially First Amendment) questions these days, so I am a good deal more familiar with that doctrine than I am with, say, the Bankruptcy Code, the Administrative Procedure Act, or the law of search and seizure. But I generally come to these constitutional questions more as an advocate—as in this case, where, along with several colleagues, I submitted an amicus brief to the Court supporting the respondents. See Brief of First Amendment Scholars (Professors Cole, Karst, Post, Redish, Van Alstyne, Varat and Winkler) as Amici Curiae in Support of Respondents, Brown v. Entm't Merch. Ass'n, 131 S. Ct. 2729 (2011) (No. 08-1448). I have described my own views about the First Amendment as being "pretty simple" and "absolutist," see David G. Post, In Search of Jefferson's Moose: Notes on the State of Cyberspace 188 (2009), and I candidly acknowledge that the many intricacies of much constitutional doctrine (and scholarship) often elude me.

[5] Brown, 131 S. Ct. at 2733 (quoting Ashcroft v. ACLU, 535 U.S. 564, 573 (2002)).

the "strict scrutiny" such efforts will receive in the courts. The government's burden of justification in such cases—to demonstrate that it has "a compelling interest" in achieving the goal it is pursuing, that it has taken action "narrowly tailored" to advance that interest, and that there are no "less speech-restrictive alternatives" available to accomplish that purpose as effectively[6]—is not only substantial, it is well-nigh insurmountable.[7] "Strict in theory, fatal in fact,"[8] as we were taught in law school.

Regulation of "obscene" speech, however, gets no special First Amendment-imposed scrutiny at all. Though it may indeed be "speech," obscene speech stands outside "the freedom of speech" that the First Amendment protects:

> From 1791 to the present, . . . the First Amendment has "permitted restrictions upon the content of speech in a few limited areas," and has never "include[d] a freedom to disregard these traditional limitations." *United States v. Stevens*, [130 S. Ct. 1577, 1584 (2010)] (quoting *R. A. V. v. St. Paul*, 505 U. S. 377, 382–83 (1992)). These limited areas—such as obscenity, *Roth v. United States*, 354 U. S. 476, 483 (1957), incitement, *Brandenburg v. Ohio*, 395 U. S. 444, 447–49 (1969) (per curiam), and fighting words, *Chaplinsky v. New Hampshire*, 315 U. S. 568, 572 (1942)—represent "well-defined and narrowly limited classes of speech, the prevention and punishment of which have never been thought to raise any Constitutional problem," *id.*, at 571–72.[9]

So the government is free, subject only to whatever constraints arise elsewhere (that is, outside the First Amendment), to regulate,

---

[6] *Id.* at 2738; see also Ashcroft v. ACLU, 542 U.S. 656, 665–66 (2004).

[7] See United States v. Playboy Entm't Group, Inc., 529 U.S. 803, 818 (2000) ("It is rare that a regulation restricting speech because of its content will ever be permissible."); Brown, 131 S. Ct. at 2747 (Alito, J., concurring) (describing strict scrutiny burden as "perhaps insurmountable").

[8] See Fullilove v. Klutznick, 448 U.S. 448, 519 (1980) (Marshall, J., concurring).

[9] Brown, 131 S. Ct. at 2733 (some internal citations omitted); see also Ashcroft, 535 U.S. at 574 ("Obscene speech, for example, has long been held to fall outside the purview of the First Amendment.") (citing Roth v. United States, 354 U.S. 476, 484–85 (1957)).

or to prohibit entirely, the production, sale, and distribution—though not, interestingly, the possession[10]—of "obscene" material. The rationale for this exception? In *Roth v. United States*, the first case squarely holding that obscenity stands outside the First Amendment, the Court, speaking through Justice William Brennan, explained it as follows:

> The guaranties of freedom of expression in effect in 10 of the 14 States which by 1792 had ratified the Constitution, gave no absolute protection for every utterance. Thirteen of the 14 States provided for the prosecution of libel, and all of those States made either blasphemy or profanity, or both, statutory crimes. As early as 1712, Massachusetts made it criminal to publish "any filthy, obscene, or profane song, pamphlet, libel or mock sermon" in imitation or mimicking of religious services. Thus, profanity and obscenity were related offenses.
>
> In light of this history, it is apparent that the unconditional phrasing of the First Amendment was not intended to protect every utterance. This phrasing did not prevent this Court from concluding that libelous utterances are not within the area of constitutionally protected speech. *Beauharnais v. Illinois*, 343 U.S. 250, 266 [(1952)]. At the time of the adoption of the First Amendment, obscenity law was not as fully developed as libel law, but there is sufficiently contemporaneous evidence to show that obscenity, too, was outside the protection intended for speech and press.
>
> The protection given speech and press was fashioned to assure unfettered interchange of ideas for the bringing about of political and social changes desired by the people. . . . All ideas having even the slightest redeeming social importance—unorthodox ideas, controversial ideas, even ideas hateful to the prevailing climate of opinion—have the full protection of the guaranties, unless excludable because they encroach upon the limited area of more important interests. But implicit in the history of the First Amendment is the rejection of obscenity as utterly without redeeming social importance. . . . "[S]uch utterances are no essential part of any exposition of ideas, and are of such slight social value as a step to truth that any benefit that may be derived from

[10] Stanley v. Georgia, 394 U.S. 557, 568 (1969) (mere private possession of obscene material cannot constitute a criminal offense).

30

them is clearly outweighed by the social interest in order and morality. . . ."[11]

Notice the two separate doctrinal justifications for the obscenity exception: the historical ("In light of this history, . . . At the time of the adoption of the First Amendment . . .") and the sociological (obscenity is "no essential part of any exposition of ideas" and is of "slight social value as a step to truth").

Predictably enough, a good deal of the early confusion in the obscenity cases centered on the definitional question: What *is* "obscene" speech? And who gets to decide what is, or is not, obscene? After a decade or so "during which [the] Court struggled with the intractable obscenity problem,"[12] and despite "considerable vacillation over the proper definition of obscenity,"[13] and notwithstanding Justice Potter Stewart's oft-quoted aphorism ("I know it when I see it"),[14] the Court ended "over a decade of turmoil"[15] in *Miller v. California*,[16] promulgating the now-familiar formula:

> *Miller* set forth the governing three-part test for assessing whether material is obscene and thus unprotected by the First Amendment: "(a) Whether the average person, applying contemporary community standards, would find that the work, taken as a whole, appeals to the prurient interest; (b) whether the work depicts or describes, in a patently offensive way, sexual conduct specifically defined by the applicable state law; and (c) whether the work, taken as a whole, lacks serious literary, artistic, political, or scientific value."[17]

The *Miller* formula has two noteworthy features. First, the Court's characterization of it as a "test for assessing whether material is obscene and thus unprotected by the First Amendment" is not quite

[11] Roth v. United States, 354 U.S. 476, 482–85 (1957) (quoting Chaplinsky v. New Hampshire, 315 U.S. 568, 571–72 (1942) (internal citations omitted).

[12] New York v. Ferber, 458 U.S. 747, 754 (1982) (quoting Interstate Circuit, Inc. v. City of Dallas, 390 U.S. 676, 704 (1968) (Harlan, J., concurring in part and dissenting in part)).

[13] *Id.*

[14] Jacobellis v. Ohio, 378 U.S. 184, 197 (1964) (Stewart, J., concurring) (referring to the category of "hard-core" pornography).

[15] Ashcroft, 535 U.S. at 574.

[16] Miller, 413 U.S. 15 (1973).

[17] Ashcroft, 535 U.S. at 574 (quoting Miller, 413 U.S. at 24).

accurate. It doesn't enable you to look at any particular item and answer the question, "Is this photograph, or magazine, or video 'obscene' and thus unprotected by the First Amendment?" Instead, it specifies the process that the government must follow when it gets around to defining something as obscene. It's a meta-definition, if you will. It enables you to determine, if the government is punishing, or threatening to punish, you for the content of your photograph, or magazine, or video, whether the particular definition of prohibited speech contained in "applicable state law" under which such punishment is being imposed comports with the Constitution; it asks, that is, whether there was a finding that "the average person, applying contemporary community standards, would find that the work, taken as a whole, appeals to the prurient interest," and that the work depicts "sexual conduct specifically defined by the applicable state law," and that it does so "in a patently offensive way," and so on.

Second, by declaring that speech can be deemed "obscene" only if "the average person, applying contemporary *community standards*" deems it to be so, the *Miller* standard clearly contemplates that First Amendment protection will expand and contract as one moves from one community to another. "People in different States vary in their tastes and attitudes, and this diversity is not to be strangled by the absolutism of imposed uniformity,"[18] and it is "neither realistic nor constitutionally sound to read the First Amendment as requiring that the people of Maine or Mississippi accept public depiction of conduct found tolerable in Las Vegas, or New York City."[19] This feature of obscenity doctrine (though some might deem it a bug, not a feature) has led us into some difficult doctrinal thickets, as legislatures and courts have struggled to define the relevant "community" whose standards apply to an obscenity determination in the Internet age.[20]

But putting those complications aside, *Roth-Miller* draws a fairly clear line between the protected and the unprotected: *Roth* tells us

---

[18] Miller, 413 U.S. at 33.

[19] *Id.* at 32.

[20] See Ashcroft, 535 U.S. 564 (2002), where the Court struggled, in a series of fractured opinions, to define the correct interpretation of "community standards" regarding Internet speech.

that speech is either "in" (and subject to the full panoply of First Amendment protection against content regulation) or "out" (in which case the First Amendment is indifferent to its regulation), and *Miller* tells us how the line between in and out is to be drawn. That's where things stood—and where, by and large, they still stand—with respect to the obscene. Considerable confusion was introduced into this simple scheme early on, however, as the Court confronted attempts to regulate the distribution of the "nasty-but-not-quite-obscene" to minors. Most people, I suspect, would agree that there is material that is not obscene but that we might nonetheless not like to see in the hands of nine-year-olds. Rigid line-drawing of the *Roth-Miller* variety, however, doesn't lend itself terribly well to adjustment for context, and the Court's struggles with this issue have led to a great deal of doctrinal confusion—to which, as we'll see below, the *Brown* decision may have contributed its fair share.

Ginsberg v. New York,[21] one of the earliest of these "distribution to minors" cases, is the source of a great deal of that confusion and of a great deal of subsequent mischief. In *Ginsberg*, the owner of a Bellmore, Long Island, luncheonette had been convicted of selling "girlie magazines"—concededly *not* obscene[22]—to a 16-year-old boy in violation of a New York statute that made it unlawful "knowingly to sell . . . to a minor . . . (a) any picture . . . which depicts nudity . . . and which is harmful to minors, [or] (b) any . . . magazine . . .

---

[21] 390 U.S. 629 (1968). As Justice Breyer points out, *Ginsberg* is "often confused with a very different, earlier case, *Ginzburg v. United States*, 383 U.S. 463 (1966)." Brown, 131 S. Ct. at 2763 (Breyer, J., dissenting).

[22] The material in question "contained pictures which depicted female "nudity" in a manner defined in subsection 1(b) [of the statute], that is "the showing of . . . female . . . buttocks with less than a full opaque covering, or the showing of the female breast with less than a fully opaque covering of any portion thereof below the top of the nipple . . . , " and (2) that the pictures were "harmful to minors" in that they had, within the meaning of subsection 1(f) "that quality of . . . representation . . . of nudity . . . [which] . . . (i) predominantly appeals to the prurient, shameful or morbid interest of minors, and (ii) is patently offensive to prevailing standards in the adult community as a whole with respect to what is suitable material for minors, and (iii) is utterly without redeeming social importance for minors." Ginsburg, 390 U.S. at 632–33. In declaring that these materials fall outside the bounds of the "obscene," the Court cited *Redrup v. New York*, 386 U.S. 767 (1967), a case holding that the paperback books *Lust Pool, Shame Agent, High Heels,* and *Spree,* as well as the magazines *Gent, Swank, Bachelor, Modern Man, Cavalcade, Gentleman, Ace,* and *Sir,* were not "obscene" and unprotected.

which contains [such pictures] and which, taken as a whole, is harmful to minors."[23]

The Court—speaking, as in *Roth,* through Justice Brennan—upheld the conviction, though its opinion is somewhat less than pellucid in regard to its reasons for doing so. Although there is some language in the majority opinion that suggests that the decision rested on a ground involving lesser First Amendment rights for minors,[24] most of the opinion can be read as "adjust[ing] the definition of obscenity,"[25] placing additional material into the "obscenity" category (and therefore entirely outside First Amendment protection). The Court endorses (though it never quite articulates or explains) the theory of "variable obscenity":

> Material which is protected for distribution to adults is not necessarily constitutionally protected from restriction upon its dissemination to children. In other words, the concept of obscenity or of unprotected matter may vary according to the group to whom the questionable material is directed or from whom it is quarantined.[26]

---

[23] Ginsberg, 390 U.S. at 631–32.

[24] See, e.g.:

> We have no occasion in this case to consider the impact of the guarantees of freedom of expression upon the totality of the relationship of the minor and the State. It is enough for the purposes of this case that we inquire whether it was constitutionally impermissible for New York, insofar as § 484-h does so, to accord minors under 17 *a more restricted right than that assured to adults* to judge and determine for themselves what sex material they may read or see. [W]e cannot say that the statute invades the area of *freedom of expression constitutionally secured to minors.*

Id. at 636–37 (emphasis added).

[25] *Id.* at 638.

[26] *Id.* at 636 (quoting Bookcase, Inc. v. Broderick, 218 N.E.2d 668, 671 (N.Y. 1966):

> The concept of variable obscenity is developed in Lockhart & McClure, Censorship of Obscenity: The Developing Constitutional Standards, 45 Minn. L. Rev. 5 (1960). At 85 the authors state: "Variable obscenity . . . furnishes a useful analytical tool for dealing with the problem of denying adolescents access to material aimed at a primary audience of sexually mature adults. For variable obscenity focuses attention upon the make-up of primary and peripheral audiences in varying circumstances, and provides a reasonably satisfactory means for delineating the obscene in each circumstance."

Id. at 635 n.4.

Though they are not obscene, these "girlie magazines," the Court seemed to be saying, are "not . . . constitutionally protected"—at least, as far as their dissemination to children is concerned. The Court described its action as "sustain[ing] state power to *exclude material defined as obscenity*" by the New York statute.[27] So just as New York may prohibit the sale or distribution *to anyone* of material that is obscene (*as to everyone*), subject only to non-First-Amendment rational basis review, so too may it prohibit the sale and distribution *to minors* of material that is obscene (*as to minors*), subject only to that rational basis review.

> Two interests justify the limitations in § 484-h upon the availability of sex material to minors under 17, *at least if it was rational for the legislature to find that the minors' exposure to such material might be harmful.* First of all, constitutional interpretation has consistently recognized that the parents' claim to authority in their own household to direct the rearing of their children is basic in the structure of our society. . . . The State also has an independent interest in the well-being of its youth . . . "to protect the welfare of children," and to see that they are "safe-guarded from abuses" which might prevent their "growth into free and independent well-developed men and citizens."[28]

The "only question," then, was "whether the New York Legislature might *rationally conclude*, as it has, that exposure to the materials proscribed by § 484-h constitutes such an 'abuse'" from which minors should be safeguarded.[29]

> [O]bscenity is not protected expression. . . . To sustain state power to *exclude material defined as obscene by § 484-h* requires only that we be able to say that *it was not irrational for the legislature to find that exposure to material condemned by the statute is harmful to minors.* . . . [We] cannot say that § 484-h, *in defining the obscenity of material on the basis of its appeal to minors under 17,* has no *rational relation* to the objective of safeguarding such minors from harm.[30]

[27] *Id.* at 641 (emphasis added).
[28] *Id.* at 639–41 (emphasis added).
[29] *Id.* at 641 (emphasis added).
[30] *Id.* at 641–43 (emphasis added).

Thus was a new constitutional category born: "obscene-as-to-minors."[31]

Ginsberg, then, technically speaking, isn't a First Amendment case at all—it's a *not* First Amendment case. It's about the regulation of *unprotected* speech—speech that is obscene as to minors—about which the First Amendment has nothing to say (at least, when the state regulates its distribution to minors).

One doesn't have to be Hugo Black or Thomas Jefferson to see the camel poking its nose under this particular tent. How capacious is the category of speech that is "obscene as to minors"? How much leeway will the state be permitted in placing speech into that category?

II. The California Statute

The California statute at issue here

> prohibits the sale or rental of "violent video games" to minors, and requires their packaging to be labeled "18." The Act covers games "in which the range of options available to a player includes killing, maiming, dismembering, or sexually assaulting an image of a human being, if those acts are depicted" in a manner that "[a] reasonable person, considering the game as a whole, would find appeals to a deviant or morbid interest of minors," that is "patently offensive to prevailing standards in the community as to what is suitable for minors," and that "causes the game, as a whole, to lack

---

[31] As the Ninth Circuit put it when ruling on the case that is the subject of this article:

> The *Ginsberg* Court applied a rational basis test to the statute at issue because it placed the magazines at issue within a sub-category of obscenity—obscenity as to minors—that had been determined to be not protected by the First Amendment . . .

Video Software Dealers Ass'n v. Schwarzenegger, 556 F.3d 950, 959 (9th Cir. 2009). See also Ferber, 458 U.S. at 749 n.2 (noting that two states prohibit dissemination only "if the material is *obscene as to minors*") (emphasis added); Erznoznik v. Jacksonville, 422 U.S. 205, 213–14 (1975) ("Speech that is neither *obscene as to youths* nor subject to some other legitimate proscription cannot be suppressed solely to protect the young from ideas or images that a legislative body thinks unsuitable for them.") (emphasis added); Brown, 131 S. Ct. at 2743 (Alito, J., concurring) ("The law at issue in *Ginsberg* prohibited the sale to minors of materials that were deemed 'harmful to minors,' and the law defined 'harmful to minors' simply by adding the words 'for minors' to each element of the definition of obscenity set out in what were then the Court's leading obscenity decisions.").

serious literary, artistic, political, or scientific value for minors." Violation of the Act is punishable by a civil fine of up to $1,000.[32]

The district court applied strict scrutiny and invalidated the act, enjoining its enforcement. California appealed to the Ninth Circuit, arguing that *Ginsberg* controlled and validated what the state had done:

> The State's argument on appeal [is] that we should not apply strict scrutiny and instead should . . . analyze the Act's restrictions under what has been called the "variable obscenity" or "obscenity as to minors" standard first mentioned in *Ginsberg*. In essence, the State argues that the Court's reasoning in *Ginsberg* that a state could prohibit the sale of sexually-explicit material to minors that it could not ban from distribution to adults should be extended to materials containing violence. This presents an invitation to reconsider the boundaries of the legal concept of "obscenity" under the First Amendment.[33]

The Ninth Circuit rejected the invitation:

> *Ginsberg* is specifically rooted in the Court's First Amendment obscenity jurisprudence, *which relates to non-protected sex-based expression*—not violent content, which is presumably protected by the First Amendment. *See* 390 U.S. at 640. *Ginsberg* explicitly states that the New York statute under review "simply adjusts the definition of obscenity to social realities by permitting the appeal of this type of material to be assessed in term of the sexual interests of such minors." . . . The *Ginsberg* Court applied a rational basis test to the statute at issue because it placed the magazines at issue within a sub-category of obscenity—obscenity as to minors—that had been determined to be not protected by the First Amendment, and it did not create an entirely new category of expression excepted from First Amendment protection.[34]

---

[32] Brown, 131 S. Ct. at 2732–33.

[33] Schwarzenegger, 556 F.3d at 957–58.

[34] *Id.* at 959 (emphasis added).

III. The Supreme Court's Opinion(s)

When the Supreme Court granted California's cert petition in April 2010, Court-watchers were left scratching their heads: Why did the Court agree to hear the case? The lower courts had been unanimous thus far; every court (including the courts of appeals in the Seventh and Eighth Circuits, in addition, now, to the Ninth) that had considered similar (or identical) statutes had (1) applied strict scrutiny and (2) struck them down as violating the First Amendment.[35] Moreover, the Court had just, the previous week, issued its decision in *United States v. Stevens*, invalidating by an 8-1 margin a federal statute that criminalized depictions of animal cruelty.[36] *Stevens* squarely and resoundingly rejected the government's argument that such depictions should be "added to the list" of categorically unprotected speech (joining "obscenity, defamation, fraud, incitement, and speech integral to criminal conduct").[37] The Court made it abundantly clear that it was not interested in attempts to expand these categories beyond their "traditional limitations":[38]

> The Government contends that . . . categories of speech may be exempted from the First Amendment's protection without any long-settled tradition of subjecting that speech to regulation. Instead, the Government points to Congress's "legislative judgment that . . . depictions of animals being intentionally tortured and killed [are] of such minimal redeeming value as to render [them] unworthy of First Amendment protection," and asks the Court to uphold the ban on the same basis. The Government thus proposes that a claim of categorical exclusion should be considered under a simple balancing test: "Whether a given category of speech enjoys

[35] Entm't Software Ass'n v. Swanson, 519 F.3d 768 (8th Cir. 2008); Interactive Digital Software Ass'n v. St. Louis County, 329 F.3d 954 (8th Cir. 2003); Am. Amusement Mach. Ass'n v. Kendrick, 244 F.3d 572 (7th Cir.), cert. denied, 534 U.S. 994 (2001); Entm't Merchants Ass'n v. Henry, No. Civ-06-675-C, 2007 WL 2743097 (W.D. Okla. Sept. 17, 2007); Entm't Software Ass'n v. Foti, 451 F. Supp. 2d 823 (M.D. La. 2006); Entm't Software Ass'n v. Granholm, 426 F. Supp. 2d 646 (E.D. Mich. 2006); Entm't Software Ass'n v. Blagojevich, 404 F. Supp. 2d 1051 (N.D. Ill. 2005), aff'd, 469 F.3d 641 (7th Cir. 2006); Video Software Dealers Ass'n v. Maleng, 325 F. Supp. 2d 1180 (W.D. Wash. 2004).

[36] 130 S.Ct. 1577 (2010).

[37] *Id.* at 1584–85 (internal citations omitted).

[38] *Id.* (quoting R.A.V. v. St. Paul, 505 U.S. at 383).

First Amendment protection depends upon a categorical balancing of the value of the speech against its societal costs." As a free-floating test for First Amendment coverage, that sentence is startling and dangerous. The First Amendment's guarantee of free speech does not extend only to categories of speech that survive an *ad hoc* balancing of relative social costs and benefits. The First Amendment itself reflects a judgment by the American people that the benefits of its restrictions on the Government outweigh the costs. Our Constitution forecloses any attempt to revise that judgment simply on the basis that some speech is not worth it. . . .

When we have identified categories of speech as fully outside the protection of the First Amendment, it has not been on the basis of a simple cost-benefit analysis. . . .[39]

Strong words indeed. With uniformity in the lower courts, and a near-unanimous declaration, still ringing in our ears, that the Court will be very stingy when asked to expand the categories of unprotected speech at a legislature's behest—more or less *precisely* what California was asking for here, and precisely what the Ninth Circuit had rejected—the cert grant really was puzzling; four justices (at least) were unhappy, for some reason, with this status quo. It looked like a real battle was shaping up—at least a 5-4 cliffhanger.[40] That the Court subsequently took so long to issue its decision—the case had been argued on November 2, 2010, and the decision was delayed until the very last day of the 2010 term, June 27, 2011—seemed to confirm that something complicated and possibly important was happening behind the wizard's curtain: some dramatic reformulation of First Amendment doctrine, perhaps, or some new law about the state's relationship with minors, or some shifting alliances among the justices.

When the decision was finally handed down, Linda Greenhouse wasn't the only person surprised that the Court not only had affirmed the Ninth Circuit, but that it had done so by a vote of 7-2. That hardly clears up the question as to why the Court granted

---

[39] *Id.* at 1585–86 (internal citations omitted).

[40] See Lyle Denniston, Argument preview: Kids and Video Games, SCOTUSblog, Oct. 26, 2010, http://www.scotusblog.com/?p=107224 (opining that "at least four Justices—the number needed to grant review—seemed at least temporarily persuaded by California's argument that the issue was one of 'national importance' because of the rise of what the state called 'a new, modern threat to children'").

cert in the first place. But even more surprising was the lineup, which was not only unusual but unique; in almost two decades of service together on the Court, this was the first time, as far as I have been able to determine, that Justices Breyer and Thomas were together, alone, in dissent.

Justice Scalia's opinion for the Court (joined only by Justices Ginsburg, Kennedy, Sotomayor, and Kagan for a majority—another unusual alliance) is straightforward: *Ginsberg* is not a shield from heightened First Amendment scrutiny any time a legislature deems speech "harmful to minors"; it only applies to speech that is harmful to minors because it is *obscene* as to minors. The decision relies heavily on *Stevens* for the proposition that "new categories of unprotected speech may not be added to the list by a legislature that concludes [that] certain speech is too harmful to be tolerated."[41] As Scalia says,

> without persuasive evidence that a novel restriction on content is part of a long (if heretofore unrecognized) tradition of proscription, a legislature may not revise the "judgment [of] the American people," embodied in the First Amendment, "that the benefits of its restrictions on the Government outweigh the costs."[42]

And just as the Court rejected the federal government's attempt in *Stevens* to "shoehorn" speech about animal cruelty into the category of the "obscene," so too does it reject California's "attempt to make violent-speech regulation look like obscenity regulation":[43]

> Our cases have been clear that the obscenity exception to the First Amendment does not cover whatever a legislature finds shocking, *but only depictions of "sexual conduct"* ... [V]iolence is not part of the obscenity that the Constitution permits to be regulated.[44]

If violent speech, like depictions of animal cruelty, can't be shoehorned into the category of the "obscene," it follows almost *a fortiori*

---

[41] See Brown, 131 S. Ct. at 2734 ("That holding [in *Stevens*] controls this case.").
[42] *Id.* (quoting Stevens, 130 S. Ct. at 1585).
[43] *Id.*
[44] *Id.* at 2734–35.

that it can't be shoehorned into the category of speech that is "obscene-*as-to-minors*." *Ginsberg*, the Court declares, did not permit the New York legislature to regulate material that (merely) had been deemed "harmful to minors," it permitted the New York legislature to regulate *sexual* material that had been deemed harmful to minors. The statute that was upheld in *Ginsberg* was, the Court emphasizes, "a prohibition on the sale to minors of *sexual* material that would be obscene from the perspective of a child";[45] it merely "adjust[ed] the definition of *obscenity*," taking an already-existing category of unprotected speech and adjusting its contours to fit the "'social realities by permitting the appeal of this type of material to be assessed in terms of the sexual interests' [of] minors.'"[46]

Rational legislative judgments that those materials are harmful to children because of their *sexual content* will be upheld (as in *Ginsberg*); but the legislature is not free to expand the boundaries of that obscene-as-to-minors category to include whatever material it (rationally or not) has declared harmful to minors:

> Speech that is neither obscene as to youths nor subject to some other legitimate proscription cannot be suppressed solely to protect the young from ideas or images that a legislative body thinks unsuitable for them.[47]

The Court declares that it might entertain the creation of a new exception for "violent-as-to-minors" speech "if there were a long-standing tradition in this country of specially restricting children's access to depictions of violence."[48] But there is no such tradition.[49] So the California statute is (simply) "a restriction on the content of

---

[45] *Id.* at 2735 (emphasis in original).

[46] *Id.* (quoting Ginsberg, 390 U.S. at 638).

[47] *Id.* at 2736 (quoting Erznoznik v. Jacksonville, 422 U.S. 205, 213–14 (1975)).

[48] *Id.*

[49] *Id.* The opinion here goes off into a short riff on the widespread depiction of violence in books and movies to which we give children access, citing *Grimm's Fairy Tales*, *The Inferno*, *The Odyssey*, and *The Lord of the Flies* (while somehow managing to omit "The Itchy & Scratch Show" from *The Simpsons*, which is both a parodic cartoon commentary on the availability of hyper-violent cartoon fare consumed by (fictional) children, and also itself watched by millions of children (and adults) tuning in to *The Simpsons*).

protected speech" and receives the Full Monty of strict scrutiny.[50] California must show more than that the California legislature was not acting irrationally in declaring violent videogames a threat to the health or well-being of the state's minors; it must show that the statute "is justified by a compelling government interest and is narrowly drawn to serve that interest."[51]

If you're like me, this is the point, in Supreme Court First Amendment opinions, where you stop reading closely and begin skimming. The hard, outcome-determinative battle is over; now it only remains for the Court to find reasons why the statute fails strict scrutiny, which it virtually always does.[52] But it's worth taking a quick look at this portion of the Court's opinion, for I will return to it in the discussion below. The Court holds that the statute fails both strict scrutiny prongs. It fails the "compelling interest" requirement because while there is certainly *some* evidence that violent video games cause harm—enough, certainly, for a rational legislature to act on—California "cannot show a direct causal link between violent video games and harm to minors"[53] with the "degree of certitude *that strict scrutiny requires.*"[54] A belief—even a reasonable belief—in that causal link is not sufficient; under this most assertive form of judicial scrutiny, California "bears the risk of uncertainty, [and] ambiguous proof will not suffice."[55]

Second, even if California were able to demonstrate the existence of that causal link between violent speech and harm to minors, the statute would nonetheless be unconstitutional because it is not narrowly tailored to achieve its asserted goal. It is "wildly underinclusive" because it only covers violent video games, and not the wide range of other violent speech (in movies, cartoons, nursery rhymes, fairy tales . . .) to which children are exposed, and because the statute is content to "leave this dangerous, mind-altering material in the hands of children so long as one parent (or even an aunt or

---

[50] *Id.* at 2738; see also *id.* at 2757 (Alito, J., concurring) ("[T]he Court now holds that any law that attempts to prevent minors from purchasing violent video games must satisfy strict scrutiny instead of the more lenient standard applied in *Ginsberg*").

[51] *Id.* at 2738.

[52] See *supra* notes 7–8 and accompanying text.

[53] Brown, 131 S. Ct. at 2738.

[54] *Id.* at 2739 n.8 (emphasis added).

[55] *Id.*

uncle) says it's OK."[56] This alone, the majority declares, is enough to defeat the legislation.[57] Moreover, the statutory coverage is also "vastly overinclusive":[58] though the state asserted that the statute was designed to "aid parental authority,"

> [n]ot all of the children who are forbidden to purchase violent video games on their own have parents who *care* whether they purchase violent video games. While some of the legislation's effect may indeed be in support of what some parents of the restricted children actually want, its entire effect is only in support of what the State thinks parents *ought* to want. This is not the narrow tailoring . . . that restriction of First Amendment rights requires.[59]

Justice Alito, concurring for himself and Chief Justice Roberts, would hold the statute unconstitutional on the "narrower ground that the law's definition of 'violent video game' is impermissibly vague."[60] Due process requires that "laws give people of ordinary intelligence fair notice of what is prohibited"—especially in the context of speech regulation because of "the obvious chilling effect" that vagueness has on speech.[61] The obscenity doctrine (as I noted above) doesn't define obscenity, but it does require that it *be* defined, with specificity; statutes targeting unprotected obscenity must target "depict[ions] or descri[ptions of] sexual conduct *specifically defined* by the applicable state law."[62] But the California law does not meet this vital threshold requirement; it does not define "violent video games" with the "'narrow specificity' that the Constitution

---

[56] *Id.* at 2740; see also *id.* ("That is not how one addresses a serious social problem.").

[57] *Id.*

[58] *Id.* at 2741.

[59] *Id.* (emphasis in original).

[60] *Id.* at 2742 (Alito, J., concurring).

[61] *Id.* at 2743.

[62] *Id.* at 2744 (citing Miller, 413 U.S. at 24). The Court in *Miller* gave "a few plain examples of what a state statute could define for regulation" under the standard announced in the opinion, including "[p]atently offensive representations or descriptions of ultimate sexual acts [and] [p]atently offensive representations or descriptions of masturbation, excretory functions, and lewd exhibition of the genitals." 413 U.S. at 25.

demands."[63] Reasonable people could disagree about exactly *what* the California statute prohibited:

> The threshold requirement of the California law does not perform the narrowing function served by the limitation in *Miller*. . . . It provides that a video game cannot qualify as "violent" unless "the range of options available to a player includes killing, maiming, dismembering, or sexually assaulting an image of a human being."
>
> For better or worse, our society has long regarded many depictions of killing and maiming as suitable features of popular entertainment, including entertainment that is widely available to minors. The California law's threshold requirement would more closely resemble the limitation in *Miller* if it targeted a narrower class of graphic depictions.[64]

The other definitional provisions of the statute—targeting speech that "a reasonable person . . . would find appeals to a deviant or morbid interest of minors [and] patently offensive to prevailing standards in the community as to what is suitable for minors"—are also "not up to the task," because (unlike obscenity) there are no "generally accepted standards regarding the suitability of violent entertainment for minors."[65]

> The California Legislature seems to have assumed that these [community] standards are sufficiently well known so that a person of ordinary intelligence would have fair notice as to whether the kind and degree of violence in a particular game is enough to qualify the game as "violent."
>
> There is a critical difference, however, between obscenity laws and laws regulating violence in entertainment. . . . Although our society does not generally regard all depictions of violence as suitable for children or adolescents, the prevalence of violent depictions in children's literature and entertainment creates numerous opportunities for reasonable people to disagree about which depictions may excite "deviant" or "morbid" impulses.[66]

[63] Brown, 131 S. Ct. 2741.
[64] *Id.*
[65] *Id.* at 2745.
[66] *Id.* at 2746.

IV. The Dissents

If you're looking for a good illustration, perhaps to show friends or students, of just how odd the discourse in the Supreme Court can be at times, look no further. With only a little bit of imaginative effort, the four opinions in this case could be seen as coming out of four entirely different legal systems; it's as though the same statute had been presented for consideration to the highest court in the United States, Romania, Morocco, and Australia, and these are the opinions that emerged from that process.

Justice Thomas's dissenting opinion expresses the hard-headed and uncompromising originalism for which he is well known:

> When interpreting a constitutional provision, "the goal is to discern the most likely public understanding of [that] provision at the time it was adopted." *McDonald v. Chicago,* [130 S. Ct. 3020, 3072 (2010)] (Thomas, J., concurring in part and concurring in judgment). Because the Constitution is a written instrument, "its meaning does not alter." *McIntyre v. Ohio Elections Comm'n,* 514 U. S. 334, 359 (1995) (Thomas, J., concurring in judgment) (internal quotation marks omitted). "That which it meant when adopted, it means now." *Ibid.* (internal quotation marks omitted). . . .
>
> As originally understood, the First Amendment's protection against laws "abridging the freedom of speech" did not extend to all speech. . . . In my view, the "practices and beliefs held by the Founders" reveal another category of excluded speech: speech to minor children bypassing their parents. The historical evidence shows that the founding generation believed parents had absolute authority over their minor children and expected parents to use that authority to direct the proper development of their children. It would be absurd to suggest that such a society understood "the freedom of speech" to include a right to speak to minors (or a corresponding right of minors to access speech) without going through the minors' parents. . . . The founding generation would not have considered it an abridgment of "the freedom of speech" to support parental authority by restricting speech that bypasses minors' parents.[67]

In support of this latter proposition—which, more or less, ends the constitutional inquiry for Justice Thomas—he relies, *inter alia,*

---

[67] Brown, 131 S. Ct. at 2751–52 (Thomas, J., dissenting).

on Wadsworth's *The Well-Ordered Family* (1712), Cotton Mather's *A Family Well-Ordered* (1699), *The History of Genesis* (1708), Locke's *Some Thoughts Concerning Education* (1692), Burgh's *Thoughts on Education* (1749), along with a number of more recent scholarly studies focused on child-rearing practices during the Founding period.[68]

That is originalism on steroids and, to my eye, rather poignantly illustrates the weakness of the approach. I understand, and am sympathetic to, the notion that the meaning of a constitutional provision should be informed by the meaning given to it by those who drafted and ratified it. But can that really mean that we will look to the child-rearing principles of Cotton Mather and John Locke to define, for all time, the scope of the constitutional protection for free speech? Even assuming that Justice Thomas (or anyone else) can reconstruct the sociology of the 18th century to definitively support the notion that parents possessed "absolute authority" over their children, and that "total parental control over children's lives" was the governing societal norm—what then? The question in this case is not "do parents have absolute authority over their children?" The question in the case is, rather, "how does what the state did *here* relate to (1) the authority of parents over their children, (2) the power of the state to protect the well-being of children, and (3) the constitutional protection for 'the freedom of speech'?" That's a hard question in 2011, and it would have been a hard question in 1791, because it involves *categorization*: Is this, actually, a case about the authority of parents over their children? Or is it a case about the extent of the state's power to protect minors? The scope of the First Amendment rights of video game manufacturers? Or the scope of the First Amendment rights of minors? Nothing in Justice Thomas's historical research tells me, or can possibly tell me, how people in the 18th century would have answered *those* questions. Let me put it this way: I know enough about discourse in the late 18th century to know that if you had walked into a bar in, say, Richmond, or Boston, or Philadelphia, in 1791 and made any of the following statements, you would have gotten a nice little argument going:

- "The government has just decreed that children can't attend religious services. Can it do that?"

[68] See *id.* at 2752–57.

- "The government has just decreed that all schoolbooks must include endorsements of John Adams's candidacy for the presidency, and a defense of the Alien and Sedition Act. Can it do that?"
- "The government has just decreed that adults may not sing to children who are not their own. Can it do that?"

Justice Thomas believes that all those questions can be answered in the affirmative—and, more importantly, that "18th century society" would have answered all those questions in the affirmative. (Indeed, he believes the former precisely *because* he believes the latter.) His belief is misplaced, in my opinion. No amount of historical research can tell us what "the answer" to any of those questions would have been—in 1791, 1891, or 1991—because there is no "answer" that "society" can give to those questions. They're contested and contestable propositions, depending on (among other things) how you characterize what the government was doing: helping parents or usurping their role, for example.[69]

---

[69] Another reason that the opinions in this case may well end up in First Amendment casebooks is the *sotto voce* argument between Justices Scalia and Thomas, the Court's most committed originalists, on this very point. Here is Scalia responding to Thomas's dissent:

> Justice Thomas . . . denies that persons under 18 have any constitutional right to speak or be spoken to without their parents' consent. Most of his dissent is devoted to the proposition that parents have traditionally had the power to control what their children hear and say. This is true enough. And it perhaps follows from this that the state has the power to enforce parental prohibitions— to require, for example, that the promoters of a rock concert exclude those minors whose parents have advised the promoters that their children are forbidden to attend. *But it does not follow that the state has the power to prevent children from hearing or saying anything without their parents' prior consent.* The latter would mean, for example, that it could be made criminal to admit persons under 18 to a political rally without their parents' prior written consent—even a political rally in support of laws against corporal punishment of children, or laws in favor of greater rights for minors. . . . It could be made criminal to admit a person under 18 to church, or to give a person under 18 a religious tract, without his parents' prior consent. . . . Such laws do not enforce parental authority over children's speech and religion; they impose governmental authority, subject only to a parental veto. In the absence of any precedent for state control, uninvited by the parents, over a child's speech and religion (Justice Thomas cites none), and in the absence of any justification for such control that would satisfy strict scrutiny, those laws must be unconstitutional.

Brown, 131 S. Ct. at 2736 n. 3.

At the far other end of the spectrum from Justice Thomas's rigid and uncompromising stance, Justice Breyer's dissent is all balance and nuance. The most eye-catching feature of his dissenting opinion (and the one that earned it Ms. Greenhouse's designation as "most unusual judicial performance" of the 2010 term[70]) are the two lengthy appendices, listing "peer-reviewed academic journal articles"[71]—the "vast preponderance of which," the majority opinion informs us, "is outside the record"[72]—on the topic of "psychological harm resulting from playing violent video games," categorized as either supporting (Appendix A, the longer of the two) or not supporting (Appendix B) the hypothesis that violent video games are harmful to minors.

I cannot say for certain exactly why Justice Breyer thought that this extensive listing would advance the constitutional discussion (as opposed to, say, a sentence or two along the lines of "There are lots of studies, some on one side and some (fewer) on the other."). He begins with his own recharacterization of the case—thereby nicely illustrating the point I made above concerning the significance of characterization—as being about neither the authority of parents over their children nor depictions of violence:

> [T]he special First Amendment category I find relevant is not (as the Court claims) the category of "depictions of violence," but rather the category of "protection of children."[73]

Categorized that way, of course, *Stevens*—which the majority, you will recall, found controlling[74]—is entirely irrelevant, for it had nothing to do with the "protection of children." Justice Breyer applies what he calls "a strict form of First Amendment scrutiny"[75] to review of the California statute, although it is clearly not the "strict scrutiny" of ordinary usage:

---

[70] See Greenhouse, note 1, *supra*.

[71] Brown, 131 S. Ct. at 2771 (Breyer, J., dissenting).

[72] *Id.* at 2739 n.8 (majority opinion).

[73] *Id.* at 2762 (Breyer, J., dissenting).

[74] See *supra* note 41 and accompanying text.

[75] Brown, 131 S. Ct. at 2762 (Breyer, J., dissenting); see also *id.* at 2765 ("I would determine whether the State has exceeded [constitutional] limits by applying a strict standard of review.").

> Like the majority, I believe that the California law must be "narrowly tailored" to further a "compelling interest," without there being a "less restrictive" alternative that would be "at least as effective." I would [however] not apply this strict standard "mechanically." Rather, in applying it, I would *evaluate the degree to which the statute injures* speech-related interests, *the nature of* the potentially-justifying "compelling interests," *the degree to which* the statute furthers that interest, *the nature and effectiveness of* possible alternatives, and, in light of this evaluation, whether, *overall*, "the statute works speech related harm . . . *out of proportion to the benefits* that the statute seeks to provide."[76]

It's a kind of multifactor cost-benefit balancing test, meant to be difficult, though "not impossible" to satisfy.[77] As applied to the statute at issue, it reveals no constitutional flaw. The California law "imposes no more than a modest restriction on expression."[78] The "interest that California advances in support of the statute is compelling"—both "(1) the basic parental claim to authority in their own household to direct the rearing of their children, which makes it proper to enact laws designed to aid discharge of [parental] responsibility, and (2) the state's "independent interest in the well-being of its youth."[79] There is "considerable evidence that California's statute significantly furthers this compelling interest."[80] And Justice Breyer finds "no 'less restrictive' alternative to California's law that would be 'at least as effective'" as the statutory scheme it enacted.[81]

The most revealing portion of his opinion comes when introducing the material in those appendices. After a fairly lengthy discussion of the social science literature on the harm to children from exposure

---

[76] *Id.* at 2765–66 (emphasis added).

[77] *Id.* at 2766.

[78] *Id.*

[79] *Id.* at 2767 (quoting Ginsberg, 390 U.S. at 639–40).

[80] *Id.*

[81] *Id.* at 2770; see also *id.* at 2771:

> The upshot is that California's statute, as applied to its heartland of applications (i.e., buyers under 17; extremely violent, realistic video games), imposes a restriction on speech that is modest at most. That restriction is justified by a compelling interest (supplementing parents' efforts to prevent their children from purchasing potentially harmful violent, interactive material). And there is no equally effective, less restrictive alternative.

to violent video games and the "many scientific studies that support California's views,"[82] Justice Breyer acknowledges that "[e]xperts debate the conclusions of all these studies [and that] some of those critics have produced studies of their own in which they reach different conclusions."[83] He continues: "I, like most judges, lack the social science expertise to say definitively who is right. But . . . ."[84]

At this point, I admit I expected something like: "But I defer to the legislative judgment of the people of California." Instead, he writes that

> associations of public health professionals who do possess that expertise have reviewed many of these studies and found a significant risk that violent video games, when compared with more passive media, are particularly likely to cause children harm.[85]

After a review of these "meta-analyses"[86] (by such groups as the American Academy of Pediatrics, the American Academy of Child and Adolescent Psychiatry, the American Psychological Association, the American Medical Association, the American Academy of Family Physicians, and the American Psychiatric Association), he concludes:

> Unlike the majority, I would find sufficient grounds *in these studies and expert opinions* for this Court to defer to an elected legislature's conclusion that the video games in question are particularly likely to harm children.[87]

So he would "defer" to the legislature here, but only because of his independent (and off-record) examination of the studies and expert opinions in the academic literature.

---

[82] *Id.* at 2768.
[83] *Id.* at 2769.
[84] *Id.*
[85] *Id.*
[86] *Id.* at 2768.
[87] *Id.* at 2770 (emphasis added).

V. Discussion

The *Brown* decision was hailed by many, and probably most, commentators as a big victory for free speech and the First Amendment,[88] and I suppose it is. It does seal up a crack—when read along with *Stevens, two* cracks—in what we might call the wall of separation between speech and state: "obscenity" may be outside the scope of the First Amendment, but the government can't get away with simply defining any speech it wishes to suppress as "obscene" (*Stevens*) or "obscene as to minors" (*Brown*) and avoid the heightened scrutiny to which content-based regulation is ordinarily subject under the First Amendment.

Two things, though, might give us pause. To begin with, on the legal question at the heart of the case—will a legislature's decision to prohibit the distribution of purportedly harmful but non-obscene speech receive the highest level of First Amendment scrutiny?—the Court appears to be split into a somewhat more fragile 5-4 alignment than the overall vote might suggest. Justice Alito and Chief Justice Roberts did not, technically speaking, reach the level-of-scrutiny question in their concurrence, having decided the threshold (vagueness) question in the respondents' favor; but their "brief[] elaborat[ion]" of the "reasons for questioning the wisdom of the Court's

---

[88] See, e.g., Catherine J. Ross, The Supreme Court Was Right to Strike Down California's Video Game Law, Wash. Post, June 27, 2011, http://www.washingtonpost.com/opinions/the-supreme-court-was-right-to-strike-down-californias-video-game-law/2011/06/27/AG6jYDoH;usstory.html ("The justices rejected a radical challenge to free speech—in the process protecting all of us, not just children."); David G. Savage, Supreme Court Strikes Down California Video Game Law, L.A. Times, June 28, 2011, http://www.latimes.com/entertainment/news/la-na-0628-court-violent-video-20110628,0,5099090.story (noting that the decision "highlights a consistent theme of the high court under Chief Justice John G. Roberts Jr.: Freedom of speech is almost always a winner, even if the context is unusual"); Brent Jones, Our View: Even Violent Video Games Are Protected, USA Today, Jun. 27, 2011, http://www.usatoday.com/news/opinion/editorials/2011-06-27-Even-violent-video-games-are-protected;usn.htm (describing "why the Supreme Court was right Monday in giving the makers of violent video games the same protections as the pamphleteers, printers and orators of the 18th century"); Tony Mauro, Roberts Court Extends Line of Permissive First Amendment Rulings in Video Game Case, The AmLaw Daily, June 28, 2011, http://amlawdaily.typepad.com/amlawdaily/2011/06/scotusfirst amendmentvideo.html (*Brown* decision continues an "undeniable trend line" in favor of "classic First Amendment protection for even the most objectionable speech").

approach"[89] makes it fairly clear that they are inclined to answer
the question in the negative:

> [T]he Court is far too quick to dismiss the possibility that
> the experience of playing video games (and the effects on
> minors of playing violent video games) may be very different
> from anything that we have seen before. . . . In some of
> these games, the violence is astounding. . . . When all of the
> characteristics of video games are taken into account, there
> is certainly a reasonable basis for thinking that the experience
> of playing a video game may be quite different from the
> experience of reading a book, listening to a radio broadcast,
> or viewing a movie. And if this is so, then for at least some
> minors, the effects of playing violent video games may also
> be quite different. The Court acts prematurely in dismissing
> this possibility out of hand. . . . I would not squelch legislative
> efforts to deal with what is perceived by some to be a signifi-
> cant and developing social problem. If differently framed
> statutes are enacted by the States or by the Federal Govern-
> ment, we can consider the constitutionality of those laws
> when cases challenging them are presented to us.[90]

So whether this particular crack is truly sealed up or just papered
over for the moment remains to be seen.

A more troubling feature of the decision concerns what Justice
Breyer refers to in his dissent as the "serious anomaly in First
Amendment law"[91] created by the majority's holding:

> *Ginsberg* makes clear that a State can prohibit the sale to
> minors of depictions of nudity; today the Court makes clear
> that a State cannot prohibit the sale to minors of the most
> violent interactive video games. But what sense does it make
> to forbid selling to a 13-year-old boy a magazine with an
> image of a nude woman, while protecting a sale to that 13-
> year-old of an interactive video game in which he actively,
> but virtually, binds and gags the woman, then tortures and
> kills her? What kind of First Amendment would permit the
> government to protect children by restricting sales of that

[89] Brown, 131 S. Ct. at 2746 (Alito, J., concurring).
[90] *Id.* at 2748, 2749, 2751.
[91] *Id.* at 2771 (Breyer, J., dissenting).

extremely violent video game only when the woman—
bound, gagged, tortured, and killed—is also topless?[92]

It's a very good question: What kind of First Amendment is that,
and is it indeed the one that we now have? Justice Alito noted the
same anomaly:

> As a result of today's decision, a State may prohibit the sale
> to minors of what *Ginsberg* described as "girlie magazines,"
> but a State must surmount a formidable (and perhaps insur-
> mountable) obstacle if it wishes to prevent children from
> purchasing the most violent and depraved video games
> imaginable.[93]

It appears to be, unfortunately, a correct reading of First Amendment doctrine post-*Brown*. Tellingly, the majority opinion—notwithstanding Justice Scalia's usual penchant for engaging directly with
objections raised in the other opinions, as he does in regard to a
number of other matters several times in his opinion here—contains
no reference or response to this charge, an implied concession, in
my view, that the majority recognizes that it has no good rejoinder
to the point.

It is unfortunate, because the system of legal doctrine has any
number of self-correction and self-repair mechanisms, and serious
anomalies—points of doctrine that look silly, as this one does—
often lead to re-assessments and revisions, with no guarantee that
any such a revision will be a more speech-protective one. And it's
also unfortunate because it was so unnecessary; the majority had
ample opportunity to bring this area of First Amendment doctrine
more closely into line with common sense, and failed to seize it.

To see that, we need to go to the majority's treatment of *Ginsberg*.
The majority reads *Ginsberg* to declare that material that is "obscene
as to minors," like other "obscene" speech, is outside the protection
of the First Amendment, and that a legislature's decision to regulate
or prohibit such speech will be given only the lightest touch of
rational basis review. To which, in *Brown*, the Court simply adds:
we will strictly enforce the boundaries around this category, and

---

[92] *Id.*

[93] *Id.* at 2747 (Alito, J., concurring).

only allow the legislature to place sexually themed material into it, not just anything the legislature deems "harmful to minors."

It's a plausible reading of *Ginsberg*, entirely consistent with the language in the *Ginsberg* opinion itself. It is, however, *not* the reading that courts, including the Supreme Court itself, had been giving *Ginsberg* over the past 20 years or so.

To see this, consider this rather unexceptional statement of the "strict scrutiny" test, from the Ninth Circuit's opinion in this case:

> We ordinarily review content-based restrictions on protected expression under strict scrutiny, and thus, to survive, the Act "must be narrowly tailored to promote a compelling Government interest." *United States v. Playboy Entm't Group, Inc.*, 529 U.S. 803, 813 (2000). "If a less restrictive alternative would serve the Government's purpose, the legislature must use that alternative." *Id.; see also Sable Comm'ns of Cal., Inc. v. FCC*, 492 U.S. 115, 126 (1989) ("The Government may . . . regulate the content of constitutionally protected speech in order to promote a compelling interest if it chooses the least restrictive means to further the articulated interest."); *Reno v. ACLU*, 521 U.S. 844, 876–77 (1997) (finding relevant the fact that a reasonably effective method by which parents could prevent children from accessing internet material which parents believed to be inappropriate "will soon be widely available").[94]

It's all very familiar, almost boilerplate, First Amendment "strict scrutiny" language. But notice: each of the cases cited (*United States v. Playboy, Sable Comm. v. FCC,* and *Reno v. ACLU*) deal with *restrictions on the distribution of sexually themed material to minors*[95]—*Ginsberg*

---

[94] Schwarzenegger, 556 F.3d at 958.

[95] In *Playboy,* cable operators successfully challenged a federal statute requiring operators "who provide channels 'primarily dedicated to sexually-oriented programming' either to 'fully scramble or otherwise fully block' those channels or to limit their transmission to hours when children are unlikely to be viewing, set by administrative regulation as the time between 10 p.m. and 6 a.m.," 529 U.S. at 806. In *Sable,* the challenged federal statute "made it a crime to use telephone facilities to make 'obscene or indecent' interstate telephone communications 'for commercial purposes to any person under eighteen years of age or to any other person without that person's consent'," 492 U.S. at 120. Finally, in *Reno,* the statute criminalized both "the knowing transmission of obscene or indecent messages to any recipient under 18 years of age" and the "sending or displaying of patently offensive messages in a manner that is available to a person under 18 years of age," 521 U.S. at 857–60.

cases—and yet they all are being cited as exemplars of "strict scrutiny." How can that be?

Or consider another case in this recent line, *Ashcroft v ACLU*, where the Court again upheld a challenge to a statute "enacted by Congress to protect minors from exposure to sexually explicit materials on the Internet."[96] Here, without even so much as a nod in *Ginsberg*'s direction,[97] the Court again applied heightened scrutiny to the statutory scheme, demanding that the government show that there were no "less restrictive alternatives" available to it and that "speech is restricted no further than necessary to achieve the goal" of shielding minors from harm. The Court struck down the statute on the grounds that "there are a number of plausible, less restrictive alternatives to the statute" that would allow the government to achieve its purpose of protecting minors from harm—primarily, software filters that impose only "selective restrictions" on speech and that "may well be more effective" than the statutory restrictions at keeping harmful material out of the hands of minors.[98]

It's more than a little curious. In all these cases, attempts to regulate the distribution of sexually themed material to minors received (and, as it happens, failed) heightened scrutiny—*not* the rationality review seemingly called for by *Ginsberg*.

Ginsberg, I would suggest, had all but vanished from the scene, along with the notion that speech in the "obscene as to minors" category could be suppressed without being subject to any First Amendment scrutiny at all. Under these and a host of other post-*Ginsberg* precedents, a regulation targeting the distribution of even sexually themed material to minors must be narrowly tailored to

---

[96] 542 U.S. 656, 659 (2002).

[97] The majority opinion in *Ashcroft* does not even mention *Ginsberg*.

[98] *Id.* at 667. The opinion cites *Playboy* for support:

> The closest precedent on the general point is our decision in *Playboy Entertainment Group*. *Playboy Entertainment Group*, like this case, involved a content-based restriction designed to protect minors from viewing harmful materials. The choice was between a blanket speech restriction and a more specific technological solution that was available to parents who chose to implement it. Absent a showing that the proposed less restrictive alternative would not be as effective, we concluded, the more restrictive option preferred by Congress could not survive strict scrutiny.

> *Id.* at 670 (citations omitted).

achieve its purposes, and it must be the least restrictive alternative available to solve the problem being addressed; it must, in short, survive strict First Amendment scrutiny.

The majority here in *Brown* could easily have taken this approach, treating this case not as a *Ginsberg* case, but as a *Playboy-Reno-Sable-Ashcroft* case: The statute must satisfy the "narrow tailoring" requirement, *not because it is targeted at something other than sexually themed material, but because it is a content-based suppression of speech that gets, as always, the strictest of scrutiny.* There's no "anomaly" here at all; this "wildly overinclusive" and "vastly underinclusive" statute is *not* narrowly tailored to achieve its purpose, and it is therefore unconstitutional—*whether or not it targets depictions of topless, or merely maimed, women.*

So all the ink spilled in this case, and all the fighting, about whether or not this statute falls within "the *Ginsberg* 'obscene-as-to-minors' exception," were entirely irrelevant to the outcome of the case; under this long line of post-*Ginsburg* precedent, the statute would receive (and cannot satisfy) strict First Amendment scrutiny—proving, once again, I suppose, how important characterization can be in constitutional litigation.

What is most troubling, then, about *Brown* is that it appears to resurrect a version of *Ginsberg* that had been, if not exactly sent to the glue factory, at least turned out to pasture some time ago. The entire Court has now endorsed a version of *Ginsberg* that shields some speech from First Amendment scrutiny altogether. Two cheers to the Court for making that category smaller than California wanted it to be. But the post-*Ginsberg* precedent had virtually eliminated the category altogether. This may, or may not, matter down the road; we'll see. But a home run for the First Amendment it's not, and I'm not prepared to jump on that bandwagon quite yet.

Snyder v. Phelps: A Hard Case That Did Not Make Bad Law

*Paul E. Salamanca**

In *Snyder v. Phelps*,[1] the Court stood by the First Amendment in hard times. A religious group conducted a protest some 1,000 feet from a fallen marine's funeral, holding such pickets as "God Hates the USA," "Thank God for Dead Soldiers," and "You're Going to Hell." Despite the empathy that virtually anyone would feel for the marine's grieving father, the Court held by a vote of eight to one that his action for intentional infliction of emotional distress and intrusion upon seclusion could not survive, owing largely to the public nature of the issues the protesters had raised.[2] "Hard cases," a British judge once wrote, "are apt to introduce bad law."[3] "Great cases," Justice Holmes elaborated, "like hard cases make bad law. For great cases are called great, not by reason of their real importance in shaping the law of the future, but because of some accident of immediate overwhelming interest which appeals to the feelings and distorts the judgment."[4] The "accident of immediate overwhelming interest" at work in *Snyder v. Phelps* was the very real and compelling humanitarian claim presented by that grieving father, Albert Snyder.

As a doctrinal matter, *Snyder* may have involved little more than the application of settled law to difficult facts. More than a dozen

* Wyatt, Tarrant & Combs Professor of Law, University of Kentucky, College of Law. I am grateful to Richard Ausness, Jean Ellen Cowgill, Josh Douglas, Jon Fleischaker, Michael Healy, Cynthia Marks, Chad Meredith, John Nalbandian, John Roach, David Royse, and Christina Wells for their comments on this article.

[1] 131 S. Ct. 1207 (2011).

[2] See *id.* at 1219 (intentional infliction of emotional distress); see also *id.* at 1220 (intrusion upon seclusion).

[3] Winterbottom v. Wright, (1842) 152 Eng.Rep. 402, 406; 10 M.&W. 109, 116 (Rolfe, B.).

[4] Northern Securities Co. v. United States, 193 U.S. 197, 400 (1904) (Holmes, J., dissenting). See also Christina E. Wells, Privacy and Funeral Protests, 87 N.C. L. Rev. 151, 233 (2008).

times, the Court has recognized that the Constitution protects sharp discourse over matters of public concern. The list of words and phrases it has used to make this point is long. The First Amendment protects "disagreeable" speech,[5] "distasteful" speech,[6] speech that has "profound unsettling effects,"[7] "misguided" speech,[8] "scurrilous" speech,[9] speech that "stirs people to anger,"[10] "unseemly expletive[s],"[11] "four-letter word[s],"[12] "execrations,"[13] "contemptuous" speech,[14] "offensive" speech,[15] "embarrass[ing]" speech,[16] "insulting" speech,[17] "outrageous" speech,[18] even "hurtful" speech.[19] With this language in mind, some of which the Court first used more than 70 years ago, one might plausibly be surprised that the litigation between Mr. Snyder and the church went as far as it did. The answer might lie in the circumstances of the case: a father in grief, a son who gave his life for his country, and a religious group that took advantage of the son's funeral to express a message that many consider outrageous. The cultural pressure on the Court to uphold the verdict against the church was unquestionably intense. The Court

---

[5] Texas v. Johnson, 491 U.S. 397, 414 (1989) (burning of the flag).

[6] Cohen v. California, 403 U.S. 15, 21 (1971) (wearing of a jacket bearing the words "Fuck the Draft" in a courthouse).

[7] Terminiello v. Chicago, 337 U.S. 1, 4 (1949) (provocative speech).

[8] Hurley v. Irish-American Gay, Lesbian and Bisexual Group of Boston, Inc., 515 U.S. 557, 574 (1995) (exclusion of a group from a private parade); Cantwell v. Connecticut, 310 U.S. 296, 310 (1940) (religious speech).

[9] Cohen, 403 U.S. at 22.

[10] Terminiello, 337 U.S. at 4.

[11] Cohen, 403 U.S. at 23.

[12] Id. at 25.

[13] Id. at 23.

[14] Street v. New York, 394 U.S. 576, 593 (1969) (burning of the flag accompanied by derogatory words relating thereto).

[15] Hill v. Colorado, 530 U.S. 703, 715 (2000) (statute prohibiting certain expressive activity within 100 feet of the entrance to a medical facility); Texas v. Johnson, 491 U.S. at 414; Cohen, 403 U.S. at 23, 25; Street, 394 U.S. at 592.

[16] NAACP v. Claiborne Hardware Co., 458 U.S. 886, 910 (1982) (boycott of commercial establishments).

[17] Boos v. Barry, 485 U.S. 312, 322 (1988) (signs near an embassy that might bring the foreign government into "public odium" or "public disrepute").

[18] Id.

[19] Hurley, 515 U.S. at 574.

therefore deserves credit for adhering to previously recognized principles and for not constructing an artificial category to sustain an otherwise desirable result.

To be sure, *Snyder* did break some new ground. For example, the Court may have recast *Hustler Magazine, Inc. v. Falwell*—albeit without being explicit—as a case depending more on the status of the speech at issue therein (a crude parody suggesting that Jerry Falwell had committed incest with his mother) than on Falwell's status as a public figure.[20] Had *Hustler* depended entirely on Falwell's status, it would not have supported the holding in *Snyder*, assuming Mr. Snyder was a private figure—an issue the Court did not address.[21] In fact, by the principle of *expressio unius est exclusio alterius* ("to say the one is to exclude the other"), it might have supported a holding against the church.

The Court could have explained exactly why the protest did not fall into any recognized category of unprotected speech, such as fighting words. Instead, it took the incremental tack of reiterating the importance of speech on matters of public concern and putting the protest in that category. In doing this, the Court responded to arguments that the protesters had sought to exploit the funeral for their own benefit and that Mr. Snyder was part of a "captive audience." In a potentially important development, the Court indicated that merely hitching speech on a matter of public concern to someone else's wagon, without more, does not exclude it from protection.[22] With respect to captive audiences, the Court may have nudged this doctrine back toward its proper boundaries, where people in public places subjected to speech they find offensive are ordinarily expected to look or walk away.

The following is a brief description and largely positive critique of *Snyder*.

I. Facts

On March 3, 2006, Marine Lance Corporal Matthew A. Snyder died in the line of duty in Iraq.[23] His father, Albert Snyder, arranged

---

[20] Hustler Magazine, Inc. v. Falwell, 485 U.S. 46 (1988).

[21] Although the Court did not address this issue, Justice Samuel Alito in his dissent twice described Mr. Snyder as a private figure. See Snyder, 131 S. Ct. at 1222, 1226 (Alito, J., dissenting).

[22] See Snyder, 131 S. Ct. at 1217–18.

[23] Snyder v. Phelps, 533 F. Supp. 2d 567, 571 (D. Md. 2008).

for the funeral to take place on March 10 at St. John's Catholic Church in Westminster, Maryland. Local papers gave notice of the service.[24]

On March 8, members of the Westboro Baptist Church of Topeka, Kansas, founded in 1955 by Fred W. Phelps, announced their intention to travel to Maryland to conduct a protest of the funeral. In fact, they conducted three protests in Maryland, one near the capitol in Annapolis, one near the Naval Academy, and one near the funeral itself.[25]

The funeral procession passed within 200 or 300 feet of the last protest.[26] Although Mr. Snyder could see only the tops of Westboro's signs, and did not learn their contents until he saw them on television that evening,[27] they bore messages that would deeply offend the average citizen, let alone a grieving father. Reflecting their belief that "God hates and punishes the United States for its tolerance of homosexuality, particularly in [its] military,"[28] the signs read: "God Hates the USA/Thank God for 9/11," "America Is Doomed," "Don't Pray for the USA," "Thank God for IEDs," "Fag Troops," "Maryland Taliban," "Fags Doom Nations," "Not Blessed Just Cursed," "Thank God for Dead Soldiers," "Pope in Hell," "Priests Rape Boys," "You're Going to Hell," and "God Hates You."[29]

The protest took place approximately 1,000 feet from the church, on public land next to a public way, in a plot designated by police. Although the protesters sang hymns and recited verses from the Bible, they did not yell or utter profanities. There was no violence,[30]

---

[24] In their brief and throughout oral argument, respondents contended or suggested that Mr. Snyder had made himself a public figure by notifying the press about the funeral, by giving interviews to the media about his son, and perhaps by engaging in other expressive activities. See Brief for Respondents at 5–6, 32, Snyder, 131 S. Ct. 1207 (No. 09–751); Transcript of Oral Argument at 32, 34, 36, 39, 40, 51, 52, Snyder, 131 S. Ct. 1207 (No. 09–751).

[25] Snyder, 131 S. Ct. at 1213. See also Brief of Amicus Curiae American Civil Liberties Union et al. at 2, Snyder, 131 S. Ct. 1207 (2011) (No. 09–751).

[26] According to Mr. Snyder, the procession would have passed closer to the protest had it not been rerouted. See Brief for Petitioner at 4, Snyder, 131 S. Ct. 1207 (No. 09–751).

[27] See Snyder, 131 S. Ct. at 1213.

[28] Id.

[29] Id. at 1216–17. "God Hates the USA" and "Thank God for 9/11" were on opposite sides of the same sign. The words "God's View" were opposite the words "Not Blessed Just Cursed." See Brief of Amicus Curiae ACLU, supra note 25, at 3.

[30] See Snyder, 131 S. Ct. at 1213.

but there appear to have been a number of people in the area, owing in part to counterprotests against Westboro.[31] The protest lasted about half an hour and ended as the funeral began.[32]

Some weeks later, one of Westboro's members, Shirley L. Phelps-Roper, posted an "epic" on the church's website. In this tract, Ms. Phelps-Roper made pointed criticisms of Mr. Snyder and his ex-wife, specifically that they had "taught Matthew to defy his creator," that they had "raised him for the devil," and that they had "taught him that God was a liar."[33] Mr. Snyder discovered the epic while conducting a search on Google.[34]

On June 5, 2006, Mr. Snyder filed a lawsuit in federal court against Mr. Phelps and the church.[35] He later added Ms. Phelps-Roper and Rebekah A. Phelps-Davis as defendants. Mr. Snyder sought damages on five different theories: defamation, intrusion upon seclusion, publicity given to private life, intentional infliction of emotional distress, and civil conspiracy. In October 2007, the district court granted defendants' motion for summary judgment on the claims of defamation and publicity given to private life.[36] The court justified its decision as to defamation on the ground that the epic "was essentially Phelps-Roper's religious opinion and would not realistically tend to expose Snyder to public hatred or scorn."[37] It rejected the claim of publicity given to private life because defendants had not published any information that had previously been private. The case went to the jury on the remaining three claims.

---

[31] See Brief of Amicus Curiae ACLU, *supra* note 25, at 4, ("'More than 20 Patriot Guard Riders . . . carried American flags and stood between Respondents and the church. The Patriot Guard made a 'tunnel' of flags from Mr. Snyder's car to the church entrance. . . .'") (citation omitted); see also J. Joshua Wheeler, The Road Not Taken: How the Fourth Circuit Reached the Right Result for the Wrong Reason in *Snyder v. Phelps*, 2010 Cardozo L. Rev. de novo 273, 277–78 (2010) ("An organized group of motorcycle riders. . . . were stationed at two places during the funeral service, both of which were closer to the church than the location of the Phelps protest.").

[32] See Snyder, 131 S. Ct. at 1213; Brief of Amicus Curiae ACLU, *supra* note 25, at 3; Brief for Respondents, *supra* note 24, at 8.

[33] Snyder, 533 F. Supp. 2d at 572.

[34] *Id.*

[35] *Id.* Jurisdiction rested on diversity of citizenship.

[36] *Id.* Mr. Snyder did not seek review of these decisions. See Snyder v. Phelps, 580 F.3d 206, 213 n.3 (4th Cir. 2009).

[37] *Id.* at 572–73. The claim for defamation appears to have depended entirely on the epic.

The jury then brought in a plaintiff's verdict of $10.9 million, including $2.9 million in compensatory and $8 million in punitive damages.[38] Although the court rejected most of defendants' motions after trial, it did reduce punitive damages to $2.1 million, making the total award $5 million.[39]

The Fourth Circuit Court of Appeals reversed, concluding that Westboro's speech addressed matters of public concern,[40] made no assertions that were susceptible to proof or disproof,[41] and consisted largely of "rhetorical hyperbole and figurative expression."[42]

The Supreme Court affirmed, in an opinion written by Chief Justice John Roberts and joined by every member of the Court except Justice Samuel Alito (with Justice Stephen Breyer writing a short concurring opinion). The Court divided its analysis into two parts, one relating to Mr. Snyder's claim for intentional infliction of emotional distress[43] and another relating to his claim for intrusion upon seclusion.[44]

II. The Court Precludes Recovery for Intentional Infliction of Emotional Distress

In the first analytical part of *Snyder*, the Court devoted much of its attention to reiterating the importance of speech on matters of public concern, allocating the signs to this category, and defending

---

[38] *Id.* at 573.

[39] *Id.* at 597.

[40] Snyder, 580 F.3d at 222–23.

[41] *Id.* at 223.

[42] *Id.* at 224. Judge Dennis Shedd concurred in the judgment, concluding that Mr. Snyder had not satisfied the elements of either intentional infliction of emotional distress or intrusion upon seclusion under Maryland law. See *id.* at 227 (Shedd, J., concurring in the judgment). The majority rejected this tack on the ground that the appellants had not presented it for review. See *id.* at 216–17. The Supreme Court acknowledged Judge Shedd's view but assumed for the sake of argument that the protest would constitute a tort. See Snyder, 131 S. Ct. at 1215 n.2. In his dissent, Justice Alito emphatically maintained that Mr. Snyder had made out a proper claim for intentional infliction of emotional distress. See *id.* at 1223 (Alito, J., dissenting) ("Although the elements of the IIED tort are difficult to meet, respondents long ago abandoned any effort to show that those tough standards were not satisfied here.").

[43] See Snyder, 131 S. Ct. at 1215–19 (Part II).

[44] See *id.* at 1219–20 (Part III).

this allocation against Mr. Snyder's most salient objections.[45] Although this part ran to only 19 paragraphs, the Court devoted at least 13 of them to this one issue. As the Court explained, speech on matters of public concern "is the essence of self-government" in a democracy, where the people themselves are the ultimate source of authority.[46] Quoting previous cases, the Court then gave a broad conception of such speech. "Speech deals with matters of public concern," wrote the Chief Justice, "when it can 'be fairly considered as relating to any matter of political, social, or other concern to the community,' or when it 'is a subject of legitimate news interest; that is, a subject of general interest and of value and concern to the public.'"[47] The Court then explained that whether speech pertains to public or private matters depends on its "content, form, and context," "as revealed by the whole record,"[48] and that courts have a duty to conduct "an independent examination" of the record to ensure that the principles of free speech are protected.[49]

The Court applied that precedent to the protest, beginning with the signs' content. Although most would reject Westboro's theology, the Court properly recognized that the signs spoke to matters of public importance—"the political and moral conduct of the United States and its citizens, the fate of our nation, homosexuality in the military, and scandals involving the Catholic clergy."[50]

The Court then turned to Mr. Snyder's objections. He had argued that at least some of the signs, particularly those that included the

---

[45] The Court rendered its decision without reference to the epic, concluding that petitioner had not presented it for review. See Snyder, 131 S. Ct. at 1214 n.1.

[46] *Id.* at 1215 (quoting Garrison v. Louisiana, 379 U.S. 64, 75 (1964)).

[47] *Id.* at 1216 (quoting Connick v. Myers, 461 U.S. 138, 146 (1983); San Diego v. Roe, 543 U.S. 77, 83–84 (2004) (per curiam)) (internal citations omitted).

[48] *Id.* (quoting Dun & Bradstreet, Inc. v. Greenmoss Builders, Inc., 472 U.S. 749, 761 (1985) (opinion of Powell, J.) (quoting Connick, 461 U.S. at 761)) (internal quotation marks omitted).

[49] *Id.* (quoting Bose Corp. v. Consumers Union of the United States, Inc., 466 U.S. 485, 499 (1984) (quoting N.Y. Times v. Sullivan, 376 U.S. 254, 284–86 (1964))). At this point in the opinion, the need at least for a remand became obvious, because the Maryland district court had allowed the jury to decide whether the First Amendment protected at least some of the signs. See Snyder, 533 F. Supp. 2d at 578 ("While signs expressing general points of view are afforded . . . protection," the court wrote, certain other signs, "which could be interpreted as being directed at the Snyder family, created issues for the finder of fact.").

[50] Snyder, 131 S. Ct. at 1217.

word "you," referred directly to his son or his family as a whole and therefore spoke only to private matters.[51] He also argued that speech on a matter of public concern loses some of its protection when it is attached to an event like the funeral.[52] Even if the factual premises underlying these arguments were valid, the Court said, they did not lessen the protest's claim to protection, given both its "overall thrust and dominant theme" and its location "on public land next to a public street."[53] In other words, the Court indicated, the fact that speech takes place in a traditional public forum renders more likely its status as speech on a matter of public concern. By taking this tack, the Court was able to pretermit the issue of whether the signs "related to" the Snyders.[54] It was also able to concede that Westboro had set up its protest in "connection" or "conjunction" with the funeral.[55] "There is no doubt," wrote the Chief Justice, "that Westboro chose to stage its picketing at the Naval Academy, the Maryland State House, and Matthew Snyder's funeral to increase publicity for its views and because of the relation between those sites and its views . . . ."[56]

Although the Court acknowledged the pain the protest must have caused Mr. Snyder, it nevertheless refused to allow his claim for intentional infliction of emotional distress to go forward.[57]

---

[51] See Brief for Petitioner, *supra* note 26, at 36 ("'The [Fourth Circuit] declined to analyze whether the Phelpses' numerous other signs, including those saying, 'You're Going to Hell' and 'God Hates You,' raised a matter of public concern, despite acknowledging that the signs could reasonably be interpreted as targeted specifically at Mr. Snyder."). Justice Alito emphasized this point in his dissent. See Snyder, 131 S. Ct. at 1226 (Alito, J., dissenting) ("[I]t is abundantly clear that respondents, going far beyond commentary on matters of public concern, specifically attacked Matthew Snyder.").

[52] See Brief for Petitioner, *supra* note 26, at 40 ("[E]ven matters of 'public concern' lose some of their protection when interjected into the context of a private funeral.").

[53] Snyder, 131 S. Ct. at 1217.

[54] *Id.*

[55] *Id.*

[56] *Id.*

[57] See *id.* at 1217–19. At this point, the Court might also have explained why Mr. Synder's likely status as a private figure did not put the protest outside the First Amendment. See *infra* notes 72–82 and accompanying text for a discussion of this issue.

III. The Court Precludes Recovery for Intrusion upon Seclusion

The Court then turned to Mr. Snyder's claim for intrusion upon seclusion, with particular reference to his contention that he was part of a "captive audience" at his son's funeral.[58] In making this argument, Mr. Snyder relied on a line of cases in which the Court had held that the First Amendment does not protect speech that invades a "substantial privacy interest . . . in an essentially intolerable manner."[59] The difficulty with such precedent is always in the details, of course. But the Court made relatively short work of this issue, resolving it in only five paragraphs.[60] It began by emphasizing a salutary rule of default, that people in public places subjected to speech they dislike have a presumptive duty to avert their eyes (from a visual message) or walk away (from an aural message). "In most circumstances," wrote the Chief Justice, "the Constitution does not permit the government to decide which types of otherwise protected speech are sufficiently offensive to require protection for the unwilling listener or viewer. Rather," he continued, "the burden normally falls upon the viewer to avoid further bombardment of [his] sensibilities simply by averting [his] eyes."[61] The Court then described the doctrine of captive audiences as one "applied . . . only sparingly," giving two examples of its application to the home.[62] It then refused to apply this narrow doctrine to Mr. Snyder's situation, rendering his claim for intrusion upon seclusion untenable.[63]

---

[58] See Brief for Petitioner, *supra* note 26, at 45 ("Even assuming . . . that the Phelpses' *speech alone* would be entitled to First Amendment protection in other circumstances, Mr. Snyder is entitled to governmental protection from the Phelpses' conduct because he was a captive audience at his son's funeral.").

[59] Cohen, 403 U.S. at 21.

[60] See Snyder, 131 S. Ct. at 1219–20 (Part III).

[61] *Id.* at 1220 (quoting Erznoznik v. City of Jacksonville, 422 U.S. 205, 210–11 (1975)) (brackets original) (quotation marks omitted).

[62] See *id.* (citing Rowan v. Post Office Dep't, 397 U.S. 728 (1970) (delivery of offensive mail to the home); citing and quoting Frisby v. Schultz, 487 U.S. 474, 484–85 (1988) (pickets "before or about" a residence)).

[63] See Snyder, 131 S. Ct. at 1220. Mr. Snyder's claim for civil conspiracy, on which the jury had also found in his favor, required liability for at least one substantive tort. Because the First Amendment was a bar to both intentional infliction of emotional distress and intrusion upon seclusion, the Court held that Mr. Snyder could not recover on this claim. See *id.*

IV. The "Outrageousness" of Speech Should Not Exclude It from Protection

In *Snyder*, the Court stood by its own precedent in difficult circumstances, which is the test of any principle. The First Amendment would not be worth much if it gave way when *truly* unpopular speech were at issue,[64] and practitioners will now have *Snyder* as an example of how far the Constitution extends in protecting unpalatable speech. The Court also deserves credit for not constructing an artificial category to sustain the verdict in favor of Mr. Snyder. Any such category would have had porous walls and therefore would have posed a threat to free expression.

Take, for example, the basic argument that "outrageous" speech is a category with real contours that public servants and juries can administer without regard to point of view. This task is virtually, if not literally, an impossible one for human beings.[65] "'Outrageousness,'" the Court correctly observed, "is a highly malleable standard with 'an inherent subjectiveness about it which would allow a jury to impose liability on the basis of the jurors' tastes or views, or perhaps on the basis of their dislike of a particular expression.'"[66] As Chief Justice William Rehnquist wrote in *Hustler*, if the Court there could have laid down "a principled standard" to distinguish *Hustler*'s parody from Thomas Nast's cartoons, "public discourse would probably [have] suffer[ed] little or no harm." "But we doubt that there is any such standard," he went on to say, "and we are quite sure that the pejorative description 'outrageous' does not supply one."[67] The Court in *Snyder* was therefore on solid ground in holding that the nature of the protest was no bar to protection. In fact, the Court quite properly observed that, had others stood next to Westboro with such pickets as "God Bless America" and "God Loves You," liability would not have attached.[68]

---

[64] See Brandenburg v. Ohio, 395 U.S. 444, 446–47 (1969) (per curiam) (speech at a meeting of the Ku Klux Klan that included extensive racial epithets). See also Brief of Amicus Curiae Reporters Committee for Freedom of the Press et al. at 12–14, Snyder, 131 S. Ct. 1207 (No. 09–751).

[65] See generally Eugene Volokh, Freedom of Speech and the Intentional Infliction of Emotional Distress Tort, 2010 Cardozo L. Rev. de novo 300, 308 (2010).

[66] Snyder, 131 S. Ct. at 1219 (quoting Hustler, 485 U.S. at 55).

[67] Hustler, 485 U.S. at 55.

[68] Snyder, 131 S. Ct. at 1219.

The principle of avoiding malleable tests appeared throughout *Snyder*, not just in the context of "outrageous" speech. Whether speech is directed at another person is also a matter of degree. Outside the context of fighting words, which merits distinct attention,[69] a large volume of powerful speech can be seen as "directed" toward someone, rendering the presence or absence of "direction" a weak limiting principle from the point of view of free speech. Imagine, for example, a university that conferred degrees in a discipline sincerely believed by a small group to be frivolous. Imagine as well a protest of its graduation with such pickets as "This Place Is a Joke," "You Never Studied," or "You Learned Nothing." The graduates may well find the signs "outrageous" and see them as "directed" toward them. This cannot be enough to render the First Amendment inapplicable. Human beings are social beings, and much of what they do is bound up with matters of public concern. Mere "relation to" another person, without more, should not exclude speech on a matter of public concern from protection. The Court was thus correct not to find this point dispositive.[70]

Much the same can be said with respect to the question of taking advantage of another's event for expressive purposes. At first impression, such speech truly does come across as opportunistic and perhaps even obnoxious. "This is my graduation," one might say. But again we find ourselves with a principle that potentially includes so much that it would inevitably facilitate uneven application and discrimination according to point of view. Speech is most powerful when given at the right place and time. Effective speech will often exploit some other event. The Gettysburg Address is one of the most famous speeches ever given on our nation's soil. Its power arose in part from its location, its proximity in time to the battle, and the blood that had earned the site its special significance. We can surely assign a positive valence to the principles Lincoln articulated in 1863 that virtually all would deny to Westboro's signs, but that contrast should be irrelevant to the scope of protection. The

---

[69] See *infra* notes 123–30 and accompanying text.

[70] See Snyder, 131 S. Ct. at 1217 ("[E]ven if a few of the signs . . . were viewed as containing messages related to Matthew Snyder or the Snyders specifically, that would not change the fact that the overall thrust and dominant theme of Westboro's demonstration spoke to broader public issues.").

Court was therefore on solid ground in finding this issue as well non-dispositive.[71]

For similar reasons, the Court was correct not to allow Mr. Snyder's likely status as a private figure to affect its conclusion. In addition to arguing that speech directed to another or that exploits the event of another deserves minimal protection, Mr. Snyder had also argued that the First Amendment should strike a different balance where the audience of harsh language is a private figure. "Where . . . a private figure has not linked himself to an issue of public concern," he maintained, "the state's interest in protecting the private figure should outweigh an attacker's First Amendment right to publicly hurl epithets in his direction."[72]

In making this argument, Mr. Snyder had some wind at his back. In its jurisprudence on defamation and the First Amendment, for example, the Court has emphasized the status of the plaintiff. Thus, a public official or figure seeking to recover for defamation must establish not only that the statement was false but also that the defendant acted with "actual malice"—"knowledge" that the statement was false or "reckless disregard" as to its accuracy.[73] This requirement holds true without regard to the relief sought. For private plaintiffs, however, the rules are different. If the statement pertains to a matter of public concern, a private plaintiff can obtain compensatory damages for defamation by establishing falsity and a degree of fault short of actual malice, such as negligence.[74] In addition, if the statement pertains to a matter of *private* concern, a private plaintiff potentially can obtain any form of relief, whether or not he or she can establish actual malice.[75] The Court has justified its differential treatment of public and private figures on two grounds. First, public figures presumably have greater access to the media to defend themselves and thus less need to vindicate themselves in court.[76] Second, public figures choose to enter the

---

[71] See *id.* at 1217–18.

[72] Brief for Petitioner, *supra* note 26, at 34.

[73] N.Y. Times, 376 U.S. at 279–80.

[74] See Gertz v. Robert Welch, Inc., 418 U.S. 323, 347 (1974).

[75] See Dun & Bradstreet, 472 U.S. at 761 (plurality).

[76] See Gertz, 418 U.S. at 344.

maelstrom of debate and thus can be seen in purely normative terms as less deserving of the courts' protection.[77]

Despite this jurisprudence on defamation, however, Mr. Snyder's best support arguably lay in *Hustler Magazine, Inc. v. Falwell*, a decision from 1988 that actually involved a claim for intentional infliction of emotional distress.[78] *Hustler* arose from a parody of an advertisement for Campari Liqueur. In a feigned interview, the magazine had Falwell describing "a drunken incestuous rendezvous with his mother in an outhouse."[79] Per Chief Justice Rehnquist, the Court foreclosed the claim unless Falwell, clearly a public figure, could establish the same kind of "actual malice" on the magazine's part as would be required to sustain a claim for defamation.[80] Because the parody was too hyperbolic to be credible, this exception was essentially a throw-away, leaving a public figure like Falwell at the mercy of such caricatures.

That case was arguably strong precedent for Mr. Snyder. If *Hustler* relied entirely on Falwell's status as a public figure, and if Mr. Snyder could establish that he was not such a figure, logic might suggest that his action should proceed. Here, the Court was perhaps called on to reconcile two lines of precedent: on the one hand, its many recognitions over the years that the Constitution protects sharp words in public discourse, and on the other, its apparent emphasis in *Hustler* on the status of the plaintiff. Although it did not resolve this issue explicitly in *Snyder*, between the lines it may have recast *Hustler* as extending to all claims arising from speech on a matter of public concern, even if the plaintiff is a private figure. If so, Mr. Snyder's likely status as a private figure mattered only in determining whether the protest spoke to an issue of public concern. As the Court observed, however, "even if a few of the signs . . . were viewed as containing messages related to Matthew Snyder or the Snyders specifically, that would not change the fact that the overall thrust and dominant theme of Westboro's demonstration spoke to broader public issues."[81]

---

[77] See *id.*
[78] 485 U.S. 46 (1988).
[79] *Id.* at 48.
[80] See *id.* at 56.
[81] *Snyder*, 131 S. Ct. at 1217.

Whatever the Court's exact analysis, it was correct not to allow Mr. Snyder's status to dictate the holding of the case. Private figures are often implicated in debates on public issues. Consider again the hypothetical university conferring degrees in a discipline thought by some to be frivolous. The graduates themselves would almost certainly be private figures.[82]

V. The "Captive Audience" Should Be a Narrow Category

As many have observed, the Court's jurisprudence on the question of captive audiences has not been entirely coherent.[83] At times, it has adhered to the idea that a captive audience is one that literally cannot avoid a particular form of expression. Thus, in *Kovacs v. Cooper*, the Court upheld a law that forbade individuals from operating trucks that emitted "loud and raucous noises" on public ways, due to the inability of those nearby to ignore such noises.[84] Likewise, in *Grayned v. City of Rockford*, the Court upheld restrictions on "[n]oisy" and "disrupt[ive]" protests near schools in session.[85] Applying the same principle to reach the opposite conclusion, the Court in *Cohen v. California* famously vacated a conviction for disturbing the peace of a man who had worn a jacket bearing the words "Fuck the Draft" in a courthouse.[86] "[P]ersons confronted with Cohen's jacket," wrote Justice Harlan by way of distinguishing *Kovacs*, "were in a quite different posture than, say, those subjected to the raucous emissions of sound trucks blaring outside their residences. Those in the Los Angeles courthouse could effectively avoid further bombardment of their sensibilities simply by averting their eyes."[87]

Other cases followed in the same vein. In *Erznoznik v. City of Jacksonville*, the Court struck down an ordinance that prohibited

---

[82] See Volokh, *supra* note 65, at 305 ("[T]he category of private figures includes many people—civil rights lawyers, authors, civic group officers, professors, criminals, and more—who are involved with matters of public concern."); see also *id.* ("Even the speech in *Hustler* could easily have inflicted emotional distress on Falwell's mother, had she been alive at the time.").

[83] See, e.g., Wells, *supra* note 4, at 156.

[84] 336 U.S. 77, 78 (1949) (plurality) (quoting the ordinance).

[85] 408 U.S. 104, 120 (1972).

[86] 403 U.S. 15, 26 (1971).

[87] *Id.* at 21.

nude images from the screens of drive-ins visible from a public way, on the ground that people could simply look away.[88] Similarly, in *Madsen v. Women's Health Center, Inc.*, the Court invalidated part of an injunction that prohibited protesters from displaying images outside a medical clinic that could be seen by patients inside.[89] In reaching this conclusion, the Court took the sensible position that the clinic could simply "pull its curtains."[90]

On the other hand, the Court has also upheld various restrictions without regard to whether the audience could just avert its eyes or walk away. In *Frisby v. Schultz*, for instance, it upheld an ordinance that prohibited prolonged pickets in front of a single residence, even though the occupants could presumably close their blinds.[91] Similarly, in *Rowan v. Post Office Department*, the Court upheld a statute that authorized people to specify erotic material that they did not want to receive in the mail, even though they could simply take one look at it and throw it away.[92] Perhaps the most extreme case in this vein was *Lehman v. City of Shaker Heights*, where the Court upheld a city's refusal to carry advertisements for political campaigns inside its municipal buses, despite patrons' ability to sit or look elsewhere.[93] Finally, in *FCC v. Pacifica Foundation* the Court upheld a reprimand against Pacifica for its broadcast of George Carlin's "Seven Dirty Words" over the radio during the day.[94] Although someone could certainly have averted his or her ears by turning off the radio after the broadcast began, Justice John Paul Stevens rejected this option, analogizing it to "saying that the remedy for an assault is to run away after the first blow."[95]

This second line of decisions is problematic. When the Court expands the concept of a "captive audience" beyond the bounds of

---

[88] 422 U.S. 205 (1975).

[89] 512 U.S. 753, 773 (1994).

[90] *Id.* The Court upheld other parts of this injunction, however. See *id.* at 770 (prohibition on pickets in certain areas); *id.* at 772–73 (prohibition on noise). The Court justified the ban on pickets as a means of protecting access. The ban on loud noises reflected the teaching of *Kovacs*.

[91] 487 U.S. 474, 488 (1988).

[92] 397 U.S. 728, 737–38 (1970).

[93] 418 U.S. 298, 304 (1974) (plurality).

[94] 438 U.S. 726, 750–51 (1978).

[95] *Id.* at 748–49.

someone who literally cannot avoid the speech at issue, it adopts a construction of "captivity" that arguably allocates too much authority to the audience. That is, instead of protecting an unwilling listener from hearing something that he or she simply cannot avoid, the Court grants that person an ability to restrict all speech within his or her zone that he or she finds offensive—however that zone may come to be defined.

There is abstract merit to this construction of "captivity," but not enough to matter. As Robert Nozick argued, our sensibilities are more fully implicated in a community than across an entire country. "In a nation," he wrote, "one knows that there are nonconforming individuals, but one need not be directly confronted by these individuals or by the fact of their nonconformity. Even if one finds it offensive that others do not conform," he went on, "even if the knowledge that there exist nonconformists rankles and makes one very unhappy, this does not constitute being harmed by the others or having one's rights violated." But, he concluded, "in a face-to-face community one cannot avoid being directly confronted with what one finds to be offensive. How one lives in one's immediate environment is affected."[96] In other words, people will often feel better if their daily movements and transactions do not bring them into contact with ways of life and forms of expression that they find unorthodox and unsettling.

This utopian vision has intuitive appeal. Indeed, it may be compelling with respect to private property owned by people who prefer harmony over cacophony. But it has never found support in our cases with respect to public property, especially such traditional public forums as streets, walks, and parks—and rightly so. Given our pluralistic culture, our belief that answers come from unexpected directions, and our inveterate mistrust of the censor's hand—who, after all, is always a human being—we have properly eschewed the idea that the government or any group of citizens can edit the content of expression in a public place for the sake of decorum or the protection of sensibilities. As Justice Oliver Wendell Holmes once wrote, "time has upset many fighting faiths." "[T]he best test of truth," he added, "is the power of the thought to get itself accepted

[96] Robert Nozick, Anarchy, State, and Utopia 322 (1974).

in the competition of the market...."[97] "The Constitution exists precisely so that opinions and judgments, including esthetic and moral judgments about art and literature, can be formed, tested, and expressed," observed Justice Anthony Kennedy. "[T]hese judgments are for the individual to make, not for the Government to decree, even with the mandate or approval of a majority."[98]

At least some of the variant precedent described above can be defended on alternate grounds. *Frisby*, for example, can perhaps be defended on the ground that an omnipresent protest in front of one's house implicates the physical security of oneself and one's family. Arguably, few heads of household would relax knowing that someone was continually present just outside. In a completely different context, the Court has observed that being able to maintain control over the proximity of others is causally related to physical security.[99] On balance, however, this approach may not prove persuasive. After all, many people live on streets full of pedestrians, and even a Hyde Park of the United States may have neighbors.[100]

Frisby might also be defended on the ground that the home is unique, the "last citadel of the tired, the weary, and the sick."[101] (The Fourth Amendment also provides a textual hook.) This approach might also go some way to explain *Pacifica* and *Rowan*. The problem here is that empiric categories are inevitably porous at their outer edges. At one time, many might have put the Pledge of Allegiance in a unique juridical category,[102] or the flag.[103] Mr.

---

[97] Abrams v. United States, 250 U.S. 616, 630 (1919) (Holmes, J., dissenting).

[98] United States v. Playboy Entm't Group, Inc., 529 U.S. 803, 818 (2000).

[99] See Boos v. Barry, 485 U.S. 312, 321 (1988) (identifying "the need to protect the security of embassies" as a potentially valid basis for regulating protests near such buildings); see also Dolan v. City of Tigard, 512 U.S. 374, 394 (1994) (observing that, were the city to exact a "permanent recreational easement" along the edge of Dolan's property, she would "lose all rights to regulate the time in which the public entered onto the greenway, regardless of any interference it might pose with her retail store").

[100] I refer, of course, to London's famous public green, not our current president's formative Chicago neighborhood.

[101] 487 U.S. at 484 (quoting Gregory v. City of Chicago, 394 U.S. 111, 125 (1969) (Black, J., concurring)).

[102] See Bd. of Educ. v. Barnette, 319 U.S. 624 (1943).

[103] See Texas v. Johnson, 491 U.S. 397 (1989).

Snyder might well have seen the venue for his son's funeral as comparably special.[104]

The Court might have used *Snyder v. Phelps* as a vehicle for clarifying this area of the law. For example, it could have adopted the position that a captive audience is one that literally cannot avoid particular speech, and that Mr. Snyder was not such a person. The latter, minor premise is certainly true, as Mr. Snyder did not have to look at the Phelpses' signs, nor in fact was he able to, according to his own testimony, until he saw them on television after both the protest and the funeral were over. Instead of adopting such an aggressive approach, however, the Court simply recognized the concept of a captive audience and held that, whatever its contours, it did not embrace Mr. Snyder's situation.[105]

The Court provided some guidance on captive audiences. Along with describing the doctrine as one it applies only "sparingly,"[106] the Court also reiterated the important language from *Erznoznik* (quoting *Cohen*) that "the burden normally falls upon the viewer to avoid further bombardment of [his] sensibilities simply by averting [his] eyes."[107] Recognizing aversion as a default emphasizes the primacy of the approach taken by such cases as *Kovacs*, *Cohen*, *Grayned*, *Erznoznik*, and parts of *Madsen*, to the effect that a captive audience is one that cannot avoid being subject to unwanted speech either by looking or walking away. On the other hand, the Court cited *Frisby* and *Rowan* with approval, confirming their validity as precedent.[108]

The Court also referred to *Frisby* and *Madsen* in its analysis of Mr. Snyder's claim for intentional infliction of emotional distress. There are "a few limited situations," the Chief Justice wrote, "where the

---

[104] See Snyder, 131 S. Ct. at 1227–28 (Alito, J., dissenting) ("[F]unerals are unique events. . . .). But see Wells, *supra* note 4, at 231 ("Extending the *Frisby* rationale to funeral services because they are particularly unique [is] a mistake. One can make that claim about a host of events, ranging from graduation ceremonies to weddings and bar mitzvahs.").

[105] Snyder, 131 S. Ct. at 1220 ("We decline to expand the captive audience doctrine to the circumstances presented here.").

[106] *Id.*

[107] *Id.* (quoting Erznoznik v. City of Jacksonville, 422 U.S. 205, 210–11 (1975)) (brackets in the original).

[108] See *id.* (citing Frisby, 487 U.S. at 484–85; Rowan, 397 U.S. at 736–38).

location of targeted picketing can be regulated under provisions the Court has determined to be content neutral."[109] He then gave the ban on "picketing 'before or about' a particular residence" from *Frisby* and the "buffer zone between protesters and an abortion clinic entrance" from *Madsen* as examples.[110] This language is important both for what it says and for what it does not say. The Court obviously wrapped its arms around *Frisby*. On the other hand, by giving *Madsen* and not the later case of *Hill v. Colorado* as an example of a valid regulation of protests near a clinic, the Court may have suggested a subtle retreat from the latter precedent.

In *Hill*, the Court upheld a Ptolemaic bubble around people within a certain radius of the entrance to a medical facility.[111] Specifically, the cycle was within 100 feet of the door, and the epicycle was within eight feet of the person.[112] The Court justified its holding on the ground that the statute was neutral as to content and satisfied the test applicable to such regulations—that it served a significant public interest, was narrowly tailored, and left open ample alternative channels of communication.[113] Some of the Court's language, however, was quite broad.[114] For example, it suggested that the state's interest in the health and safety of citizens might allow a "special focus on unimpeded access to health care facilities and the avoidance of potential trauma to patients associated with confrontational protests."[115] Preventing impediments to "access" is an obvious regulation of the place or manner of speech,[116] but preventing "trauma" appears to serve interests both related and unrelated to content. A loud noise or rapid approach could certainly be "traumatic" without regard to content, reflecting the general approach of *Kovacs*, but so too could a peaceful message that a person simply does not want to hear.

---

[109] *Id.* at 1218.

[110] *Id.* (quoting Frisby, 487 U.S. at 477; Madsen, 512 U.S. at 768).

[111] See Hill v. Colorado, 530 U.S. 703, 730 (2000).

[112] See *id.* at 707.

[113] See *id.* at 725–26. The statute allowed some approach within the bubble, giving some support to the argument that it was not in fact neutral as to content. See *id.* at 742 (Scalia, J., dissenting).

[114] See generally Wells, *supra* note 4, at 208–12.

[115] Hill, 530 U.S. at 715.

[116] See Boos, 485 U.S. at 321.

The Court also sought to justify the bubble as a device to "protect listeners from unwanted communication,"[117] thus implying that a person can be a part of a "captive audience" in a public place 100 feet from the entrance to a clinic. Almost certainly, however, people do not have "substantial privacy interests," as per *Cohen*,[118] in a bubble 16 feet wide in a public place 100 feet from a clinic or hospital, absent a prophylactic need, demonstrated in the circumstances of the case, to prevent loud noises or other forms of unprotected expressive activity.[119] Perhaps the Court's decision in *Snyder* not to cite *Hill* portends a willingness to retreat from the breadth of *Hill*'s language.

VI. Going Forward

Under such precedent as *Madsen* and *Hill*, the Court has allowed lower courts and legislatures to forbid certain forms of speech in close proximity to medical clinics. If the Court stands by these decisions, a legislature perhaps may impose similar limits on protests very near funerals. Various scholars have made this observation,[120] and the Court in *Snyder* was careful to reserve this issue.[121] The question then arises whether expressive activity that would violate such restrictions would give rise to an action for intentional infliction of emotional distress or intrusion upon seclusion. Perhaps so. There is general parity between what the government may forbid in the first instance and what a jury may later deem tortious.[122]

Such a conclusion may depend on the presence or absence of some form of unprotected conduct or expression, such as "fighting words."

---

[117] Hill, 530 U.S. at 715–16.

[118] 403 U.S. at 21.

[119] See Hill, 530 U.S. at 761 (Scalia, J., dissenting); see generally Wells, *supra* note 4, at 212 (raising this general issue).

[120] See, e.g., Stephen R. McAllister, Funeral Picketing Laws and Free Speech, 55 U. Kan. L. Rev. 575, 612 (2006–2007) ("Is it possible to enact a constitutional funeral picketing law? The short answer is yes."); *id.* at 601 (reading *Frisby, Madsen*, and *Hill* to indicate that a buffer around funerals "may be permissible for purposes such as limiting noise and ensuring ingress and egress, but not simply to prevent persons from seeing messages or images that they may find disturbing or offensive"); Wells, *supra* note 4, at 231 ("What then can states do to protect mourners' privacy at funerals? More than many people realize given the seemingly all or nothing manner in which this debate has been framed.").

[121] See Snyder, 131 S. Ct. at 1218.

[122] See N.Y. Times, 376 U.S. at 265.

Snyder v. Phelps: *A Hard Case That Did Not Make Bad Law*

The original and perhaps sole justification for excluding such words from the ambit of the First Amendment was to prevent immediate breaches of the peace. By the Court's analysis, "fighting words" are words so insulting, both in content and delivery, that they are likely to induce the listener to violence.[123] The immediacy of this reaction explains why more speech or better speech cannot serve as the antidote for bad speech. To the extent it has taken this approach, the Court has adopted for fighting words the same justification it has used for excluding incitement from constitutional protection.[124]

But query whether *Madsen* and *Hill* depend entirely on this justification. To some extent, of course, they reflect a simple concern with access to places where people have a lawful right to be, a concern neutral as to content and therefore unobjectionable if drawn with enough precision. A corresponding civil action for some kind of trespass might therefore have been available in these cases.[125] But both *Madsen* and *Hill* appear to go beyond such concerns in their analysis, taking up the legal status of words that do not literally deny access. Query further, then, whether the Court would allow civil liability for non-impeding, expressive activity that would be subject to one of the restrictions upheld in these cases, and if so, on what theory.

This issue arose during the oral arguments in *Snyder*. In particular, some of the justices asked whether "fighting words," as a category of unprotected speech, could only be directed to an individual literally capable of resorting to violence.[126] The justices also asked whether

---

[123] See Cohen, 403 U.S. at 20 (defining "fighting words" as "those personally abusive epithets which, when addressed to the ordinary citizen, are, as a matter of common knowledge, inherently likely to provoke violent reaction"); Street, 394 U.S. at 592; Chaplinsky v. New Hampshire, 315 U.S. 568, 572 (1942) ("'Fighting words" are "those which by their very utterance inflict injury or tend to incite an immediate breach of the peace.").

[124] See Brandenburg v. Ohio, 395 U.S. 444 (1969) (per curiam).

[125] See generally Prosser and Keeton on the Law of Torts 47 (W. Page Keeton gen. ed.) (5th ed. 1984).

[126] Transcript of Oral Argument, *supra* note 24, at 32:

JUSTICE ALITO: Well, it's an older—it's an elderly person. She's really probably not in—in a position to punch this person in the nose.

JUSTICE SCALIA: And she's a Quaker, too.

persistent following, stalking, or harassment might support liability.[127] Although the Phelpses' counsel denied that any such activity, expressive or otherwise, was at issue in the case,[128] and the Court later confirmed the absence of such activity,[129] the justices' questions certainly support the conclusion that a case that did present fighting words or the like could support liability. In fact, Justice Breyer was quite clear in his concurrence that the First Amendment would not protect a message communicated via fighting words.[130]

Conclusion

In *Snyder*, the Court took the modest tack of identifying a category of protected speech—speech on a matter of public concern—and refusing to make an exception to that category for Westboro's protest. The Court was therefore justified in describing its holding as "narrow." This approach has the advantage of being minimalist, which a court would undoubtedly prefer in a case with strong cultural implications. On the other hand, this approach perhaps has the disadvantage of creating false implications about the scope of unprotected speech.

When a court starts by defining a category of unprotected expression, it suggests that speech outside the category is protected, unless it falls into yet another category of unprotected expression. The default, thus, is protection, or at least presumptive protection. (The government may regulate even protected speech if it can satisfy "strict scrutiny" by showing that the regulation is necessary and narrowly tailored to serve a compelling public interest, with no less

---

[127] See *id.* at 27 (question by Justice Kagan) ("Ms. Phelps, suppose—suppose your group or another group or—picks a wounded soldier and follows him around . . . . Does that person not have a claim for intentional infliction of emotional distress?"); *id.* at 43 (remark by Justice Kennedy) ("But . . . the hypotheticals point out that there can be an intentional infliction of emotional distress action for certain harassing conduct.").

[128] See *id.* at 29–30 (fighting words); *id.* at 41 ("[A]pproaching an individual up close and in their grill to berate them gets you out of the zone of protection, and we would never do that."); *id.* at 42 ("[W]e don't do follow-around in this church.").

[129] See Snyder, 131 S. Ct. at 1215 n.3.

[130] See *id.* at 1221 (Breyer, J., concurring). A few months after *Snyder*, Justice Scalia also gave "fighting words" as an example of unprotected speech. See Brown v. Entm't Merch. Ass'n, 131 S. Ct. 2729, 2733 (2011). This might have been an oblique reference to *Snyder*.

restrictive alternatives.[131]) In two recent cases, *United States v. Stevens* and *Brown v. Entertainment Merchants Association*,[132] the Court has taken this approach, beginning with categories of unprotected expression and emphasizing that such categories require a strong historical basis.[133] "'From 1791 to the present,'" wrote the Chief Justice in *Stevens*, a case about depictions of cruelty to animals, "the First Amendment has 'permitted restrictions upon the content of speech in a few limited areas.'"[134] "These 'historic and traditional categories long familiar to the bar,'" he went on, "'—including obscenity, defamation, fraud, incitement, and speech integral to criminal conduct—are 'well-defined and narrowly limited classes of speech, the prevention and punishment of which have never been thought to raise any Constitutional problem.'"[135] Because the United States has no legal tradition of excluding depictions of cruelty to animals from First Amendment protection, the defendant's films of fights between animals (principally dogs) did not fall into an unprotected category.[136] The Court reached a similar conclusion in *Brown* with respect to video games.[137]

On the other hand, when the Court starts out by defining a category of protected speech, it suggests that speech outside the category is not protected. This implication was perhaps a latent weakness of *Hustler*, where the Court's emphasis on Falwell's status as a public figure arguably meant that the First Amendment would not protect crude speech on a matter of public concern that did not pertain to a public figure. Given the posture of *Snyder*, in terms of both its

---

[131] See Nadine Strossen, *United States v. Stevens*: Restricting Two Major Rationales for Content-Based Speech Restrictions, 2009–2010 Cato Sup. Ct. Rev. 67, 77–78 (2010).

[132] Stevens, 130 S. Ct. 1577 (2010); Brown, 131 S. Ct. 2729 (2011).

[133] See, e.g., Stevens, 130 S. Ct. at 1584.

[134] *Id.* (quoting R.A.V. v. City of St. Paul, 505 U.S. 377, 382–83 (1992)).

[135] *Id.* (citations omitted).

[136] See *id.* at 1585.

[137] See Brown, 131 S. Ct. at 2733–34. Justice Scalia's taxonomy of unprotected speech in *Brown* differed slightly from that of Chief Justice Roberts in *Stevens*. The Chief Justice gave five examples of such speech—obscenity, defamation, fraud, incitement, and speech integral to criminal conduct, see Stevens, 130 S. Ct. at 1584—whereas Justice Scalia gave only three: obscenity, incitement, and fighting words. See Brown, 131 S. Ct. at 2733. The distinctions may not be material, although Scalia's mention of fighting words might constitute an oblique reference to *Snyder*, which preceded *Brown* by a few months.

cultural implications and the remote applicability of any such unprotected category of speech as fighting words, the Court was justified in taking the minimalist approach. In doing so, however, it left it to future cases to clarify the law in the area between the categories of protected and unprotected speech.

Don't Feed the Alligators: Government Funding of Political Speech and the Unyielding Vigilance of the First Amendment

Joel M. Gora*

"Every dollar I spend over the threshold starts feeding the alligator trying to eat me."

That was the description of Arizona's system for public financing of political campaigns from the perspective of a candidate who financed his campaign privately without government funds. What he meant was that once his campaign funding exceeded the amount that the government established as sufficient for that election, every time he raised or spent a dollar more, the government would give one dollar to his publicly funded opponent. If he had two such opponents, they *each* received a dollar to match his spending and counterattack his speech, multiplying the government resources available against him and his speech. Hence his rather graphic lament about alligators.[1]

A generation earlier, a slightly more elegantly expressed objection to government funding of politics came from Eugene McCarthy, the great liberal senator from Minnesota whose 1968 primary challenge to President Lyndon B. Johnson over the Vietnam War helped end the Johnson presidency. One of the two marquee plaintiffs in the 1976 landmark case of *Buckley v. Valeo*,[2] McCarthy was vehemently

* Professor of Law, Brooklyn Law School. I want to thank Dean Michael Gerber and the Brooklyn Law School Dean's Summer Research Stipend Program for supporting the work on this article.

[1] The quote from the unidentified candidate appears in Michael Miller, Gaming Arizona: Public Money and Shifting Candidate Strategies, 41 PS: Pol. Sci. & Pol. 527–32 (2008).

[2] Buckley v. Valeo, 424 U.S. 1 (1976). The lead plaintiff was then-Senator James L. Buckley, Conservative from New York.

opposed to all aspects of the Federal Election Campaign Act challenged in that case, particularly the brand-new government financing of presidential campaigns. In his typically wry way, McCarthy suggested that government financing of presidential campaigns was like the colonists in 1776 asking King George III to finance the American Revolution. Since politics was all about challenging and changing the government, it was ludicrous, he thought, for the government to be funding politics.[3] So he and other plaintiffs challenged *any* provision that involved government financing of politics, complaining further that it would discriminate against insurgents, third parties, and new points of view.[4]

The effort to turn Senator McCarthy's perception into constitutional doctrine proved unsuccessful in *Buckley*. The Court, with only two dissenters, held that the Constitution did not forbid the federal government from funding presidential political campaigns. The contention that government funding of politics was a constitutionally inappropriate task fell on deaf ears.

While the Court has decided around 20 campaign finance cases since then, not until this year did the Court revisit the constitutional validity of public funding of political campaigns. This time, although the Court did not embrace Senator McCarthy's insistence on complete separation of government funding and politics, it did reject a

---

[3] Here's how his former aide described McCarthy's view:

> During the American Revolution, [McCarthy] said, "One of the complaints was that the Crown was controlling politics in this country and controlling government. We now say that the government can control politics and through politics it can control the government, which really closes the whole circle as I see it." McCarthy asked people to imagine King George III saying to the colonists, "'Why don't you raise a few thousand pounds? We will provide matching funds, and you can run a pure revolution with matching funds from the Crown. We will have a few things to say about how you run the revolution and where it goes. . . .'"

Mary Meehan, The Federal Election Commission, Cato Policy Analysis No. C at 8, Nov. 1, 1980.

[4] McCarthy and Buckley were well positioned to challenge another feature of the new law, strict contribution limits, since each man had run a successful outsider campaign with help from a small number of large contributions, McCarthy's successful campaign against a sitting president had famously been underwritten by a handful of wealthy liberals, prominent among them General Motors heir Stewart Mott, whose large contributions would have been illegal under the new law.

scheme that used the levers of public funding to bring about results inconsistent with First Amendment safeguards of political speech. And the Court also expressed the kind of skepticism about government funding of politics that recalls Senator McCarthy's observations about asking King George to fund the American Revolution.

In its 5-4 ruling in *Arizona Free Enterprise Club's Freedom Club PAC v. Bennett,*[5] the Court invalidated a key feature of Arizona's self-proclaimed "Clean Election" scheme for funding state politics.[6] As Chief Justice John Roberts's opinion for the Court explained, under the Arizona Citizens Clean Elections Act, passed by voter initiative in 1998, candidates for statewide and legislative office who raise a specified amount of small private contributions can have their primary and general election campaigns funded by the government, rather than relying on their own and contributed funds. But if they choose that option, they cannot raise or spend a penny more than the government-determined amount they are given.

But the Arizona scheme went considerably further than the presidential general election flat-grant scheme upheld in *Buckley*. It also contained a trigger provision, giving additional "matching" funds to participating candidates whenever nonparticipating candidates, or independent groups supporting them, spent more than the allotment given to the participating candidate. In other words, the government decided how much would be an appropriate amount to spend on a political campaign for, say, the state senate, and gave that amount to a participating candidate. Any participating candidate then receives more money if the total amount spent by a privately funded rival, *plus* independent groups supporting that rival— or opposing the participating candidate—exceeded the designated amount. The more money spent against a government-funded candidate, the more money the government would give that candidate

---

[5] 131 S. Ct. 2806 (2011). The act is set forth at Ariz. Rev. Stat. Ann. §§ 16-940-961. The trigger matching provisions are contained in § 16-952(A)-(C).

[6] Of course, the official characterization of those who accept public financing as "clean" politicians suggests that those who eschew the "Clean Elections" program are somehow dirty or unclean, a powerful psychological inducement for candidates to go the public-funding route in the first place and for voters to incline toward those who do. Indeed in a "clean election" scheme in Maine, there was a proposal with the potential to have the official Election Day ballot identify those candidates who were "clean." See Daggett v. Comm. on Gov't Ethics & Election Practices, 205 F.3d 445, 467 (1st Cir. 2000).

to counter the spending, up to a ceiling of three times the original government-set spending limits. Beyond that level, no additional government funds would be made available to the publicly financed candidate.[7]

The pivotal issue for the Court was whether this "trigger" device would advance or hinder the First Amendment goal of facilitating "more speech." Supporters of the law claimed that since government funding would subsidize more speech by the participating candidate, it was almost by definition a "more speech" system. Challengers claimed that the availability of so-called matching funds would deter and discourage speech by outside candidates and independent groups who would be, in effect, "drowned out" by government-funded counterattacks. The more they spoke, the more the government would fund "counter-speech" against them. This prospect, in turn, would deter the outside candidates and independent groups from spending and drive the candidates into the public-financing system with its strict limits on how much speech they could have. The result would ultimately be less speech, not more, which opponents claimed to be the real purpose of the scheme.

The Court viewed the trigger provision as aimed at the heart of the First Amendment's concerns: to keep government from suppressing electoral speech. As the Court saw it, the purpose and effect of the triggered matching-funds structure were to deter and discourage campaign speech by imposing a substantial burden and penalty on the speech of privately funded candidates and independent groups, thereby undercutting the very purpose of the First Amendment to

---

[7] The lawyer who won *Arizona Free Enterprise*, rebutting claims that the system was a valid populist measure to expand political opportunity, has pointed out that, perversely, it has had the opposite effect:

> Because trigger matching funds were capped at two times the initial grant, the very wealthy could spend beyond the cap and not have the government level their speech after that. Instead, the burden in the case fell most heavily on those political speakers with little money, who were either too small or not rich enough to spend beyond the cap, such as my clients. So, the law mostly "leveled" the speech of middle-class candidates and small independent groups, while leaving the speech of wealthy and large groups like the NRA, the Sierra Club, or the SEIU far less affected.

Bill Maurer, Email to Election Law Listserv, Election Law Listserv Website/Law-Election Archives (Jun. 27, 2011, 11:26 a.m.), http://department-lists.uci.edu/piper-mail/law-election/2011-June/000494.html (last visited Aug. 8, 2011).

ensure the most robust and vigorous debate about government and politics. The ultimate result would be less speech, not more.

Thus, the Court applied strict First Amendment scrutiny, requiring the state to prove a compelling interest for the suppression of political speech. Prevention of corruption was not being furthered because none of the private political funding being burdened and deterred— by self-financed candidates, severely limited campaign contributions, or totally independent groups—could be called corrupt under the Court's precedents. To the extent that corruption might be prevented by inducing more candidates to accept public financing, this was too attenuated and indirect a justification for burdens on speech. Therefore, the clean election plan would not directly combat corruption.

As to the goal of "leveling the playing field," that had been condemned ever since *Buckley* as wholly inconsistent with the central point of the First Amendment: keeping government from controlling the quality and quantity of political speech. Accordingly, the Court properly recognized that the Arizona "trigger" mechanism was an unconstitutional state-financed counterattack that undercut the First Amendment. The government would not be allowed to do indirectly something it could not do directly: limit and level political speech. That kind of public financing of political campaigns is not constitutionally acceptable.

The four dissenters, in a spirited opinion by Justice Elena Kagan, saw the situation quite differently. To them, *Buckley* had put beyond doubt the constitutional validity of public funding of political campaigns, and the new feature of triggered matching funds was a clever way to ensure that as many candidates as possible would opt in to the public-funding system and therefore avoid the inherent corruption of wide-scale private financing of politics. Since "clean" government-funded elections would provide less opportunity for political corruption, and since the trigger mechanism would help encourage candidates to foreswear private financing and its inherent corruption, the trigger mechanism served the interests of preventing corruption, albeit in a roundabout way.

The disagreement in *Arizona Free Enterprise* over the validity of triggered matching funding is, of course, emblematic of the larger battles that have raged over campaign finance regulation for 40 years now, ever since the passage of the Federal Election Campaign Act of 1971. The battles focused on the meaning of the First Amendment and the best way to ensure a robust and well-functioning democracy, with minimum corruption and maximum participation.

On one side are justices who feel that First Amendment values have to be balanced against electoral fairness and opportunity—that is, that individual or group liberty must be tempered by constitutional concerns regarding equality and political corruption. Those justices would permit government to limit *all* political funding in the service of "leveling the playing field" and combating corruption, which they feel is endemic to private financing. Accordingly, such financing must be driven out of the system. The four *Arizona Free Enterprise* dissenters are largely in that camp.

Other justices take a more libertarian position of minimum regulation of political funding in order to protect the speech and association that it embodies and implements. They would resolve the clash between liberty and equality by hewing to the liberty side of the ledger. Indeed, they see political liberty as the source of equal political opportunity for all different points of view.

Finally, there have been justices, largely in the middle, who have straddled these issues—as did the *Buckley* decision—with a nod to liberty and a nod to equality, while trying to avoid "undue influence."

There is another way, one which insists that the clash between liberty and equality in the campaign finance area is a false one; that limits on liberty do not achieve equality but disable those without power from challenging and changing the status quo. This view also assumes that expanding political opportunity and participation are valid goals of government. For quite some time, the ACLU advocated a position that came close to achieving this synthesis. The ACLU's mantra was: (1) no limits on contributions or expenditures, so that free speech will remain unfettered by government; (2) full disclosure of large contributions to major party candidates, so that the people, not the government, can decide who has too much access or influence; and (3) public funding to all legally qualified candidates, but *without* limits and conditions—so-called floors without ceilings—to enhance and expand political speech without limiting it.[8] With public

---

[8] Regrettably, the ACLU has recently changed its policy and now supports both "reasonable" limits on contributions and conditioned limits on candidates who accept public funding. See Floyd Abrams, Ira Glasser & Joel Gora, Editorial, The ACLU Approves Limits on Speech, Wall St. J., Apr. 30, 2010, available at http://online.wsj.com/article/SB10001424052748704423504575212152820875486.html (last visited Aug. 2, 2011).

funding as a welcome part of the mix, such a policy might have been less palatable to Senator McCarthy, and certainly to the Cato Institute, but it entailed less government control than the policy approved by the Court majority in *Buckley* or the dissenters in *Arizona Free Enterprise*.

I. The *Buckley* Baseline

Almost all questions of the constitutional validity of campaign finance rules trace back to the fountainhead of *Buckley v. Valeo.* *Buckley* involved an across-the-board challenge to the sweeping changes in federal campaign finance law wrought by the Federal Election Campaign Act of 1971 and its post-Watergate amendments in 1974.

The initial FECA was a surprising mix of speech protection and regulation. First, it limited the use of media for political advertising to address skyrocketing increases in TV campaign ads during the 1960s. Some of the restrictions applied to both the media and independent groups, but they were held to violate the First Amendment—an early indication that efforts to control independent political speech would be an Achilles' heel of campaign finance regulations, as later reflected in *Arizona Free Enterprise.*[9] Second, having dealt with what appeared to be the major campaign finance problem of the time—excessive media advertising by campaigns—FECA also eliminated limits on contributions by individuals to candidates, a deregulatory surprise that would be short-lived. Third, and alternatively, FECA severely tightened porous federal disclosure requirements to deal with allegedly undue influence by large contributors. Finally, the separate Revenue Act of 1971 authorized the use of the "taxpayer checkoff," which allowed people to designate one dollar of their tax returns for a presidential public-financing fund, an important first step toward presidential election public funding.

But the original FECA did not survive a single election cycle. Instead, Congress enacted the major 1974 amendments to FECA, driven by the campaign finance excesses associated with Watergate and embodying a sweeping overhaul of federal campaign finance

---

[9] ACLU v. Jennings, 366 F. Supp. 1041 (D.D.C. 1973) (three-judge court), vacated sub nom. Staats v. ACLU, 422 U.S. 1030 (1975).

law. The new law contained severe limitations on campaign expenditures by candidates and independent groups, and similarly austere limits on contributions to candidates and political committees. The amendments carried-forward strong and intrusive disclosure provisions from the 1971 act, created a new Federal Election Commission whose members would be under the thumb of the House and Senate leadership, and, for the first time, provided for public funding of presidential elections—at least for those candidates and parties who could qualify.[10]

The law was challenged by a diverse coalition of political dissenters and outsiders, led by Senators Buckley and McCarthy, who came together over the firm conviction that the law, cheered as necessary reforms and antidotes to Watergate, was, in reality, a flawed incumbents' protection act that would entrench the political status quo, freeze out the voices of change, and systematically violate the First Amendment's commands in the process.[11] They saw the law as a seamless web of anti-democratic and anti-change devices, a systematic assault on freedoms of speech and association in the area where they had their most urgent application—elections for public office—and a regime to be enforced by the very officials whom elections are designed to challenge.

The Supreme Court only partially agreed, in a landmark decision that seemed to split as many differences as possible.[12]

On the key question of campaign funding, the Court ruled expenditures could not be restrained, since limits on political spending were direct limits on political speech. But large contributions to candidates and committees could be sharply limited because they were less directly exercises of First Amendment rights and could pose dangers of corruption and its appearance. Thus, rather than recognize that giving and spending political funds were two sides

---

[10] One early version of the Senate bill even included public funding of House and Senate campaigns as well, a far-reaching provision that was omitted during the later stages of the legislative process. See S. Rep. No. 93-689 (1974).

[11] In the interests of full disclosure, I should note that I was one of the lawyers for the *Buckley* challengers.

[12] I have been a staunch defender of *Buckley*; or at least the parts of it that vindicated First Amendment rights. See generally Joel M. Gora, *Buckley v. Valeo*: A Landmark of Political Freedom, 33 Akron L. Rev. 7 (1999). But it certainly fell short of the ideal protection of such rights against campaign finance restraints.

of the same First Amendment coin, the Court freed one but allowed government to control the other, without acknowledging the distortions and disparities that would result. This maneuver was especially questionable, considering that a candidate's contributions to his own campaign were properly held to be protected expenditures and not limitable contributions.

On disclosure, the Court upheld reporting of contributions to candidates of as little as $101, but tempered the privacy-invading speech- and association-chilling effects of that ruling by noting that controversial minor parties might escape disclosure and, where independent expenditures were concerned, ruling that only those expressly advocating the election or defeat of specified candidates could be subject to reporting and disclosure. "Issue advocacy" that criticized the stances of politicians on issues was thus declared off-limits from any form of federal regulation, a welcome safe haven that would remain for the next 25 years.

On the composition of the Federal Election Commission, the Court unanimously determined that giving a majority of its powers to officials appointed by Congress was a clear violation of the Constitution's Appointments Clause, which vests the president, not Congress, with the power to appoint such important officers. (After the ruling, Congress quickly reformed the selection method, but stipulated that no more than three of the six members could come from any one party. Only Democratic and Republican representatives have ever been appointed.)

On the public-funding aspect of *Buckley*, the Court approved. The 1974 FECA amendments had launched the first federal campaign financing in our history by providing public funds for presidential campaigns.[13] It had three components: (1) primary election matching

---

[13] At around the same time, the federal government also provided for a different kind of "public financing" of politics by allowing taxpayers to claim a modest tax credit or deduction for any political donation to a candidate or party, federal, state or local. See Buckley, 424 U.S. at 108, n.146. Some believe that encouraging citizen participation in funding politics in this fashion is the best kind of "public financing": private choices, publicly incentivized. Interestingly, when President Barack Obama was criticized for rejecting public financing and raising all his money privately, his excuse was that he was raising money from "the public." (Of course, to equate tax credits with public "subsidies" is to endorse the "tax expenditure" logic that the Court rejected this past term in *Ariz. Christian School Tuition Org. v. Winn*, 131 S. Ct. 1436 (2011), whereby the government owns all income and allows taxpayers to retain some of it.)

funds for those seeking the presidential nomination of a major party—those parties whose presidential candidates had gotten more than 25 percent of the popular vote in the prior election; (2) a direct grant of funds for the nominating conventions of a major party; and (3) a lump-sum payment for the general election presidential campaign of a major party candidate. Notice that all three of these components heavily favor the two established parties: the Democrats and Republicans. Of course, there being no free lunch, these various benefits came with lots of terms, conditions, and strings attached.

The matching-funds program for primary elections provided that a major party candidate who had raised at least $5,000 in 20 or more states, counting only donations of $250 or less, was eligible for matching funds. These funds matched the first $250 of any such donation up to a total of 50 percent of the spending limits to which the candidate had to agree—$10 million overall nationwide, *plus* state-by-state spending limits determined by an incredibly complex formula. The arrangement was structured to discourage regional candidacies of the kind represented by Alabama Governor George Wallace in 1968, or ideological candidacies like those of Senator Eugene McCarthy. Thus, from the very outset, public funding was abused to manipulate political outcomes.

The party convention funding, initially set at $2 million, came with one major string: the party could spend no more than that amount on its convention, and the same amount was made available to any party that qualified as a major party—again, Democrats and Republicans.[14]

The general election public funding was a flat grant of $20 million.[15] But the candidate receiving the grant could not raise or spend a

[14] These limits have not prevented lavish corporate and interest-group funding of convention-related activities in recent years through payments for "host city" events. Astoundingly, in 2008, while the two parties were each allotted $16.8 million of public funds for their conventions, interest-group and wealthy-donor spending on these host activities totaled over $124 million. See 35 F.E.C.R. 7, at 8 (July 2009).

[15] All three amounts were adjustable for inflation, so that the spending limits over the decades have been automatically raised. But they clearly have not kept pace with the costs of campaigning. In 2008, the basic primary limit was $42 million, the convention funding was $16.3 million, and the basic general election limit was $84 million. John McCain took the money and that was all he could spend. Barack Obama turned it down and spent almost 10 times that much: $746 million. By comparison, contribution limits were not adjusted for inflation until 2003, so that the effect of those limits each year from 1976 forward was a gradual de facto *decrease* in the contribution limits and a concomitant increase in the difficulty of fundraising for

dollar more than that for his campaign. In other words, expenditure limits were an integral feature of the presidential public funding for both the primaries and general elections. This was not a program of "floors without ceilings"; this was a program of "floors are ceilings."

The *Buckley* challengers made two basic arguments against the presidential campaign finance scheme. First, they claimed government had no business funding the political process, which was designed to be a check on government. By analogy to separation of church and state, there needed to be a separation of government and the funding of politics to avoid the dangerous "entanglement" that would result. A related submission was that funding political campaigns was not a proper exercise of Congress's spending power. The other key contention was that the funding arrangements fatally discriminated against new parties and outsider candidates and would starve them of any sustenance before they could gain a foothold in politics, in violation of both First Amendment requirements and equal protection safeguards.

The Court, by a 6-2 vote, dispatched these arguments and legitimized the constitutionality of public financing of political campaigns. Indeed, the Court warmly embraced what it considered to be the positive features of the funding program: "In this case, Congress was legislating for the 'general welfare'—to reduce the deleterious influence of large contributors on our political process, to facilitate communication by candidates with the electorate, and to free candidates from the rigors of fundraisers."[16]

First, the Court would not second-guess the congressional determination that presidential public funding would further the general welfare, a traditional form of judicial deference to congressional spending choices.[17] Second, the "entanglement" contention was rejected on the ground that the statute was a congressional effort "not to abridge, restrict, or censor speech, but rather to use public money to facilitate and enlarge public discussion and participation in the electoral process, goals vital to a self-governing people. Thus

---

those without personal wealth or connections to well-heeled interest groups and supporters. The result was more pressure to take the government money and the spending limits.

[16] 424 U.S. at 91 (citing S. Rep. No. 93-689, at 1–10 (1974)).

[17] *Id.* at 90–92.

[the statute] furthers, not abridges, pertinent First Amendment values."[18] This language was cited repeatedly by the defenders of the Arizona scheme. Finally, the Court rejected the discrimination claims: that the system entrenched the two major parties at the expense of third parties and independent candidates and new voices generally.[19]

Absent from the majority's justification was an answer to this question: How could spending limits that had just been declared unconstitutional earlier in the opinion be imposed as a condition on the receipt of public funding? Indeed, the Court had no sooner finished a stirring affirmation of the limited role of government and the maximum role of political freedom in our constitutional system,[20] when it abruptly reversed course with the attached footnote:

> For the reasons discussed in Part III, *infra*, Congress may engage in public financing of election campaigns and may condition acceptance of public funds on an agreement by the candidate to abide by specified expenditure limitations. Just as a candidate may voluntarily limit the size of the contributions he chooses to accept, he may decide to forgo private fundraising and accept public funding.[21]

The problem was that Part III explains why Congress may engage in public financing of campaigns, but it nowhere explains why the receipt of a government financial benefit (campaign subsidies) can be conditioned on the imposition of an otherwise unconstitutional condition (spending limits). That invitation to mischief has been accepted by a number of the campaign public-funding programs enacted in *Buckley*'s wake.

There were two dissenters on public financing in the *Buckley* era. Chief Justice Warren Burger, essentially channeling McCarthy's King

---

[18] *Id.* at 92–93.

[19] *Id.* at 93–108. Minor parties were three-time losers in *Buckley*, unfortunately. Contribution limits denied them the help of the occasional financial angel, public funding froze them out, and disclosure laws still applied to them.

[20] *Id.* at 57 ("In the free society ordained by our Constitution it is not the government, but the people—individually as citizens and candidates and collectively as associations and political committees—who must retain control over the quantity and range of debate on public issues in a political campaign.").

[21] *Id.* at 57 n.65.

George III theme, would have struck down the entire statute: expenditure limitations, contribution limitations, intrusive and overbroad disclosure requirements—the works.[22] He was similarly unimpressed with the constitutional justifications for public financing. Indeed, in his view, "the use of funds from the public treasury to subsidize political activity of private individuals would produce substantial and profound questions about the nature of our democratic society."[23] Quoting former Senator Howard Baker—"I think there is something incestuous about the Government financing and, I believe, inevitably then regulating, the day-to-day procedures by which the Government is selected"—Chief Justice Burger concluded that "the inappropriateness of subsidizing, from general revenues, the actual political dialogue of the people—the process which begets the Government itself—is as basic to our national tradition as the separation of church and state . . . or the separation of civilian and military authority."[24] He also viewed the program as an open invitation to government scrutiny and control of the inner workings of our campaigns and parties.

Then-Justice William Rehnquist also would have invalidated the public funding, on First Amendment grounds, because "Congress . . . has enshrined the Republican and Democratic Parties in a permanently preferred position" at the constitutional expense of minor party and independent candidates.[25]

For the next 35 years, the Court would remain virtually silent on the subject, having decreed that public financing of campaigns is constitutional and otherwise unconstitutional limitations can be imposed as a condition of accepting the public largesse.[26]

---

[22] *Id.* at 236–46 (Burger, C.J., dissenting in part).

[23] *Id.* at 247.

[24] *Id.* at 248–49.

[25] *Id.* at 293 (Rehnquist, J., dissenting in part).

[26] There was one effort, in the aftermath of *Buckley*, to challenge the limits imposed on those accepting public funds. Based on the experience of the 1976 presidential campaigns, when the major party candidates took the public funds and were barred from raising and spending a penny more, the Republican National Committee filed suit contending that presidential candidates were compelled to take the public funding because private fundraising with sharp contribution restrictions was unavailing, that the campaigns required additional assistance to be anything more than television campaigns, that any grassroots participation could no longer be financed by the parties—which had a crippling effect on robust campaigns—and that imposing the spending limits on the receipt of the public funds constituted a classic unconstitutional

II. Public Financing Since *Buckley*

Following the Court's somewhat uncritical acceptance of the constitutionality of public financing of political campaigns, a number of significant developments have occurred.[27]

A. Presidential Public Funding

In recent years, we have witnessed the dismal failure of the system of public funding of presidential elections. The Court approved public funding on two grounds: First, it served the valid purpose of substituting for private funding and thus reducing whatever improper potential private funding might have; and second, it was designed to enhance and not restrain political communication. Neither of those objectives has been achieved.

Presidential public funding seemed to proceed uneventfully and perhaps usefully in the first two or three elections where it was available, at least from the vantage point of the two major parties. But starting in the 1980s and reaching a crescendo in the 1990s, it became clear that the expenditure limits mandated by the law were inadequate to run an effective presidential campaign. Enter "soft money."

Soft money took many forms, but one notorious instance happened in 1996, when President Bill Clinton basically auctioned off overnights in the Lincoln Bedroom in exchange for large five- or six-figure contributions to the Democratic National Committee for use in his re-election campaign. This and less scandalous soft-money stories ultimately led to the ban in the McCain-Feingold bill on such soft-money raising and spending by national political parties, upheld in *McConnell v. FEC.*[28] But until then, the major parties raised major

---

condition on the presidential candidates, attempting to accomplish indirectly what could not be commanded directly. These claims were rejected in a decision summarily affirmed by the Supreme Court. See Republican Nat'l Comm. v. FEC, 487 F. Supp. 280 (S.D.N.Y.) (three-judge court), aff'd, 445 U.S. 955 (1980). *Buckley* and the summary affirmance in the *RNC* case were invoked in the *Arizona* dissent.

[27] For a general discussion of public financing, see Public Financing in American Elections (Costas Panagopolous ed., 2011), Welfare for Politicians? Taxpayer Financing of Campaigns (John Samples ed., 2005), Peter J. Wallison & Joel M. Gora, Better Parties, Better Government: A Realistic Program for Campaign Finance Reform 62–79 (2009).

[28] McConnell v. FEC, 540 U.S. 93 (2003).

amounts of money outside the FECA limits on contributions and publicly funded campaigns. Whether or not one thinks of this as corruption, it certainly undercuts the premise that public funding served the purpose of relieving candidates from the burdens and obligations that may accompany private contributions.

Second, the idea that public funding would provide ample subsidies for "more speech" was called into question as campaign costs increased and government allotments of public funds could not keep pace. Even though they were adjusted for inflation, the limits on the amount of money that could be spent for either primary or general election campaigns were entirely too low. The original $20 million lump-sum grant for the general election might have seemed adequate in 1976 (even though it was quite a bit lower than President Nixon's 1972 re-election campaign cost), but by 2000 it was clearly not. Major party candidates—Bush and Kerry in 2004, Clinton and Obama in 2008—therefore began abandoning public financing in the primaries so they could raise and spend well beyond the spending ceilings. But what really drove a stake through the heart of presidential public financing was then-Senator Obama's decision to reject public financing in the *general election* as well, the first significant major party candidate to ever do so. That was quite stunning for someone who had long championed campaign finance reform. But Obama and his advisors determined that they could raise much more than they would be allowed to spend under public financing and, wow, were they right! Obama raised and spent approximately $750 million—that's right three quarters of a *billion* dollars—the most expensive political campaign in American history, and a privatizer's delight since not a penny of that money was publicly provided and much of it came from well-heeled individuals and groups. So the public-funding system has certainly not reduced the effect of private funding on presidential politics.

Finally, to the extent that public financing may involve an important kind of democratic legitimacy and participation, the presidential public financing scheme has been a dismal failure as well. As staggering as the amount of money that candidate Obama raised and spent in his 2008 campaign is the unwavering decline in support for the program, as measured by citizen participation through the check-off feature on Form 1040 tax returns. Although this procedure is nowhere near as democratic as a system that would let each taxpayer direct, say, $100 of his tax liability to the political party or candidate of his choice, it is nonetheless a rough barometer of public support for the program. The participation rate has declined relentlessly from around 30 percent following *Buckley* to well below 10 percent today, hardly a democratic vote of confidence. Indeed, the declining levels of participation caused Congress to raise the check-off amount from one to three dollars in 1993 to avoid a potential shortfall in funds.[29]

B. Congressional Public Funding

Public funding of congressional campaigns has not been much more promising. In the 35 years since *Buckley*, no such provision has been enacted, despite bills having been introduced almost every session. Some have passed the House. Some have passed the Senate. One passed both but was vetoed by President George H. W. Bush in 1992 because he did not approve of the mandated spending limits that would protect incumbents. That is one of the reasons incumbents like to vote for public funding: Even though they would be authorizing funds for their opponents, they can impose spending limits that almost inevitably benefit themselves. All things being equal—the playing field being "leveled"—incumbents have enormous institutional and inherent advantages. (Reformers like public funding because they believe that almost all private funding is inherently corrupt.)

Until 2008, many of the proposals for public financing of congressional campaigns, like the perennial Fair Elections Now Act, also had trigger provisions that allowed for increased fundraising and spending to counter well-financed, privately funded opposition campaigns—as insurance against the occasional well-heeled or well-supported challenger or opposing group. Following the decision

---

[29] Most state and local public-funding schemes do not even have the fig leaf of direct public support like a tax check-off mechanism. Instead, the legislators simply enact public financing to finance their own campaigns. That practice has been the experience in New York City, with its lavish matching-funds program. The New York city council simply raises the match whenever it sees fit and provides more public monies for its reelection campaigns. The basic match is now 6 to 1: six dollars of public funding for every dollar of private contributions (up to $175 per contributor). Many have claimed the New York City program can be a model for the post-*Arizona Free Enterprise* future. We will see, Part V, *infra*, if that is the case.

in *Davis v. FEC*,[30] the versions of FENA no longer contained such mechanisms—the sponsors correctly having seen the *Davis* handwriting on the wall, as discussed further in Part III below.

C. State and Local Public Funding

At the state and local level, the results have been mixed. The Congressional Research Service has estimated that public funding of political campaigns exists in one form or another in 16 states, either in statewide elections or at the local level only, like New York.

The programs take a variety of forms. Some follow the presidential primary model and offer matching funds to enhance the effect of private contributions, usually up to a certain level. Some follow the presidential general election approach and give one lump-sum payment for the whole campaign. Both systems almost always impose spending limits on those who receive the matching funds or lump-sum subsidies and may impose other conditions and restrictions as well, such as a limitation on the use of the candidate's personal funds, a restriction on the source of contributions that will be matched, or required participation in televised debates.[31] These programs seem anchored in the *Buckley* approach where candidates choose for themselves between public funding accompanied by spending limits or private financing without such limits. But, unlike in *Arizona Free Enterprise*, the actions of one candidate or group have no direct effect on the fundraising prospects of any other candidate.

The most ambitious schemes are the "clean election" systems, of the kind at issue in *Arizona Free Enterprise*. Advancing the twin goals of imposing limits on campaign spending and driving private funding out of campaigns, these "clean" public-financing systems have often been enacted by popular referendum, supported by well-funded liberal advocacy groups and well-financed publicity campaigns claiming that the program will level the playing field and

---

[30] Davis v. FEC, 554 U.S. 724 (2008) (striking down a trigger provision raising contribution limits for certain federal candidates but not their opponents).

[31] This was not always the case. When public funding of campaigns first got started, there were a few jurisdictions that did enact the "floors without ceilings" approach, but they were quickly abandoned, especially after *Buckley* said that imposing spending limits on public funding of campaigns was acceptable. In recent years, some mainstream political figures have suggested that we should consider taking the same floors-without-ceilings approach to presidential funding, since the limits have become so counterproductive to participation.

cure the evils of corruption, "pay to play" politics, and special-interest dominance of our political agendas. The elixir has proved alluring to some. Under these schemes, the candidate is typically required to raise a respectable amount of money, but in very small amounts—such as five dollars—in order to qualify for full public funding of primary and general election campaigns. From that point forward, no private money is allowed.

Two devices are used to pressure candidates into these public-funding systems and the spending limits that come with them. First, the public-funding option is usually coupled with very low private contribution limits, thus making it extremely hard for candidates who are not either personally wealthy or well-connected (usually incumbents) to raise money. If that scheme seems coercive, its defenders claim that the candidate made a "voluntary" choice to accept the limits that go with the subsidies, relying on footnote 65 in the *Buckley* decision.[32]

The other device is the trigger mechanism embedded in many "clean election" schemes, like Arizona's. This mechanism is a way to help induce candidates, especially incumbents, into public funding by giving them some insurance against being outspent. The one thing that might keep incumbents from giving up their normal fundraising advantage—even though they would retain all the other playing-field-tilting perquisites of incumbency—is the fear that the low spending limits on a publicly funded campaign would render them vulnerable to a high-spending campaign by a well-heeled challenger or independent group. The trigger addresses that problem by enhancing the funding of the participating candidate in response to speech by either the nonparticipating opponent or independent groups. The enhancement can take the form of raising the spending limit, raising the contribution limit, or providing additional government funds to counter the speech of the adversaries of the favored, government-funded candidate. Some have objected that the purpose and effect of these triggers are to deter the privately funded candidate in the first place—in order to achieve the impermissible goal of limiting and leveling campaign speech. The defenders of such

---

[32] See *supra* note 21 and accompanying text. In *Randall v. Sorrell*, 548 U.S. 230 (2006), the Court reviewed Vermont's financing scheme for statewide elections of governor and lieutenant governor. The Court held that the contribution limits were so low as to render competitive campaigns extremely unlikely and were thus unconstitutional.

schemes have responded, almost smugly, that these "trigger" funds or "fair fight" funds or "rescue" funds are simply an example of providing "more speech," a First Amendment touchstone, and therefore could not possibly violate the First Amendment.

This argument persuaded some pre-*Davis* courts, but only one post-*Davis* court—the Ninth Circuit in *Arizona Free Enterprise*.[33] The whole purpose and effect of these schemes are to reduce political electoral speech and the reliance on private financing of that speech. And, as the prevailing attorney in the Supreme Court pointed out, the effect of the law is almost pernicious in restraining the speech of middle-class candidates.[34]

The effect of these various state and local public-funding schemes in terms of the claimed benefits of increasing electoral competition and reducing official corruption is questionable. Government and academic studies have not shown any significant evidence of positive accomplishments in these regards.[35] Where First Amendment rights are burdened, equivocal results fall well short of what the Court's demanding scrutiny requires.

In summary, public funding has been provided, but in ways designed to coerce candidates into accepting it and the other limitations that go with it. The schemes seek to achieve indirectly— through "voluntary" participation and acceptance—what the First Amendment overwhelmingly denies government the power to achieve directly: expenditure limits. Normally, such circumvention of constitutional rights is condemned by the unconstitutional conditions doctrine. But, as we saw, *Buckley* blew right past that barrier and, until recently, lower courts have followed suit.

Expenditure limits are critical to public-funding schemes. Incumbent legislators will not consider any "floors without ceilings"

---

[33] It is telling, however, that the primary congressional election public-financing bill, FENA, eliminated the trigger mechanism in versions proposed after *Davis* was decided.

[34] See *supra* note 7.

[35] See Brief for Center for Competitive Politics as Amicus Curiae in Support of the Petitioners at 5–9, Arizona Free Enterprise, 131 S. Ct. 2806 (Nos. 10-238 & 10-239) (summarizing studies). See also, Wallison & Gora, *supra* note 27, at 63 (discussing whether New York City public-financing program has promoted competition or countered corruption).

approach because they will not provide a free lunch to their challenger opponents without knowing that it will not be very nourishing. And ceilings effected by popular referendum are vulnerable to the claim that they "level the playing field."

Still, the current Court has shown increasing skepticism for campaign finance schemes that seem to be end runs around core First Amendment principles. These schemes have been shown to exploit campaign finance rules and regulations to manipulate the ways candidates and groups speak out on electoral matters, or force them to do so in the way that the incumbents want. In *Arizona Free Enterprise*, the Court once again rejected such manipulative and intrusive restrictions on how we choose to organize our political and electoral speech (see Part IV below). By calling into question many key features of the system for public financing of elections, *Arizona Free Enterprise* will significantly effect future campaigns (see Part V below). As the Court continues to see these restrictions not as combating corruption but as suppressing speech, the programs will continue to be in constitutional jeopardy.

III. Constitutional Doctrine Since *Buckley*

For 25 years, the Court's handling of campaign finance issues was relatively consistent, with no clear patterns discernable.[36] The Court accepted the *Buckley* baselines and then determined on which side of them a particular case fell. Some decisions gave aid and comfort to the pro-regulatory camps, while others cheered the deregulatory forces. If cases involved restrictions on independent expenditures, the Court tended to wheel out its heavy First Amendment fire power. Such speech and its funding were at the very core of the First Amendment protections, implicated the essence of citizen criticism of government, and posed little or no danger of corruption because, by definition, they could not be in concert with candidates and might often be unwelcome by the very candidates they seemed to support. For these reasons also, deference to the legislative branch that fashioned the restraints was minimal and First Amendment scrutiny of asserted ends and means was at its maximum. The incumbents

---

[36] See generally Lillian BeVier, Campaign Finance and Free Speech: First Amendment Basics Redux: *Buckley v. Valeo* to *FEC v. Wisconsin Right To Life*, 2006–2007 Cato Sup. Ct. Rev. 77 (2007).

imposing those restraints were dimly viewed as protecting their own turf rather than benignly viewed as protecting the public weal. In such situations, the Court struck down limitations on corporate expenditures in referendum campaigns, on political action committee spending (whether for or against publicly financed presidential candidates), on candidate criticism by non-profit corporations, and on independent spending by political parties that would benefit their own candidates.[37]

On the other hand, in cases involving contributions, especially made to candidates or for the benefit of candidates, the Court hewed to the *Buckley* divide and tended to uphold such restrictions, without offering much pushback against justifications based on countering corruption or the appearance of corruption.[38] Finally, in two significant cases involving disclosure, the Court saw the situations as far removed from the core of corruption reflected by large contributions to mainstream candidates and used strong political privacy and association-protecting language and analysis to strike down the disclosure or registration requirements.[39]

These various cases were not all decided by ideologically partisan 5-4 majorities. The pendulum swung back and forth from case to case. In 2000, however, the Court decided the first of four cases where the pendulum swung only one way: in the direction of greater judicial deference to campaign finance controls.

The first case rejected an effort to revisit *Buckley*'s upholding of contribution limits.[40] The case involved a Missouri statute containing

---

[37] First Nat'l Bank of Boston v. Bellotti, 435 U.S. 765 (1978); FEC v. Nat'l Conservative Political Action Comm., 470 U.S. 480 (1985); FEC v. Mass. Citizens for Life, Inc., 479 U.S. 238 (1986); and Colo. Republican Fed. Campaign Comm. v. FEC, 518 U.S. 604 (1996); but see Austin v. Mich. State Chamber of Commerce, 494 U.S. 692 (1990), overruled by Citizens United v. FEC, 130 S. Ct. 876 (2010).

[38] Calif. Med. Asso. v. FEC, 453 U.S 182 (1981); and FEC v. Nat'l Right to Work Comm., 459 U.S. 197 (1982); but see Citizens Against Rent Control v. City of Berkeley, 454 U.S. 290 (1981) (contribution limits to a referendum campaign struck down as far removed from the potential for *candidate* corruption).

[39] Brown v. Socialist Workers '74 Campaign Comm., 459 U.S. 87 (1982) (delivering on *Buckley*'s promise of disclosure protection for controversial minor parties); McIntyre v. Ohio Elections Comm. 514 U.S. 334 (1995) (citing the anonymously written Federalist Papers in protecting citizen's right to circulate anti-tax flyer without putting her name on it).

[40] Nixon v. Shrink Missouri Gov't Now PAC, 528 U.S. 377 (2000).

basically the same $1,000 ceiling that *Buckley* had sustained for federal elections. Time and inflation had, in effect, lowered that amount to around $300, and the challengers argued that such a low contribution limit disadvantaged candidates who were not able to self-finance. The Court rejected these arguments in a way that expressed a sharp distrust of private financing of campaigns and a deference to the legislature's efforts to police the potential for corruption, undue influence, and improper access, which the Court believed were handmaidens of such private financing.

One year later, the Court declined to expand an earlier ruling that allowed parties to make independent expenditures in support of their own candidates but not party expenditures coordinated with those same candidates.[41] Since all the funding would be limited as to source and amount and fully disclosed—so-called hard money— the plaintiffs argued that no corruption potential was present. The Court held, however, that prophylactic rules were appropriate. There was the risk that such newfound freedom might be used *indirectly* by unscrupulous donors who would give large contributions to parties to circumvent the more restrictive limits on contributions directly to candidates.

In early 2003, the Court again rejected efforts to loosen the reins of campaign-finance controls. The Court had held previously that nonprofit advocacy corporations, like a Right to Life group, could make independent expenditures supporting or opposing particular candidates, even though the group was a corporation.[42] Building on that premise, such a group sought permission to make contributions directly to candidates, once again, limited in amount and fully disclosed. Again, the Court said no, citing the concerns with corruption and corporate dominance of our politics, even though these were nonprofit corporations who wanted to make limited-in-amount contributions.[43]

Most sweepingly, at the end of 2003, the Court decided the broad challenge to the McCain-Feingold bill, the Bipartisan Campaign Reform Act of 2002.[44] In an unusual opinion jointly authored by

---

[41] FEC v. Colo. Republican Fed. Campaign Comm., 533 U.S. 431 (2001).

[42] FEC v. Mass. Citizens for Life, Inc., 479 U.S. 238 (1986).

[43] FEC v. Beaumont, 539 U.S. 146 (2003).

[44] McConnell v. FEC, 540 U.S. 93 (2003).

Justices John Paul Stevens and Sandra Day O'Connor, the Court upheld the law, building on the themes of its recent cases: the dangers of corporate and union dominance of our politics, the need for prophylactic rules to prevent circumvention of limits on contributions by corporations and unions, the willingness to allow limits on independent expenditures by unions and corporations (including nonprofits), and, underlying all these new or revised restrictions, a broad deference to the judgment of Congress about the need to impose these controls to prevent undue access and influence as a fair tradeoff against First Amendment values.

To opponents of campaign finance limitations, the 5-4 ruling was the nadir of the Court's campaign finance jurisprudence. In both its ruling and its approach, the *McConnell* majority displayed the kind of deference to legislative choices rarely seen in a First Amendment case, and especially one involving such sweeping restraints on political speech. The great divide between the five justices in the majority who upheld all the key features of McCain-Feingold and the four dissenters who strenuously rejected those restraints was that, where the proper functioning of democracy was concerned, the majority viewed more political speech as the problem, while the dissenters saw more political speech as the solution.[45]

As is well known, the membership of the Supreme Court was constant from 1994 until 2005, the longest such period in its history. Then, in short order, Justice Sandra Day O'Connor, a "swing" vote and co-author of *McConnell*, retired to care for her ailing husband and was eventually replaced by Justice Samuel Alito. Chief Justice William Rehnquist took ill and died, and was replaced by Chief Justice John Roberts. That change in the Court would help set in motion the dramatic pendulum swing in the opposite direction that we have witnessed for the last five years in five cases, culminating in *Arizona Free Enterprise*.

At first, the movement seemed small. In a 2006 case, the Court for the first time struck down a state's extremely low contribution limits on the ground that such restraints improperly stifled political competition and entrenched the status quo. The Court also invalidated spending limits as flat violations of *Buckley*.[46] An interesting

---

[45] For further development of these themes, see Joel M. Gora, The First Amendment . . . United, 27 Ga. St. U.L. Rev. 935 (2011).

[46] Randall, 548 U.S. at 236.

harbinger of the new Chief Justice Roberts's views came during oral argument when he sharply challenged the Vermont attorney general's claim that the low limits were necessary to combat "corruption," pressing the lawyer to demonstrate in detail why and how Vermont was "corrupt" and required a potentially unconstitutional measure to combat the problem. It seemed clear that the chief justice was not about to accept the talismanic incantation of "corruption" as a carte blanche immunity for any campaign finance restriction or regulation that came down the pike.

The pendulum gathered momentum the next year in a case that was a partial do-over of the 2003 *McConnell* ruling, which upheld federal bans on corporate, union, and nonprofit broadcast ads that simply mentioned federal candidates, even without electoral advocacy.[47] The *McConnell* Court had surprisingly upheld that ban on the ground that so many of the independent ads criticizing or attacking politicians were "sham issue ads" and the functional equivalent of "express advocacy," which such entities were already banned from promoting. This ruling caused a great deal of consternation among groups like the ACLU whose election season commentary on elected officials was now banned by the law upheld in *McConnell*.

This ruling was now challenged by a Right to Life group that wanted to run ads critical of Wisconsin's two senators, one of whom, Senator Russell Feingold, ironically, was up for re-election. His law, McCain-Feingold, made it illegal for that group to criticize him during the election season. The Court held, 5-4, that the law could not constitutionally be applied to such ads. In a powerful use of the *McConnell* precedent, Chief Justice Roberts neatly unpacked the government's arguments as follows: if ads can be restrained only because many of them are "the functional equivalent of express advocacy," then ads that are *not* the functional equivalent of express advocacy should not be banned. Otherwise, the law would be allowing the invasion of protected "issue advocacy." That doctrinal maneuver effectively gutted the statutory section that, on its face and as upheld in *McConnell*, prohibited all ads that even mentioned a politician.

---

[47] FEC v. Wisconsin Right To Life (WRTL), 551 U.S. 449 (2007); see generally, BeVier, *supra* note 36.

More broadly, Chief Justice Roberts insisted that every case raising the issue of where to draw the "functional equivalent of express advocacy" line was a First Amendment case, and all procedures and standards for making that determination have to be First-Amendment friendly, including high barriers against chilling political speech. For example, we must "give the benefit of any doubt to protecting rather than stifling speech." "When it comes time to defining what speech [qualifies for protection] we give the benefit of the doubt to speech, not censorship." "Where the First Amendment is implicated, the tie goes to the speaker, not the censor."[48] From these premises, the opinion easily concluded that the issue advocacy of the group posed no threat of "corruption" that would justify a restraint of speech. And his opinion ends by quoting the words of the Free Speech Clause of the First Amendment, a signature textualism that would have made the "absolutist" Justice Hugo Black proud.

These two cases evidence a distrust for easy assertions that campaign finance restrictions are necessary to prevent corruption and a strong First Amendment thumb on the scale for resolving the clash of campaign finance rules and free speech rights. The third case in our pendulum's swing is the so-called Millionaire's Amendment case, *Davis v. FEC*, improperly named since the amount that could trigger penalties was well beneath that amount, and not much more than a second mortgage on a New York City co-op. Under the provision, if a candidate spent more than a certain amount of personal funds, the contribution limits of his opponent were raised three-fold. It was sold to Congress as a way for the members to protect themselves against a high spending, self-financed opponent, one of the two risks that incumbents try to minimize (criticism by independent groups is the other). And, as is true of most campaign finance restrictions, while neutrally applicable to incumbents and challengers alike, the real world effect is to tilt the playing field in favor of incumbents, not just to level it. Indeed, the Millionaire's Amendment has almost never been invoked *against* an incumbent because they invariably do not have to rely on their own funds to campaign for re-election; they are easily able to raise money from

---

[48] WRTL, 551 U.S. at 474.

individual and group supporters. The amendment is overwhelmingly used against challengers.

The Court saw right through the corruption argument, pointing out that the law itself cynically undercut that rationale by *raising* contribution limits. If it was necessary to have limits to guard against corruption in the first place, how could you justify raising them three-fold when an opponent self-finances his own campaign? Moreover, if large contributions are more likely to cause corruption, why exacerbate that problem—particularly in response to the one campaign that is *least* likely to be corrupt: the self-financed candidate beholden to no one. The Court rejected this charade as a cover for the law's obvious purpose and effect: to discourage candidates—again mostly challengers—from self-financing their campaigns (and thereby threatening incumbents). Such manipulation of campaign finance rules—burdening speech by enabling the opponent to raise more funds to counter that speech—was a net loss, not gain, for the volume of political expression. The trigger was constitutionally defective. The Court saw the statute as a cynical attempt to use campaign finance restrictions to control political speech, manipulate electoral outcomes, and penalize those who would use their own personal funds to support their own campaign speech. Gone was any effort at placating Congress, in either outcome or attitude. Evident instead was the new majority's deep skepticism of the motives and methods of campaign finance controls.[49]

That brings me to the final piece put into place: It would almost dictate the outcome in *Arizona Free Enterprise*. I refer, of course, to the well-known, and in so many quarters reviled and condemned, decision in the *Citizens United* case.[50] The Court's holding—that the

---

[49] Davis v. FEC, 554 U.S. 724 (2008). Frankly, the only disappointment of this case was that the four liberal dissenters in *Wisconsin Right to Life* would continue to embrace sloganeering support for frankly unsupportable efforts by Congress either to flout *Buckley*'s principles or to exploit them cynically.

[50] Citizens United v. FEC, 130 S. Ct. 876 (2010). For my own view that the decision was an historic reaffirmation of classic First Amendment principles, see Gora, The First Amendment . . . United, *supra* note 45. For other takes on the case, see Ilya Shapiro & Nicholas M. Mosvick, *Stare Decisis* after *Citizens United*: When Should Courts Overturn Precedent, 16 Nexus J. L. & Pub. Pol'y 121 (2011); James Bopp, Jr. & Richard E. Coleson, A Big Year for the First Amendment: Citizens United v. Federal Election Commission: "Precisely what *WRTL* Sought to Avoid," 2009–2010 Cato Sup. Ct. Rev. 29 (2010).

First Amendment prevents the use of campaign finance restrictions to prohibit independent political speech of entities like corporations, unions, or nonprofit organizations—and the principles applied have telling implications for *Arizona Free Enterprise*:

- Government may not limit or burden political speech, especially independent speech, which is inherently not corrupting or problematic;
- Government may not determine how much political speech there should be or that speech from certain sources will "distort" or "imbalance" the debate or prevent "a level playing field";
- Government may not circumvent these principles by forcing political speech into burdensome channels like requiring that all organizations speak through political action committees;
- Government may not manipulate and design campaign finance rules to favor or advantage certain kinds of speakers and disfavor or disadvantage others;
- Government may not impose burdensome requirements or vague rules and regulations that have the effect of requiring people and organizations to get the government's permission before engaging in political speech or that may chill and deter political speech in the first place;
- Government may not simply cry "corruption" to deflect deep judicial distrust and strict scrutiny of campaign finance regulations; and
- Government may define "corruption" only in terms of quid pro quo arrangements, and may not invoke broader notions that contributions or independent expenditures can be restrained because they might allow "undue influence" on or "improper access" to political officials.

The *Citizens United* Court demonstrated a deep skepticism of the fairness and neutrality of permitting government to enforce campaign finance rules. The pendulum of judicial review had clearly swung from *McConnell's* broad deference to the embodiment of strict scrutiny. *Citizens United* was a game changer for First Amendment review of campaign finance restrictions. While not quite the equivalent of the exceptionally potent doctrine against prior restraints, one could say, to adopt the language of the Pentagon Papers case, that any system of campaign finance limitations "comes to this Court bearing a heavy presumption against its constitutional validity."[51] *Davis* invalidated the use of trigger mechanisms to manipulate the level of campaign funding and deter and penalize those who finance their own campaigns. *Citizens United* reaffirmed the *Buckley* principle that the people, not the government, get to determine how much political speech is appropriate or necessary or enough. Yet in *Arizona Free Enterprise*, the law empowered the *government* to set the level that it thought was enough to run a viable political campaign and then gave the government the further power to manipulate that level to favor those who participated in the program and to penalize those who used or benefited from private funding—all in a manner that favored some forms and choices of campaign financing and disfavored others. These precedents would seem to cover and condemn the Arizona program and, perhaps ultimately, call into question the *Buckley* opinion that upheld public funding more generally.

IV. Rounding Up the Alligators: The Court's *Arizona* Decision

These cases were pretty much all the Court needed to condemn Arizona's scheme. The Court's holding was clear: "Arizona's matching funds scheme substantially burdens protected political speech without serving a compelling state interest and therefore violates the First Amendment."[52] *Arizona Free Enterprise* divided along the same 5-4 conservative/liberal lines as did the three previous campaign finance decisions. Chief Justice Roberts wrote for the majority with Justices Sonia Sotomayor and Elena Kagan comfortably stepping into the roles of their predecessors, Justices David Souter and John Paul Stevens, respectively. The majority opinion was straightforward in its framing and resolution of the issues, use of precedent, and invocation of broader principles. The ultimate issue was whether the triggering scheme was about encouraging more electoral speech or suppressing it.

A. The Nature of the Scheme

Candidates for state office could seek public financing for their campaigns by raising a significant number of small donations and

---

[51] N.Y. Times Co. v. United States, 403 U.S. 713, 714 (1971) (quoting Bantam Books, Inc. v. Sullivan, 372 U.S. 58, 70 (1963)).

[52] Arizona Free Enterprise, 131 S. Ct. at 2813.

then agree to raise or spend no more than the primary or general election government allotment for the particular election. The distinctive feature of the plan was the "matching" funds provision. It gave the participating candidates additional state monies for their campaigns if opposing privately financed candidates raised or spent more than the state-determined limit or if independent groups spent funds in support of the privately financed candidate or in opposition to the publicly funded candidate in excess of those limits. All such spending against a participating candidate was aggregated to trigger the flow of state monetary support. Where *two* publicly financed candidates faced one privately financed candidate, any funds the latter spent beyond the government-decreed limits were matched by the state, which then gave those amounts to *each* of the publicly financed candidates. The same was true of any outside group spending: if it benefited an "outside" candidate, *both* inside candidates received the same amount of money from the government. These triggers and possible multiple matches continued to operate so long as outside speech opposed the inside candidates, up to three times the amount of the initial grant. Beyond that level, there was no more matching. Outside candidates could spend as much as they had or could raise, but under the very low contribution limits of $840 for statewide offices or $410 for legislative offices. Independent spending was subject to no direct limitation.

The Court detailed the scheme's disparities and anomalies—ones that tended to tilt the playing field toward the "clean" publicly financed candidates:

- If the privately funded candidate spent $1,000 of his own money for a direct mailing, the government would give *each* of his publicly financed opponents $940 (an unrealistically low 6 percent discount for fundraising costs avoided);
- If the privately funded candidate held a fundraiser that generated $1000 in contributions, each of his publicly funded opponents would receive $940 from the government;[53]

---

[53] A perfect example of this: When Arizona Democrat Janet Napolitano, now secretary of homeland security, was running for governor, she joked that President George W. Bush, in effect, held a fundraiser for her when he spoke at a dinner to raise money for her privately funded opponent. The government gave her $750,000 in matching tax dollars.

- If an independent group spent $1,000 on a brochure expressing its support for the privately funded candidate—wholly without that candidate's authorization or approval—each publicly funded candidate would receive $940 from the government;
- If an independent group spent $1,000 on a brochure opposing one publicly financed candidate, but saying nothing about the privately financed candidate, the publicly funded candidate would receive $940 directly from the government to counter that speech;
- If an independent group spent $1,000 on a brochure supporting one of the publicly financed candidates, the other publicly financed candidate would receive $940 from the government, but the privately financed candidate would receive nothing.
- If an independent group spent $1,000 on a brochure opposing the privately financed candidate, the government would not give him anything to help him respond.[54]

Privately funded candidates and independent groups who claimed they were burdened and disadvantaged by these campaign finance disparities sued to declare the triggers unconstitutional. The triggers penalized their speech by using it as the predicate for funding their opponents. In effect, the government was "drowning out" their speech through a state-financed counterattack on it.[55] A district court declared the matching-funds trigger unconstitutional, largely on the basis of *Davis* and enjoined its enforcement.[56] A panel of the Ninth Circuit subsequently reversed the district court, held the matching-funds trigger scheme constitutional and vacated the injunction against its enforcement.[57] That court concluded that the system did not impose a significant burden or direct restraint on speech and was justified by the government's interest in combating quid pro quo political corruption inherent in private financing of campaigns. Shortly thereafter, the Supreme Court reinstated the district court's injunction so that the triggers would not operate

---

[54] Arizona Free Enterprise, 131 S. Ct. at 2815.

[55] They did not challenge the basic constitutionality of public financing of political campaigns or the specific mechanism for presidential public financing upheld in the *Buckley* case. See *id.* at 2833.

[56] McComish v. Brewer, 2010 U.S. Dist. LEXIS 4932 (D. Ariz. 2010).

[57] McComish v. Bennett, 611 F.3d 510 (9th Cir. 2010).

during the fall 2010 state and local elections in Arizona.[58] The Court's action reinforced the expectation that *Davis* and *Citizens United* had put the *Arizona Free Enterprise* scheme on borrowed time. That expectation, of course, became reality.

In order to decide the case, the Court had to resolve two basic issues: First, did the matching-funds trigger scheme substantially burden the First Amendment rights of the privately financed candidates and independent speakers or groups whose speech was being countered by the provision of government funds? Second, if so, was such a burden justified as advancing a compelling government interest? The Court answered the first question yes and the second question no: "Laws like Arizona's matching fund provision that inhibit robust and wide-open political debate without sufficient justification cannot stand."[59]

B. The Speech Burdens Created

The *Davis* case made the Court's task so much easier because the burdens on speech in *Arizona Free Enterprise* were so similar to the Millionaire's Amendment harms. Indeed, *Arizona Free Enterprise* was even worse. In *Davis*, the disadvantaged, self-financing candidate suffered the harm of having his own campaign funding trigger the *opportunity* for his opponents to raise money more easily by lifting the contribution ceilings on donations to their campaigns. In *Arizona Free Enterprise*, the Court observed, the effect was even more severe because the government gave the outside candidate's opponent funds *directly*, without even the need to raise the money. Moreover, in elections where there were multiple inside candidates, the match was multiple as well, so that one dollar of speech made by an outside candidate would trigger two dollars or perhaps three dollars of government-funded speech against that candidate. Third, the outside candidate had absolutely no control over money given to inside candidates triggered by the speech of independent groups or individuals. Furthermore, that independent speech might have been unwelcome and counterproductive to the outside candidate (for example, "Nazis for the outside candidate").

---

[58] McComish v. Bennett, 130 S. Ct. 3408 (2010).

[59] Arizona Free Enterprise, 131 S. Ct. at 2829.

Moreover, the Arizona scheme had an additional, novel set of burdens, completely different from both *Buckley* and *Davis*: the government-funded counterattack against *independent* speech. The triggered match was not just for spending by the outside candidate, but for speech by independent groups. That was a new feature of the second generation of public-funding laws, designed to give the inside candidates an insurance policy against high-spending outside groups and induce incumbents to participate in the public-funding system. The Court pointedly noted that the triggered match imposed an even more severe burden on independent groups; unlike candidates, they were obviously not eligible to seek public funds for their speech in the first place. There was then not even the fiction of a "voluntary" choice between public funding and private financing of political speech. For these groups, the only way they could avoid the government's triggered financing of counter-speech against their message would either be to change their message or not speak at all. For government to impose such a "choice" on the speaker's decision whether to speak or what to say cuts against the core First Amendment protection of speaker autonomy heralded by both *Buckley* and *Citizens United* and applied to the trigger scheme in *Davis*.

Responding to the dissenters' complaint that a scheme like this could not be a burden because it provided for "more speech," the Court said that any added speech was one-sided, only aiding the speech of the publicly funded candidate and burdening (thus reducing) the speech of the privately funded candidate. Such a consequence is a defining characteristic of expenditure limits—namely, they burden and limit the speech of some "to enhance the speech of others," a leveling-down concept "wholly foreign to the First Amendment."[60]

The Court also found strong support in two cases outside the campaign finance area that held that government regulations requiring speakers to provide a forum for those they oppose was a violation of the First Amendment. *Miami Herald v. Tornillo* struck down a

---

[60] *Id.* at 2811 (quoting Buckley, 424 U.S. at 48–49). The whole *Buckley* passage, usually omitted by critics of the ruling, is as follows: "But the concept that government may restrict the speech of some elements of our society in order to enhance the relative voice of others is wholly foreign to the First Amendment, which was designed 'to secure the widest possible dissemination of information from diverse and antagonistic sources' and 'to assure unfettered interchange of ideas for the bringing about of political and social changes desired by the people.'"

"right of reply" statute that required newspapers to give editorial space to those politicians they criticized.[61] *Pacific Gas & Electric v. Public Utilities Commission of California*, invalidated a requirement that utility companies allow their public policy opponents to include opposing messages in monthly bill mailings.[62] In both cases, the Court ruled that such requirements not only improperly expropriated the speaker's property and gave it to his ideological opponents, but the very prospect of having to do so deterred the speaker's own speech: He would be inclined to tailor his remarks rather than giving a speech benefit to his ideological opponents.

The fact that the speaker was not compelled to express a message with which he disagreed was beside the point; the gravamen of the harm was that the state provided a monetary subsidy to the speaker's political rival—triggered by the speaker's own speech. *That* was the burden on speech—that it would force the speaker to think twice before engaging in speech that the government would use to provide a direct, tangible benefit to the speaker's adversary. "The Arizona law imposes a similar penalty: The State grants funds to publicly financed candidates as a direct result of the speech of privately financed candidates and independent expenditure groups. The argument that this sort of burden promotes free and robust discussion is no more persuasive here than it was in *Tornillo.*"[63] By similar reasoning, the challengers' concession that Arizona could have provided a three-times larger grant in the first place without triggers did not lessen the particular harm of the trigger mechanism, which directly penalized one candidate's or group's speech by giving government funds to the other candidates in response to that speech.[64]

---

[61] 418 U.S. 241 (1974).

[62] 475 U.S. 1 (1986).

[63] Arizona Free Enterprise, 131 S. Ct. at 2821.

[64] The Court also rejected the dissent's suggestion that the Arizona scheme was acceptable under cases permitting government broad leeway in subsidizing speech so long as the scheme did not amount to a penalty. See, e.g., Rust v. Sullivan, 500 U.S. 173 (1991); Nat'l Endowment for the Arts v. Finley, 524 U.S. 569 (1998); Regan v. Taxation With Representation, 461 U.S. 540 (1983). In this case, the Court noted, "The direct result of the speech of privately financed candidates and independent expenditure committees is a state-provided monetary subsidy to a political rival." Arizona Free Enterprise, 131 S. Ct. at 2821. The Court likewise rejected the analogy to the lower standard of review that *Citizens United* applied to disclosure and disclaimer requirements in the campaign finance area, observing that disclosure does not result in a cash windfall to one's political opponents because of one's own speech.

Finally, contradicting the dissent, the Court noted significant evidence of the actual chilling effect the triggers had on outside candidates and independent groups. But the real problem was not how many outside candidates had refrained from speaking, but that every outside candidate and group had to confront the question of whether to speak and, by so doing, provide a direct financial benefit to their opponents. As in *Davis*, the harm was the very existence of the trigger mechanism and the inherent effect it had on the speech choices of outside candidates: "It is clear not only to us but to every other court to have considered the question after *Davis* that a candidate or independent group might not spend money if the direct result of that spending is additional funding to political adversaries."[65] Accordingly, the Court concluded, "Because the Arizona matching fund provision imposes a substantial burden on the speech of privately financed candidates and independent expenditure groups, "that provision cannot stand unless it is 'justified by a compelling state interest.'"[66]

C. The Justifications Found Wanting

That brought the Court to the second critical branch of the inquiry: Did the trigger mechanism's substantial burden on speech serve a compelling governmental interest? Two interests were considered: one that the state disclaimed and one that it advanced.

The compelling interest treated like the plague was the one that, in the Court's opinion, was the real motivating force behind the Arizona scheme: "to level the playing field." Few phrases are more poll-tested to produce good feelings than that one. It has been a key mantra of the campaign finance control movement: In order to improve our political and electoral speech and competition, we need to find ways to reduce the financial disparities among candidates—to level the playing field. That was the avowed purpose of the *Buckley* statute: trying to ensure that no one person could spend more than a nominal amount on politics and no one candidate could spend more than any other. And it is one of the two motivating forces behind the "clean elections" movement, to drive more and

[65] Arizona Free Enterprise, 131 S. Ct. at 2823.
[66] *Id.* at 2824 (citations and internal quotation marks omitted).

more candidates into the publicly funded system where all candidates get the same amount to spend, and even more if outside candidates or groups speak.

The problem is, "if there is any fixed star in our constitutional constellation," it is that campaign finance laws cannot attempt to level the playing field and equalize political speech.[67] *Buckley* condemned that rationale in no uncertain terms, branding it "wholly foreign to the First Amendment." Liberals and campaign finance control groups have bitterly attacked that part of *Buckley* for a generation and came close to putting a major doctrinal dent in that theme in *Austin* and *McConnell*, which limited campaign funding to counter the influence of "immense aggregations of wealth" that might, one could say, tilt the playing field. But after *Citizens United* reaffirmed the *Buckley* ban on equalizing campaign speech, "level the playing field," as good as it sounded to proponents of more regulation, was constitutional anathema.[68]

For these reasons, Arizona understandably disclaimed an interest in "leveling the playing field." Conjuring up the old Groucho Marx line, "Who are you going to believe, me or your lying eyes?" the Court pointed to a number of factors to show the illicit purpose. These factors included the rhetoric used to support the "clean election" law when it was enacted by referendum, the text used in the law ("equal funding of candidates," "equalizing funds"), and the structures and mechanisms of the law designed to induce participation by providing trigger funds to help, though not guarantee, a level playing field. Accordingly, the Court concluded that one of the goals was to equalize campaign funding and therefore campaign speech, a clearly illicit, let alone not a compelling, interest.[69] "'Leveling the playing field' can sound like a good thing. But in a democracy,

---

[67] W. Va. State Bd. of Educ. v. Barnette, 319 U.S. 624, 642 (1943).

[68] In addition, leveling the political playing field simply will not work. To the extent leveling limits are effective, they simply freeze the political status quo and magnify the enormous advantages of incumbency. In addition, to the extent they do not cover all political speech—because of things like the statutory media exemption and the constitutional protection for issue advocacy—they are anything but fair and equal. Rather they simply privilege the individuals and groups whose speech is not subject to the controls. Wholly apart from the First Amendment, leveling the playing field simply makes no democratic sense.

[69] The state's disclaimer of this purpose was not aided by the fact, noted at oral argument, that the website of the Clean Election Commission, the agency responsible

campaigning for office is not a game. It is a critically important form of speech. The First Amendment embodies our choice as a nation that, when it comes to such speech, the guiding principle is freedom—the 'unfettered exchange of ideas'—not whatever the state may view as fair."[70]

Preventing corruption, of course, is the only compelling interest the Court recognizes now and, courtesy of *Citizens United*'s reaffirmation of *Buckley*'s formulation, an interest concerned only with quid pro quo dangers, not the more gossamer claims of undue access or influence. Drawing carefully on settled doctrine in the area, Chief Justice Roberts showed why the Arizona scheme, and the burdens and penalties it visited on private and independent speech, could not be justified on the ground of preventing corruption. First, none of the speech that Arizona countered, deterred, and penalized was the product of any campaign finance practice that the Court had deemed corrupting. The state matched a candidate's own spending, but ever since *Buckley*, reaffirmed by *Davis*, the Court has said that self-financing was the most protected and least corrupting form of campaign finance—on the self-evident basis that a candidate cannot corrupt himself. Second, Arizona could not be seeking to prevent corruption in the form of large donations to candidates that might influence their official behavior because, quite simply, Arizona allowed no such donations. On the contrary, the state's contribution limits were extremely low—indeed, "ascetic"—and subject to rigorous and timely reporting and disclosure.[71] Properly, the Court concluded that low contribution limits and full-disclosure requirements were more than ample antidotes to cognizable quid pro quo corruption. Finally, Arizona's scheme could not be seeking to prevent corruption by countering independent expenditures: The Court,

---

for administering the law, contained the following statement: "The Citizens Clean Elections Act passed by the people of Arizona in 1998 to level the playing field when it comes to running for office." After oral argument, the website was changed—scrubbed?—to state that the purpose of the law was "to restore citizen participation and confidence in our political system." Arizona Free Enterprise, 131 S. Ct. at 2825 n.10.

[70] *Id*. at 2826 (citing Buckley, 424 U.S. at 14).

[71] *Id*. at 2827. Indeed, they were so low that they came perilously close to violating the *Randall* ban on low contribution levels that suppressed electoral competition. Of course, that is part of the "clean election" strategy: setting contribution limits so low that all but the well-heeled or well-connected candidates are coerced into the public-funding system with its severe expenditure limits.

from *Buckley* through *Citizens United*, had consistently said that such expenditures, at the core of the First Amendment, could not be corrupting because, by definition, they are not coordinated in any way with candidates.[72]

Accordingly, none of the campaign financing that Arizona claimed it had a compelling interest in countering posed any risk or danger of corruption, and the triggered funding system was not directly serving the anti-corruption interest.

In a nutshell, the trigger provisions *could not* constitutionally serve a leveling purpose and *did not* directly serve a corruption-preventing function. But could they be justified in any other way? The state's answer was that the triggers prevented corruption by herding candidates into the public-financing system in the first place. "They contend that the provision indirectly serves the anticorruption interest, by insuring that enough candidates participate in the State's public funding system, which in turn helps combat corruption."[73] Though noting *Buckley's* approval of public financing as a means of eliminating the influence of large private contributions, the Court was unwilling to extend that general principle to validate the matching-funds provision at issue in *Arizona Free Enterprise*. None of the deterred campaign financing was corruption-threatening. Moreover, the Court observed:

> How the State chooses to encourage participation in its public funding system matters, and we have never held that a State may burden political speech—to the extent the matching funds provision does—to ensure adequate participation in a public funding system. Here the State's chosen method is unduly burdensome and not sufficiently justified to survive First Amendment scrutiny.[74]

In effect, the Court refused to circumvent First Amendment rights for the indirect accomplishment of a purportedly compelling objective: "Laws like Arizona's matching fund provision that inhibit

---

[72] The Court suggested otherwise in both *Austin* and *McConnell* but those cases were ultimately overruled in *Citizens United*. See *supra* note 37 and accompanying text.

[73] Arizona Free Enterprise, 131 S. Ct. at 2827.

[74] *Id.* at 2828.

robust and wide-open political debate without sufficient justification cannot stand."[75]

D. The Dissenters' Different Perspective

The Court let pass the real full-throated justification for the law—namely, as the title of the statute implies, only public money supports "clean elections"; private money is unclean or dirty or inherently corrupting. Thus, by pressuring candidates into taking public funding, the trigger serves the goal of preventing corruption; the "clean" public-funding system, unlike its private counterpart, cannot by definition be corrupt.

That is really what clean election laws have always been about: *any* private financing of political campaigns is corrupting. If it is the candidate's own money, it violates democratic equality of one person, one vote and allows the wealthy to "buy elections." Likewise, private contributions larger than specified "qualifying" amounts are corrupting because of quid pro quo and undue influence by "special interests." That is not quite what Arizona and its supporters argued, but its basic defense of the trigger mechanism was that it was necessary to induce candidates to become "clean"—almost like a reformed drug user—and participate in the public-funding system. The more candidates who participated, the less corruption there would be; therefore, Arizona had a compelling interest in the triggers as a way to get more candidates to give up private funding and go into the system. Sadly, the dissenters bought this theory hook, line, and sinker.

Justice Kagan's dissent contained two parts. First, she maintained, triggers did not significantly burden or penalize speech, were not condemned by *Davis*—which was about disparities—and were justified by cases giving government greater leeway when it was subsidizing speech, not directly restricting it.

But the heart of the dissent was a sweeping condemnation of the American campaign-financing system's heavy reliance on private funding. Here are ways that the dissent characterized the nature and dangers of privately financed election campaigns:

- "Candidates accept large contributions in exchange for the promise that, after assuming office, they will rank the donors'

[75] *Id.* at 2829.

interests ahead of all others. As a result of these bargains, politicians ignore the public interest, sound public policy languishes, and the citizens lose their confidence in government."
- There is "a cancerous effect of this corruption."
- "[T]he greatest hope of eliminating corruption lies in creating an effective public financing system, which will break candidates' dependence [there's that drug user theme again] on large donors and bundlers."
- Public financing like Arizona's "produces honest government, working on behalf of all the people" and can "break the stranglehold of special interests on elected officials."
- "Campaign finance reform has focused for a century on one key question: how to prevent massive pools of private money from corrupting our political system."
- "By supplanting private cash in elections, public financing eliminates the source of political corruption."
- The Court "wrongly prevents Arizona from protecting the strength and integrity of its democracy."
- "When private contributions fuel the political system, candidates will make corrupt bargains to gain the money needed to win election. And voters, seeing the dependence of candidates on large contributors (or on bundlers of smaller contributions), may lose faith that their representatives will serve the public interest."[76]

[76] *Id.* at 2829–30, 2841–42 (Kagan, J., dissenting). Some wags might point out that these claimed corruptions might have been at work recently when a major state enacted a controversial bill that the governor endorsed the very day he received a $60,000 contribution from a powerful special-interest lobby that supported the bill; or when various state legislators received five-figure campaign contributions from lobby groups and obscenely rich donors who also supported the bill. (Notably, millions were spent on expensive media campaigns urging politicians to vote for the bill or face defeat at the polls in the next election.) The bill at issue was New York's legalization of same-sex marriage, passed, ironically, within days of the Supreme Court's *Arizona Free Enterprise* decision. See Gay Rights Groups Gave Cuomo $60,000 as He Pushed Marriage Bill, Records Show, N.Y. Times, July 15, 2011 at A17. The *Wall Street Journal* enjoyed editorially tweaking its cross-town rival, the *New York Times*, for the powerful role of *private* campaign financing in bringing about a cherished liberal objective. See Editorial, Campaign Speech and Gay Marriage, Wall St. J., June 29, 2011, at A16. The *Times*, though lauding the marriage equality legislation, made no editorial mention of its support by wealthy special interests, many of whom would benefit economically from the legislation. No "pay-to-play" problems there, apparently, or at least none the *Times* thought worth mentioning. I wonder if Justice Kagan thinks the new legislation in her home state was the result of "corruption."

These buzzwords and phrases sound like they came out of a Common Cause press release. Such a jaundiced view of our system of private funding of political campaigns is certainly in vogue in such quarters. Some academics and editorialists support those views, and a majority of Americans—after a generation of brainwashing by the mainstream media—may even feel the same way. It is a stunning and alarming thought that the Supreme Court would be only one justice away from allowing every state and locality, not to mention Congress, to impose a "clean election" system on American politics, despite the injunctions of the First Amendment.

The gap between the majority and the dissent almost seems unbridgeable. One prominent election law scholar, reacting contemporaneously to the ruling, said the Court was in a "[d]octrinal death match."[77] One view holds that government can and really should be the primary or even exclusive source of campaign funding and that the First Amendment should welcome this development or, at least, get out of the way unless the funding entails overt viewpoint discrimination. The other view holds that the First Amendment bars the government from managing or funding the political process. The dissenters think more private funding of political speech is the problem for democracy, while the majority think it is the solution. The different perspectives sometimes seem as powerfully divisive as the schism over abortion, affirmative action, and other hot button issues, where people see fundamental things totally differently and the notion of bridging the gap seems quixotic.

But, finally, at least the *Arizona Free Enterprise* case has put to rest the vexing question: "Is money speech?" All nine justices now seem to agree that it is: The Court majority thinks it should come from the people; the dissenters are content to let it be supplied by the government. Indeed, Justice Kagan praised the Arizona scheme for generating the "just right" level of political speech, and then using monetary incentives to encourage candidates to stick to that level.[78] Clearly, Justice Kagan sees the relationship between money and speech, even though the Framers no doubt would have rejected her

---

[77] See Heather Gerken, Campaign Finance and the Doctrinal Death Match, Balkinization Blog, June 27, 2011, http://balkin.blogspot.com/2011/06/campaign-finance-and-doctrinal-death.html (last visited Aug. 2, 2011).

[78] Arizona Free Enterprise, 131 S. Ct. at 2832.

preference for government's deciding how much political speech is "just right" and penalizing people who speak "too much" by giving money to their political opponents.

V. The Future for Public Financing of Election Campaigns

What does *Arizona Free Enterprise* augur for the future of public financing of political campaigns? Doctrinally, the Court reaffirmed, in word and deed, that strict scrutiny means strict scrutiny. Even in the context of public funding, campaign finance regulations that directly or indirectly restrain the amount of speech and undermine the autonomy of political speakers must be justified in the most careful way. In terms of precedent, most "triggers" are now presumptively unconstitutional, whether they result in more public funding or higher private-funding limits for favored candidates.

More intriguing is the question of whether *any* otherwise First Amendment-unfriendly limits can continue to be imposed on the recipients of public funding as a condition of getting those benefits. In other words, is the basic *Buckley* bargain—public funding in exchange for expenditure limits and no private funding—now called into question? Supporters of public funding were quick to claim that *Arizona Free Enterprise* left this aspect of *Buckley* unscathed. But that is yet to be determined.

Finally, what are the political ramifications of the decision? The now-defunct triggers were designed to enforce the expenditure limits supposedly integral to public funding. With that hammer gone, those limits may have outlived their usefulness. Some form of floors without ceilings may make sense after all, politically, whether or not constitutionally.

A. Doctrinal Possibilities

First, will the strict scrutiny applied in *Arizona Free Enterprise* spill over into other challenged areas of campaign finance law, such as the continued ban on contributions by certain entities? Or indeed will the Court revisit the very propriety of limits on contributions that have been consistently upheld? One scholar suggests there is no such danger since the Court pointed to various restraints on contributions as not meriting strict scrutiny because they were considered less onerous.[79] Remember, however, that *Arizona Free Enterprise*'s broader themes included the need to preserve speaker autonomy regarding funding, the application of strict scrutiny to restraints

---

[79] Rick Hasen, The Arizona Campaign Finance Case: The Surprisingly Good News in the Supreme Court's Decision, The New Republic, June 27, 2011, available at

that had a chilling effect, and the refusal to find that the corruption interest—concededly compelling—was being directly protected. At the very least, the Court will take a closer look at these traditionally accepted campaign finance limitations.

Second, all forms of triggered public financing to counteract privately funded campaign speech are almost per se unconstitutional. Whether the provisions provide for additional public funds being granted, as in Arizona and Maine—the other well-known "clean election" state—or additional private-fundraising rights and opportunities, or spending limits being increased. They all appear fatally flawed under the Court's analysis in *Arizona Free Enterprise*. Some lower courts have already agreed—based on either *Arizona Free Enterprise* or *Davis*.[80]

A particularly interesting case will be the New York City public-financing program, in existence for a quarter of a century and much beloved of local editorial writers and public-funding advocacy groups. After *Arizona Free Enterprise*, the spokespeople for both the New York City program and one of the main public-finance advocacy groups rushed to declare the New York program bulletproof, even after the decision, and a model for the country. The program provides six dollars of public money for each dollar of private money a candidate raises in small contributions, up to $175—which is almost the equivalent of a flat-grant system. Spending limits are imposed as a "voluntary" condition of accepting the match, as well as mandatory debates and various other restraints. As a practical matter, it is questionable whether the New York City program has succeeded in fostering competitive elections or preventing corruption.[81] In addition, the program contains trigger mechanisms that

---

http://www.tnr.com/article/politics/90834/arizona-campaign-finance-supreme-court (last visited Aug. 2, 2011).

[80] A number of "trigger" schemes have been declared unconstitutional or are being rewritten in Arizona, Maine, Florida, Albuquerque, San Francisco and Los Angeles. But a former student of mine, Nicholas I. Bamman, Brooklyn Law School Class of 2011, has suggested in an unpublished paper on file with the author that there may be some trigger schemes that might still pass constitutional muster and make good public policy sense.

[81] See Wallison & Gora, Better Parties, Better Government, *supra* note 27; Michael Howard Saul & James Oberman, Indicted Councilman Hands Out Cash, Wall St. J., June 29, 2011, at A19; see also, Sean Parnell, Opposing View: Reject Tax-Financed Campaigns, USA Today, June 27, 2011 (noting press reports that 12 New York City

are certainly vulnerable under *Arizona Free Enterprise*.[82] Finally, there is a good argument that the system forces almost all candidates to participate and abide by the requisite spending limits unless, of course, the candidate is named Bloomberg.

Which brings us to the $64,000 question: Did the Court in *Arizona Free Enterprise* really put its Good Housekeeping Seal of Approval on the no-triggers *Buckley* system, which awarded matching funds for small contributions, conditioned on spending limits, plus a lump sum conditioned on no private contributions? As a practical matter, we've seen how that worked out at the presidential level. From a constitutional perspective, are *Buckley*'s limits-mandated matching funds and lump sum funds still good law?

Here too, the editorialists and public-financing advocates were quick to claim that the *Arizona Free Enterprise* Court turned aside efforts to challenge *Buckley*'s approval of public financing. But, in fact, only one or two amicus curiae briefs criticized *Buckley* or suggested revisiting it, and the parties challenging the law stipulated that they were not arguing that a lump-sum payment in advance, à la Buckley, would be problematic. Their only targets were the triggers, which they claimed put a special and different burden on private speech by having government fund a counterattack to that speech. The Court agreed.

At the end of its opinion, the Court did say, after declaring the Arizona trigger scheme a substantial and unjustified burden on First Amendment rights: "We do not today call into question the *wisdom* of public financing as a means of funding political candidacy."[83] Public-funding advocates have seized on this sentence as proof positive of their narrow reading of the effect of the decision. But I think they may be whistling past the graveyard. Conservative justices like to say they are not getting into the "wisdom" of legislation. That

---

Council members, all elected with public financing, have been caught up in graft and corruption inquiries).

[82] See Larry Levy & Andrew Rafalaf, High Court's Recent Decision on Public Matching Funds Renders New York City's Campaign Finance System Ripe for Constitutional Attack, Albany Gov. L. Rev. Fireplace, July 11, 2011, available at http://aglr.word press.com/2011/07/11/high-courts-recent-decision-on-public-matching-funds-renders-new-york-citys-campaign-finance-system-ripe-for-constitutional-attack-2/ (last visited Aug. 2, 2011).

[83] Arizona Free Enterprise, 131 S. Ct. at 2828 (emphasis added).

would be "legislating from the bench," and conservatives presumably do not do that. But the Court did call into question the *constitutionality* of some public-financing provisions. Indeed, in the very next sentence, Chief Justice Roberts made this point explicitly: "[D]etermining whether laws governing campaign finance violate the First Amendment is very much our business."[84] Then the Court went on to note: "We have said governments 'may engage in public financing of election campaigns' and that doing so can further 'significant governmental interest[s],' such as the state interest in preventing corruption in *Buckley*. . . . But the goal of creating a viable public financing scheme can only be pursued in a manner consistent with the First Amendment."[85] After *Arizona Free Enterprise*, any public-funding scheme will have to meet the tougher tests applied to strike down the particular arrangement there.

How will *Buckley* fare under those more robust standards? *Buckley* identified three interests properly served by public funding: (1) facilitating speech, not abridging it; (2) eliminating the improper influence of large contributions; and (3) relieving major party candidates of the rigors of fundraising. The last interest has been undermined by *Randall v. Sorrell* where the Court held that sparing candidates—particularly incumbents with a government to run—the rigors of private fundraising was not an interest sufficiently compelling to justify direct expenditure limits. With regard to corruption, public funding as an antidote to potential corruption from private contributions was the ultimate justification for the Arizona scheme, and it was rejected as insufficient to justify even indirect restraints on privately funded candidates

The first interest, facilitating speech, is in considerable tension with *Arizona Free Enterprise*. There the Court found that the scheme gave money for speech but had the purpose and effect of *abridging* speech, not facilitating it. Moreover, one of *Arizona Free Enterprise*'s critical themes is that government may not decide how much campaign speech is enough. That's nothing new: *Buckley* said in no uncertain terms that government could not directly limit speech, and *Arizona Free Enterprise* said in no uncertain terms that government could not indirectly limit speech. So if the purpose of public

---

[84] *Id.*
[85] *Id.*

funding with limits attached is to cap the amount of campaign speech, not merely replace private fundraising, that "level the playing field" rationale has been sharply rejected by the Court.

In my view, the dirty little secret of public funding—unless it takes the form of floors without ceilings—has always been to limit spending. The *Buckley* statute did it both directly and through public funding. No presidential candidate could spend more than $20 million and the government would give each exactly that amount for his campaign, just as long as he "voluntarily" agreed not to spend a penny more. That sounds like leveling the playing field to me. And the ultimate driving force, which comes mostly from the left, is viewpoint-based preference—that is, muting the voices of the right and the rich on the theory, however mistaken, that the policy views of those groups will prevail unfairly and undemocratically unless there's a level playing field. Necessary "progressive" change cannot occur, it is claimed, without changing the campaign finance system to stop favoring the "special interests."[86]

That is not to say *Buckley* is in jeopardy on this issue. But the presidential funding system upheld in that case—with its comparatively low limits, its impotence at preventing corruption (think soft money and big checks for party accounts), and its effect on speech (recall Obama's $750 million privately raised versus McCain's $100 million public-funding cap)—might well be overturned if *Buckley* were revisited. If the *Davis/Citizens United/Arizona Free Enterprise* toolbox of strict First Amendment doctrines and presumptions were applied to *Buckley*-style matching contributions or lump-sum mechanisms, with low spending limits and other speech-suppressing or speech-managing requirements (for example, mandatory participation in candidate debates), how would the current Court respond?

Indeed, the Court's sensitivity to public-funding mandates to speak less may even call into question the basic justification for

---

[86] See Brief of Petitioners-Appellants at 8–12, Arizona Free Enterprise, 131 S. Ct. 2806 (2011) (Nos. 10-238 & 10-239), for examples of such viewpoint-based themes in the language of the Clean Election referendum. More broadly, the complaint for 40 years has been that "good" legislation in the "public interest" has been systemically stymied by the private funding of our politics and the special-interest power this facilitates. Only one of the most recent iterations of this trope is from Harvard's Professor Lawrence Lessig, see Lessig, Democracy after *Citizens United*, Boston Review, September/October 2010, available at http://bostonreview.net/BR35.5/lessig.php (last visited Aug. 2, 2011).

conditioned spending limits: that they are accepted "voluntarily" and therefore pose no First Amendment problem. Remember *Buckley*'s footnote 65, which said that, though spending limits were unconstitutional, candidates could "voluntarily" agree to them as a condition of getting the public funding. But there were two problems with this footnote. First, the Court never really discussed why a "voluntary" agreement to surrender First Amendment rights was permissible. Second, had there been such a discussion, it would have had to engage the Court's "unconstitutional conditions" doctrine. As previously described by Richard Epstein in these pages, that doctrine holds that "even if a state has absolute discretion to grant or deny any individual a privilege or a benefit, it cannot grant the privilege subject to conditions that improperly coerce, pressure or induce the waiver of that person's constitutional rights."[87] Another version of the doctrine holds that the government cannot accomplish indirectly what it cannot achieve directly—it cannot purchase what it cannot command.

Partly the issue is whether the particular campaign finance system stacks the deck against private fundraising and spending, for example, with very low contribution limits, so the choice to accept public funding is not "voluntary." But the broader issue is whether you can ever "voluntarily" be made to surrender a constitutional right to obtain a government benefit. Put in the *Buckley* context, if you have a First Amendment right to spend as much as you can raise on your campaign, how can the government make you surrender that right in order to get government funding for your campaign? In this context, can the government purchase what it cannot command? Perhaps the *Buckley* justices had an unstated bargain to split the difference: strike down direct limits but allow indirect limits. But this judicial bargain might well fly in the face of the unconstitutional conditions doctrine. If quantity controls are content controls, as the Court has maintained ever since *Buckley*, then government is using its control over funding to control content. The less you can spend, the less you can say, and the less control you have over how you can say it. Does the new *Arizona Free Enterprise* vigilance over First

---

[87] Richard Epstein, Church and State at the Crossroads: *Christian Legal Society v. Martinez*, 2009–2010 Cato Sup. Ct. Rev. 105, 109 n.7 (2010) (quoting Richard A. Epstein, Bargaining with the State 5 (1993)).

Amendment rights in the context of public funding call into question even the bargain that may have been struck in *Buckley*?

B. Political Possibilities

What else does the future likely hold for public financing of politics? Given the current economic crisis and the constraints on more government spending, there seems to be absolutely no appetite for lavish public funding of politics—"Food Stamps for Politicians" as some have derisively called it. The politics of this issue has always been that incumbents want limits as part of any public-financing scheme because they do not want to give large campaign benefits to their usually underfunded opponents. Liberal reform groups want limits because the less money in politics the better so far as they are concerned—except, of course, the small "qualifying" contributions embedded into "clean election" systems. If those groups had their way, we might have complete public funding of campaigns and no private money allowed—however irrational as a practical matter and impermissible as a constitutional matter.

But political realities are influenced by constitutional constraints. When it seemed that the Court had taken a hands-off approach to public financing of political campaigns, reformers pushed through all manner of Rube Goldberg schemes, like the one in Arizona. Now that the Court has made limits-driven public-funding arrangements constitutionally questionable, there may be an incentive to push for approaches that emphasize different values. The later versions of the FENA—the perennial vehicle for public financing of congressional campaigns—quietly deleted any trigger provisions after the *Davis* handwriting on the wall. Similar bills now emphasize limits but allow them to be adjusted upward if there are matching small-donor contributions, without regard to what opponents do. So, in incremental steps we may be slowly moving toward a system with more of an emphasis on "floors" and less of an emphasis on "ceilings."

That would, of course, still ruffle Senator McCarthy and libertarians, who believe passionately that government should have no role in funding its opposition. But to those who feel that public support for political speech can be reconciled with freedom of speech, "floors without ceilings" may be looking better all the time.

Sorrell v. IMS Health: Protecting Free Speech or Resurrecting Lochner?

*Richard Samp**

*Richard Samp**

The Supreme Court's latest foray into commercial speech doctrine, *Sorrell v. IMS Health*,[1] confirms a remarkable trend in First Amendment jurisprudence over the past 30 years. In recent years, the Court's conservative justices have been far more likely than its liberal ones to strike down government speech restrictions on First Amendment grounds. But 35 years ago, those roles were largely reversed.

That trend is no more evident than in case law addressing commercial speech—that is, speech, such as advertising, that proposes a commercial transaction. When the Court first concluded in a 1976 decision that commercial speech was entitled to First Amendment protection, liberal justices unanimously joined Justice Harry Blackmun's majority decision.[2] Then-Justice William Rehnquist dissented, while Justice Potter Stewart and Chief Justice Warren Burger filed concurring opinions that expressed hesitancy over the new doctrine. But every conservative justice joined Justice Anthony Kennedy's sweeping, pro-First Amendment majority opinion in *Sorrell*, while three of the Court's four liberals (all but Justice Sonia Sotomayor) signed on to Justice Stephen Breyer's passionate dissent.[3] In 1976's *Virginia Board*, the plaintiffs were represented by the liberal Public Citizen Litigation Group. In *Sorrell*, Public Citizen filed an amicus brief in support of government speech restrictions.

But while the new battle lines in commercial speech litigation have become increasingly clear, what is far less clear is what the *Sorrell* decision portends for the development of First Amendment doctrine. On the one hand, Justice Kennedy's opinion several times

---

* Chief Counsel, Washington Legal Foundation.
[1] Sorrell v. IMS Health, Inc., 131 S. Ct. 2653 (2011).
[2] Va. Bd. of Pharmacy v. Va. Citizens Consumer Council, Inc., 425 U.S. 748 (1976).
[3] 131 S. Ct. at 2673 (Breyer, J., dissenting).

suggested that government restrictions on commercial speech should frequently be subjected to some sort of "heightened" scrutiny. (Heretofore, such restrictions have generally been subject to an "intermediate" level of First Amendment scrutiny, first articulated in *Central Hudson Gas & Electric Corp. v. Public Services Commission of New York*.[4]) But *Sorrell* never explained how its "heightened" scrutiny was to be applied. Indeed, the Court ultimately determined that because the speech restrictions at issue could not pass muster even under the less exacting *Central Hudson* test, there was no reason to decide whether a more rigorous First Amendment test should be applied.[5]

It thus remains to be seen whether *Sorrell* marks a major expansion of First Amendment protection for commercial speech. Several justices have expressed a willingness to eliminate the doctrinal distinctions between commercial speech and other forms of speech. *Sorrell* indicates that the Court's majority is not yet willing to take that step.

I. The Vermont Statute

At issue was a Vermont statute (Act 80) that sought to restrict the access of pharmaceutical companies to information about the prescribing habits of Vermont doctors. Drug companies want that information because it permits them to identify those doctors most likely to prescribe their drugs, and because it allows them to ascertain how best to present their sales pitches when making sales calls at the doctors' offices—a process called "detailing." Vermont articulated two reasons why it wanted to restrict access to prescriber-identifying information. First, it sought to protect doctors' privacy interests. Second, it noted that the economics of the pharmaceutical industry are such that only higher-priced, brand-name drugs are promoted through the detailing process. Vermont concluded that by restricting access to prescriber-identifying information, it could interfere sufficiently with the detailing process to effect a shift in overall drug sales away from brand-name drugs and toward lower-priced generic drugs (which Vermont concluded were often at least as safe and effective as equivalent brand-name drugs). Vermont

---

[4] 447 U.S. 557 (1980).
[5] 131 S. Ct. at 2667.

contended that such a shift would result in reduced health care costs and in improvements in health care.

Pharmacies are the principal source of information about doctors' prescribing habits. Federal law prohibits them from dispensing a prescription drug unless the customer presents a prescription signed by a licensed doctor. Pharmacies have a strong financial interest in retaining information regarding who prescribed dispensed drugs: medical insurance companies generally require them to reveal the prescriber's name before they will pay a share of the drug's costs. Data publishers (sometimes pejoratively referred to as "data miners") purchase prescription information from pharmacies, analyze it to determine which doctors prescribe which drugs, and then provide the analyzed data to their customers, most of whom are drug companies.

Act 80 restricted access to prescriber-identifying information in three ways. First, it prohibited pharmacies, insurers, and similar entities from selling or leasing such information. Second, it prohibited them from permitting the use of such information "for marketing or promoting a prescription drug, unless the prescriber consents." Third, it imposed an identical prohibition on pharmaceutical manufacturers and marketers, in the absence of prescriber consent.[6] The first two prohibitions contained several broad exceptions;[7] according to the Supreme Court, those exceptions "made prescriber-identifying information available to an almost limitless audience"— that is, just about everyone other than drug companies.[8]

II. The First Amendment Challenge

Before Act 80 took effect, the nation's three largest data publishers challenged the statute on First Amendment grounds.[9] A trade group of drug manufacturers filed a similar challenge, and the two suits were consolidated. The U.S. Court of Appeals for the Second Circuit agreed that the statute violated their First Amendment rights and

---

[6] Vt. Stat. Ann. tit. 18, § 4631(d) (2011).

[7] Vt. Stat. Ann. tit. 18, § 4631(e) (2011).

[8] Sorrell, 131 S. Ct. at 2669.

[9] The data publishers are referred to collectively as "IMS Health," the largest of the three publishers.

enjoined enforcement.[10] The U.S. Court of Appeals for the First Circuit previously rejected First Amendment challenges that IMS Health had brought against similar statutes adopted in New Hampshire and Maine.[11] The U.S. Supreme Court granted review to resolve the conflict.

In affirming the Second Circuit's decision, the Court applied the four-part *Central Hudson* test that it has traditionally applied in commercial speech cases over the past 30 years. Under that test, courts consider as a threshold matter whether the commercial speech concerns unlawful activity or is inherently misleading. If so, the speech is not protected by the First Amendment. If the speech concerns lawful activity and is not misleading, the challenged speech regulation violates the First Amendment unless government regulators can establish that: (1) they have identified a substantial government interest; (2) the regulation "directly advances" the asserted interest; and (3) the regulation "is no more extensive than is necessary to serve that interest."[12]

Because Act 80 applied even to speech that was not inherently misleading and that did not propose an illegal transaction, the first *Central Hudson* prong was not relevant. Vermont identified two interests, both of which the Court assumed to be "substantial," that were served by Act 80: (1) medical privacy and (2) lowering the costs of medical services and improving public health. The Court held that neither rationale was sufficient to survive *Central Hudson* scrutiny.

The Court concluded, in light of the broad statutory exceptions that permitted widespread distribution of physician-identifying information, that Act 80 did not sufficiently "advance the State's asserted interest in physician confidentiality," and thus that the statute flunked the third prong of the *Central Hudson* test.[13] It left open the possibility that a more broadly based privacy provision—one that regulated even more speech—might have passed the test.[14]

---

[10] IMS Health, Inc. v. Sorrell, 630 F.3d 263 (2d Cir. 2010).

[11] IMS Health, Inc. v. Ayotte, 550 F.3d 42 (1st Cir. 2008), cert. denied, 129 S. Ct. 2864 (2009) (New Hampshire); IMS Health, Inc. v. Mills, 616 F.3d 7 (1st Cir. 2010) (Maine).

[12] Central Hudson, 447 U.S. at 566.

[13] Sorrell, 131 S. Ct. at 2668.

[14] *Id.*

The Court deemed the second interest identified by Vermont as constitutionally insufficient because, it held, Act 80 did not advance that interest "in a permissible way."[15] It noted that Vermont was seeking to achieve its health care goals by restraining truthful speech by drug companies that, Vermont feared, would cause doctors to write inappropriate and costly prescriptions. The Court held that regulation of truthful commercial speech can never be justified based on concern over how others might react to the speech. It repeated its prior admonition that "the 'fear that people would make bad decisions if given truthful information' cannot justify content-based burdens on speech."[16] Such justifications for burdening speech were particularly inappropriate given that the targets of the speech—prescribing physicians—were "sophisticated and experienced consumers."[17]

III. Content-Based and Speaker-Based Restrictions

Had the Court confined itself to consideration of whether Act 80 could survive intermediate scrutiny under *Central Hudson*, the *Sorrell* decision would likely have attracted little attention. But the Court went well beyond a typical *Central Hudson* analysis in its discussion of speech restrictions based on the content of the speech and the identity of the speaker. Instead, it stated unequivocally that "heightened judicial scrutiny is warranted" whenever a "content-based burden" is imposed on protected speech, and it concluded that Act 80 imposes just such a content-based burden.[18] We will have to await future cases to discover what sort of heightened judicial scrutiny the majority had in mind.

Although the majority suggested that "heightened" scrutiny had been applied in previous commercial speech cases involving content-based speech restrictions, none of the cases cited by the majority were commercial speech cases.[19] *Turner Broadcasting System, Inc. v. FCC* was a First Amendment challenge to a federal "must carry" statute that required cable television systems to carry the signals of

---

[15] *Id.* at 2670.
[16] *Id.* at 2670–71 (quoting Thompson v. W. States Med. Ctr., 535 U.S. 357, 374 (2002)).
[17] *Id.* at 2671.
[18] *Id.* at 2663.
[19] *Id.* at 2663–64.

over-the-air television stations.[20] *United States v. Playboy Entertainment Group, Inc.* challenged a federal statute that prohibited cable stations from providing sexually explicit programming except during late-night hours.[21] *Simon & Schuster, Inc. v. Members of New York State Crime Victims Board* challenged a New York State law that imposed financial burdens on those who sought to publish books describing their criminal activities.[22] In each of those cases, the Court indicated that burdens imposed on speech based on its content are subject to heightened scrutiny even if the government does not ban the speech altogether, but none of those cases involved commercial speech—speech proposing a commercial transaction—and in none of the decisions did the Court suggest that its call for heightened scrutiny extended to commercial speech cases.

In noncommercial speech cases, the issue of "heightened" scrutiny usually arises in the context of determining whether the time-place-or-manner doctrine applies to a challenged speech restriction. Under that doctrine, "the government may impose reasonable restrictions on the time, place, or manner of protected speech, provided the restrictions are justified without reference to the content of the regulated speech, that they are narrowly tailored to serve a significant government interest, and that they leave open ample alternative channels for communication of the information."[23] Thus, for example, the Court applied this somewhat relaxed standard of review to uphold a New York City ordinance that controlled music volume at rock concerts in Central Park because the controls were imposed without regard to the content of the music and reasonably accommodated the needs of individual musicians.[24] An essential prerequisite to application of the time-place-or-manner doctrine is that the government's motivation for regulating speech not be based on the content of the speech; the doctrine is inapplicable and heightened scrutiny is applied whenever "the government has adopted a regulation of speech because of disagreement with the message it conveys."[25] But the Court has never considered the time-place-or-manner doctrine in the context of commercial speech and none of its

[20] 512 U.S. 622 (1994).

[21] 529 U.S. 803 (2000).

[22] 502 U.S. 105 (1991).

[23] Ward v. Rock Against Racism, 491 U.S. 781, 791 (1989).

[24] *Id.* at 803.

[25] *Id.* at 791.

time-place-or-manner decisions has suggested that the doctrine is applicable to restrictions on commercial speech. Accordingly, *Sorrell*'s assertion that "heightened" scrutiny applies to *any* content-based burdens imposed on speech, even when the speech is commercial in nature, suggests that the Court may be contemplating a substantial expansion of First Amendment protection for commercial speech.

Moreover, as the *Sorrell* dissent points out, most statutes restricting commercial speech are, by their very nature, to some degree content-based:

> Regulatory programs necessarily draw distinctions on the basis of content. . . . Electricity regulators, for example, oversee company statements, pronouncements, and proposals, but only about electricity. . . . The Federal Reserve Board regulates the content of statements, advertising, loan proposals, and interest rate disclosures, but only when made by financial institutions. . . . And the FDA oversees the form and content of labeling, advertising, and sales proposals of drugs, but not of furniture.[26]

If heightened scrutiny is to be applied to any commercial speech regulation that is based on the content of the speech being regulated, one could reasonably conclude that *all* such regulations will be subject to heightened scrutiny.

Indeed, it is reasonable to surmise that the Court ultimately disposed of *Sorrell* on relatively narrow grounds because it recognized the potentially wide-ranging implications of its "heightened scrutiny" language and wished to avoid committing itself irrevocably to a position whose ramifications remain unclear. By striking down Act 80 under the less exacting *Central Hudson* test, the Court bought time to work out precisely when commercial speech restrictions should be subject to "heightened scrutiny"—scrutiny more exacting than the *Central Hudson* test—and what "heightened scrutiny" should consist of in the commercial speech context.

IV. "Neutral Justifications" for Commercial Speech Restrictions

One hint regarding how the Court may answer those questions is contained in *Sorrell*'s discussion of speech restrictions designed

---

[26] Sorrell, 131 S. Ct. at 2677 (Breyer, J., dissenting).

to protect consumers against fraud. The Court recognized that commercial speech restrictions may pass First Amendment muster when adopted to protect against fraud, even if they are content-based: "The Court has noted, for example, that 'a State may choose to regulate price advertising in one industry but not in others, because the risk of fraud . . . is in its view greater there.'"[27] The Court contrasted such permissible content-based commercial speech restrictions with Act 80, stating that "Vermont has not shown that its law has a neutral justification."[28]

Of course, a statute that regulates price advertising in the used-car industry but not, for example, in the retail grocery industry cannot be said to have a "neutral" justification as that term is normally understood. Instead of treating all price advertising neutrally, it imposes greater burdens on one type of commercial speech based on its content (statements about used-car prices) than on other price advertising. And it likely does so precisely because legislators disfavor used-car price advertising; they deem it more susceptible to fraud than other forms of price advertising. Indeed, given that the Court was referring to "neutral justification[s]" for laws that by definition are not "neutral" with respect to the content of speech, the Court could not have intended the word "neutral" to be accorded its everyday meaning. Rather, the Court's statement that content-based commercial speech restrictions are constitutionally permissible only when they possess a "neutral justification" may simply indicate that the Court intended to limit such restrictions to a small number of narrowly defined and well-accepted categories.

As *Sorrell* indicates, one such category covers speech restrictions designed to protect consumers from fraud: "Indeed, the government's legitimate interest in protecting consumers from commercial harms explains why commercial speech can be subject to greater governmental regulation than noncommercial speech."[29] Even where commercial speech is not inherently misleading, it can be regulated to reduce the possibility that some consumers might nonetheless be misled. Disclaimers may appropriately be required in advertisements, "in order to dissipate the possibility of consumer confusion

---

[27] *Id.* at 2672 (majority opinion) (quoting R.A.V. v. St. Paul, 505 U.S. 377, 388–89 (1992)).

[28] *Id.*

[29] *Id.*

or deception."[30] Thus, for example, states may require a lawyer to attach a disclaimer to an advertisement offering contingency fee services, to make clear to potential clients that even though they will owe no "fees" unless they win their case, they may still be responsible for court costs.[31] The Court has never tolerated the imposition of similar burdens on noncommercial speech.

A second (and less controversial) "neutral justification" is the suppression of commercial speech that is false or that proposes an illegal transaction. While false noncommercial speech is generally accorded a modicum of First Amendment protection in order to guard against the chilling of truthful speech,[32] false commercial speech has never been deemed entitled to any First Amendment protection.[33] Moreover, a ban on false commercial speech arguably could never properly be described as "content-based" suppression of speech because it applies to *all* false commercial speech, not merely false commercial speech touching on specific topics. While a ban on commercial speech that proposes an illegal transaction generally qualifies as content-based (because it undoubtedly has been adopted based on government disapproval of the specific message being conveyed), the Court has long recognized that such speech restrictions are compatible with the First Amendment,[34] and *Sorrell* characterized such restrictions as "restrictions directed at commerce or conduct" that impose no more than "incidental burdens on speech."[35]

A third "neutral justification" implicitly endorsed by *Sorrell* is protection of privacy. *Sorrell* rejected Vermont's privacy-based justifications for Act 80, but the Court did so primarily because the statute permitted dissemination of prescriber-identifying information in so many circumstances that it did not directly advance Vermont's claimed privacy interests (and thus did not satisfy prong three of the *Central Hudson* test). The Court indicated, however, that the Vermont statute might have been upheld had it more broadly

[30] In re R.M.J., 455 U.S. 191, 201 (1982).
[31] Zauderer v. Office of Disciplinary Counsel, 471 U.S. 626, 651–52 (1985).
[32] Gertz v. Robert Welch, Inc., 418 U.S. 323 (1974).
[33] Central Hudson, 447 U.S. at 563.
[34] Pittsburgh Press Co. v. Human Relations Comm'n, 413 U.S. 376, 388 (1973).
[35] Sorrell, 131 S. Ct. at 2664.

protected the privacy of doctors by restricting more speech.[36] A broader statute would still likely be deemed content-based because it would prohibit speech about what drugs a doctor prescribes but not speech that would entail a similar invasion of privacy, for example, speech about analogous conduct by a dentist or speech about a doctor's income. But *Sorrell* indicates that the government's interest in protecting privacy can, in at least some instances, serve as an adequate "neutral justification" for imposing content-based burdens on truthful commercial speech.[37]

Such privacy-based speech restrictions are likely permissible even when the First Amendment would prohibit similar restrictions on noncommercial speech. In the noncommercial context, the Court has explained that "[a]s a general matter, state action to punish the publication of truthful information seldom can satisfy constitutional standards."[38] Thus, the Court upheld the First Amendment right of a radio station to air a tape of an illegally intercepted telephone conversation despite a federal law prohibiting such broadcasts, finding that the public interest in airing matters of public concern outweighed the privacy interests of the parties to the intercepted conversation.[39] Because commercial speech is less likely to be deemed a matter "of public concern," the Court appears more likely to uphold a government's interest in protecting privacy when the regulated speech is commercial in nature.

There is no indication in *Sorrell* that the Court is willing to recognize "neutral justification[s]" for content-based commercial speech restrictions outside these three areas, which are (1) prophylactic rules designed to protect against the possibility that consumers will be misled, (2) laws prohibiting commercial speech that is false or proposes an illegal transaction, and (3) laws designed to protect privacy. The Court made abundantly clear that one justification for content-based commercial speech restrictions is never compatible

---

[36] *Id.* at 2668.

[37] As an example of a statute that "would present quite a different case"—it might well survive First Amendment challenge—the Court cited the Health Insurance Portability and Accountability Act of 1996, 42 U.S.C. § 1320d-2 (2006), which broadly protects the privacy of patients' medical records, at least in a commercial context. Sorrell, 131 S. Ct. at 2668.

[38] Bartnicki v. Vopper, 532 U.S. 514, 527 (2001).

[39] *Id.* at 534.

with the First Amendment: a desire to influence the conduct of third parties indirectly, by restraining speech that might cause the third parties to act in a manner that the government deems undesirable.[40] *Sorrell* concluded that just such a desire had been among Vermont's principal motivations for adopting Act 80. The Court explained:

> The State seeks to achieve its policy objectives through the indirect means of restraining certain speakers—that is, by diminishing detailers' abilities to influence prescription decisions. Those who seek to censor or burden free expression often assert that disfavored speech has adverse effects. But the fear that people would make bad decisions if given truthful information cannot justify content-based burdens on speech. . . . The First Amendment directs us to be especially skeptical of regulations that seek to keep people in the dark for what the government perceives to be their own good. . . . The State can express [its] views through its own speech. . . . But a State's failure to persuade does not allow it to hamstring the opposition. The State may not burden the speech of others in order to tilt public debate in a preferred direction.[41]

The *Sorrell* dissent was correct, of course, that economic regulation will often impose burdens on speech, whether intended or not.[42] The majority made clear, however, that "the First Amendment does not prevent restrictions directed at commerce or conduct from imposing incidental burdens on speech."[43] But when a statute imposes "more than an incidental burden on protected expression" and does so based on the content of speech or the identity of the speaker, it will be subject to "heightened scrutiny" and can never be undertaken to tilt public debate in a preferred direction.[44]

V. Application to Existing Federal Speech Restrictions

Sorrell's pronouncement that content-based restrictions on commercial speech are subject to "heightened scrutiny" calls into question the constitutionality of speech restrictions imposed under a

---

[40] Sorrell, 131 S. Ct. at 2671.

[41] *Id.* (citations omitted).

[42] *Id.* at 2675 (Breyer, J., dissenting).

[43] *Id.* at 2664 (majority opinion).

[44] *Id.* at 2664–65.

variety of federal regulatory programs. Such federal speech restrictions in most instances are content-based. In response to previous First Amendment challenges, the federal government has raised a variety of defenses, some of which may not meet *Sorrell*'s definition of a "neutral justification" for burdening speech and thus may no longer be sufficient to withstand constitutional challenge. This article briefly examines *Sorrell*'s potential effect on two federal regulatory programs: the regulation of prescription drugs and the regulation of sales of securities.

A. Prescription Drugs

The Food and Drug Administration comprehensively regulates the manufacture and sale of prescription drugs pursuant to the Federal Food, Drug, and Cosmetic Act.[45] No "new drugs" may be introduced into interstate commerce unless they are approved by the FDA for a specified use.[46] As part of the approval process, the FDA specifies the precise labeling for the approved product. The agency does not permit a manufacturer to market an approved product for a use that it has not approved; indeed, if an approved product is marketed for an unapproved new use, the FDA deems the product an unapproved new drug that is subject to seizure. The FDA also considers such a product to be "misbranded" (and thus subject to seizure) because its labeling will not provide directions for administering the drug for the new use, and federal law deems prescription drugs to be misbranded if not properly labeled for each of their intended uses.[47]

But the medical community's knowledge regarding the safety and effectiveness of FDA-approved drugs inevitably outpaces FDA-approved labeling. Physicians who regularly work with such drugs learn of safe and effective uses for the drugs that are not included within the labeling; such uses are generally referred to as off-label uses. The FDA does not control the practice of medicine and thus does not seek to regulate the speech or conduct of physicians, who routinely prescribe FDA-approved products to their patients for off-label uses. But the FDA has repeatedly cracked down on drug

---

[45] 21 U.S.C. §§ 301–399d (2006).
[46] 21 U.S.C. § 355(a) (2006).
[47] 21 U.S.C. § 352(f)(1) (2006).

companies that speak truthfully about off-label uses of their products. The courts have made clear that the First Amendment imposes some limits on the FDA's authority to sanction manufacturers that discuss off-label uses.[48]

In defending against First Amendment challenges, the FDA has asserted that its restrictions on truthful manufacturer speech serve two important government interests: (1) manufacturers have a natural tendency to provide a biased summary of their products' attributes, and a ban on manufacturer off-label speech is the only means of ensuring that doctors and patients are not misled; and (2) prohibiting off-label speech provides manufacturers with an incentive to conduct the extensive product testing necessary to obtain agency approval for the new use, and conducting such testing is the only way to determine for sure that the off-label use is actually safe and effective. *Sorrell* will make it significantly harder for the FDA to sustain each of those arguments.

The FDA undoubtedly has a strong interest in preventing misleading speech about off-label use. But current enforcement policy entails a high degree of the content-based and speaker-based speech regulation of which *Sorrell* was so critical. For example, although the manufacturer of a drug is likely to be as well-acquainted as anyone with medical research regarding off-label uses of that drug, the manufacturer is the *only* entity that is prohibited from speaking truthfully about those uses. If any sort of "heightened scrutiny" is applied to the FDA's misleading-speech rationale for suppressing manufacturer off-label speech, the agency will have a very difficult time justifying its total ban on truthful speech and explaining why, for example, use of disclaimers would be insufficient to ameliorate any potentially misleading aspects of the speech.

The FDA's second rationale for its content-based speech regulation (providing an incentive for increased product testing) is unlikely to survive *Sorrell*. Nothing in the Court's decision indicated that content-based speech suppression as a means of inducing a censored party to engage in additional scientific research is the sort of "neutral justification" that can survive First Amendment scrutiny. Indeed, even under a traditional *Central Hudson* analysis, one can posit

---

[48] See, e.g., Wash. Legal Found. v. Friedman, 13 F. Supp. 2d 51 (D.D.C. 1998), appeal dismissed, 202 F.3d 331 (D.C. Cir. 2000).

numerous ways to provide a drug manufacturer with incentives to engage in research without restricting its right to speak truthfully.

B. The Sale of Securities

The Securities Act of 1933 sets forth detailed rules regarding the public offering of securities by an issuer or a controlling shareholder.[49] It provides that such public offerings may be made only pursuant to a prospectus, and it contains detailed rules regarding precisely what information must be included in that prospectus.[50] Among the Act's many other provisions regulating speech is Section 17(b), which prohibits anyone from writing about a security in return for compensation from the issuer, unless the compensation is fully disclosed.[51]

These provisions undoubtedly constitute content-based and speaker-based restrictions on speech. Many courts nonetheless have declined to subject the federal securities laws to more than cursory First Amendment review. One federal appellate decision frequently cited by federal government attorneys held that rules relating to the "exchange of information regarding securities" are subject to only "limited First Amendment scrutiny."[52] The appeals court justified that limited scrutiny by noting that securities law was an area that traditionally had been subject to extensive federal regulation. The court explained, "In areas of extensive federal regulation—like securities dealing—we do not believe that the Constitution requires the judiciary to weigh the relative merits of particular regulatory objectives that impinge upon communications occurring within the umbrella of an overall regulatory scheme."[53] The appeals court thus concluded that a newsletter publisher was entitled to only limited First Amendment protection from a Securities and Exchange Commission lawsuit alleging that he published articles in violation of Section 17(b).[54]

Sorrell will likely lead to significantly increased First Amendment scrutiny for restrictions imposed on truthful speech by the federal

---

[49] 15 U.S.C. §§ 77a–77aa (2006).

[50] 15 U.S.C. § 77j (2006).

[51] 15 U.S.C. § 77q(b) (2006).

[52] SEC v. Wall St. Publ'g Inst., 851 F.2d 365, 373 (D.C. Cir. 1988).

[53] *Id.*

[54] *Id.* at 373–74.

securities laws. Because such restrictions are virtually always content-based—for example, Section 17(b) applies to journalists who have received compensation from a securities issuer but not to journalists who have received no compensation—*Sorrell* suggests that they will be subject to "heightened scrutiny," above the level prescribed by *Central Hudson*. The fact that the sale of securities is an area of extensive federal regulation will no longer justify providing deferential review to securities regulations that burden speech.

It is unquestionably true that a principal purpose of the federal securities laws is to protect purchasers from fraud. *Sorrell* recognizes that combating potential fraud can be a valid basis for imposing content-based speech restrictions. But even under those circumstances, the content-based restrictions on truthful speech imposed by the securities laws must still survive heightened scrutiny. Contrary to the law as it existed pre-*Sorrell*, the judiciary will now be required "to weigh the relative merits of particular regulatory objectives that impinge upon communications occurring within the umbrella of an overall regulatory scheme."[55] The SEC may have considerable difficulty demonstrating that consumers are likely to be misled by an issuer's omission of statutorily required items from a prospectus or by a journalist's truthful article about an issuer that fails to mention compensation received by the journalist. In the absence of such a demonstration, burdens imposed by the federal securities laws on the speakers in question would not withstand First Amendment challenge.

VI. First Amendment Protection for Data

One interesting aspect of the Supreme Court's 6–3 decision striking down Act 80 is that it focused exclusively on the burdens imposed on the speech of pharmaceutical companies. Although the First Amendment claims of IMS Health and the other data publishers formed a significant portion of the plaintiffs' case, neither the majority nor the dissent chose to address those claims.

IMS Health argued that Act 80 violated its First Amendment rights in two ways. First, the statute prevented it from receiving truthful information from pharmacies. Second, the statute prevented it from conveying its analyzed data to pharmaceutical companies. Vermont

[55] *Id.* at 373.

argued that IMS Health's data were unworthy of First Amendment protection, asserting that publication of the data was more akin to commercial conduct than to commercial speech. Without directly responding to that assertion, the Court appeared skeptical:

> This Court has held that the creation and dissemination of information are speech within the meaning of the First Amendment. See, e.g., Bartnicki, [532 U.S.] at 527 ("[I]f the acts of 'disclosing' and 'publishing' information do not constitute speech, it is hard to imagine what does fall within that category, as distinct from the category of expressive conduct" (some internal quotation marks omitted)); Rubin v. Coors Brewing Co., 514 U.S. 476, 481 (1995) ("information on beer labels" is speech); Dun & Bradstreet, Inc. v. Greenmoss Builders, Inc., 472 U.S. 749, 759 (1985) (plurality opinion) (credit report is "speech"). Facts, after all, are the beginning point for much of the speech that is most essential to advance human knowledge and to conduct human affairs. There is thus a strong argument that prescriber-identifying information is speech for First Amendment purposes.[56]

The Court ultimately concluded that it did not need to rule on Vermont's request that it create "an exception to the rule that information is speech," given that it had already concluded that Act 80 infringed on the First Amendment rights of drug makers.[57]

By ducking the is-it-conduct-or-speech issue, the Court avoided an issue that has lurked in the background of commercial speech case law for many years. Had the Court ruled that IMS Health's data are constitutionally protected speech, it would then have been required to consider whether to classify the data as commercial or noncommercial speech. The answer almost surely is that IMS Health is engaged in noncommercial speech because even though its information is sold for a profit, it is not uttered for the purpose of proposing a commercial transaction. IMS Health's noncommercial speech presumably would be entitled to full constitutional protection, thereby depriving the government of virtually all ability to regulate it as such. Yet, at the same time, the Court has been reluctant to accord the same First Amendment status to compiled data that it

[56] Sorrell, 131 S. Ct. at 2667.
[57] Id.

accords to traditional political speech.[58] By avoiding the is-it-speech-or-conduct issue, the Court was able to put off having to decide whether to grant the highest levels of First Amendment protection to a form of speech (prescription data) that is a matter of limited public concern and thus may not be viewed by some justices as lying at the heart of the First Amendment's protections. Justice Breyer's failure to address the issue in his dissent is less understandable because the dissenters could not logically have voted to uphold Act 80 unless they had some reason for rejecting IMS Health's First Amendment claims.

VII. Burdening Speech vs. Directly Regulating Speech

Sorrell's reliance on the First Amendment rights of pharmaceutical companies rather than the First Amendment rights of data publishers introduced an additional wrinkle. Unlike IMS Health, whose entire business was directly affected by Act 80, drug manufacturers faced only minimal direct regulation under the statute. In particular, Act 80 did not seek to regulate the detailing process; manufacturers' sales representatives were free to continue to make all the visits to doctors' offices that they desired and were not restricted regarding the types of truthful information they were permitted to convey.

Accordingly, the Court's decision striking down Act 80 was not based on a finding that the statute directly regulated manufacturers' speech, but on a finding that it imposed "more than an incidental burden" on their speech.[59] The Court found that the statute made it significantly more difficult for drug manufacturers to convey their desired message to doctors and "is directed at certain content and is aimed at particular speakers."[60]

The Court's conclusion—that the First Amendment protects not only against direct restrictions on speech but also against statutes that impose substantial burdens on speech—was hardly novel. In support of its conclusion, *Sorrell* cited numerous Court precedents, including a decision striking down, on First Amendment grounds,

---

[58] Dun & Bradstreet, 472 U.S. at 759.
[59] Sorrell, 131 S. Ct. at 2665.
[60] Id.

CATO SUPREME COURT REVIEW

a Minnesota "use tax" imposed on the cost of paper and ink consumed by a small group of Minnesota newspapers and magazines.[61]
In concluding that Act 80 imposed a more-than-incidental burden
on the speech of drug manufacturers, the Court stated, "Vermont's
statute could be compared with a law prohibiting trade magazines
from purchasing or using ink. . . . Like that hypothetical law, [Act
80] imposes a speaker- and content-based burden on protected
expression, and that circumstance is sufficient to justify application
of heightened scrutiny."[62]

But by relying on the speech "burdens" imposed on drug manufacturers rather than on the direct speech restrictions imposed on
IMS Health, the majority opened the door to Justice Breyer's criticism
that the majority was unduly interfering with "ordinary economic
regulatory programs."[63] He argued that Act 80 should be judged
under the lenient "rational basis" standard of review normally applicable to economic legislation. He argued:

> To apply a strict First Amendment standard virtually as a
> matter of course when a court reviews ordinary economic
> regulatory programs (even if that program has a modest
> impact upon a firm's ability to shape a commercial message)
> would work at cross purposes with this more basic constitu-
> tional approach. Since ordinary regulatory programs can
> affect speech, particularly commercial speech, in myriad
> ways, to apply a "heightened" First Amendment standard
> of review whenever such a program burdens speech would
> transfer from legislators to judges the primary power to
> weigh ends and to choose means, threatening to distort or
> undermine legitimate legislative objectives.[64]

Breyer concluded that Act 80 satisfied the "less demanding standards that are more appropriately applied in this kind of commercial
regulatory case—a case where the government seeks typical regulatory ends" and where the "speech-related consequences . . . are indirect, incidental, and entirely commercial."[65] Accusing the majority
of resurrecting substantive due process, he concluded:

[61] Minneapolis Star & Tribune Co. v. Minn. Comm'r of Revenue, 460 U.S. 575 (1983).
[62] Sorrell, 131 S. Ct. 2667.
[63] Id. at 2675 (Breyer, J., dissenting).
[64] Id.
[65] Id. at 2685.

> At best the Court opens a Pandora's Box of First Amendment challenges to many ordinary regulatory practices that may only incidentally affect a commercial message. . . . At worst, it reawakens *Lochner's* pre-New Deal threat of substituting judicial for democratic decisionmaking where ordinary economic regulation is at issue.[66]

Justice Breyer's accusation that the majority was seeking to "reawaken *Lochner*" was not well taken. As Justice Kennedy responded for the majority:

> Vermont's law does not simply have an effect on speech, but is directed at certain content and is aimed at particular speakers. The Constitution "does not enact Mr. Herbert Spencer's Social Statics." Lochner v. New York, 198 U.S. 45, 75 (1905) (Holmes, J., dissenting). It does enact the First Amendment.[67]

It is difficult to find support for Justice Breyer's contention that Act 80's effect on the speech of drug manufacturers was "incidental" when the Vermont legislature stated explicitly that Act 80's principal purpose was to impose a burden on manufacturers' speech and thereby interfere with their marketing efforts.[68] Justice Breyer's only response to those legislative findings was to assert (without citation to case law) that "[w]hether Vermont's regulatory statute 'targets' drug companies (as opposed to affecting them unintentionally) must be beside the First Amendment point."[69] But Justice Breyer failed to reconcile his assertion with the Court's numerous commercial speech decisions that have concluded that the government may not impose content-based burdens on truthful commercial speech out of fear that listeners may use the information in a manner the government does not approve of.[70]

Indeed, the relaxed standard of review espoused by Justice Breyer (and joined by Justices Ruth Bader Ginsburg and Elena Kagan) appears to be nothing short of a repudiation of the Court's entire

---

[66] *Id.*
[67] *Id.* at 2665 (majority opinion).
[68] *Id.* at 2663.
[69] *Id.* at 2679 (Breyer, J., dissenting).
[70] W. States Med. Ctr., 535 U.S. at 374; Va. Bd., 425 U.S. at 769–70.

body of commercial speech case law. It is difficult to see how any of the Court's commercial speech decisions could have been decided in favor of those challenging government speech regulations if the Court had applied Justice Breyer's relaxed standard of review. Justice Breyer (along with Justice Ginsburg) has dissented in the major commercial speech cases in the past decade,[71] so his disagreement with the Court's majority is not of recent origin.

Nonetheless, by relying on "burdens" imposed on the speech of drug manufacturers, rather than on the direct and substantial regulation of IMS Health's efforts to disseminate physician-identifying information, the majority left itself open to criticism that its First Amendment standards are too open-ended. Few would dispute that Act 80 imposed a substantial, content-based burden on drug manufacturers' truthful speech, but the majority's opinion leaves unanswered how much lower the statute's burden on manufacturer speech would have to be before Act 80 could pass First Amendment muster. A decision striking down Act 80 based on its direct, content-based regulation of IMS Health's speech (regardless of whether that speech was deemed commercial or noncommercial in nature) would have provided clearer guidance to lower courts when asked to address future First Amendment challenges to similar statutes.

Conclusion

Sorrell represents a broad reaffirmation of the Court's commercial speech doctrine and—depending on how its "heightened scrutiny" standard is applied in the future—may mark a substantial expansion in First Amendment protection for commercial speech. It also illustrates just how far apart the Court's conservative and liberal wings are in their approaches to commercial speech. While conservatives appear to be contemplating expanded commercial speech rights, liberals (led by Justice Breyer, whose dissent three times cited Justice Rehnquist's *Central Hudson* dissent) appear ready to abolish the entire commercial speech doctrine. Justice Sotomayor's decision to join the *Sorrell* majority—one of only three times all term that she disagreed with Justice Kagan—suggests that the conservative justices are likely to maintain the upper hand on this issue for the foreseeable future.

---

[71] W. States Med. Ctr., 535 U.S. 357; Lorillard Tobacco Co. v. Reilly, 533 U.S. 525 (2001).

Arizona Christian School Tuition Organization v. Winn: Does the Government Own the Money in Your Pocket?

*Tim Keller**

For 20 years, beginning soon after the enactment of the nation's first modern private school voucher program in Milwaukee, not a day passed that school choice advocates were not in court somewhere in the nation defending parents' right to choose the best school for their child. From Wisconsin to Florida, Illinois to Colorado, and Ohio to Arizona, the Institute for Justice and its allies have been in state and federal courts arguing that empowering parents to choose from among public and private schools, including religious schools, accords with federal and state constitutional guarantees of religious freedom.

But that 20-year "everyday" litigation streak came to a gratifying end on April 4, 2011, when the U.S. Supreme Court dismissed *Arizona Christian School Tuition Organization (ACSTO) v. Winn.*[1] In *ACSTO,* the Court held that taxpayers do not have standing to assert an Establishment Clause challenge to a state income-tax credit granted to individuals who donate their money to private nonprofit organizations that use these donations to help families pay tuition at private and religious elementary and secondary schools.

The respite from school choice litigation did not last long, however. Just over two months after *ACSTO* was decided, two lawsuits

* Executive Director, Institute for Justice Arizona Chapter. Keller represented the parent intervenors in *Arizona Christian School Tuition Organization v. Winn,* as well as the Arizona School Choice Trust, a nonprofit scholarship-granting organization that receives contributions eligible for the tax credit at issue in the case. He would like to thank Thomas Grier, an Institute for Justice law clerk and a student at the Ohio State University Moritz College of Law for his help with this article.

[1] Ariz. Christian Sch. Tuition Org. v. Winn, 131 S. Ct. 1436 (2011).

were filed against a voucher program recently enacted by the school district in Douglas County, Colorado, and soon thereafter a legal challenge was filed against Indiana's new statewide voucher program.[2] The Institute for Justice has moved to intervene in those cases on behalf of parents and children in desperate need of educational choice. And it is gearing up to intervene in yet another school choice case in Arizona, where the teachers' unions have threatened a lawsuit challenging the state's innovative education savings account program for children with special needs.

Given the holdings in *ACSTO* and its predecessor case *Zelman v. Simmons-Harris*,[3] future school choice cases will most certainly be filed only in state courts and will focus on state constitutional claims. There will undoubtedly be a long, drawn-out, state-by-state battle requiring the same type of perseverance and hard work that marked the first 20 years of school choice litigation. But defenders of choice are energized, passionate, and, perhaps most importantly, on solid legal ground.

I. A Story within a Story

For me, the *ACSTO* decision came as a bit of a surprise. Throughout the more than 10 years of litigation, the standing argument gained no traction—at least not until the case reached the U.S. Supreme Court for the *second* time. Upon reflection, however, the decision should not have been a surprise. In the final months of briefing, the merits argument became substantially intertwined with the taxpayer-standing argument. Indeed, the *ACSTO* plaintiffs declared in their merits brief that the "controlling issue" in the case was whether the program involved private charity or government spending.[4] If the program involved private, not government, spending, it should have been obvious that the "narrow exception" to the

---

[2] Institute for Justice Files to Intervene to Defend New Colorado School Choice Program, http://ij.org/about/3874 (last visited July 15, 2011); Institute for Justice Will Defend Indiana's New School Choice Program Against Legal Attack, http://ij.org/about/3898 (last visited July 15, 2011).

[3] Zelman v. Simmons-Harris, 536 U.S. 639 (2002) (upholding a publicly funded private school scholarship program permitting families to select both religious and nonreligious private schools under the Establishment Clause because the program was religiously neutral and controlled by private choice).

[4] Brief for Respondents at 1, ACSTO v. Winn, 131 S. Ct. 1436 (2011) (Nos. 09-987, 09-991), 2010 WL 3624706.

prohibition against taxpayer standing created by *Flast v. Cohen* would not apply.[5] Why? Because *Flast* involved the government's taxing *and spending* power.

But I'm getting ahead of myself. While the Court's holding in *ACSTO* is important, the case was first and foremost about private school choice and the lengths that school choice opponents will go to halt school choice programs. That is why this article will start at the beginning of the school choice fight.

School Choice in a Nutshell

The philosophy of school choice is simple: If the government is going to spend money on public education, then it should be done in a way that maximizes parental choice and minimizes government monopolization. Parents know better than bureaucrats what kind of educational environment best suits their children's needs, and choice-driven competition between schools is essential to any education reform effort that seeks to ensure that public schools perform at acceptable levels.

All parents, regardless of means, should enjoy a reasonable measure of choice in deciding what schools their children attend. Just above 10 percent of Americans exercise school choice by sending their K–12 children to private school.[6] Many more exercise school choice by moving to neighborhoods with (what they believe to be) good public schools.[7] But most Americans lack the financial means to do either of those things and must instead accept whatever public schools happen to serve the neighborhood they can afford to live in.[8] Public school officials know that their "customers" have nowhere

---

[5] Flast v. Cohen, 392 U.S. 83, 105–06 (1968) (creating an exception to the general rule that taxpayers do not have standing to challenge a government spending program because the Establishment Clause specifically limits congressional "taxing and spending power").

[6] Nat'l Ctr. for Educ. Statistics, Percentage distribution of students ages 5 through 17 attending kindergarten through 12th grade, by school type or participation in homeschooling and selected child, parent, and household characteristics: 1999, 2003, and 2007, Table 39, available at http://nces.ed.gov/programs/digest/d09/tables/dt09_039.asp (last visited July 12, 2011).

[7] See Lance T. Izumi, Vicki E. Murray, and Rachel S. Chaney, Not as Good as You Think: Why the Middle Class Needs School Choice, Pac. Res. Inst. (2007).

[8] In 2007, 70.6 percent of children attended a public school assigned to them by the government. See Nat'l Ctr. for Educ. Statistics, *supra* note 6.

else to turn, so those officials lack any meaningful incentive to provide a high-quality education.[9]

Per-pupil public school funding has *octupled* since the end of World
War II—even though the U.S. population has only doubled—and
it has *tripled* since the 1970s.[10] Yet performance during that time has
remained stagnant. America spends more on public education per
pupil than any other industrialized nation and receives far worse
results. Currently, Washington, D.C., spends approximately $16,500
per pupil per year, but still has one of the nation's most atrocious
public school systems.[11] And contrary to popular mythology, public
school teachers are not underpaid, but actually earn roughly the
same amount as architects, accountants, engineers, nurses, and other
professionals of similar stature—about $30 per hour.[12] So more
money is not the answer; choice-driven competition is.

There are four basic ways of delivering true[13] school choice:

First are scholarships or "vouchers" given directly by the government to parents, who may then select the private (and sometimes
public) school of their choice, using the voucher as partial or total
payment, depending on the terms of the particular program.

Second are personal tax credits and deductions for educational
expenses. Under the terms of personal-use tax benefits, parents who
spend their own money on private (and many times public) school
expenses, including the cost of tuition, may claim a personal tax
credit or deduction on their state income taxes.

Third are scholarships awarded by private scholarship-granting
organizations and funded by personal or corporate contributions.

---

[9] See generally John E. Chubb and Terry M. Moe, Politics, Markets, and America's
Schools, The Brookings Inst. (1990).

[10] Jay P. Greene, Education Myths: What Special Interest Groups Want You to Believe
About Our Schools—And Why It Isn't So 10 (2005).

[11] Leah Fabel, D.C., Maryland Rank Near Top in Per-Pupil Spending, Wash. Examiner,
May 25, 2011, at 4, available at http://washingtonexaminer.com/local/dc/2011/05/
dc-maryland-rank-near-top-pupil-spending.

[12] Greene, *supra* note 10, at 78.

[13] "True" is used to denote school choice programs that enable parents to escape the
public school system altogether. Within the public school system, there is a slowly
increasing tendency to provide greater parental choice through inter- and intra-
district transfer options, charter schools, magnet schools, etc. While important, those
measures are insufficient in themselves because they usually present no competitive
threat to the public school system itself, which is the root of the problem.

Contributors are then eligible to claim a state income tax credit when they file their tax return. This is the type of program that was at issue in *ACSTO*.

Finally, there has been recent interest in publicly funded education savings accounts.[14] Education savings accounts differ from traditional voucher programs in that parents can use the funds deposited in their child's account for a wide variety of educational services, including tutoring, purchasing curriculum, online instruction, saving for college tuition—and, of course, for tuition at private schools.

Currently, 20 voucher or scholarship tax credit programs operate in 12 states and Washington, D.C.[15]

2011: A Blockbuster Year for School Choice

In fall 2010, the Gleason Family Foundation hosted a school choice conference in San Francisco to announce plans for the first annual School Choice Week to be held the third week of January 2011. The conference galvanized the school choice movement around the shared values of expanding educational options for families and increasing student achievement. There was a particular emphasis on bipartisanship because there is no reason that school choice should be identified as either a Republican or Democrat issue. School Choice Week resulted in 200 organizations putting on over 150 events with tens of thousands of activists, parents, educators, policy wonks, and legislators participating.[16] Those events were publicized in more than 550 news stories.

School Choice Week's momentum carried over into state legislatures. Since November 2010, for example, the Institute for Justice (my organization) has provided legislative counseling in more than 20 states—an unprecedented number for a single legislative season. Careful drafting of school choice legislation is not only the key to a successful program, it is an essential part of maximizing the likelihood a program will withstand a constitutional challenge.

---

[14] See generally Matthew Ladner & Nick Dranias, Education Savings Accounts: Giving Parents Control of Their Children's Education, Goldwater Inst., No. 11-01 (Jan. 28, 2011).

[15] American Federation for Children, Facts, http://www.federationforchildren.org/facts (last visited July 12, 2011).

[16] See National School Choice Week, http://schoolchoiceweek.com/Video?video_id=32 (last visited July 12, 2011).

The six-month period following School Choice Week was the most productive ever for school choice legislation. Forty-two states introduced 96 bills to create or expand private school choice programs. As of this writing, 11 states and the U.S. Congress have passed school choice legislation of some type (either school voucher or scholarship tax credit programs), including five expansions of existing programs and seven new programs.[17] In addition, Congress reauthorized and expanded the Washington D.C. Opportunity Scholarship Program, a voucher program that only last year appeared to have been sentenced to a slow, lingering death from the Obama administration's decision not to allow any new students to apply for scholarships.

Arizona was the first state to create a significant new school choice program this year. It adopted the nation's first publicly funded education savings account program, targeted at children with disabilities.[18] The school district in Douglas County, Colorado, was the next to enact a new program. Colorado is one of the few states that give school districts real authority to innovate, and the result is a publicly funded scholarship program for private school tuition.[19] Indiana not only expanded its existing scholarship tax credit program and authorized a new personal tax deduction for educational expenses, it also created a means-tested statewide voucher program.[20] Oklahoma created a new scholarship tax credit program.[21] North Carolina adopted a personal-use tax credit for families with special-needs children.[22] And Wisconsin, where the modern school choice movement was born, eliminated the cap on enrollment in the Milwaukee program, made more families eligible, and expanded choice to the city of Racine.[23]

---

[17] American Federation for Children, School Choice Makes History, http://www.federationforchildren.org/articles/402 (last visited July 18, 2011).

[18] S. Bill 1553, 50th Leg., 1st Reg. Sess. (Ariz. 2011).

[19] Douglas County School District, Choice Scholarship Pilot Program, http://www.dcsdk12.org/portal/page/portal/DCSD/District_Information/School_Choice/Option_Certificates, (last visited July 15, 2011).

[20] The School Scholarship Act, H. Bill 1003, 117th Gen. Assem., 1st Reg. Sess. (Ind. 2011).

[21] The Oklahoma Equal Opportunity Education Scholarship Act, S. Bill 969, 53rd Leg., Reg. Sess. (Okla. 2011).

[22] H. Bill 344, Gen. Assem., Reg. Sess. (N.C. 2011).

[23] Governor Walker's 2011-13 biennial budget (2011 Wisconsin Act 32).

There are at least three reasons to believe that the level of interest in adopting new and expanding existing private school choice programs will continue for the foreseeable future.

First, school choice works. A recent report by Foundation for Educational Choice summarized all the empirical studies examining the effectiveness of school choice programs in improving educational outcomes both for children participating in the program and for public schools that face competitive pressure from school voucher programs.[24] The report demonstrated that 9 out of 10 empirical studies found positive educational gains for children participating in the program—and the one study that did not find a positive impact found no visible impact of any kind.[25] Indeed, no empirical study has ever found a school voucher program to negatively affect educational outcomes. Nineteen empirical studies examined the effect of school choice programs on public schools. With one immaterial exception, they all concluded that vouchers improve educational outcomes in public schools.[26]

Second, school choice programs—if designed to do so—can save states money. Considering that many states are in severe financial straits and looking for ways to save money—particularly on educational expenses that often make up one of the largest budget items— school choice is a natural alternative. Arizona's Individual Tax Credit Scholarship program was not even designed as a cost-saving measure, yet an analysis by the *Arizona Republic* concluded that the tax credit saves the state at least $8.3 million each year.[27]

---

[24] Greg Forster, A Win-Win Solution: The Empirical Evidence on School Vouchers, Found. for Educ. Choice 1–3 (2nd ed. 2011).

[25] *Id.* at 8 (six had positive gains across all students, while three had positive gains for only some students).

[26] *Id.* at 15. The exception is the recent study of Washington, D.C.'s voucher program, which holds public schools "harmless" by continuing to provide funding to public schools for the students who have left and now receive a voucher. *Id.* at 25.

[27] Ronald J. Hansen, Private School Tax Credits Save $8.3 Million, Arizona Republic, Oct. 20, 2009, available at http://www.azcentral.com/news/election/topstories/articles/1020taxcredits1020.html. A more generous examination of the Arizona tax credit program by Dr. Charles North at Baylor University argues that the program saves the state a minimum of $99.8 million and possibly as much as $241.5 million per year. See Charles M. North, Estimating the Savings to Arizona Taxpayers of the Private School Tuition Tax Credit, Center for Ariz. Policy, available at http://www.azpolicy.org/sites/azpolicy.org/files/downloads/ArizonaSTOTaxCreditCM North.pdf.

Finally, school choice is constitutional. Indeed, many new school choice programs over the past several years—particularly tax credit programs and voucher programs for special-needs students—have gone unchallenged in court. Four years ago, the Institute for Justice and the American Legislative Exchange Council published a nationwide analysis of each state's constitution to determine the legal viability of school choice programs and concluded that nearly every state's constitution will permit some form of private school choice.[28]

Of course, some types of school choice programs and some states are more likely to generate legal challenges than others. While there will likely be interest in and consideration of all four types of school choice programs, the *ACSTO* decision may spur some states to seriously consider tax credit programs because they are now effectively immune from federal court challenges by state taxpayers. Tax credit programs have also survived or avoided legal challenges in states where voucher programs have been held unconstitutional.[29]

II. Arizona's Path to Genuine Education Reform (and its Road to the Supreme Court)

In the mid-'90s, the Arizona legislature charted a course toward genuine educational freedom. Like those early explorers who set sail on uncharted waters, Arizona's journey has been long, sometimes choppy, and filled with hardship, sacrifice, and triumph.

Arizona's first step, in 1994, was to enact a robust charter school law.[30] Charter schools are nontraditional public schools funded by the state, but typically operated by private nonprofit or for-profit

---

[28] Richard D. Komer & Clark Neily, School Choice and State Constitutions, Inst. for Justice and Am. Legis. Exchange Council (2007), available at http://www.ij.org/ images/pdf_folder/school_choice/50statereport/50stateSCreport.pdf. The principal exceptions are Massachusetts and Michigan.

[29] Compare Kotterman v. Killian, 972 P.2d 606 (Ariz. 1999) (upholding scholarship tax credit program under Arizona Constitution) with Cain v. Horne, 202 P.3d 1178 (Ariz. 2009) (striking down voucher programs under Arizona Constitution). In Florida, the Supreme Court declared a voucher program for children attending failing schools unconstitutional in Bush v. Holmes, 919 So. 2d 392 (Fla. 2006), but Florida's corporate scholarship tax credit program has never been challenged.

[30] Ariz. Rev. Stat. Ann. § 15-181 et seq. (1994).

organizations.[31] According to the Arizona Charter School Association, there are now 511 charter schools in Arizona constituting 25 percent of the public schools in the state.[32]

The following year, the legislature took its next step by requiring school districts to establish open enrollment policies—so that students could attend any traditional public school, either within or outside their school district, without being charged tuition.[33]

Two years later, the legislature took another bold educational reform step by "seek[ing] to bring private institutions into the mix of educational alternatives open to the people" of Arizona.[34] It did so by establishing a modest tax credit, up to $500, for contributions from individuals to nonprofit organizations called school tuition organizations.[35] School tuition organizations, in turn, award tuition scholarships to families who desire to enroll their children in private schools.

Arizona's tax credit program was inspired by the Arizona School Choice Trust, an organization founded in 1993 to award privately funded private school scholarships to low-income families.[36] Within 10 days of the trust's publishing a request for applications for scholarships in the *Arizona Republic*, 500 students applied. The trust was able to issue 54 privately funded scholarships. The other children were placed on a waiting list.

The demand for the Arizona School Choice Trust's privately funded scholarship program spurred the legislature to adopt "a tax credit . . . for contributions to a tuition scholarship organization, such as the Arizona School Choice Trust Fund."[37] The individual

---

[31] Ariz. Rev. Stat. Ann. § 15-183(A) (2011).

[32] About Arizona Charter Schools, http://www.azcharters.org/pages/schools-basic-statistics (last visited May 17, 2011).

[33] Ariz. Rev. Stat. Ann. § 15-816.01 (1995).

[34] Kotterman, 972 P.2d at 611 (upholding Arizona's individual scholarship tax credit program under both the U.S. and Arizona Constitutions).

[35] Ariz. Rev. Stat. Ann. § 43-1089 (2009). The legislature has amended the tax credit program numerous times over the years, including adjusting the amount of the tax credit. This article cites the current version of the program.

[36] Arizona School Choice Trust, ASCT's Generous Founders, http://www.asct.org/Founders.shtml (last visited July 12, 2011).

[37] Hearing Before H. Comm. on Educ., 43d Leg., 1st Reg. Sess. (Ariz. 1997) (minutes of Jan. 29 meeting), ALIS Online, http://www.azleg.gov/FormatDocument.asp?inDoc=legtext/43leg/1R/comm_min/House/0129%2EED.htm (last visited July 12, 2011).

tax credit program essentially changed what was "a tax deduction to a tax credit, enhancing the ability of these organizations to raise funds and [thereby] allowing more low-income children the opportunity to attend the school of their choice."[38]

By the Numbers: Arizona's Individual Scholarship Tax Credit Program

The Individual Scholarship Tax Credit program authorizes individuals to claim a dollar-for-dollar state income tax credit up to $500 per individual (or $1,000 for married couples filing jointly) for donations to qualified school tuition organizations.[39] A qualified school tuition organization must be a tax-exempt charity under 26 U.S.C. § 501(c)(3)[40] and must allocate 90 percent of the donations it receives to scholarships to help children attend private schools.[41] They may not restrict their grants to students attending only one school.[42] Nor may they award grants to students who attend schools that discriminate on the basis of race, color, handicap, familial status, or national origin.[43] Donors may not request that their contribution be used to benefit a dependent.[44]

In 2010, the 53 school tuition organizations operating in Arizona collectively awarded 26,453 tuition scholarships.[45] These diverse organizations serve a wide variety of needs, pedagogies, and geographic areas. Four organizations offer grants only to families seeking a nonreligious Montessori-style education. Other organizations

---

[38] *Id.*

[39] Ariz. Rev. Stat. Ann. § 43-1089(A)(1)–(2) (2011).

[40] To qualify as a tax-exempt organization, an entity must be "organized and operated exclusively" for, among other purposes, "religious, charitable, scientific . . . literary, or educational purposes . . . ." 26 U.S.C. § 501(c)(3) (2011). Consequently, even organizations devoted to promoting religion—such as churches—enjoy direct economic tax benefits, including deductibility of contributions. See 26 U.S.C. § 170 (2011).

[41] Ariz. Rev. Stat. Ann. §§ 43-1089(A), 43-1603(B)(1) (2011).

[42] Ariz. Rev. Stat. Ann. § 43-1603(B)(2) (2011). The obvious result of this provision is that school tuition organizations may serve less than the entire private school market, but they may not exist to serve only one school.

[43] Ariz. Rev. Stat. Ann. § (H)(2)(a) (2011). The implication of this provision is that school tuition organizations may operate precisely like any other federally tax-exempt organization and prefer coreligionists or like minded individuals.

[44] Ariz. Rev. Stat. Ann. § 43-1603(B)(4) (2011).

[45] Ariz. Dep't of Revenue, Individual Income Tax Credit for Donations to Private School Tuition Organizations: Reporting for 2010 (2011).

exist to meet the needs of particular geographic areas, such as children attending private schools in cities or regions outside the state's major metropolitan areas.

Considering that a large percentage of Arizona's private schools are religious, it should not be surprising that many organizations affiliate themselves with particular religious beliefs and/or denominations.[46] At least 30 of the 55 school tuition organizations in terms of both donations and grants have no obvious religious affiliation, however, including 5 of the top 10.[47] Of the 367 different private schools attended by scholarship recipients, well over 100 had no obvious religious affiliation.[48]

Moreover, research shows that the program has given families access to private schooling options that they likely could not have afforded otherwise. Data from nearly 80 percent of scholarship recipients reveal that the median family income of participants is almost $5,000 lower than both Arizona's statewide median and the median income of recipients' neighborhoods.[49]

The Empire Strikes Back

My friend and fellow school choice litigator Clint Bolick is fond of saying that if there is one thing *Star Wars* teaches us, it is that the empire always strikes back.[50] That is particularly true in the school choice context. For two decades, proponents of educational freedom have not only had to work hard to overcome the teachers' unions powerful lobbyists in state legislatures in order to pass new school choice programs, but they have also had to fight a rear-guard action in court in order to keep their hard-won legislative victories.

---

[46] See, e.g., Kotterman, 972 P.2d at 626 ("At least seventy-two percent of [Arizona private] schools are sectarian.") (Feldman, J., dissenting) (citing Coffey, A Survey of Arizona Private Schools (1993)).

[47] Ariz. Dep't of Revenue, *supra* note 47 at 8–9.

[48] *Id.* at 14–20.

[49] Vicky E. Murray, An Analysis of Arizona Individual Income Tax-Credit Scholarship Recipients' Family Income, 2009–10 School Year, at 1, available at http://www.hks.harvard.edu/pepg/PDF/Papers/PEPG10-18_Murray.pdf.

[50] Clint Bolick, Voucher Wars: Waging the Legal Battle over School Choice 198, 207 (2003).

First Legal Challenge to Arizona Tax Credit Program: Kotterman v. Killian

Arizona's school choice opponents are a particularly litigious bunch. The first lawsuit challenging Arizona's Individual Tax Credit program, *Kotterman v. Killian,* was filed in 1997 by the Arizona Education Association before the first tax-credit-eligible donation was ever given to a school tuition organization. The Arizona Supreme Court rejected the union's claims under both the federal and state constitutions.

In a prescient decision three years before the primary federal constitutional issue was settled by *Zelman,* the Arizona Supreme Court determined that Arizona's tax credit program was religiously neutral, allowed a broad spectrum of private choice, and therefore did not have the impermissible effect of either advancing or inhibiting religion under the Establishment Clause.[51]

Kotterman also involved claims under the Arizona Constitution's religion clauses—commonly known as Blaine Amendments.[52] As the *Kotterman* majority recognized, Blaine Amendments are vestiges of Maine Representative James G. Blaine's attempt to ride a wave of anti-Catholic bigotry to the White House in the 1870s and 1880s.[53] Blaine rose to prominence at a time when the public schools were predominantly Protestant.[54] Finding the public schools inhospitable to their doctrine, Catholics pushed for a separate system of publicly funded Catholic schools. Blaine thus attempted to amend the U.S. Constitution to prohibit any public funding for "sectarian" schools—and it was an open secret that "sectarian" was code for "Catholic."[55]

---

[51] Kotterman, 972 P.2d at 616.

[52] The Arizona Constitution, Article 2, Section 12 states in relevant part: "No public money or property shall be appropriated for or applied to any religious worship, exercise, or instruction, or to the support of any religious establishment." The Arizona Constitution, Article 9, Section 10 says, "No tax shall be laid or appropriation of public money made in aid of any church, or private or sectarian school, or any public service corporation."

[53] Kotterman, 972 P.2d at 624.

[54] Richard D. Komer, School Choice and State Constitutions' Religion Clauses, 3 J. of Sch. Choice 331 (2009).

[55] Mitchell v. Helms, 530 U.S. 793, 828 (2000) (plurality) ("Opposition to aid to 'sectarian' schools acquired prominence in the 1870's with Congress's consideration (and near passage) of the Blaine Amendment, which would have amended the Constitution to bar any aid to sectarian institutions. Consideration of the amendment arose at a

While finding no direct link between the original Blaine Amendment and Arizona's Blaine Amendments, the Arizona Supreme Court was nevertheless "hard pressed to divorce the amendment's language from the insidious discriminatory intent that prompted it."[56] The court therefore refused to interpret the provisions beyond the scope of their plain language and concentrated on the meaning of the phrases "public money" and "appropriation of public money." Given that no money from the tax credit program ever enters the state treasury or is ever controlled by the government, the Arizona Supreme Court declared that "under any common understanding of the words, we are not here dealing with 'public money.'"[57]

The *Kotterman* plaintiffs made the same argument that the plaintiffs in *ACSTO* would later make, namely that "because taxpayer money *could* enter the treasury if it were not excluded by way of the tax credit, the state effectively controls and exerts quasi-ownership over it."[58] But the Arizona Supreme Court found such an expansive interpretation "fraught with problems."[59] It dealt specifically with two of those problems. First, "under such reasoning all taxpayer income could be viewed as belonging to the state because it is subject to taxation by the legislature."[60] And second, if tax credits "constitute public funds, then so must other established tax policy equivalents like deductions and exemptions."[61]

The Arizona Supreme Court also rejected the notion that the tax credit was the equivalent of laying a tax. "We cannot say that the legislature has somehow imposed a tax by declining to collect potential revenue from its citizens."[62] Indeed, the court went on to say that if it were the equivalent of laying a tax that the justices "would be hard pressed to identify the citizens on whom it is assessed."[63]

---

time of pervasive hostility to the Catholic Church and to Catholics in general, and it was an open secret that 'sectarian' was code for 'Catholic.'").

[56] Kotterman, 972 P.2d at 624.

[57] *Id.* at 618.

[58] *Id.*

[59] *Id.*

[60] *Id.*

[61] *Id.*

[62] *Id.* at 621.

[63] *Id.*

The *Kotterman* plaintiffs filed a petition for certiorari to the U.S. Supreme Court on the federal constitutional question. The Institute for Justice, which had intervened in *Kotterman* on behalf of parents and children who would benefit from the program, actually supported the petition because we and our clients believed so strongly that Arizona's tax credit program would pass constitutional muster. The petition, however, was denied.

Federal Court Challenge to Arizona's Tax Credit Program: Winn v. Killian (*ultimately* ACSTO v. Winn)

Soon after the U.S. Supreme Court denied the petition for certiorari, the ACLU of Arizona filed a federal court challenge, *Winn v. Killian*, alleging that Arizona's Individual Tax Credit program violated the Establishment Clause. The complaint asserted both a facial and an as-applied challenge to the statute.

The ACLU claimed that the program violated the Establishment Clause by (1) "affirmatively authorizing and permitting [school tuition organizations] to use State income-tax revenues to pay tuition for students at religious schools"; (2) "affirmatively authorizing and permitting [school tuition organizations] to use State income-tax revenues to make tuition grants to students attending only religious schools or schools of only one religious denomination or to students of only one religion"; and (3) "affirmatively authorizing and permitting [school tuition organizations] to use State income-tax revenues to pay tuition for students at schools that discriminate on the basis of religion in selecting students."[64]

The Institute for Justice immediately moved to intervene on behalf of parents and children relying on the scholarship program. The Arizona Christian School Tuition Organization also moved to intervene, represented by separate counsel. The state of Arizona, before the motions to intervene were ruled on, filed a motion to dismiss, arguing that the Federal Tax Injunction Act deprived the district court of jurisdiction.[65] The district court granted the state's motion

---

[64] Complaint at 6–7, Winn v. Killian, No. CV-00-0287 EHC, on file with the Institute for Justice.

[65] The Federal Tax Injunction Act, 28 U.S.C. § 1341, reads: "The district courts shall not enjoin, suspend or restrain the assessment, levy or collection of any tax under State law where a plain, speedy and efficient remedy may be had in the courts of such State."

to dismiss pursuant to the Tax Injunction Act and denied the motions to intervene as moot.

Of course, in 2000, Arizona was not the only state actively defending school choice programs. In Ohio, after that state's supreme court upheld Cleveland's school voucher program,[66] a federal court challenge was filed—a challenge that would ultimately take the Cleveland program to the U.S. Supreme Court. The early school choice cases always began in state court and included both federal and state constitutional claims. But school choice opponents—led by the National Education Association—knew they needed a knockout blow. The union's opportunity came in *Zelman v. Simmons-Harris,* decided by the U.S. Supreme Court in June 2002. But it was the unions who were knocked out.

In *Zelman,* the Court struck a tremendous blow for freedom of educational choice and opportunity. For decades, students in the Cleveland public school system were trapped in public schools that failed miserably on every imaginable performance measure. Things were so bad that in 1995 "a Federal District Court declared a 'crisis of magnitude' and placed the entire Cleveland school district under state control."[67] It is no wonder that the legislature sought to enact some meaningful education reforms. One of those measures was the Pilot Project Scholarship Program, which provided tuition aid from the state treasury to students to attend any participating public or private school of their parents' choice.[68] While the program permitted any public school district adjacent to the district's boundaries to participate in the program, no public school district elected to do so.[69] Of the 56 private schools that signed up to participate, 46 (or 82 percent) had a religious affiliation; of the more than 3,700 students who participated, 96 percent enrolled in a religious school.[70]

Against this backdrop, and in light of decades of prior precedent upholding government programs that permitted public aid to flow

---

[66] Simmons-Harris v. Goff, 711 N.E.2d 203 (Ohio 1999).

[67] Zelman, 536 U.S. at 644 (noting that "[o]nly 1 in 10 ninth graders could pass a basic proficiency examination, and students at all levels performed at a dismal rate compared with students in other Ohio public schools").

[68] *Id.* at 644–45.

[69] *Id.* at 645–47.

[70] *Id.* at 647.

to religious institutions at the direction of private individuals, a 5-4 majority upheld the voucher program.[71] In summarizing the prior precedent establishing the appropriate legal test to be applied to the Cleveland voucher program, the Court said:

> *Mueller, Witters,* and *Zobrest* thus make clear that where a government aid program is neutral with respect to religion, and provides assistance directly to a broad class of citizens who, in turn, direct government aid to religious schools wholly as a result of their own genuine and independent choice, the program is not readily subject to challenge under the Establishment Clause.[72]

The majority in *Zelman* concluded that the Cleveland voucher program shared these features and that, as a program of true private choice that provided benefits to families on neutral terms with no governmental preference for or against religion, it easily passed constitutional muster. *Zelman* should have put an end to the Arizona federal case. As Notre Dame law professor Nicole Stelle Garnett recently opined, after *Zelman* the claims in *ACSTO* "bordered on frivolous."[73]

But before *Zelman,* the ACLU had appealed *Winn's* dismissal under the Tax Injunction Act to the U.S. Court of Appeals for the Ninth Circuit. The Ninth Circuit heard oral argument on June 11, 2002—a mere 16 days before the U.S. Supreme Court announced its decision in *Zelman.* The Ninth Circuit opinion, released on October 3, 2002, and written by Judge Stephen Reinhardt, reversed the district court's dismissal pursuant to the Tax Injunction Act. The decision did not address the merits of the case—and therefore did not discuss *Zelman* or its predecessor cases—but it did include a lengthy footnote attempting to distinguish tax credits from tax deductions, suggesting

---

[71] *Id.* at 649 ("Three times we have confronted Establishment Clause challenges to neutral government programs that provide aid directly to a broad class of individuals, who, in turn, direct the aid to religious schools or institutions of their own choosing. Three times we have rejected such challenges.").

[72] *Id.* at 652.

[73] Nicole Stelle Garnett, A Winn for Educational Pluralsim, 121 Yale L.J. Online 31, 33 (2011), available at http://yalelawjournal.org/2011/05/26/garnett.html.

the panel was sympathetic to the *Winn* plaintiffs' argument that tax-credit-eligible contributions were the equivalent of state tax revenues.[74]

The state filed a petition for certiorari on the Tax Injunction Act issue, which the U.S. Supreme Court granted. In *Hibbs v. Winn,* the Supreme Court, in yet another 5-4 decision—with Justice Sandra Day O'Connor siding with the oft-described liberal wing of the Court—affirmed the Ninth Circuit's decision and remanded the case to the district court for further proceedings.[75]

In *Hibbs,* the Court noted that there was half a century of federal court precedent adjudicating claims involving tax credits and that not once had any jurist or attorney suggested that the Tax Injunction Act—enacted in 1937—stood as a jurisdictional bar.[76] Foreshadowing some of the arguments to come later in *ACSTO,* the state argued that those cases—which did not address jurisdiction—were mere *sub silentio* holdings entitled to no deference now that the issue was squarely before the Court. The Court very quickly "reject[ed] that assessment."[77] Of course, it would be a different story when the taxpayer-standing issue was raised. But before the *Winn* plaintiffs would learn that they never had standing to raise their claims in federal court in the first instance, there would be another six years of litigation.

Return to the District Court

Frankly, it was not at all obvious that the plaintiffs would continue to press their Establishment Clause claim after *Hibbs v. Winn.* They had set a favorable precedent on the Tax Injunction Act that would preserve future challenges to state tax credit programs. But the Arizona tax credit program appeared, at least to those of us who were defending the program, to be on all fours with *Zelman.* Between the majority opinion's emphasis on the importance of private choice—

---

[74] Winn v. Killian, 307 F.3d 1011, 1015 n.5 (9th Cir. 2002) ("We note that a tax credit differs from a tax deduction in that where a tax deduction is involved, giving money to a religious institution is not, as is the case of a tax credit, a free gift.").

[75] Hibbs v. Winn, 542 U.S. 88 (2004). J. Elliott Hibbs replaced Mark Killian as the director of the Department of Revenue in the period between the Ninth Circuit and the Supreme Court decisions on the Tax Injunction Act issue.

[76] *Id.* at 92.

[77] *Id.* at 94.

and Justice O'Connor's concurrence stressing that the private choice inquiry should encompass "all reasonable alternatives to religious schools that are available to parents'"[78]—the Arizona program seemed constitutionally bulletproof.

Private choice imbues *every* aspect of Arizona's tax credit program. The government is at least four times removed from any money that flows to religious organizations. Private individuals or groups must create a school tuition organization. Those privately created and operated school tuition organizations must then decide to provide scholarships to students attending religious schools. Taxpayers then have to choose to contribute to the school tuition organization. And parents must apply for a scholarship for their student from that school tuition organization. As Judge Diarmuid O'Scannlain would later write, "the state's involvement stops with authorizing the creation of [school tuition organizations] and making tax credits available. After that, the government takes its hands off the wheel."[79]

In light of *Zelman*, it was difficult to see how *Mueller's* statement that the "historic purposes of the [Establishment] Clause simply do not encompass the sort of attenuated financial benefit, ultimately controlled by the private choices of individual parents, that eventually flows to parochial schools from the neutrally available tax benefit at issue in this case" would not be applied to Arizona's tax credit.[80]

And yet, what we viewed as the program's constitutional shield, the plaintiffs viewed as the program's Achilles' heel. The plaintiffs would argue that it was the multiple layers of private choice that made the tax credit program unconstitutional. This view, of course, is informed by the plaintiffs' belief that tax-credit-eligible funds are the equivalent of state tax revenues and that, therefore, school tuition organizations are just like government grantees. The plaintiffs' basic argument would be that the same strictures that applied to government programs providing aid directly to religious institutions should be applied to the Arizona program.

The plaintiffs relied on cases like *Bowen v. Kendrick*, where the Supreme Court upheld, on its face, the Adolescent Family Life Act—

---

[78] Zelman, 536 U.S. at 663 (O'Connor, J., concurring).

[79] Winn v. ACSTO, 586 F.3d 649, 660 (9th Cir. 2009) (denying rehearing en banc) (O'Scannlain, J., dissenting).

[80] Mueller v. Allen, 463 U.S. 388, 400 (1983).

a government program that allowed both religious and nonreligious institutions to receive direct grants from Congress to pay for services related to adolescent sexuality and family planning—but said that this type of direct government grant could not be used to promote religion or inculcate the views of a particular religious doctrine.[81] If the Supreme Court's direct aid line of cases applied to the Arizona program, then school tuition organizations could not affiliate with religious schools or prefer coreligionists when awarding scholarships. In other words, the plaintiffs were not going to raise the white flag of surrender.

Thus, on remand, the Institute for Justice immediately renewed its motion to intervene on behalf of the Arizona School Choice Trust and the parents, including Glenn and Rhonda Dennard, who became the human faces of the case.[82] The Arizona Christian School Tuition Organization, now represented by the Alliance Defense Fund, also renewed its motion to intervene. Those motions were granted and both IJ and ADF submitted motions to dismiss, arguing that the taxpayers lacked standing and that the plaintiffs failed to state a claim after *Zelman*. The state filed a motion for judgment on the pleadings arguing that *Zelman* controlled, but the state declined to challenge the taxpayer plaintiffs' standing.

The district court assumed standing and granted IJ's motion to dismiss, holding that the "Tuition Tax Credit program is a program of 'true private choice'" and that *Zelman* controlled.[83] The district court found that the decisions of some school tuition organizations to fund religious schools did not implicate the Establishment Clause because those decisions were based on private choices—not government control.[84]

The ACLU appealed and the parties received notice that the Ninth Circuit panel that heard and decided *Winn v. Killian* was going to retain jurisdiction of the case. But it would be almost three years before that panel would hear oral arguments in the case. Given

---

[81] Bowen v. Kendrick, 487 U.S. 589, 621–22 (1988).

[82] See, e.g., Institute for Justice, Arizona School Choice Fight Goes to U.S. Supreme Court, available at http://www.youtube.com/watch?v=weipY6rpMss.

[83] Winn v. Hibbs, 361 F. Supp. 2d. 1117, 1120 (D. Ariz. 2005).

[84] *Id.* at 1122.

Reinhardt's previous opinion and the panel's willingness to distinguish between credits and deductions—essentially tipping its hand that it would view credits as the equivalent of tax revenue, the ACLU was content to wait for what it expected would be a very favorable panel.

The Ninth Circuit, Again

A few months before the argument, the panel *sua sponte* ordered supplemental briefing in light of the Supreme Court's decision in *DaimlerChrysler Corp. v. Cuno*, which held that state taxpayers did not have standing to challenge a local municipality's grant of certain tax breaks to an auto manufacturer as a violation of the Commerce Clause.[85] IJ and ADF continued to argue that the taxpayer plaintiffs lacked standing. The state once again refused to contest standing.

When the day for oral argument finally came, school choice supporters did not walk away very encouraged. During the argument, the plaintiffs' attorney, Arizona State University College of Law Professor Paul Bender, while not fully abandoning some of his more audacious claims, was definitely open to relief far narrower in scope than the original complaint had requested.

At one point, when pushed by Judge Reinhardt, Professor Bender even conceded that the plaintiffs were only challenging school tuition organizations that restricted their scholarships along religious lines. He went so far as to say that, absent a very narrow reading of *Zelman*—that is, absent cabining *Zelman* to its specific facts of a school district in dire straits—his clients had no problem with school tuition organizations like the Arizona School Choice Trust because it provides scholarships to students choosing both religious and nonreligious schools.

Once the state stood to argue, the state's attorney, Paula Bickett, announced our planned division of time. She would argue the Establishment Clause and I would argue the taxpayer-standing issue. The court instructed us, however, not to address standing. Fortunately, I prepared for the merits as well. When I reached the podium, due to Professor Bender's concession on the narrowing of issues, Judge Reinhardt pressed me as to whether my clients, the Arizona School

[85] DaimlerChrysler Corp. v. Cuno, 547 U.S. 332, 344–46 (2006).

Choice Trust and parents receiving scholarship funds from the trust, had any real interest in the case.

Of course the Arizona School Choice Trust had an interest in the case. The ACLU had not explicitly abandoned its facial claims and its briefing argued forcefully that the tax credit program had been passed for an improper religious purpose. (Any law passed for an improper purpose—even a law that is facially neutral—must be struck down in its entirety.) It also maintained its claim that *Zelman* was an exception to the general rule that public funds may not be used to attend religious institutions absent the extraordinary facts present in that case. I had to waste precious time arguing these points with Judge Reinhardt before getting to my merits argument. The time clock ran quickly down to zero.

It would be more than a year—April 21, 2009—before the Ninth Circuit issued its written opinion reversing the district court. The court concluded that the plaintiffs had standing as taxpayers. It cited *Hibbs v. Winn* for the proposition that the Supreme Court "has rejected the suggestion that its consistent past practice of exercising jurisdiction [in cases challenging tax credits, deductions, and exemptions] amounts to mere *sub silentio* holdings that command no respect."[86]

On the merits, the panel said that even though the tax credit was religiously neutral on its face and there was no legislative history suggesting an improper religious motivation for passing the program,[87] a program's *operation* "may, in some circumstances, reveal its ostensible purpose to be a sham."[88] The only such "evidence" proffered by the plaintiffs in this case was the fact that school tuition organizations "are permitted to restrict the use of their scholarships to use at certain religious schools." But it is the plain language of the statute itself that "permits" the scholarship organizations to restrict scholarships to less than the entire population of private

---

[86] Winn v. ACSTO, 562 F.3d 1002, 1011 (9th Cir. 2009) (internal quotations omitted).

[87] To the contrary, the panel admitted that the only legislative history demonstrated that the tax credit program's "primary sponsor's concern in introducing the bill was providing equal access to a wide range of schooling options for students of every income level by defraying the costs of educational expenses incurred by parents." *Id.* at 1011–12.

[88] *Id.* at 1012.

schools.[89] Indeed, no party contested the fact that school tuition organizations operated in precisely this manner. And yet, the panel said that "[s]uch allegations, *if proved*, could belie defendants claim that [the tax credit] was enacted primarily to provide Arizona students with equal access to a wide range of schooling options."[90]

The panel further stated that the plaintiffs could demonstrate that the primary effect of the tax credit program was to advance religion because parental choices were constrained by the choice of taxpayers as to which school tuition organizations taxpayers choose to donate their money. Neither the panel nor the plaintiffs disputed that the tax credit program "is neutral with respect to taxpayers who direct money to [school tuition organizations], or that any of the program's aid that reaches a [school tuition organization] does so only as a result of the genuine and independent choice of an Arizona taxpayer."[91] And yet, both were willing to argue that because a majority of taxpayers contributed to religious institutions, those private choices amount to government endorsement of religion. They reached that conclusion by suggesting that a "reasonable observer" would view the large number of religious donations as somehow being encouraged by the state.[92]

These conclusions ignored the Supreme Court's repeated admonition that it would be "loathe to adopt a rule grounding the constitutionality of a facially neutral law on annual reports reciting the extent to which various classes of private citizens claimed benefits under the law"[93] and that "the constitutionality of a neutral choice program does not turn on annual tallies of private decisions made in any given year by thousands of individual recipients."[94]

---

[89] Ariz. Rev. Stat. Ann. § 43-1603(B)(2) (2011) ("To be eligible for certification and retain certification, the school tuition organization . . . [s]hall not limit the availability of educational scholarships or tuition grants to only students of one school.").

[90] ACSTO, 562 F.3d at 1012 (emphasis added).

[91] *Id.* at 1018.

[92] *Id.* at 1022 ("Significantly, plaintiffs' allegations suggest the taxpayers' role in the structure of the [tax credit program] *encourages* them to use the tax credits to promote sectarian goals . . . .").

[93] Mueller, 463 U.S. at 401.

[94] Zelman, 536 U.S. at 658 n.4.

Once More into the Breach: Back to the Ninth Circuit
The Ninth Circuit's decision in *Winn v. Arizona Christian School Tuition Organization* was nothing short of outrageous. It warranted a petition for certiorari, and there was a strong belief that a petition would be granted. But the decision was so far afield from Supreme Court precedent that we felt there was some chance—however slight—that the Ninth Circuit might grant a motion to rehear the case *en banc*. After conferring with other appellate lawyers and Ninth Circuit practitioners, one thing became clear: Even if the Ninth Circuit declined to rehear the case, the panel opinion was so out of touch with Establishment Clause jurisprudence that we were likely to draw an opinion dissenting from a denial of rehearing. Such a dissent, it was strongly advised, would increase the likelihood of our petition for certiorari being granted.

It took another six months to receive the decision denying rehearing, but it was well worth the wait. We had hoped that, if the court voted to reject rehearing, at least one judge would write a dissent that would become useful to us in further litigation. Our hope was realized—and then some. Judge Diarmuid O'Scannlain wrote a blistering attack on the *Winn* panel's opinion, and his dissent was joined by *seven* other judges. The original panel even felt compelled to write a separate opinion concurring in the decision to deny the petition for rehearing so it could respond to O'Scannlain's dissent.

O'Scannlain's dissent meticulously demonstrates that "nothing in the panel opinion grapples with the fact that Arizona does nothing to encourage, to promote, or otherwise to incentivize private actors to direct aid to religious schools. Nothing explains how 'the *government itself*' has advanced religion through its own activities and influence."[95] He concludes by saying that the panel can hardly be faulted for this failure because "it cannot manufacture what does not exist."[96]

III. Back to the U.S. Supreme Court
Judge O'Scannlain's dissent emboldened IJ to take an unusual and risky tactic. We did not simply ask for certiorari; we asked that the Ninth Circuit be summarily reversed. The state of Arizona sought certiorari on the merits. Our ADF allies focused their petition on

---

[95] ACSTO, 586 F.3d at 670 (denying rehearing en banc) (O'Scannlain, J., dissenting).
[96] *Id.* at 671.

the issue of taxpayer standing (while concurring with the petitions filed by IJ and the state on the merits).

There is no such thing as a certainty when it comes to Supreme Court litigation, and even though we felt like we had positioned ourselves as well as possible for Supreme Court review, we were all nervous waiting for the orders to be filed after the case was conferenced. So when we saw the order granting the petitions for certiorari, there was much celebration. There was only one slight disappointment. The Court granted the state's and ADF's petitions, but held ours—leaving our clients in the relatively rare position of "Respondents in Support of Petitioners" pursuant to Supreme Court Rule 12.6. Our clients thus had full party status, entitling them to file briefs on the merits, but this odd arrangement foreshadowed that I would not be participating in the oral argument.

During the merits briefing, it became increasingly clear that the question of standing and the merits arguments were closely connected because they both involved the question of whether tax-credit-eligible contributions were the equivalent of state tax revenue. The ACLU pegged its entire argument on the notion that (1) all tax-credit-eligible contributions were state tax revenues, not private charitable contributions; and (2) this transformed the program into a government spending program and meant that school tuition organizations should therefore be treated like direct government grantees.

We received a pleasant surprise during the briefing, when the United States joined our side by filing an amicus brief arguing both that the plaintiffs lacked standing and that the tax credit program passed muster under the Establishment Clause. The United States argued in no uncertain terms that "[a] tax credit, by definition, does not extract one cent from taxpayers. To the contrary, it *forgoes* the extraction of state income taxes."[97] That led the United States to argue that the program "merely provides a beneficial tax consequence for private citizens who donate their own funds to [school tuition organizations] of their own choosing."[98]

---

[97] Brief of United States at 15, ACSTO v. Winn, 131 S. Ct. 1436 (2011) (Nos. 09-987, 09-991), 2010 WL 3066230.

[98] *Id.* at 14.

A total of 18 amicus briefs were filed in support of the program. Three were filed in opposition. While the supporting amicus briefs were all excellent, three stood out as particularly helpful. The Becket Fund for Religious Liberty's brief hammered home the fact that the Supreme Court has repeatedly rejected the Ninth Circuit's notion that "private choices can be mistaken for government endorsement" of religion.[99] The Cato Institute brief took on the plaintiffs' notion that the numerous private choices under the Arizona program limited parental choice and autonomy.[100] This brief demonstrated that giving individuals the freedom to create and operate school tuition organizations consistent with their values and beliefs has led to more funding and more options for parents.[101] And the Jewish Tuition Organization's brief, written by Bennett Cooper and Robert Destro, dismantled not only the Ninth Circuit's many erroneous legal arguments, but corrected many of the factual misrepresentations made by both the plaintiffs and the Ninth Circuit regarding how school tuition organizations fundraise, award scholarships, and work with private schools.[102]

When it came time to decide who would argue the case, IJ and ADF strongly agreed that it was important for an ADF attorney to argue the taxpayer standing issue. After all, it was ADF's petition that asked the Court to grant certiorari on the standing issue. And moreover, for 10 years the state of Arizona had conceded that the plaintiffs had standing. The state was not opposed to splitting the argument time, but the United States' participation as an amicus added a new wrinkle because the acting solicitor general, Neal Katyal, also intended to ask for argument time.

---

[99] Brief of Becket Fund for Religious Liberty, ACSTO v. Winn, 131 S. Ct. 1436 (2011) (Nos. 09-987, 09-991), 2010 WL 4150190. The Becket Fund also appended a partial list of over 600 tax laws, including federal and state tax credits, tax deductions, and tax exemptions that could be negatively affected if the Supreme Court let stand the Ninth Circuit's reasoning.

[100] Brief of Cato Institute at 26–29, ACSTO v. Winn, 131 S. Ct. 1436 (2011) (Nos. 09-987, 09-991), 2010 WL 3066228. Cato's brief was joined by the Foundation for Educational Choice, the American Federation for Children, the Council for American Private Education, the Center for Education Reform, and the director of Cato's Center for Educational Freedom, Andrew Coulson.

[101] *Id.* at 27.

[102] Brief of Jewish Tuition Org. et al., ACSTO v. Winn, 131 S. Ct. 1436 (2011) (Nos. 09-987, 09-991), 2010 WL 3167316.

IJ felt very strongly that the only way a three-way split would be granted was if the parties filed a joint motion for divided argument time. Several friends and colleagues warned me about how heated things could become when it came to matters in the U.S. Supreme Court, but up until this point the parties had worked solidly together toward a common goal. Unfortunately, no agreement was reached and two separate motions were filed asking the Court to divide the argument time.

Arizona and the United States moved first and asked that the time be divided only between the two governments. ADF proposed a three-way split but also argued that if the time was divided in two, the solicitor general should not supplant the party whose petition had been granted. The government's motion was granted, but the Court's decision to deny ADF an opportunity to argue set the stage for post-argument briefs—briefs that the ACLU used to dig even deeper the hole its clients found themselves in at argument.

At oral argument on November 3, 2010, Chief Justice John Roberts and Justices Antonin Scalia, Anthony Kennedy, and Samuel Alito showed particular skepticism at the notion that the challenged tax credit program was a government spending program. Justice Kennedy—who would subsequently write the majority opinion—asked Professor Bender about his theory that tax-credit-eligible contributions to school tuition organizations are the equivalent of state tax revenues:

Justice Kennedy:	I'll give you credit, Mr. Bender. In your brief, you say if you're wrong on that point, that you're folding your tent and leaving. There's -- that there's no standing and that there's no -- no violation. But I must say, I have some difficulty that any money that the government doesn't take from me is still the government's money.
Prof. Bender:	But it does take it.
Justice Kennedy:	Let me ask you. If -- if you reach a certain age, you can get a -- a card and go to certain restaurants, and they give you 10 percent credit. I think it would be rather

offensive for the cashier to say, "and be careful how you spend my money." But that's the whole theory of your case.[103]

Building on Justice Kennedy's questions, Justice Alito sounded the same note as the majority in *Kotterman v. Killian* did more than 10 years earlier:

Justice Alito:	There's a very important philosophical point here. You think that all the money belongs to the government --
Prof. Bender:	No.
Justice Alito:	-- except to the extent that it deigns to allow private people to keep some of it.[104]

Needless to say, school choice supporters walked away far more encouraged after the Supreme Court argument than they had been after the Ninth Circuit argument. It appeared that the ACLU had, in fact, correctly framed the issue. The Court was going to decide if the moneys contributed to school tuition organizations were private or government funds. If the Arizona program did not involve any government money, what possible interest or stake could a taxpayer who sat on the sidelines have in the program?

Post-Argument Briefing

The government advocates in *ACSTO* performed capably at argument. There were important distinctions, however, in the way in which ADF—and IJ—would have responded to some of the questioning. Indeed, there were even differences between IJ and ADF (differences that were irrelevant to the taxpayer-standing issue). Both organizations, therefore, filed motions asking to file post-argument briefs. And in that subsequently granted post-argument briefing, the ACLU continued to pound the argument—to its detriment— that the tax credit contributions were state tax revenues and that the program was therefore a government spending program.

---

[103] Transcript of Oral Argument at 31, ACSTO, 131 S. Ct. 1436 (Nos. 09-987, 09-991), available at http://www.supremecourt.gov/oral_arguments/argument_transcripts/09-987.pdf.

[104] *Id.* at 35.

ADF, in its post-argument brief, argued that there was no record evidence of religious discrimination. The word "discrimination" certainly has a strong negative connotation, but the fact is that school tuition organizations are permitted to—and do—"discriminate" in a variety of ways, as pointed out by IJ's post-argument brief. As private, nonprofit organizations—and not government actors—school tuition organizations enjoy substantial discretion in awarding scholarships, under both state law and section 501(c)(3) of the federal tax code.

Nonreligious school tuition organizations can and do offer scholarships on a selective or "discriminatory" basis. For example, several school tuition organizations provide scholarships only to families seeking Montessori education. The state neither encourages nor discourages such pedagogical "discrimination," but rather remains appropriately neutral, just as it does towards religion.[105]

The neutrality principle thus allows religious nonprofit organizations to prefer coreligionists.[106] Jewish tuition organizations may permissibly award scholarships only to Jewish children attending Jewish schools, while Catholic tuition organizations may permissibly award scholarships only to Catholic children attending Catholic schools. Allowing religious school tuition organizations the freedom to prefer coreligionists is not government endorsement of religion. It is, at most, government accommodation of religion.[107]

This argument—that the Establishment Clause does not prevent the government from even-handedly authorizing private, nonprofit scholarship organizations to serve a variety of discrete and diverse

---

[105] See Walz v. Tax Comm'n of New York, 397 U.S. 664, 669 (1970) (holding that the Establishment Clause allows "benevolent neutrality which will permit religious exercise to exist without sponsorship and without interference").

[106] Indeed, in *Corp. of the Presiding Bishop of the Church of Jesus Christ of Latter-Day Saints v. Amos*, 483 U.S. 327 (1987), the Supreme Court held that the Establishment Clause is not offended when religious organizations make employment decisions based on religion. And in *Hernandez v. Comm'r*, 490 U.S. 680 (1989), the Supreme Court upheld the Internal Revenue Code's section 170, which permits deductions for charitable contributions to religious organizations and churches, even though they are permitted to prefer coreligionists both when hiring staff and when delivering aid or resources to the community.

[107] See Amos, 483 U.S. at 349 (O'Connor, J., concurring) ("[T]he objective observer should perceive the Government action as an accommodation of the exercise of religion rather than as a Government endorsement of religion.").

constituencies, including both religious and nonreligious groups—did not sit well with the ACLU. Its response agreed that "religious organizations may prefer coreligionists in distributing benefits in situations where those benefits are paid for *with their own money*," but argued that "[t]his case involves benefits paid for *entirely with state income-tax revenues*."[108] They concluded by saying, "*all of the money in the Arizona program—every penny—is tax revenue*."[109]

As the final words presented to the Court in the case, we believed this put the school choice program in a very favorable position. It seemed unlikely that a majority of the Court would agree with the plaintiffs that the funds involved were public dollars. And if they were not public funds, the plaintiffs had just admitted that school tuition organizations were free to distribute funds "to classes of beneficiaries chosen by them," including those preferring "co-religionists."[110]

The only thing left to do was sit back and wait for the decision.

IV. The Final Decision

I arrived at my Tempe, Arizona, office early on Monday, April 4. My practice was to arrive early, grab a cup of coffee, and watch the live blog at SCOTUSblog each morning the Court announced decisions. Even though the case had been argued in November, I was not expecting the decision until the end of May. Fatefully, that morning our internet service was down. So I called home and asked my wife to watch the live blog and tell me which cases were decided. She put me on the phone with our three-and-a-half-year-old son while she watched the blog.

Suddenly, in the middle of our innocent chat, I heard my wife scream and (I can only presume) rip the phone from my little boy's hand to excitedly tell me that we had won. I waited for her to give me a few more details—the vote was 5–4, Kennedy wrote the majority opinion, there was no taxpayer standing—and then I was off and running. I immediately phoned IJ's headquarters in Arlington, Virginia, to relay the good news while on my way to Starbucks to read the decision and pound out a quick press release.

---

[108] Post-Argument Brief of Appellee-Respondent at 5, ACSTO v. Winn, 131 S. Ct. 1436 (2011) (Nos. 09-987, 09-991), 2010 WL 5487485 (emphasis in original).
[109] *Id.*
[110] *Id.* at 6.

Digesting the Standing Ruling

The Court's holding—that state taxpayers do not have standing to challenge a tax credit program that is implemented by private action, funded by private contributions, and involves no state intervention—should not have come as a big surprise, given the way the standing and merits questions had become entwined. And yet, for me, it did. The standing arguments had gained *no traction* in the previous 10 years of litigation, and the case had already been in front of the Supreme Court on a jurisdictional issue. As Justice Elena Kagan wrote in her dissent, the Court had faced similar issues at least five times—"including in a prior incarnation of this very case"—and standing was never even mentioned.[111]

My surprise also flowed from my personal view of the doctrine of standing[112]—particularly the doctrine of *taxpayer* standing. I do not conceptualize the doctrine as being rooted in the text of the U.S. Constitution. I view it instead as a judicial doctrine rooted in concerns about judicial economy and, in particular, the danger of issuing an advisory opinion regarding matters of constitutional law. While the latter is a legitimate concern, as a lawyer who most often represents plaintiffs in constitutional challenges to government laws and regulations, I am less sympathetic to the former. In my opinion, the doctrine of taxpayer standing is easily gerrymandered when judges are inclined—or disinclined—to reach the merits of a particular case. And, as discussed below, my slightly jaded view of standing requirements is not far off from those articulated by the Supreme Court.[113] Notwithstanding my generally skeptical view of standing

[111] ACSTO, 131 S. Ct. at 1452–53 (Kagan, J., dissenting).

[112] Lujan v. Defenders of Wildlife, 504 U.S. 555 (1992), outlines the general standing requirements. "First, the plaintiff must have suffered an 'injury in fact'—an invasion of a legally protected interest which is (a) concrete and particularized, and (b) actual or imminent, not 'conjectural or hypothetical.' Second, there must be a causal connection between the injury and the conduct complained of—the injury has to be fairly traceable to the challenged action of the defendant, and not the result of the independent action of some third party not before the court. Third, it must be likely, as opposed to merely speculative, that the injury will be redressed by a favorable decision." *Id.* at 560–61 (citations and some internal quotations omitted). An "injury in fact" requires "that the injury must affect the plaintiff in a personal and individual way." *Id.* at 560 n.1.

[113] "The 'many subtle pressures' which cause policy considerations to blend into the constitutional limitations of Article III make the justiciability doctrine one of uncertain and shifting contours." Flast v. Cohen, 392 U.S. 83, 97 (1968) (quoting Poe v. Ullman, 367 U.S. 497, 508 (1961)).

doctrine, however, the Court was right in *ACSTO* to conclude that the plaintiffs lacked standing as taxpayers.

The Supreme Court first declared that taxpayers lacked standing to challenge the constitutionality of a government appropriation or program in *Frothingham v. Mellon*.[114] The Court said that it had "no power per se to review and annul acts of Congress on the ground that they are unconstitutional."[115] Such questions may only be considered when the party has suffered or been threatened with a "direct injury."[116] The Court could not find the requisite injury because a U.S. taxpayer's "interest in the moneys of the Treasury—partly realized from taxation and partly from other sources—is shared with millions of others; is comparatively minute and indeterminable; and the effect upon future taxation, of any payment out of the funds, so remote, fluctuating and uncertain, that no basis is afforded for an appeal to the preventive powers of a court of equity."[117]

In *Flast v. Cohen*, the Supreme Court punctured the "impenetrable barrier" erected by *Frothingham* that had stood for 45 years and prevented federal taxpayers from "challeng[ing] the constitutionality of a federal statute."[118] It did so to allow taxpayers to attack a statute on the grounds that it violated the Establishment Clause.[119] *Flast* involved an allegation that federal funds had been appropriated to pay for instruction, textbooks, and other instructional materials in religious schools.[120] In the time between *Frothingham* and *Flast*, a split of opinion had developed as to whether the taxpayer-standing doctrine was "a rule of self-restraint" or whether it was "constitutionally compelled."[121] The Court in *Flast* believed that *Frothingham* could be read to support either position.[122]

---

[114] Frothingham v. Mellon, 262 U.S. 447, 487–88 (1923).

[115] *Id.* at 488 ("The party who invokes the power must be able to show not only that the statute is invalid but that he has sustained or is immediately in danger of sustaining some direct injury as the result of its enforcement, and not merely that he suffers in some indefinite way in common with people generally.").

[116] *Id.*

[117] *Id.* at 487.

[118] Flast v. Cohen, 392 U.S. 83, 85 (1968).

[119] *Id.*

[120] *Id.* at 85–86.

[121] *Id.* at 92.

[122] *Id.* at 93.

If the doctrine was constitutionally compelled, it would be grounded in Article III's "cases" and "controversies" language.[123] The Court said that those words "limit the business of federal courts to questions presented in an adversary context."[124] From this, the Court in *Flast* reiterated that Article III imposes a rule against advisory opinions on federal courts.[125] "In other words, when standing is placed in issue in a case, the question is whether the person whose standing is challenged is a proper party to request an adjudication of a particular issue and not whether the issue itself is justiciable."[126] And a "proper party is demanded so that federal courts will not be asked to decide ill-defined controversies over constitutional issues or a case which is of a hypothetical or abstract character."[127] Thus, the question becomes "whether the party invoking federal court jurisdiction has a personal stake in the outcome of the controversy."[128]

The Court in *Flast* therefore found "no absolute bar in Article III to suits by federal taxpayers challenging allegedly unconstitutional federal taxing and spending programs."[129] The Court concluded its discussion by saying that "a taxpayer will be a proper party to allege the unconstitutionality only of exercises of congressional power under the taxing and spending clause of Article I, § 8, of the Constitution."[130] And moreover, that "[t]he taxpayer's allegation in such cases would be that *his tax money is being extracted and spent* in violation of specific constitutional protections against such abuses of legislative power."[131]

In the years since *Flast*, however, the Court has rejected every effort to expand the taxpayer-standing doctrine beyond the Establishment

---

[123] *Id.* at 94–95.
[124] *Id.* at 95.
[125] *Id.* at 95–96.
[126] *Id.* at 99–100.
[127] *Id.* at 100 (internal quotations and citations omitted).
[128] *Id.* at 101 (internal quotations and citations omitted).
[129] *Id.*
[130] *Id.* at 102.
[131] *Id.* at 106 (emphasis added).

Clause.[132] In fact, it has been slowly plugging the hole in the "impenetrable barrier" erected by *Frothingham* and punctured by *Flast*.[133]

Flast's focus on whether the particular *plaintiffs* are the proper party to bring a claim is essential to understanding the outcome in *ACSTO*. The outcome certainly could not have been rooted in concerns about issuing an advisory opinion. The case had been vigorously litigated for more than 10 years. The plaintiffs' lawyers were tenacious, smart, and entirely opposed to Arizona's tax credit program. The issues in the case were well defined. The concerns regarding issuing an advisory opinion were not present. I am sure the plaintiffs also opposed the program, but the question in *ACSTO* was whether they had a personal stake in the outcome of the case.

Justice Kennedy's opinion in *ACSTO* begins by rooting the lack of taxpayer standing far more firmly in the text of Article III than did *Flast*. "Under Article III, the Federal Judiciary is vested with the 'Power' to resolve not questions and issues but 'Cases' or 'Controversies.'"[134] Thus, "a plaintiff who seeks to invoke the federal judicial power must assert more than just the 'generalized interest of all citizens in constitutional governance.'"[135] The plaintiffs in *ACSTO* were unable to prove this. Nor did they try to make such a showing. Rather, they sought to rely on the *Flast* exception to the general rule against taxpayer standing. But even under *Flast*, there must be some showing of particular injury to the taxpayer bringing the suit.[136]

The plaintiffs in *ACSTO* could not show a particular injury because the tax credits at issue did not extract and spend the plaintiffs'

---

[132] See, e.g., DaimlerChrysler Corp., 547 U.S. at 332 (declining to expand the *Flast* exception to the doctrine of taxpayer standing to Commerce Clause challenges).

[133] See, e.g., Hein v. Freedom From Religion Found., Inc., 551 U.S. 587 (2007) (plurality opinion) (no standing under *Flast* to challenge federal executive actions funded by general appropriations); Valley Forge Christian Coll. v. Am. United for Separation of Church & State, Inc., 454 U.S. 464 (1982) (no standing under *Flast* to challenge an agency's decision to transfer a parcel of federal property to a religious institution).

[134] ACSTO, 131 S. Ct. at 1441.

[135] Id. at 1441-42 (quoting Schlesinger v. Reservists Comm. to Stop the War, 418 U.S. 208, 217 (1974)).

[136] See Doremus v. Bd. of Educ. of Hawthorne, 342 U.S. 429 (1952) (plaintiffs lacked taxpayer standing to bring Establishment Clause challenge to a law providing for the reading of the Bible in public schools because they lacked a direct financial interest in the case).

money.[137] "When Arizona taxpayers choose to contribute to [school tuition organizations], they spend their own money, not money the State has collected from respondents or from other taxpayers."[138] Echoing the merits arguments that the program did not violate the Establishment Clause because of the multiple layers of private choice, Justice Kennedy wrote that the "contributions result from the decisions of private taxpayers regarding their own funds."[139] He then stressed the multiple layers of private choice in the program. This language goes to the heart of the Establishment Clause challenge and will most certainly preclude the ACLU from attempting to find some other plaintiff to challenge the program.[140]

Concluding Thoughts

The Court's rejection of the plaintiffs' view of tax credits as the equivalent of state revenues was a welcome one. It should be a commonsense notion that funds that never enter the government's coffers remain private funds. When a taxpayer writes a check from her private bank account to a school tuition organization in December, there should be no doubt that the money contributed belongs to the taxpayer. That the state allows the taxpayer to reduce her tax bill the following April based on that contribution should not transform the contribution into tax revenue belonging to the state.

As the Arizona Supreme Court said in *Kotterman*, the tax credit merely "reduces the tax liability of those choosing to donate to

---

[137] ACSTO, 131 S. Ct. at 1447.

[138] *Id.*

[139] *Id.* at 1448 ("Private citizens create private [school tuition organizations]; [school tuition organizations] choose beneficiary schools; and taxpayers then contribute to [school tuition organizations]. While the State, at the outset, affords the opportunity to create and contribute to a[] [school tuition organization], the tax credit system is implemented by private action and with no state intervention. Objecting taxpayers know that their fellow citizens, not the State, decide to contribute and in fact make the contribution. These considerations prevent any injury the objectors may suffer from being fairly traceable to the government.").

[140] "[I]f a law or practice, including a tax credit, disadvantages a particular religious group or a particular nonreligious group, the disadvantaged party would not have to rely on *Flast* to obtain redress for a resulting injury." *Id.* at 1449 (citing Texas Monthly, Inc. v. Bullock, 489 U.S. 1, 8 (1989) (plurality opinion) (finding standing where a general interest magazine sought to recover tax payments on the ground that religious periodicals were exempt from the tax)).

[school tuition organizations].["141] It cannot be said, therefore, "that the legislature has somehow imposed a tax by declining to collect potential revenue from its citizens."[142] And yet, the U.S. Supreme Court came within one vote of holding that "all wealth belongs to the government, and then government allows citizens to keep some of it by declining to tax it."[143]

The ramifications of deciding who initially owns privately generated income extend far beyond education policy. If *ACSTO* had come out the other way on this issue, the U.S. Supreme Court would essentially have been holding that tax dollars fund every church, mosque, synagogue, and religious institution in America. Indeed, it would have been holding that *every* charitable organization that receives tax-deductible contributions—including IJ, ADF, and the ACLU—receives state funds from its donors. Such reasoning could have led to the elimination of tax deductions for donations to religious institutions. It could even have led to the elimination of tax-exempt status for religious institutions because, by declining to collect "potential revenue," the government would have arguably been directly subsidizing religion with state funds. An opposite holding would also have jeopardized the independence of nonreligious organizations that receive tax-deductible contributions because the receipt of state funds always comes with strings, limitations, and government controls. Nothing short of intellectual freedom and liberty of conscience rode on the correct outcome in *ACSTO*.

Given the way the Supreme Court ruled, however, we were spared that parade of horribles. Fortunately, the money in your wallet still belongs to you and not the government.

---

[141] Kotterman, 972 P.2d at 621.

[142] *Id.*

[143] Editorial, Supreme School Choice: A Narrow Decision Averts a Legal Assault on Private Schools, Wall St. J., Apr. 5, 2011, at A14, available at http://online.wsj.com/article/SB10001424052748703712504576242942552010676.html?mod = WSJ_article_MoreIn_Opinion.

Will Mrs. Bond Topple *Missouri v. Holland?*

*John C. Eastman**

Game on!

No, not the one waged by Carol Anne Bond against her former best friend and husband's paramour, upon learning that the paramour was carrying the husband's love child. The old adage "hell hath no fury like a woman scorned" probably needs to be updated to something like, "Don't mess with the husband of someone who works in a chemical lab!" Mrs. Bond "borrowed" some toxic chemicals from her workplace and sprinkled them on the paramour's car and mailbox in her effort to show her displeasure with her former friend's conduct. That game is not going to end well for Carol Anne Bond no matter what happens in her current case. Either she gets prosecuted by the feds, or by her local district attorney. Whatever the jurisdiction, assaulting someone with chemicals is going to land you in a heap of trouble. Thus far, the Supreme Court has entered only a narrow ruling, holding simply that Mrs. Bond has legal standing to challenge the constitutionality of the *federal* statute under which she was convicted, a statute that was meant to implement the international treaty against the use of chemical weapons.[1] That holding was so clearly correct that even the government declined

* Dr. Eastman is the Henry Salvatori Professor of Law & Community Service and former dean at Chapman University School of Law. He is also the founding director of the Center for Constitutional Jurisprudence, in which capacity he filed an amicus curiae brief in the Supreme Court on behalf of the Center and of the Cato Institute in support of Mrs. Bond, from which this article is drawn. He gratefully acknowledges his co-signatories on that brief: former Attorney General Edwin Meese III; Ilya Shapiro of the Cato Institute; and Anthony Caso, David Llewellyn Jr., and Karen Lugo from the Center for Constitutional Jurisprudence. Special acknowledgment to Cato's Trevor Burrus as well, for superb research and drafting assistance with the section on overcriminalization.

[1] See generally Bond v. United States, 131 S. Ct. 2355 (2011).

to defend before the Supreme Court the jurisdictional victory that the court of appeals had given it; the Court had to appoint former Supreme Court law clerk and University of Kansas Law School Dean Stephen McAllister as an amicus curiae to defend the indefensible position.[2]

No, the "Game on!" I want to discuss is the opportunity Mrs. Bond's case presents for a further restoration of the principles of federalism that underlie our constitutional system and the dangers to the notion of limited government if she loses her case on the merits—whether back in the lower courts on remand or perhaps in the Supreme Court after a return trip. Although this particular case occurs in the rather arcane arena of international treaties and the statutes Congress adopts to execute them, the fact that it presents issues of federalism, enumerated powers, and limited national government should make it of great interest to anyone awaiting Supreme Court review of other more high-profile legal disputes. Most immediately, it could even have an effect on the constitutional challenges to the Patient Protection and Affordable Health Care Act (Obamacare) currently wending their way to the Court.

From Birds to Obamacare

Here's the issue in a nutshell. Ninety years ago, in a case involving a U.S.-Canada migratory bird treaty, the Supreme Court—in a confusing and curt opinion by Justice Oliver Wendell Holmes—held that Congress could adopt domestic legislation that it would not otherwise have the constitutional authority to adopt, if it furthered a treaty commitment.[3] Then, about 50 years ago, the Court held that even statutes adopted in furtherance of the treaty power are constrained by other constitutional limitations on federal power.[4] The latter case, *Reid v. Covert*, involved a claim that a treaty provision violated rights protected by the Bill of Rights, while the limits on federal power at issue in the earlier *Missouri v. Holland* case derived from the enumerated-powers doctrine. But in principle, under our constitutional structure, Congress can no more exceed the limits of

---

[2] He did an admirable job, considering that he was dealt a hand with no cards—and received a nice "attaboy" in the Court's published opinion!

[3] Missouri v. Holland, 252 U.S. 416 (1920).

[4] Reid v. Covert, 354 U.S. 1 (1957).

the powers delegated to it in Article I than it can act in ways that violate the Bill of Rights. That most basic proposition was reaffirmed by the Supreme Court in its recent Commerce Clause cases, including the landmark decision in *United States v. Lopez*[5] and the follow-up decision in *United States v. Morrison.*[6] Even in cases such as *Gonzales v. Raich*[7] and *United States v. Comstock,*[8] the Court upheld the federal laws at issue (whether rightly or, as I think, wrongly) only after reaffirming its commitment to the enumerated-powers doctrine.

Before delving into the *Holland* versus *Reid* conflict, though, let me describe in greater detail the legal issues raised by Mrs. Bond's case and the preliminary jurisdictional question that the Supreme Court addressed in this round of litigation.

An Unusual Case Reaches the Supreme Court

Mrs. Bond, who lives outside Philadelphia, was indicted in federal district court for, among other things, two counts of violating Section 229 of Title 18 of the U.S. Code, which forbids the knowing possession or use of any chemical that "can cause death, temporary incapacitation or permanent harm to humans or animals" where not intended for a "peaceful purpose."[9] Had this statute been enacted pursuant to Congress's power to regulate commerce among the states, it would likely be unconstitutional. The statute contains no requirement of a nexus with interstate commerce (such as use of chemicals that had moved in interstate commerce, or harm to humans or animals traveling in interstate commerce); it applies to mere possession as well as use; and it is not limited to conduct that is economic in nature. In short, under the most recent precedent (*Lopez, Morrison,* and even *Raich*), Congress very likely could not enact this statute under its Commerce Clause authority.

No matter, say some in Congress and elsewhere, because the statute, part of the Chemical Weapons Convention Implementation Act of 1998,[10] implements a treaty, the Convention on the Prohibition

---

[5] 514 U.S. 549 (1995).
[6] 529 U.S. 598 (2000).
[7] 545 U.S. 1 (2005).
[8] 130 S. Ct. 1949 (2010).
[9] 18 U.S.C. §§229(a), 229F(1), 229F(7–8).
[10] 112 Stat. 2681–856, 22 U.S.C. § 229 et seq. (2011).

of the Development, Production, Stockpiling and Use of Chemical Weapons and on Their Destruction, which was ratified by the United States in 1997. Unlike ordinary laws, which form part of the supreme law of the land only if "made in Pursuance" of the Constitution, treaties are valid whenever made "under the Authority of the United States."[11] Treaties thus provide their own authority for Congress to enact implementing statutes without regard to other, enumerated-powers limitations on its power—or so the argument goes. Indeed, some interpretations of *Missouri v. Holland* hold this view to have been approved by the Supreme Court.

Mrs. Bond moved to dismiss the indictment, contending that Section 229 was unconstitutional because it intruded upon powers that our Constitution reserves to the states, as acknowledged in the Tenth Amendment. The district court denied her motion and so Mrs. Bond entered a guilty plea, reserving her right to appeal the constitutionality of Section 229.

On that appeal, the U.S. Court of Appeals for the Third Circuit requested supplemental briefing on the issue of whether Mrs. Bond even had standing to raise the "intrudes on state sovereignty" constitutional challenge and, based in part on briefing by the Department of Justice (which the department would later disavow), held that she did not. Mrs. Bond is not a state, after all, so absent the state's own objection to federal overreach, the Third Circuit Court of Appeals held that she could not herself defend the state's prerogatives. This position found some support in a sentence from a New Deal-era decision of the Supreme Court, *Tennessee Electric Power Co. v. TVA*, noting that a private party, "absent the states or their officers, have no standing in this suit to raise any question under the [Tenth] amendment."[12]

The Supreme Court agreed to review Mrs. Bond's case to consider this preliminary issue of whether Mrs. Bond had legal standing to pursue her constitutional challenge. Although technically that was the only question decided—Mrs. Bond does indeed have standing to challenge the constitutionality of the statute under which she was convicted!—the language that Justice Anthony Kennedy chose to

---

[11] U.S. Const. Art. VI cl. 2.

[12] 306 U.S. 118, 144 (1939) (after apparently conflating concepts of legal standing and legal injury).

employ on behalf of the Court, echoed by Justice Ruth Bader Ginsburg in her concurring opinion, is what makes this case of much broader interest.

A Concise, Powerful, and Unanimous Opinion

Justice Kennedy's opinion for the unanimous Court reiterates, for example, the long-standing view that the national government is one of limited and enumerated powers, not one of unlimited authority.[13] "The principles of limited national powers and state sovereignty are intertwined," Justice Kennedy wrote. "Impermissible interference with state sovereignty is not within the enumerated powers of the National Government . . . and action that exceeds the National Government's enumerated powers undermines the sovereign interests of the States."[14]

Mrs. Bond had standing to challenge Section 229 as an unconstitutional interference with state sovereignty because such "unconstitutional action can cause concomitant injury to persons in individual cases."[15] In other words, whether couched as a claim that the statute exceeds enumerated powers or violates the Tenth Amendment's proscription that the powers not delegated to the federal government are reserved to the states or to the people, the issue of Mrs. Bond's standing to challenge the constitutionality of the statute is the same.

---

[13] Bond v. United States, 131 S. Ct. 2355, 2366 (2011); see also, e.g., Wyeth v. Levine, 129 S. Ct. 1187, 1206 (2009); United States v. Morrison, 529 U.S. 598, 618 & n.8 (2000); United States v. Lopez, 514 U.S. 549, 552 (1995); New York v. United States, 505 U.S. 144, 156–57 (1992); Gregory v. Ashcroft, 501 U.S. 452, 457 (1991); A.L.A. Schechter Poultry Corp. v. United States, 295 U.S. 495, 528-29 (1935); Mayor of New Orleans v. United States, 35 U.S. (10 Pet.) 662, 736 (1836); Cohens v. Virginia, 19 U.S. (6 Wheat.) 264, 426, 428 (1821); McCulloch v. Maryland, 17 U.S. (4 Wheat.) 316, 405 (1819) ("This government is acknowledged by all to be one of enumerated powers."); Marbury v. Madison, 5 U.S. (1 Cranch) 137, 176 (1803) ("The powers of the legislature are defined, and limited; and that those limits may not be mistaken, or forgotten, the constitution is written."); cf. Federalist No. 45, at 292–93 (Madison) (Rossiter ed. 1961) ("The powers delegated by the proposed Constitution to the federal government are few and defined. Those which are to remain in the State governments are numerous and indefinite").

[14] Bond, 131 S. Ct. at 2366 (citing New York v. United States, 505 U.S. 144, 155–59 (1992) and United States v. Lopez, 514 U.S. 549, 564 (1995)).

[15] *Id.*

The Tenth Amendment is merely the "mirror image" of the enumerated-powers structure of the Constitution.[16]

Before turning to the merits of Mrs. Bond's claim, which the lower courts will now consider on remand, it is worth pausing for a moment to discuss the alternative view proffered by the United States (via Acting Solicitor General Neal Katyal), a view that the Court described as "a misconception," a "flawed" "premise," with "no basis in precedent or principle."[17] (Ouch.)

The Third Circuit had based its decision denying legal standing to Mrs. Bond on a view that the Tenth Amendment protects state sovereign interests even in the face of otherwise valid exercises of congressional power, and that only the states have standing to defend those interests. While disavowing the Third Circuit's holding, the acting solicitor general tried to salvage its premise by contending that Mrs. Bond had actually raised an enumerated-powers objection to Section 229 (for which she would have standing), not a state sovereignty objection (for which, the SG claimed, she would not have standing).[18] The Supreme Court soundly rejected the solicitor general's attempt to split the Tenth Amendment atom.

To be sure, the Supreme Court had suggested in the past that the Tenth Amendment creates a carve-out of state sovereign powers that cannot be infringed by Congress even when Congress is acting pursuant to an enumerated power.[19] The tension created by that extra-textual reading of the Tenth Amendment was subsequently cured, however, when the Court recognized that the same idea is more properly grounded in the "proper" element of the Necessary and Proper Clause than in a penumbra of the Tenth Amendment.[20]

---

[16] New York, 505 U.S. at 156 (1991) ("[T]he two inquiries are mirror images of each other. If a power is delegated to Congress in the Constitution, the Tenth Amendment expressly disclaims any reservation of that power to the States; if a power is an attribute of state sovereignty reserved by the Tenth Amendment, it is necessarily a power the Constitution has not conferred on Congress.").

[17] Bond, 131 S. Ct. at 2365, 2367.

[18] Brief for United States at 18, Bond v. United States, 131 S. Ct. 2355 (2011) (No. 09-1227).

[19] Nat'l League of Cities v. Usury, 426 U.S. 833, 842-43 (1976); Fry v. United States, 421 U.S. 542, 547 (1975).

[20] Printz v. United States, 521 U.S. 898, 923-24 (1997); see also Gonzales v. Raich, 545 U.S. 1, 39 (2005) (Scalia, J., concurring in the judgment) ("cases such as [Printz] affirm that a law is not proper for carrying into Execution the Commerce Clause when it

Will Mrs. Bond Topple Missouri v. Holland?

Printz v. United States thus recognizes that even the "state sovereignty" concern flows from the enumerated-powers doctrine, not from a separate preserve of state powers that only the states have standing to protect.

Moreover, as Justice Kennedy emphasized, the federalist structure of our Constitution does more than simply "preserv[e] the integrity, dignity, and residual sovereignty of the States."[21] "Rather, federalism [also] secures to citizens the liberties that derive from the diffusion of sovereign power."[22] "By denying any one government complete jurisdiction over all the concerns of public life," he elaborated, "federalism protects the liberty of the individual from arbitrary power. When government acts in excess of its lawful powers, that liberty is at stake."[23] Powerful stuff!

Because "[f]idelity to principles of federalism is not for the States alone to vindicate,"[24] Mrs. Bond has as much standing to challenge the constitutionality of the statute under which she was convicted as Mr. Lopez had to challenge his conviction in *United States v. Lopez*. That Congress sought to criminalize conduct in excess of its authority under the Commerce Clause in *Lopez* and in excess of its authority under the Necessary and Proper Clause (implementing the treaty power) in Mrs. Bond's case is of no moment on the jurisdictional issue. Both criminal defendants had the "concrete and particularized" "injury in fact" that the Supreme Court has deemed necessary for Article III standing,[25] and a finding of unconstitutionality would afford as much redress to Mrs. Bond as it did to Mr. Lopez. Indeed, because Mrs. Bond is the "object of the action" by the government, there was "little question" that the government's action—its criminal prosecution—"caused [her] injury, and that a judgment preventing . . . the action will redress it."[26] As Justice Ginsburg added in her concurring

---

violates a constitutional principle of state sovereignty" (emphasis in original, internal quotation marks and brackets omitted)).

[21] Bond v. United States, 131 S. Ct. at 2364.

[22] *Id.* (quoting New York v. United States, 505 U.S. 144, 181 (1992) (in turn quoting Coleman v. Thompson, 501 U.S. 722, 759 (1991) (Blackmun, J., dissenting))).

[23] *Id.*

[24] *Id.*

[25] See Lujan v. Defenders of Wildlife, 504 U.S. 555, 560-61 (1992).

[26] *Id.* at 561–62.

opinion, "'An offence created by [an unconstitutional law] . . . is not a crime.'"[27] "A conviction under [such a law] is not merely erroneous, but is illegal and void."[28]

Moreover, even if the Third Circuit's reasoning had simply been shifted to an inquiry into whether the congressional intrusion into a matter of core state concern was "proper" under the Necessary and Proper Clause, Mrs. Bond would still have standing to press her challenge to the constitutionality of the statute under which she was convicted. As we noted in the brief filed in *Bond* on behalf of the Center for Constitutional Jurisprudence and the Cato Institute, one of the principal purposes of federalism is to protect individuals against an overreaching federal government by subdividing sovereign authority between the federal and state governments, each capable of checking the other.[29] It would be anomalous to hold that an individual beneficiary of this system of checks and balances could not defend her own particularized interests when the state fails to do so. States simply cannot sublet to the federal government powers that "We the People" assigned to them or reserved to ourselves, and individuals who are particularly harmed by the attempted reallocation of power are not without recourse to the courts to challenge it.

Finally, Justice Kennedy's opinion for the Court seems to recognize the emerging national consensus that criminal law is becoming over-federalized and, as a consequence, less tethered to its core principles and aims. Indeed, in May 2010, the Heritage Foundation and the National Association of Criminal Defense Lawyers—organizations often diametrically opposed to each other—co-published a study on the proliferation of the federal criminal code and the disturbing

---

[27] Bond, 131 S. Ct. at 2367 (Ginsburg, J., concurring) (quoting Ex parte Siebold, 100 U.S. 371, 376 (1880)).

[28] *Id.* (quoting Siebold, 100 U.S. at 376–77).

[29] Brief of the Center for Constitutional Jurisprudence and Cato Institute at 7, Bond v. United States, 131 S. Ct. 2355 (2011) (No. 09-1227) (citing Gregory v. Ashcroft, 501 U.S. 452, 458 (1991) ("The 'constitutionally mandated balance of power' between the States and the Federal Government was adopted by the Framers to ensure the protection of 'our fundamental liberties.'") (in turn quoting Atascadero State Hospital v. Scanlon, 473 U.S. 234, 242 (1985))).

way in which such laws are often passed without a *mens rea* requirement.[30]

Overcriminalization

The sheer number of new federal crimes boggles the mind. To wit, the federal criminal code now includes at least 4,450 crimes.[31] Congress added an average of 56.5 crimes per year to the federal code between 2000 and 2007[32] and has raised the total number of federal crimes by 40 percent since 1970.[33] Moreover, the federal criminal code has grown not just in size but in complexity, making it difficult to both (1) determine what statutes constitute crimes and (2) "differentiat[e]" whether a single statute with different acts listed within a section or subsection includes more than a single crime and, if so, how many."[34]

Nevertheless, Congress keeps piling on. During the 109th Congress (2005–06), 446 new criminal offenses were proposed, less than half of which were sent for expert review at either the House or Senate Judiciary Committee. As a result, as the Supreme Court recently recognized in *Skilling v. United States*,[35] federal prosecutors are often left with enormously vague statutes that implicate core constitutional and due process concerns.

This complexity of criminal law, as well as the sheer number of statutes on the books, makes the systemic cleansing of the federal criminal code a difficult task. The Court's holding in *Bond* that criminal defendants have standing to challenge the laws under which they are charged as *ultra vires* congressional actions violating either Article I or the Tenth Amendment is thus a crucial piece in the overall effort to reign in the burgeoning federal criminal law. Indeed, the Supreme Court has recognized that a government of enumerated

---

[30] Brian W. Walsh & Tiffany M. Joslyn, Without Intent: How Congress Is Eroding the Intent Requirement in Federal Law (2010).

[31] John S. Baker Jr., Revisiting the Explosive Growth of Federal Crimes, Legal Memorandum No. 26, Heritage Found. (June 16, 2008).

[32] *Id.*

[33] James Strazella et al., Task Force on the Federalization of Criminal Law, Am. Bar Ass'n Criminal Justice Section, The Federalization of Criminal Law 7 (1998).

[34] John S. Baker Jr., Jurisdictional and Separation of Powers Strategies to Limit the Expansion of Federal Crimes, 54 Am. U. L. Rev. 545, 549 (2005).

[35] 130 S. Ct. 2896 (2010).

powers was created for the benefit of those living under the duly
constituted government, that the "first principles" of the Constitution "serve to prevent the accumulation of excessive power in any
one branch," and that "a healthy balance of power between the
States and the Federal Government will reduce the risk of tyranny
and abuse from either front."[36] The same "first principles" hold true
for any defendant charged with a federal crime that arguably goes
beyond the enumerated powers of Congress, whether they bring a
claim under Article I or the Tenth Amendment. Kudos to Justice
Kennedy and a unanimous Court for adhering to this important
principle.

Now for a preview of the merits of Mrs. Bond's case, to be considered on remand.

The Larger Issue

Justice Kennedy described the issue as follows: "The ultimate
issue of the statute's validity turns in part on whether the law can
be deemed 'necessary and proper for carrying into Execution' the
President's Article II, § 2 Treaty Power."[37] By so framing the question
in terms of one of the Constitution's enumerated powers (the Necessary and Proper Clause), Justice Kennedy has already signaled that
the broader interpretation some courts and commentators have
given to *Missouri v. Holland*—that provisions of a treaty can authorize
legislation that Congress would not otherwise have the power to
enact—is misplaced.

Yet that misplaced interpretation is just what the district court
provided before the Third Circuit threw the standing curveball at
the case. In rejecting Mrs. Bond's challenge, the district court simply
noted in conclusory fashion that because Section 229 "was enacted
by Congress and signed by the President under the necessary and
proper clause of the Constitution . . . [t]o comply with the provisions
of a treaty," it was constitutionally valid and, apparently, did not
contravene federalism principles, as Mrs. Bond had claimed.[38] Mrs.
Bond's constitutional challenge cannot be dispensed with so easily.

---

[36] Lopez, 514 U.S. at 552 (quoting Gregory, 501 U.S. 452 (internal quotation marks omitted)).

[37] Bond, 131 S. Ct. at 2367 (citing U.S. Const. art. I, § 8, cl. 18).

[38] Pet. App. at 28, Bond, 131 S. Ct. 2355 (No. 09-1227) (district court ruling on motion to dismiss indictment).

As noted at the outset, the root of the district court's error is the broad interpretation that has been given to *Missouri* v. *Holland*, which in the lower courts has come to stand for two related and constitutionally dubious propositions: (1) that the treaty power is not limited to the enumerated powers otherwise delegated to the national government and (2) that the Necessary and Proper Clause is likewise not limited when used in support of the treaty power.[39]

The broad interpretation of *Missouri v. Holland* that the district court relied on results in an implicit overruling of precedent. In *Mayor of New Orleans v. United States*, the Supreme Court held that because the "government of the United States . . . is one of limited powers" and "can exercise authority over no subjects, except those which have been delegated to it," the congressional police power authority over federal territories could not "be enlarged under the treaty-making power."[40] *Missouri v. Holland* does not mention that precedent, much less hold that it was being overruled.

Moreover, the broad interpretation of *Missouri v. Holland* has been severely undermined by two subsequent decisions of the Supreme Court: *Reid* and *Lopez*.

Reid addressed whether, by adopting a statute designed to give effect to a treaty, the federal government could avoid the requirements in Article III, Section 2, of the Constitution, and in the Fifth and Sixth Amendments, that civilians are entitled to indictment by grand jury and trial by jury. In a rare reversal of course after a petition for rehearing allowed the Court additional time to consider just how significant a matter of basic constitutional law was at stake, the Court held that the Constitution imposed limits even on the treaty power. "The United States is entirely a creature of the Constitution," noted Justice Hugo Black, writing for the plurality and

---

[39] See, e.g., United States v. Lue, 134 F.3d 79, 83 (2d Cir. 1998) ("the United States may make an agreement on any subject suggested by its national interests in relation with other nations"); *id.* at 84 ("If the Hostage Taking Convention is a valid exercise of the Executive's treaty power, there is little room to dispute that the legislation passed to effectuate the treaty is valid under the Necessary and Proper Clause"); *id.* at 85 ("the treaty power is not subject to meaningful limitation under the terms of the Tenth Amendment"); United States v. Ferreira, 275 F.3d 1020, 1027–28 (11th Cir. 2001) (agreeing with *Lue*); see also Nicholas Quinn Rosenkranz, Executing the Treaty Power, 118 Harv. L. Rev. 1867, 1871 n.11 (2005), and cases cited therein.

[40] 35 U.S. (10 Pet.) 662, 736 (1836).

announcing the judgment of the Court.[41] "Its power and authority have no other source. It can only act in accordance with all the limitations imposed by the Constitution."[42] "[T]he United States Government . . . has no power except that granted by the Constitution."[43]

Although Justice Black was writing for a four-justice plurality, Justice John Marshall Harlan II agreed with the essential point in his separate opinion concurring in the judgment: "Under the Constitution Congress has only such powers as are expressly granted or those that are implied as necessary and proper to carry out the granted powers."[44]

The Court plurality flatly rejected the contention that the legislation depriving Mrs. Reid of her constitutional right to a civilian jury trial could "be sustained as legislation which is necessary and proper to carry out the United States' obligations under the international agreements made with [Great Britain and Japan]." According to the plurality, "The obvious and decisive answer to this, of course, is that no agreement with a foreign nation can confer power on the Congress, or on any other branch of Government, which is free from the restraints of the Constitution."[45] And Justice Harlan specifically disclaimed reliance on an unlimited treaty power in his separate opinion concurring in the judgment:

> To say that the validity of the statute may be rested upon the inherent "sovereign powers" of this country in its dealings with foreign nations seems to me to be no more than begging the question. As I now see it, the validity of this court-martial jurisdiction must depend upon whether the

---

[41] Reid, 354 U.S. at 5–6 (citing Martin v. Hunter's Lessee, 14 U.S. (1 Wheat.) 304, 326 (1816); Ex parte Milligan, 71 U.S. (4 Wall.) 2, 119, 136–37 (1866); Graves v. People of State of New York ex rel. O'Keefe, 306 U.S. 466, 477 (1939); Ex parte Quirin, 317 U.S. 1, 25 (1942)).

[42] Id. at 6 (citing Marbury v. Madison, 5 U.S. (1 Cranch) 137, 176–80 (1803); Territory of Hawaii v. Mankichi, 190 U.S. 197, 236–39 (1903) (Harlan, J., dissenting)).

[43] Id. at 12.

[44] Reid, 354 U.S., at 66 (Harlan, J., concurring in judgment). Similarly, Justice Felix Frankfurter, who also filed a separate opinion concurring in the judgment, recognized that a "particular provision" of the Constitution "cannot be dissevered from the rest of the Constitution." Reid, 354 U.S. at 44 (Frankfurter, J., concurring in judgment).

[45] Id. at 16.

statute, as applied to these women, can be justified as an exercise of the power, granted to Congress by Art. I, § 8, cl. 14 of the Constitution, "To make Rules for the Government and Regulation of the land and naval Forces." I can find no other constitutional power to which this statute can properly be related.[46]

Hence, neither the treaty power nor the Necessary and Proper Clause may be used to expand Congress's lawmaking authority beyond the powers enumerated in the Constitution.

That brings us to *United States v. Lopez,* the second major Court decision that undermined the overly broad interpretation that has been given to *Missouri v. Holland.* In *Lopez,* the Court made clear that the doctrine of enumerated powers also serves as a significant restraint on the powers of the national government: "'Congress' authority is limited to those powers enumerated in the Constitution, and . . . those enumerated powers are interpreted as having judicially enforceable outer limits.'"[47]

Lopez's holding complements quite nicely the reasoning of *Reid,* and the two cases together cast serious doubt on the continuing vitality of the broad reading that has been given to *Missouri v. Holland.* The *Reid* plurality noted, for example, that "the shield which the Bill of Rights *and other parts of the Constitution* provide to protect his life and liberty should not be stripped away just because it happens to be in another land."[48] Further, when repudiating the holding of *In re Ross*[49] that the Constitution did not apply abroad, the *Reid* plurality specifically noted that the problem with the statutory scheme upheld in *Ross* was the "blending of executive, legislative, and judicial powers in one person or even in one branch of the Government," which it described "as the very acme of absolutism."[50] While individual provisions of the Bill of Rights were undoubtedly implicated as well, the *Reid* plurality did not discuss them, focusing

---

[46] *Id.* at 66 (Harlan, J., concurring in judgment).

[47] Lopez, 514 U.S. at 566.

[48] 354 U.S. at 6 (emphasis added). Note how this concern for liberty is echoed in Justice Kennedy's discussion of the Tenth Amendment and other structural protections for liberty. Bond, 131 S. Ct. at 2364–67.

[49] 140 U.S. 453 (1891).

[50] Reid, 354 U.S. at 11.

instead on the protection of liberty provided by the core separation-of-powers structure found in the main body of the Constitution itself.[51]

Similarly, the *Reid* plurality rejected the notion that the Supremacy Clause exempted "treaties and the laws enacted pursuant to them" from "compl[iance] with the provisions of the Constitution."[52] The only reason the Supremacy Clause does not use the "in pursuance" of the Constitution formulation for treaties that it uses for legislation was to confirm that agreements made by the United States under the Articles of Confederation "would remain in effect."[53] "It would be manifestly contrary to the objectives of those who created the Constitution," noted the plurality,

> as well as those who were responsible for the Bill of Rights—let alone alien to our entire constitutional history and tradition—to construe Article VI as permitting the United States to exercise power under an international agreement without observing constitutional prohibitions. In effect, such construction would permit amendment of that document in a manner not sanctioned by Article V. The prohibitions of the Constitution were designed to apply to all branches of the National Government and they cannot be nullified by the Executive or by the Executive and the Senate combined.[54]

Accordingly, the *Reid* plurality noted that "[t]his Court has regularly and uniformly recognized the supremacy of the Constitution over a treaty."[55] The exemplary language cited by the *Reid* plurality from one such case is particularly instructive: "The treaty power, as expressed in the constitution, is in terms unlimited *except by those restraints which are found in that instrument against the action of the government or of its departments, and those arising from the nature of the government itself and of that of the States.*"[56] The language quoted from

---

[51] *Id.* at 10–12.

[52] *Id.* at 16.

[53] *Id.* at 16–17 (citing 4 Farrand, Records of the Federal Convention 123 (rev. ed. 1937)).

[54] *Id.* at 17 (citing Virginia Ratifying Convention, 3 Elliot's Debates 500–19 (1836 ed.)).

[55] *Id.* (citing United States v. Minnesota, 270 U.S. 181, 207–08 (1926); Holden v. Joy, 84 U.S. (17 Wall.) 211, 242–43 (1872); The Cherokee Tobacco, 78 U.S. (11 Wall.) 616, 620–21 (1870); Doe ex dem. Clark v. Braden, 57 U.S. (16 How.) 635, 657 (1853)).

[56] *Id.* (citing Geofroy v. Riggs, 133 U.S. 258, 267 (1890) (emphasis added)).

Geofroy speaks of both kinds of restraints against the power of the federal government, the explicit prohibitions of the Bill of Rights and those arising from the nature of the government itself, including apparently that the federal government is one of limited, enumerated powers.[57]

The *Reid* plurality did not itself apply that necessary conclusion to *Missouri v. Holland* because, at the time, the Court had so broadly interpreted the enumerated powers at issue as to amount to almost no limitation at all: "To the extent that the United States can validly make treaties, the people and the States have delegated their power to the National Government and the Tenth Amendment is no barrier."[58] By citing *United States v. Darby*, however, the *Reid* Court indicated that it was addressing constitutional limits imposed by the scope of other enumerated powers, not asserting that the people had delegated an unlimited authority to the national government via the treaty power.

Hence the significance of *Lopez*. The *Reid* plurality's *obiter dictum* (non-binding commentary) with respect to *Holland* must be read in light of *Lopez* and the doctrine of limited, enumerated powers that it confirms. The United States cannot "validly" make a treaty that ignores the structural limits on federal power, any more than it can "validly" make a treaty that ignores the express prohibitions on federal power.[59] More to the point for *Bond*, Congress cannot "validly" exceed its enumerated powers by the simple expedient of relying on a treaty rather than Article I. At least, not without altering the limited "nature of the government itself,"[60] removing the liberty-protecting "shield" that the structural parts of the Constitution provides, or acting "manifestly contrary to the objectives of those who

---

[57] See also *id.* at 22 (discussing how the Necessary and Proper Clause is limited by both kinds of specific restraints on governmental power: the text of the enumerated powers being furthered and specific prohibitions elsewhere in the Constitution and the Bill of Rights).

[58] *Id.* at 18 & n.35 (citing, e.g., United States v. Darby, 312 U.S. 100, 124–25 (1941)).

[59] See, e.g., Virginia Ratifying Convention (June 18, 1788), in 3 Elliot's Debates 504 (Gov. Randolph) ("When the Constitution marks out the powers to be exercised by particular departments, I say no innovation can take place [by use of the treaty power]"); *id.* (June 19, 1788), in 3 Elliot's Debates 514–15 (Madison) (rejecting the claim that the treaty power "is absolute and unlimited," noting that "[t]he exercise of the power must be consistent with the object of the delegation," and that "[t]he object of treaties is the regulation of intercourse with foreign nations, and is external").

[60] Geofroy, 133 U.S. at 267.

created the Constitution, . . . let alone alien to our entire constitutional history and tradition," or permitting "amendment of [the Constitution] in a manner not sanctioned by Article V."[61]

Thus far, the lower courts have been unwilling to follow the combined reasoning of *Reid* and *Lopez* to reject the broader interpretation that has been given to *Missouri* v. *Holland*. Instead, as manifested by the district court's perfunctory dismissal of the issue below, they apparently feel bound by the view that the entire matter must be dispensed with simply by noting that the challenged act of Congress was enacted as a "necessary and proper" means of giving effect to a treaty—and therefore no further inquiry into constitutionality is required.

Such a view can yield some very absurd results. For example, a treaty with Austria that included a provision assisting its native son, the naturalized (rather than native-born) citizen and former governor of California, could allow the president, with the advice and consent of the Senate, to excise the native-born citizen eligibility requirement for the presidency.[62] A multinational treaty on age discrimination could likewise excise the 35-year-old age requirement for the same office.[63] Another one, such as the Convention on the Elimination of All Forms of Discrimination Against Women, could authorize the provisions of the Violence Against Women Act already held to be unconstitutional in *Morrison*. Yet another, such as the Convention on the Rights of Children, could authorize the provisions of the Gun-Free School Zones Act held constitutionally infirm in *Lopez*. The examples are as numerous as the imagination. This small sampling should demonstrate just how significant a threat to the concept of limited government there is from the pernicious theory that the treaty power is exempt from constitutional constraints or that, contrary to the Framers' understanding that a "treaty" could only concern the relations between nations, the treaty power can instead be used to alter how a nation deals domestically with its own citizens.[64]

---

[61] *Reid*, 354 U.S. at 17, 33.

[62] U.S. Const. art. II, § 1, cl. 5.

[63] *Id.*

[64] See *Geofroy*, 133 U.S. at 266 ("the treaty power of the United States extends to all proper subjects of negotiation between our government and the governments of other nations") (emphasis added); *id.* at 267 ("It would not be contended that [the treaty power] extends so far as to authorize what the Constitution forbids, or a change in

Looking to the Future

Happily, the district court's perfunctory rejection of Mrs. Bond's claim had already been rebuffed by the Third Circuit, which recognized that she raised important constitutional issues that, but for the lack of standing it erroneously attributed to her, would require the court to "wade into the debate over the scope and persuasiveness of" *Missouri v. Holland.*[65] The Third Circuit should now wade into that debate with the vigor that a remand from the Supreme Court demands.

Even if the Third Circuit holds that the treaty power itself allows the federal government to address issues that are not otherwise within its constitutional powers, such a holding would not answer the analytically distinct question of whether a treaty that is not self-executing could authorize Congress to act in excess of the legislative powers assigned to it. Professor Nicholas Quinn Rosenkranz's recent article in the *Harvard Law Review* persuasively argues that such a promise in a treaty must be read as a commitment to push for a constitutional amendment that would authorize the promised legislation, not as authorization for Congress to adopt unconstitutional legislation.[66] That is, textually, the Necessary and Proper Clause authorizes Congress "[t]o make all Laws which shall be necessary and proper for carrying into Execution . . . [the President's] Power, by and with the Advice and Consent of the Senate, to make Treaties. . . ."[67] Rosenkranz carefully points out that, as a simple matter of grammatical construction, Congress has the power to make laws necessary and proper for the president "to make Treaties" (such as appropriating money for diplomats to travel to treaty negotiations), not to make laws necessary and proper to implement non-self-executing treaties already made.[68]

As no less a justice than Joseph Story recognized, "the power is nowhere in positive terms conferred upon Congress to make laws

---

the character of the government or in that of one of the states"); see also, e.g., Virginia Ratifying Convention (June 19, 1788), in 3 Elliot's Debates 514–15 (Madison) (noting that "[t]he object of treaties is the regulation of intercourse with foreign nations, and is external").

[65] Bond v. United States, 581 F.3d 128, 135 (3d Cir. 2009).

[66] See Rosenkranz, *supra* note 39.

[67] U.S. Const. art. I, § 8, cl. 18; art. II, § 2, cl. 2.

[68] Rosenkranz, 118 Harv. L. Rev. at 1882–84.

to carry the stipulations of treaties into effect."[69] Justice Holmes's *ipse dixit* in *Missouri v. Holland,* conclusorily stating the opposite, that "[i]f the treaty is valid there can be no dispute about the validity of the statute under Article I, § 8, as a necessary and proper means to execute the powers of the Government,"[70] warrants a more reasoned analysis than Justice Holmes provided. If Holmes was correct, the treaty power can be used to undo the carefully wrought edifice of a limited government assigned only certain enumerated powers. That those who drafted and ratified the Constitution intended to bury such a dormant time bomb in their handiwork is too much of a stretch to be seriously entertained.

Yet that is precisely the path the lower courts have embarked on, via their broad interpretation of *Missouri v. Holland.* Hopefully, the slight nod from Justice Kennedy at the conclusion of his opinion for the Court in phase 1 of Mrs. Bond's case will be read as an invitation to the lower courts to begin grappling with these constitutional issues in the serious manner they deserve. If, as seems evident, the treaty power cannot be used as an end run around the carefully wrought limitations on the power of the federal government, it will be the solemn duty of the courts to say so.

---

[69] Prigg v. Pennsylvania, 41 U.S. (16 Pet.) 539, 618–22 (1842).
[70] 252 U.S. at 432.

Connick v. Thompson: An Immunity That Admits of (Almost) No Liabilities

David Rittgers*

The criminal prosecutor, we are told, "may strike hard blows," but "he is not at liberty to strike foul ones."[1] The reality is not so evenhanded. Prosecutors routinely strike foul blows, obtaining convictions while concealing exculpatory evidence from defendants. A boxing analogy springs to mind when distinguishing "hard" and "foul" blows, but the parallel is strained; a significant number of prosecutors' foul blows occur outside the ring of the courtroom. And neither judge nor defendant may ever know that the blow landed—or the extent of the damage it caused.

While ethical sanction and criminal prosecution provide theoretical deterrents to misconduct, they have proved ineffective in practice. Past Supreme Court rulings shield prosecutors and supervisory prosecutors from civil liability to their victims, which is the most effective deterrent to and remedy for these transgressions. This term, the Court decided that municipalities and their district attorneys' offices were likewise civilly immune for most cases of these constitutional violations.

The Court reached this conclusion in *Connick v. Thompson*,[2] an appeal by the Orleans Parish District Attorney's Office of a $14 million civil award stemming from a wrongful conviction. Prosecutorial misconduct put John Thompson in prison for 18 years, 14 years of which were on death row.[3] The facts of his case, as described by the Supreme Court, follow:

---

* Legal Policy Analyst, Cato Institute.
[1] Berger v. United States, 295 U.S. 78, 88 (1935).
[2] Connick v. Thompson, 131 S. Ct. 1350 (2011).
[3] *Id.* at 1355.

In early 1985, John Thompson was charged with the murder of Raymond T. Liuzza, Jr. in New Orleans. Publicity following the murder charge led the victims of an unrelated armed robbery to identify Thompson as their attacker. The district attorney charged Thompson with attempted armed robbery.

As part of the robbery investigation, a crime scene technician took from one of the victims' pants a swatch of fabric stained with the robber's blood. Approximately one week before Thompson's armed robbery trial, the swatch was sent to the crime laboratory. Two days before the trial, assistant district attorney Bruce Whittaker received the crime lab's report, which stated that the perpetrator had blood type B. There is no evidence that the prosecutors ever had Thompson's blood tested or that they knew what his blood type was. Whittaker claimed he placed the report on assistant district attorney James Williams' desk, but Williams denied seeing it. The report was never disclosed to Thompson's counsel.

Williams tried the armed robbery case with assistant district attorney Gerry Deegan. On the first day of trial, Deegan checked all of the physical evidence in the case out of the police property room, including the blood-stained swatch. Deegan then checked all of the evidence but the swatch into the courthouse property room. The prosecutors did not mention the swatch or the crime lab report at trial, and the jury convicted Thompson of attempted armed robbery.

A few weeks later, Williams and special prosecutor Eric Dubelier tried Thompson for the Liuzza murder. Because of the armed robbery conviction, Thompson chose not to testify in his own defense. He was convicted and sentenced to death. In the 14 years following Thompson's murder conviction, state and federal courts reviewed and denied his challenges to the conviction and sentence. The State scheduled Thompson's execution for May 20, 1999.

In late April 1999, Thompson's private investigator discovered the crime lab report from the armed robbery investigation in the files of the New Orleans Police Crime Laboratory. Thompson was tested and found to have blood type O, proving that the blood on the swatch was not his. Thompson's attorneys presented this evidence to the district attorney's office, which, in turn, moved to stay the execution and vacate Thompson's armed robbery conviction. The Louisiana Court of Appeals then reversed Thompson's murder conviction, concluding that the armed robbery conviction unconstitutionally deprived Thompson of his right to testify in his own defense at the murder trial. In 2003, the district attorney's office retried Thompson for Liuzza's murder. The jury found him not guilty.[4]

Following his acquittal, Thompson filed a civil suit against both the Orleans Parish District Attorney's Office and the individual prosecutors involved in his case, claming that they violated his constitutional rights by failing to disclose exculpatory evidence.[5] Thompson alleged that the district attorney's office was liable for (1) an unconstitutional policy that led assistant district attorneys to pursue convictions without regard for constitutional evidentiary disclosure requirements; and (2) the office's deliberate indifference to the need to train prosecutors on required disclosure to defendants.[6]

While the jury rejected Thompson's claim that the Orleans Parish District Attorney's Office maintained an unconstitutional exculpatory evidence disclosure policy, it held the office liable for failing to train prosecutors to the extent that it was deliberately indifferent to constitutional duties. The jury awarded Thompson $14 million, equivalent to $1 million for each year he spent on death row, and the district court awarded more than $1 million in attorney's fees and costs.[7]

District Attorney Harry Connick Sr. unsuccessfully appealed the ruling at the Fifth Circuit, but prevailed at the Supreme Court. In a 5-4 decision written by Justice Clarence Thomas, the Court held that a district attorney's office may not be held liable for a failure to train district attorneys on their duty to disclose exculpatory evidence. Justice Ruth Bader Ginsburg penned a dissent joined by Justices Stephen Breyer, Sonia Sotomayor, and Elena Kagan, stressing that "the conceded, long-concealed prosecutorial transgressions" in Thompson's case "were neither isolated nor atypical."[8] Justice Antonin Scalia joined the opinion of the Court in full but wrote a

---

[4] *Id.* at 1356–57 (citations omitted).

[5] See discussion of Brady v. Maryland, 373 U.S. 83 (1963), nn.5, 7 & 10–11 and accompanying text.

[6] Thompson v. Connick, No. Civ. A. 03-2045 (E.D. La., Nov. 15, 2005).

[7] Connick, 131 S. Ct. at 1357.

[8] *Id.* at 1370 (Ginsburg, J., dissenting).

concurrence (joined by Justice Samuel Alito) to rebut the dissent and stress the role of individual-prosecutor mischief in Thompson's case.[9]

In the wake of the *Connick* decision, John Thompson wrote a rebuttal of his own, in the form of an opinion piece in the *New York Times*, aptly titled "The Prosecution Rests, But I Can't":

> I don't care about the money. I just want to know why the prosecutors who hid evidence, sent me to prison for something I didn't do and nearly had me killed are not in jail themselves. There were no ethics charges against them, no criminal charges, no one was fired and now, according to the Supreme Court, no one can be sued.[10]

This article focuses on the injustice of the *Connick* holding and the current regime of immunity for constitutional violations, but the case cannot be viewed in isolation. Section I explores the natural-law roots of the Constitution and the effort to "complete" our Founding document with the post-Civil War amendments and their supporting legislation—with particular attention to the civil remedies for constitutional violations by public officials. Section II explores the history of the Supreme Court's interpretation of prosecutorial immunity and how it diverges from the intent of the authors of the Fourteenth Amendment and the Civil Rights Act of 1871. Section III tracks the development of a similarly flawed doctrine of municipal liability that treats the tortious actions of public employees differently from those of private entities, another misinterpretation of the Civil Rights Act of 1871. Section IV shows how these two lines of government immunity jurisprudence converged in *Connick v. Thompson* to produce a manifestly unjust result, and how this state of affairs will continue until either the Court or Congress reverses a regime of immunity that facilitates constitutional violations.

I. Incomplete Constitution, Continuing Injustice

As the Founders famously put it, "all Men are created equal," and "they are endowed by their Creator with certain unalienable

---

[9] "The withholding of evidence in his case was almost certainly caused not by a failure to give prosecutors specific training, but by miscreant prosecutor Gerry Deegan's willful suppression of evidence he believed to be exculpatory, in an effort to railroad Thompson." *Id.* at 1368 (Scalia, J., concurring).

[10] John Thompson, "The Prosecution Rests, But I Can't," N.Y. Times, April 10, 2011, at WK 11.

Rights, that among these are Life, Liberty, and the Pursuit of Happiness."[11] With these words they put the former colonies on the path toward a republic based on Lockean principles of natural law. That was the theory. As is often the case, applying perfect theory to an imperfect world produces mixed results.

Chief among these imperfections, the Constitution did not protect the rights of the individual as completely as the Founders envisioned. "[I]t so happened when our fathers came to reduce the principles on which they founded this Government into order, in shaping the organic law, an institution from hell appeared among them."[12] The "institution from hell" was slavery, and the political machinations necessary to accommodate slavery undermined the process of translating natural law into a parallel positive law framework. Thus, even though slaves had natural rights of life, liberty, and property, the positive law provided no mechanism for enforcing these rights at the federal level. The Bill of Rights did not apply against the states,[13] so no remedy existed until the Civil War and the constitutional amendments that would follow.

The Civil War Amendments intended to set right the balance between the individual and the state: the Thirteenth to free the slaves, the Fourteenth to protect individual rights, and the Fifteenth to extend to freedmen the right to vote. These amendments were not intended as a redrafting of the Constitution, but rather as fulfilling the intent of the Declaration, or "completing" the Constitution.[14]

The goals of the Civil War Amendments are nowhere clearer than in the three foundational clauses of Section 1 of the Fourteenth Amendment: Government must not violate the rights of the governed (Privileges or Immunities Clause), must actively secure the rights of all her citizens (Equal Protection Clause), and must provide a fair and impartial referee where the rights of the individual and

---

[11] The Declaration of Independence para. 2 (U.S. 1776).

[12] Cong. Globe, 39th Cong., 1st Sess. 536 (statement of Rep. Thaddeus Stevens) (quoted in Michael P. Zuckert, Completing the Constitution: The Fourteenth Amendment and Constitutional Rights, 22 Publius 69, 81 (Spring 1992)).

[13] Barron v. Mayor of Baltimore, 32 U.S. (7 Pet.) 243 (1833).

[14] See, e.g., Michael P. Zuckert, Completing the Constitution: The Fourteenth Amendment and Constitutional Rights, 22 Publius 69 (Spring 1992); Robert J. Reinstein, Completing the Constitution: The Declaration of Independence, Bill of Rights and Fourteenth Amendment, 47 Temp. L. Rev. 361 (1993).

the powers of the state come into conflict (Due Process Clause).[15] Indeed, the Speaker of the House presiding over the Fourteenth Amendment debates declared Section 1 the "gem of the Constitution. . .because it is the Declaration of Independence placed immutably and forever in the Constitution."[16]

While Section 1 was intended to be self-executing, the practical difficulties of asserting the Fourteenth Amendment's guarantee in the Reconstruction-era South can hardly be overstated. Members of the Ku Klux Klan, often acting with varying degrees of state sanction, visited violence on the recently freed slaves. President Ulysses S. Grant sent a message to Congress asking for legislative support of more forceful measures to enforce civil rights in the South.[17]

In response, Congress enacted the Civil Rights Act of 1871, tellingly also referred to as the "Ku Klux Klan Act."[18] A significant objective of the Act was to allow plaintiffs claiming constitutional violations by state officials to file their claims in federal court, and to provide for both financial damages and equitable remedies such as injunctions.[19] The Act's provision facilitating civil suits against

---

[15] This is not to downplay the role that due process has historically played as a guarantor of substantive liberties. The Fifth Amendment's Due Process Clause served as the basis for early constitutional objections against slavery. See Robert J. Reinstein, *supra* note 14 at 395 nn. 184–85 (1993) and accompanying text. See also Timothy Sandefur, Privileges, Immunities, and Substantive Due Process, 5 N.Y.U. J. L. & Liberty 115, 134 (2010).

[16] Cincinnati Commercial, Aug. 9, 1866, at 2 (quoted in Robert J. Reinstein, *supra* note 14 at 389).

[17] President Grant's message reads, in pertinent part:

> A condition of affairs now exists in some States of the Union rendering life and property insecure and the carrying of the mails and the collection of the revenue dangerous. The proof that such a condition of affairs exists in some localities is now before the Senate. That the power to correct these evils is beyond the control of State authorities I do not doubt; that the power of the Executive of the United States, acting within the limits of existing laws, is sufficient for present emergencies is not clear. Therefore, I urgently recommend such legislation as in the judgment of Congress shall effectually secure life, liberty, and property, and the enforcement of law in all parts of the United States. . . .

Cong. Globe, 42d Cong., 1st Sess., 244.

[18] Pub. L. No. 42-22, 17 Stat. 13 (1871).

[19] See Michael J. Gerhardt, The Monell Legacy: Balancing Federalism Concerns and Municipal Accountability under Section 1983, 62 S. Cal. L. Rev. 539, 548–49 (1989).

government officials for constitutional violations, presently codified at 42 U.S.C. § 1983, provides the basis for what we today call Section 1983 suits. Section 1983 provides, in relevant part:

> Every person who, under color of any statute, ordinance, regulation, custom, or usage, of any State or Territory or the District of Columbia, subjects, or causes to be subjected, any citizen of the United States or other person within the jurisdiction thereof to the deprivation of any rights, privileges, or immunities secured by the Constitution and laws, shall be liable to the party injured in an action at law, suit in equity, or other proper proceeding for redress.[20]

There is some evidence to suggest that Congress did not intend for traditional common-law immunities to apply to Section 1983 suits, with potentially far-reaching effects for public officials, prosecutors included.[21] As we will see, the Court has created freestanding doctrines of immunity that move significantly in the opposite direction, immunizing public officials even in cases of clear violations of constitutional rights.

The Supreme Court promptly and systematically undermined much of Congress's effort to complete the Constitution, dismantling the Fourteenth Amendment piece by piece. The Court first reduced the Privileges or Immunities Clause to incidental benefits of a national government, such as the right to "demand the care and protection of the Federal government over his life, liberty, and property when on the high seas or within the jurisdiction of a foreign government."[22] The Court further thwarted the intent of the Fourteenth Amendment's drafters by declaring that it did not place the liberties affirmed by the Bill of Rights before the laws of the states.[23] Section 1983 lay "virtually dormant" until 1961, when the Court's selective incorporation of the Bill of Rights—making certain provisions effective against the states piecemeal—breathed new life into

---

[20] 42 U.S.C. § 1983 (2010).

[21] Gerhardt, The Monell Legacy, *supra* note 19, at n.42 and accompanying text; Monell v. Dept. of Social Services of the City of New York, 436 U.S. 658, 689–90 (1978).

[22] Slaughter-House Cases, 83 U.S. (16 Wall.) 36, 79 (1873).

[23] United States v. Cruikshank, 92 U.S. 542 (1875).

the Fourteenth Amendment's constitutional guarantees and the statutes created to facilitate its enforcement.[24]

Section 1983's resurrection came to pass not through the Fourteenth Amendment's Privileges or Immunities Clause, but rather through the Due Process Clause. The Due Process Clause has since served double duty, protecting both "procedural" due process and "fundamental" due process.

Regardless of the source, rights must have remedies if they are to mean anything at all. That notion is not found solely within Section 1983, but at the heart of the Constitution. As Chief Justice John Marshall wrote in the foundational case of *Marbury v. Madison*, "The very essence of civil liberty certainly consists in the right of every individual to claim the protection of the laws, whenever he receives an injury."[25] This protection of the laws is insufficient if the remedy is so weak as to fail to deter future violations. As the *Marbury* court went on to say, "The government of the United States has been emphatically termed a government of laws, not of men. It will certainly cease to deserve this high appellation, if the laws furnish no remedy for the violation of a vested legal right."[26] Yet that is the present situation with regard to prosecutorial misconduct, where those charged with enforcing the laws are, for all intents and purposes, relieved of any personal liability for constitutional violations.[27] This state of affairs is simply unacceptable.

As we turn to the two species of immunity that shield prosecutors from accountability, we should note that the plain text of Section 1983 makes no allowance for the immunity doctrines currently in place.[28] The Supreme Court has endeavored to read the statute in light of the common law as it stood in 1871, however, reasoning

---

[24] See Michael J. Gerhardt, 62 S. Cal. L. Rev. 539, 549–51 for a discussion of sovereign immunity and civil rights jurisprudence between 1871 and 1961. For a discussion of the development of the Court's selective incorporation doctrine, see Josh Blackman & Ilya Shapiro, Keeping Pandora's Box Sealed: Privileges or Immunities, *The Constitution in 2020*, and Properly Extending the Right to Keep and Bear Arms to the States, 8 Geo. J.L. & Pub. Pol'y 1, 47–50 (2010).

[25] Marbury v. Madison, 5 U.S. 137, 163 (1803).

[26] *Id.*

[27] See *infra* Section II, nn.35, 48 & 54–55 and accompanying text.

[28] Imbler v. Pachtman, 424 U.S. 409, 417 (1976) (noting that the Civil Rights Act of 1871 "creates a species of tort liability that on its face admits of no immunities.").

that Congress would not abolish common-law tort principles "so well grounded in history and reason by covert inclusion in the general language."[29] These doctrines include official immunity from liability so "well established" within the common law that "Congress would have specifically so provided had it wished to abolish the doctrine."[30] While the Court will begin its inquiry into official immunity by determining whether "an official was accorded immunity from tort actions at common law when the Civil Rights Act was enacted in 1871, the Court next considers whether § 1983's history or purposes nonetheless counsel against recognizing the same immunity in § 1983 actions."[31]

Unfortunately, the Court's interpretation of Section 1983 is far less protective of essential liberties than the statute's authors intended, creating immunity that fails to deter official misconduct. Congress meant to make government officials liable to those citizens whose rights they violate, but the Court has let both prosecutors and municipalities off the hook.

II. *Imbler* and the Creation of Absolute Prosecutorial Immunity

Connick revolved around municipal liability, at least in part, because individual prosecutors are quickly dismissed from Section 1983 suits derived from wrongful convictions. The unwarranted application of absolute immunity to prosecutors has forced wrongly convicted plaintiffs to pursue municipal liability for prosecutors' misdeeds.

Prosecutors currently enjoy absolute immunity from prosecution for their actions because of the Court's 1976 holding in *Imbler v. Pachtman* that prosecutors are absolutely immune for their courtroom advocacy. The prospect of immunizing public officials for unethical and illegal acts that resulted in constitutional violations sparked a sharp dissent by Justice Byron White—certainly no "bleeding heart liberal"—in *Imbler*. The decades since have brought White's fears to life. Without a civil remedy available for defendants wronged

---

[29] Tenney v. Brandhove, 341 U.S. 367, 376 (1951).

[30] Pierson v. Ray, 386 U.S. 547, 554–55 (1967).

[31] Malley v. Briggs, 475 U.S. 335, 340 (1986) (quoting Tower v. Glover, 467 U.S. 914, 920 (1984)).

in court, there is clearly insufficient incentive for prosecutors to release exculpatory evidence.

This section lays a brief foundation on the duty to disclose exculpatory evidence, explores the history of immunity for prosecutors, and shows how absolute prosecutorial immunity is both a misinterpretation of the state of the common law at 1871 and a recipe for systemic injustice in criminal prosecutions.

Brady v. Maryland

The modern prosecutor's duty to disclose exculpatory evidence to the accused comes to us from the Supreme Court's holding in *Brady v. Maryland*.[32] In *Brady*, the appellant had confessed to and been found guilty of murder in connection with a robbery, but claimed at trial that his accomplice had committed the actual killing.[33] Brady had asked to see statements given by his accomplice but was not shown one statement where his accomplice confessed to the homicide. The Court held "that the suppression by the prosecution of evidence favorable to an accused upon request violates due process where the evidence is material either to guilt or to punishment, irrespective of the good faith or bad faith of the prosecution."[34]

While the Court held that both good-faith and bad-faith violations of constitutional rights require remedies such as appellate consideration of the prejudice suffered by the accused or a new trial, prosecutors remain immune from civil suit even in bad-faith cases. A bad-faith violation is no mere oversight, as Thompson's case illustrates. With a bad-faith *Brady* violation, the prosecutor deliberately suppresses or conceals evidence that she knows to be exculpatory in violation of ethical standards that require candor to the tribunal, and of laws contravening perjury. If successful, the result is not just a notch on the prosecutor's belt, but possibly an innocent citizen in jail while the real perpetrator of a serious crime roams free.

Imbler vs. Pachtman *and Absolute Immunity for Prosecutors*

A little over a decade after *Brady*, the Supreme Court faced the question of what degree of immunity prosecutors should enjoy when they violate constitutional rights. In *Imbler v. Pachtman*, the Court

[32] 373 U.S. 83 (1963).
[33] *Id.* at 84.
[34] *Id.* at 87.

declined to apply qualified immunity to prosecutors, holding instead that they enjoy absolute immunity "in initiating a prosecution and in presenting the State's case."[35] The Court did leave open the possibility for prosecutors who acted as investigators or administrators rather than as officers of the court to be granted qualified—instead of absolute—immunity. Under the qualified immunity standard, officials remain immune "insofar as their conduct does not violate clearly established statutory or constitutional rights of which a reasonable person would have known."[36] The Court left for later holdings the contours of absolute versus qualified immunity.[37]

A "functional test" has since evolved from *Imbler* that examines the type of action conducted by the prosecutor. Prosecutors (and police officers when they perform tasks that might normally be conducted by prosecutors) are not liable for missteps and mischief in the courtroom, but are subject to qualified immunity for duties further from the well of the court. A decade after *Imbler*, the Court held that a police officer filing a request for a warrant is subject to qualified, not absolute, immunity because no tradition of absolute immunity existed in 1871 that protected "one whose complaint causes a warrant to issue."[38] And while prosecutors wield absolute immunity for their participation in a probable-cause hearing against a defendant, they have only qualified immunity for legal advice provided to police officers. To hold otherwise, the Court reasoned, "would mean that the police, who do not ordinarily hold law degrees, would be required to know the clearly established law, but prosecutors would not."[39]

Prosecutors likewise enjoy only qualified immunity for participating in pre-arrest investigations,[40] for false statements made at a press

---

[35] Imbler, 424 U.S. at 431.

[36] Harlow v. Fitzgerald, 457 U.S. 800, 818 (1982).

[37] "At some point, and with respect to some decisions, the prosecutor no doubt functions as an administrator rather than as an officer of the court. Drawing a proper line between these functions may present difficult questions, but this case does not require us to anticipate them." Imbler, 424 U.S. at 432, n.31.

[38] Malley, 475 U.S. at 342.

[39] Burns v. Reed, 500 U.S 478, 495 (1991).

[40] "A prosecutor neither is, nor should consider himself to be, an advocate before he has probable cause to have anyone arrested." Buckley v. Fitzsimmons, 509 U.S. 259, 275 (1993).

conference announcing the arrest and indictment of a defendant,[41] or for false statements in an affidavit supporting a finding of probable cause.[42]

Imbler's Departure from Common Law and Justice White's Prescient Concurrence

While *Imbler*'s shield against liability set in motion the snowball of immunity for advocacy functions that would ultimately wipe out prospects for supervisory and failure-to-train liability, Justice White's *Imbler* concurrence noted both the decision's departure from the common law and its pernicious potential.

White, joined by Justices William Brennan and Thurgood Marshall, concurred on the facts before the *Imbler* Court, but wrote separately to warn against extending absolute immunity to prosecutors "on claims of unconstitutional suppression of evidence" such as *Brady* violations.[43] Justice White's concurrence focuses on the absence of a historical basis for absolute prosecutorial immunity at common law and the incentives created by civil remedies, reasoning that extending absolute immunity to *Brady* violations "would threaten to *injure* the judicial process and to interfere with Congress' purpose in enacting 42 U.S.C. § 1983."[44]

When the Civil Rights Act of 1871 was passed, prosecutors did not enjoy absolute immunity at common law for all actions. The common law recognized three forms of immunity: (1) judicial immunity, an absolute immunity that extended to judges, jurors, grand jurors, and others performing judicial functions;[45] (2) quasi-judicial immunity, commonly referred to today as "qualified immunity," or a partial immunity for "official acts involving policy discretion but not consisting of adjudication" that "could be defeated by a showing

---

[41] "[The prosecutor] does not suggest that in 1871 there existed a common-law immunity for a prosecutor's, or attorney's out-of-court statement to the press. . . . Indeed, while prosecutors, like all attorneys, were entitled to absolute immunity from defamation liability for statements made during the course of judicial proceedings and relevant to them, most statements made out of court received only good-faith immunity." *Id.* at 273 (citations omitted).

[42] Kalina v. Fletcher, 522 U.S. 118, 130–31 (1997).

[43] Imbler, 424 U.S. at 433 (White, J., concurring).

[44] *Id.* (emphasis in original).

[45] Burns, 500 U.S. at 499–500 (Scalia, J., concurring) (citing T. Cooley, Law of Torts 408–11 (1880)).

of malice";[46] and (3) defamation immunity, which extended to "all statements made in the course of court proceeding" and protected witnesses as well as attorneys to ensure candor before the court.[47]

The current immunity landscape is largely consistent with the common-law tradition. Judges[48] and legislators[49] enjoy absolute immunity for actions in their official capacity. State executive officers,[50] school board members,[51] and police officers[52] are protected only by qualified immunity.

While the public prosecutor did not exist in 1871 as it does today,[53] the functions of the modern prosecutor in some instances did enjoy absolute civil immunity at common law. As White wrote in his *Imbler* concurrence, "The general rule was, and is, that a prosecutor is absolutely immune from suit for malicious prosecution."[54] If the rule were otherwise, prosecutors would be deterred from filing charges. And "prosecutors were also absolutely immune at common law from suits for defamatory remarks made during and relevant to a judicial proceeding."[55] This is simply a manifestation of the aforementioned defamation immunity available to all witnesses at trial. And when prosecutors act not as witnesses but as complaining witnesses that make statements under oath to support warrants,[56] or act in investigatory and advisory roles, they enjoy only qualified immunity.[57]

Yet Justice White's *Imbler* concurrence spells out several reasons that *Brady* violations should be another area where qualified immunity, rather than absolute immunity, is appropriate.

---

[46] *Id.* at 500–01 (Scalia, J., concurring).

[47] *Id.* at 501 (Scalia, J., concurring) (citing J. Townshend, Slander and Libel 347–67 (2d ed. 1872); J. Bishop, Commentaries on Non-Contract Law §§ 295–300, pp. 123–25 (1889)).

[48] See Bradley v. Fisher, 80 U.S. (13 Wall.) 335 (1872).

[49] See Tenney v. Brandhove, 341 U.S. 367 (1951).

[50] See Scheuer v. Rhodes, 426 U.S. 232 (1974).

[51] See Wood v. Strickland, 420 U.S. 308 (1975).

[52] See Pierson v. Ray, 386 U.S. 547 (1967).

[53] See Imbler, 424 U.S. at 421–24.

[54] *Id.* at 437 (White, J., concurring).

[55] *Id.* at 438.

[56] See, e.g., Kalina, v. Fletcher, 522 U.S. 118 (1997).

[57] See, e.g., Burns v. Reed, 500 U.S 478 (1991); Buckley v. Fitzsimmons, 509 U.S. 259, 275 (1993).

First, no such immunity existed at common law. The common-law immunities from suits for malicious prosecution and defamation did not extend to the nondisclosure or suppression of exculpatory evidence.

Second, blanket absolute immunity is "not necessary or even helpful in protecting the judicial process. It should hardly need stating that, ordinarily, liability in damages for unconstitutional or otherwise illegal conduct has the very desirable effect of deterring such conduct."[58] As Justice White points out, the possibility of imposing liability on public officials for the violation of constitutional rights "was precisely the proposition upon which § 1983 was enacted."[59]

A qualified immunity rule with regard to *Brady* violations would establish disclosure incentives that are entirely consistent with traditional common-law immunities. Defamation liability existed in order to encourage testimony and disclosure and to aid courts in their truth-seeking role.

> It would stand this immunity rule on its head, however, to apply it to a suit based on a claim that the prosecutor unconstitutionally *withheld* information from the court. Immunity from a suit based upon a claim that the prosecutor suppressed or withheld evidence would *discourage* precisely the disclosure of evidence sought to be encouraged by the rule granting prosecutors immunity from defamation suits. *Denial* of immunity for unconstitutional withholding of evidence would encourage such disclosure.[60]

The majority disputed this point, arguing that "[a] claim of using perjured testimony simply may be reframed and asserted as a claim of suppression of the evidence upon which the knowledge of perjury rested."[61] Yet, as Justice White countered, permitting suits against prosecutors for suppressing evidence is justified by the positive incentives it creates, "that the only effect on the process of permitting such suits will be a beneficial one—more information will disclosed to the court," and this can be distinguished from allowing suits

---

[58] Imbler, 424 U.S. at 442 (White, J., concurring).
[59] *Id.*
[60] *Id.* at 442–43 (italics in original).
[61] *Id.* at 431 (majority opinion).

based on the use of perjured testimony, where "prosecutors may withhold questionable but valuable testimony from the court."[62] Yet the majority in *Imbler* created an enduring rule that continues to allow public officials to violate constitutional rights with impunity. Ironically, the qualified immunity rule that the Court feared would handicap prosecutors has proved more protective of officials than initially feared, and in retrospect the case for absolute prosecutorial immunity is weaker than when *Imbler* was written. Justice White would write the opinion of the Court in its next contemplation of immunity for functions commonly performed by prosecutors, *Malley v. Briggs*—decided only a decade after *Imbler*—noting that "[a]s the qualified immunity defense has evolved, it provides ample protection to all but the plainly incompetent or those who knowingly violate the law."[63]

Van de Kamp *Rules Out Supervisor Liability*

Yet *Imbler*'s liability protection of prosecutors for their misconduct or incompetence in the courtroom, particularly with respect to duties of disclosure to the accused, remains resolute. In 2009, the Court handed down *Van de Kamp v. Goldstein*, which barred a Section 1983 action for a wrongful conviction due to a district attorney's office's failure to institute an information-sharing system between deputy district attorneys and a failure to adequately train or supervise deputy prosecutors on disclosure of impeachment information relevant to witnesses for the prosecution.[64]

Thomas Goldstein (no relation to the Supreme Court advocate) successfully filed a *habeas corpus* petition, alleging that his murder conviction hinged on the testimony of the appropriately named jailhouse informant Edward Fink. Fink had previously received reduced sentences for providing favorable testimony in other cases, a fact that some prosecutors knew but that was never shared with Goldstein's attorney.[65] This constitutional violation, while not driven by *Brady* disclosure requirements, demanded Goldstein's release.[66]

---

[62] *Id.* at 446 n.9 (White, J., concurring).

[63] Malley, 475 U.S. at 341.

[64] Van de Kamp v. Goldstein, 129 S. Ct. 855 (2009).

[65] *Id.* at 859.

[66] The duty to disclose impeachment evidence such as prior testimony given for lenience in sentencing derives from Giglio v. United States, 405 U.S. 150 (1972).

Parallel to *Connick*, the Court refused to extend liability to supervisory prosecutors, finding that "prosecutors involved in such supervision or training or information-system management enjoy absolute immunity."[67] Indeed, the *Van de Kamp* Court explicitly foreshadowed its holding in *Connick*, declaring that absolute immunity must extend to senior prosecutors "because one cannot easily distinguish, for immunity purposes, between claims based upon training or supervisory failures related to *Giglio* and similar claims related to other constitutional matters (obligations under *Brady v. Maryland*, for example)."[68]

The Alarming Frequency of Brady *Violations*

The lack of an effective civil remedy deterrent against prosecutorial suppression of exculpatory evidence has demonstrably encouraged, or at least failed to discourage, misbehavior on the part of prosecutors.

In an article arguing for a "bad faith exception" to the absolute immunity dictated by *Imbler*, Pace University law professor Bennett Gershman points to "a large and growing body of empirical and anecdotal evidence suggesting that *Brady* violations are the most common type of prosecutorial misconduct, often occurring in the same prosecutor's office, often committed by the same prosecutor, and that appear to occur disproportionately in capital cases."[69]

Multiple studies point to an alarming prevalence of *Brady* violations. The *Chicago Tribune* reviewed 11,000 homicide convictions and found that 381 had been reversed for *Brady* violations.[70] The Center for Public Integrity looked at 11,451 convictions reviewed by appellate courts for prosecutorial misconduct, finding reversible misconduct in 2,012 of the cases, the majority for *Brady* violations.[71] The California Commission on the Fair Administration of Justice

---

[67] Van de Kamp, 129 S. Ct. at 861–62.

[68] *Id.* at 863 (citations omitted).

[69] Bennett L. Gershman, Bad Faith Exception to Prosecutorial Immunity for *Brady* Violations, Amicus, Aug. 10, 2010, at 12–13, available at http://harvardcrcl.org/wp-content/uploads/2010/08/Gershman;usPublish.pdf.

[70] Ken Armstrong & Maurice Possley, The Verdict: Dishonor, Chicago Trib, Jan. 10, 1999, at 3.

[71] Steve Weinberg, Breaking the Rules: Who Suffers When a Prosecutor Is Cited for Misconduct? The Ctr. for Pub. Integrity, 2003, at 3–4.

reviewed 2,130 cases of alleged prosecutorial misconduct, finding misconduct in 443 cases, with *Brady* violations and improper argument the leading transgressions.[72] A two-year investigation by the *Pittsburgh Post-Gazette* into 1500 allegations of prosecutorial misconduct found "hundreds of examples of discovery violations in which prosecutors intentionally concealed evidence that might have helped prove a defendant innocent or a witness against him suspect."[73]

The high rate of *Brady* violations is an expression of the inherent conflict in the roles prosecutors are asked to play. They are simultaneously participants in an adversarial system and expected to be neutral and detached officers of the court. The fact that they enjoy the absolute immunity of the latter simply exacerbates the intense career and political incentives they feel as the former. In highly publicized prosecutions, especially capital cases, these pressures are at their apex.

III. *Monell* and Municipal Liability: "Judicial Legislation of the Most Blatant Kind"

Just as the Court expanded immunity for prosecutors far beyond what they might have enjoyed in 1871, so too with liability for constitutional violations committed by public employees. Instead of applying traditional principles of vicarious liability that make employers liable for the torts of their employees, municipalities are generally only liable where the employee's error stems from his employer's policy or custom. As we will see, the history of common-law liability and the intent of the authors of the Civil Rights Act of 1871 do not support this conclusion. This doctrine is the product of, as Justice John Paul Stevens eloquently described, "judicial legislation of the most blatant kind."[74]

---

[72] California Commission on the Fair Administration of Justice, Report and Recommendations on Reporting Misconduct, Oct. 18, 2007, at 3.

[73] Bill Moushey, Hiding the Facts: Discovery Violations Have Made Evidence-Gathering a Shell Game, Pittsburgh Post-Gazette, Nov. 24, 1998, at A-1, available at http://www.postgazette.com/win/day3;us1a.asp.

[74] Oklahoma City v. Tuttle, 471 U.S. 808, 842 (1985) (Stevens, J., dissenting).

Monroe v. Pape: *Section 1983 Reborn, Municipalities Still Immune*

As previously discussed, Section 1983 lay dormant for 90 years after its passage.[75] The statute only emerged as a protector of individual rights in the 1961 case *Monroe v. Pape*.[76] The facts in *Monroe* provide a litany of rights violations:

> The complaint alleges that 13 Chicago police officers broke into petitioners' home in the early morning, routed them from bed, made them stand naked in the living room, and ransacked every room, emptying drawers and ripping mattress covers. It further alleges that Mr. Monroe was then taken to the police station and detained on "open" charges for 10 hours, while he was interrogated about a two-day-old murder, that he was not taken before a magistrate, though one was accessible, that he was not permitted to call his family or attorney, that he was subsequently released without criminal charges being preferred against him. It is alleged that the officers had no search warrant and no arrest warrant and that they acted "under color of the statutes, ordinances, regulations, customs and usages" of Illinois and of the City of Chicago.[77]

This claim carried the day on account of the incorporation of the Fourth Amendment's guarantee against unreasonable searches and seizures against the states, a change effected via the Fourteenth Amendment's Due Process Clause a little over a decade before *Monroe*.[78] The Court held that the Civil Rights Act of 1871 afforded Monroe a federal civil remedy against the officers that snatched him from his home, and that this federal remedy stood independent of any state remedies.[79]

The Court also held that Monroe's class of potential defendants did not include the City of Chicago; municipalities were not liable for the tortious constitutional violations of employees.[80] The Court

---

[75] See Section I, *supra* note 24, and accompanying text.

[76] 365 U.S. 167 (1961).

[77] *Id.* at 169.

[78] See Wolf v. Colorado, 338 U.S. 25 (1949). See also Section I, nn. 24–26 and accompanying text, discussing Due Process Clause incorporation.

[79] Monroe, 365 U.S. at 183.

[80] *Id.* at 191–92.

reviewed the history of the passage of the Civil Rights Act of 1871, focusing on the debate over a controversial amendment proposed by Senator John Sherman of Ohio.[81] The Sherman Amendment would have imposed civil liability on municipalities for the violent or destructive actions of private parties, prodding "men of property" to reject "Kukluxism" in their cities and counties with the threat of emptying the public purse wherever local authorities tolerated Klan violence.[82] The Court considered the 42nd Congress's rejection of the Sherman Amendment sufficient reason not to extend civil liability remedies to municipal corporations, even though the distinction between private and public actors is an easy one to make.[83]

Monell and Its Progeny: Municipal Liability for a "Custom or Policy"

The Court partially reversed course on the question of municipal liability in *Monell v. Dept. of Social Services of the City of New York*.[84] New York City government compelled female employees to "take unpaid leaves of absence before such leaves were required for medical reasons," sparking a civil suit under Section 1983.[85]

Reviewing the legislative history of the Civil Rights Act of 1871, the Court held that corporations, municipal corporations included, were "persons" that could be held civilly liable for constitutional violations. Section 1 of the Fourteenth Amendment clearly intended to incorporate liberties against the states, logically extending the enforcement mechanism provided in the Civil Rights Act of 1871 to local government actions.[86] The Court held that corporate personhood reached municipal corporations by virtue of both jurisprudence and legislation preceding and contemporary with the Civil Rights Act's passage. The 42nd Congress, the very same one that passed the Civil Rights Act of 1871, also passed legislation providing

---

[81] *Id.* at 187–90.

[82] Cong. Globe, 42d Cong., 1st Sess. 792 (1871) (statement of Rep. Benjamin Butler).

[83] Monroe, 365 U.S. at 190–91.

[84] 436 U.S. 658 (1978).

[85] *Id.* at 660–61.

[86] *Id.* at 686–87 (discussing intent of Rep. John Bingham to overrule *Barron v. Mayor of Baltimore* with Section 1 of the Fourteenth Amendment). "Given this purpose, it beggars reason to suppose that Congress would have exempted municipalities from suit, insisting instead that compensation for a taking come from an officer in his individual capacity from the government unit that had the benefit of the property taken."

guidance on the interpretation of federal statutes that included defining "bodies politic and corporate" as "persons."[87] While the Court correctly held that municipal corporations are "persons" liable for constitutional torts, it limited that liability to actions taken by public employees pursuant to the employer's "policy or custom."[88] The Court explicitly ruled out *respondeat superior* liability for municipal constitutional torts.[89]

Since *Monell*, the Court has elaborated on its "policy or custom" rule and expanded municipal liability to encompass some single-instance violations, but has never extended liability to a *respondeat superior* standard. As we will see, a significant number of these cases focus on the hiring and training of law enforcement officers.

In 1985, the Court held that an allegedly insufficient police training program did not support vicarious municipal liability for a single incident of excessive force in *Oklahoma City v. Tuttle*.[90] In contrast, the Court held a year later that a single decision by a municipal policymaker could, under the right circumstances, make a county liable for a constitutional tort in *Pembaur v. City of Cincinnati*.[91] In *Pembaur*, a prosecutor ordered sheriff's deputies to enter a doctor's office in search of two of the doctor's employees without a search warrant. Holding this action to be unconstitutional does not undermine absolute immunity for core prosecutorial functions under *Imbler*.[92]

In 1989, in *City of Canton v. Harris*, the Court held that the "failure to train" theory of liability common to lawsuits against police officers requires a "deliberate indifference" on the part of the municipality for potential constitutional torts such that the "shortcoming [can] be properly thought of as a city 'policy or custom' that is actionable under § 1983."[93] The plaintiff in *Canton* slumped to the floor several times in custody, and when asked if she needed medical attention,

---

[87] Act of Feb. 25, 1871 (Dictionary Act) § 2, 16 Stat. 431.

[88] Monell, 436 U.S. at 694.

[89] *Id.* at 693.

[90] 471 U.S. at 821 (1985).

[91] 475 U.S. 469, 479–80 (1986).

[92] *Id.* at 471–73. Note that the plaintiff in *Pembaur* did not sue the prosecutor in his personal capacity, believing that such a claim was foreclosed by *Imbler*. *Id.* at 474 n.2.

[93] City of Canton v. Harris, 489 U.S. 378, 389 (1989).

responded incoherently.[94] She suffered from emotional ailments and alleged that police officers should have determined that she required medical attention during her time in custody. The Court treated this claim skeptically, questioning what level of medical training police should reasonably be required to have, and distinguished this question from clear constitutional commands, such as training officers on when firearms and lethal force may be employed.[95] This hypothetical situation—a municipality's deploying a police force without rudimentary training in constitutional constraints on lethal force—became a centerpiece for the majority's discussion of municipal liability in *Connick v. Thompson.*

In 1997, the Court considered the "deliberate indifference" standard as applied to negligent hiring in *Board of the County Commissioners of Bryan County v. Brown.*[96] In *Bryan County*, a woman sustained serious leg injuries when she was forcefully pulled from a vehicle by a sheriff's deputy.[97] The deputy had been hired in spite of a criminal record that included multiple misdemeanor convictions on charges from drunken driving to assault.[98] The Court held that inadequate screening in the hiring process only rises to the level of "deliberate indifference" where a constitutional violation "would be a plainly obvious consequence of the hiring decision," and that the facts in *Bryant County* did not support such a conclusion.[99]

The Case for Municipal Respondeat Superior *Liability*

A plain reading of Section 1983 and the legislative history of the Civil Rights Act of 1871 does not support the "policy or custom" threshold for municipal liability created by the Court in *Monell.* Justice Stevens concurred in *Monell* only so far as it correctly held that municipalities are liable for constitutional torts under Section 1983 and wrote a powerful dissent in *Tuttle* that points out the Court's shameless judicial lawmaking in creating the "policy or custom" threshold for vicarious liability. Justice Stevens's objections

[94] *Id.* at 381.
[95] *Id.* at 390, n.10.
[96] 520 U.S. 397 (1997).
[97] *Id.* at 400–01.
[98] *Id.* at 401.
[99] *Id.* at 412–13.

to any liability standard other than *respondeat superior* have only gained force since the *Monell* line of cases has developed.

Congress intended to provide a remedy against municipalities for constitutional torts when it passed the Civil Rights Act of 1871. The decision to create this civil remedy must be viewed in the context of the legislative history and the legal framework of vicarious liability that existed at the time of the Act's passage. The *Monell* Court correctly recognized that where the 42nd Congress said "person," it meant to include corporations, both private and public.[100]

Not only did the 42nd Congress know what it meant when it said "person," then-existing and respected applications of *respondeat superior* doctrine against municipalities indicate that the same Congress intended to apply this liability to municipal corporations for torts committed by their employees.[101] Blackstone remarked that "the wrong done by the servant is looked upon in law as the wrong of the master himself" a hundred years before the 42nd Congress debated the Civil Rights Act of 1871, making no allowance for municipal corporations.[102] State courts in the years and decades leading up to 1871 considered it unremarkable that municipal employers were liable for the tortious actions of their employees.[103]

---

[100] See *supra* note 87, discussing the Dictionary Act of 1871.

[101] This is consistent with other Court holdings interpreting the intended scope of Section 1983. "One important assumption underlying the Court's decisions in this area is that members of the 42d Congress were familiar with common-law principles, including defenses previously recognized in ordinary tort litigation, and that they likely intended these common-law principles to obtain, absent specific provisions to the contrary." Newport v. Fact Concerts, Inc., 453 U.S. 247, 258 (1981).

[102] William Blackstone, 1 Commentaries *432.

[103] "When officers of a town, acting as its agents, do a tortious act . . . reason and justice require that the town in its corporate capacity should be liable to make good the damage sustained by an individual in consequence of the acts done." Hawks v. Claremont, 107 Mass. 414, 417–18 (1871); "Governmental corporations, then, from the highest to the lowest, can commit wrongful acts through their authorized agents for which they are responsible; and the only question is, how that responsibility shall be enforced. The obvious answer is, in courts of justice, where, by the law, they can be sued." Allen v. City of Decatur, 23 Ill. 332, 335 (1860) (cited at 471 U.S. 836 n. 8); "The liability of municipal corporations for the acts of their agent is, as a general rule, too well settled at this day to be seriously questioned." Johnson v. Municipality No. One, 5 La. Ann. 100 (1850); "That an action sounding in tort, will lie against a corporation, though formerly doubted, seems now too well settled to be questioned. And there seems no sufficient ground for a distinction in this respect, between cities and towns and other corporations." Thayer v. Boston, 36 Mass. 511, 516–17 (1837) (citations omitted).

Congressional debate over and rejection of the Sherman Amendment is not persuasive evidence of an intent to impose a liability standard other than *respondeat superior* on municipalities. The chairman of the Senate Judiciary Committee remarked that "nobody" objected to Section 1 of the Civil Rights Act of 1871, which would later be codified as Section 1983.[104] In contrast, the Sherman Amendment sparked fierce opposition because it would have imposed liability on local government for the criminal actions of private third parties, "an extraordinary and novel form of absolute liability."[105] Congressional rejection of this unprecedented civil remedy does nothing to undermine the application of commonly accepted liability doctrines.[106]

As Justice Stevens pointed out in his *Tuttle* dissent, *Monell's* "policy or custom" doctrine is "judicial legislation of the most blatant kind."[107] There is no historical or legislative basis for this constrained form of vicarious liability. The rationale for this policy choice—"concern about the danger of bankrupting municipal corporations"—is certainly a factor to take into consideration when crafting legislation affording civil remedies such as Section 1983, but that is an assessment properly made prospectively by Congress, not retroactively by the Court.[108]

The policy concerns with regard to municipal liability do not all bend the calculus in favor of the state actor, so long as adherence to the Constitution retains any force. "The interest in providing fair compensation for the victim, the interest in deterring future violations by formulating sound municipal policy, and the interest in fair treatment for individual officers who are performing difficult

---

[104] "The first section is one that I believe nobody objects to, as defining the rights secured by the Constitution of the United States when they are assailed by any State law or under color of any State law, and it is merely carrying out the principles of the civil rights bill, which has since become a part of the Constitution." Cong. Globe, 42d Cong., 1st Sess., App. 68, 80, 83–85 (statement of Sen. George Edmunds).

[105] Tuttle, 471 U.S. at 839 (Stevens, J., dissenting).

[106] "The rejection of the Sherman Amendment sheds no light on the meaning of the statute, but the fact that such an extreme measure was even considered indicates that Congress thought it appropriate to require municipal corporations to share the responsibility for carrying out the commands of the Fourteenth Amendment." *Id.*

[107] *Id.* at 842.

[108] *Id.* at 844.

and dangerous work, all militate in favor of placing primary responsibility on the municipal corporation."[109]

IV. *Connick v. Thompson*: *Imbler, Monell*, and Immunity Applied

The Court's decision in *Connick v. Thompson* can now be placed in context against the history of the Fourteenth Amendment and the Civil Rights Act of 1871. The two lines of immunity discussed in the preceding sections—prosecutorial immunity under *Imbler* and municipal liability under *Monell*—converged in *Connick v. Thompson* to bar recovery where a prosecutor committed clear constitutional violations.

While it dwells on the *Monell* case and its progeny, the majority inadvertently makes an excellent case for either (1) acknowledging that the *Monell* "policy or custom" doctrine is irretrievably flawed and should be discarded in favor of municipal *respondeat superior* liability; or (2) vitiating the absolute immunity prescribed by *Imbler*, at least as it applies to *Brady* violations.

The Opinion of the Court and the City of Canton v. Harris *Hypothetical*

Justice Thomas wrote for the majority in *Connick*, agreeing with District Attorney Connick that he was not "on actual or constructive notice of" a need for more or different training on *Brady* disclosure requirements and therefore did not meet the "deliberate indifference" standard for liability under *City of Canton v. Harris*.[110]

The Court spends a significant amount of its energy comparing the facts in *Connick* to the hypothetical "deliberate indifference" scenario postulated in *City of Canton v. Harris* that bears illustrating here. In *Harris*, the Court posed the situation as follows:

> For example, city policymakers know to a moral certainty that their police officers will be required to arrest fleeing felons. The city has armed its officers with firearms, in part to allow them to accomplish this task. Thus, the need to train officers in the constitutional limitations on the use of deadly force, *see Tennessee v. Garner*, 471 U. S. 1 (1985), can be said

---

[109] *Id.* at 843.
[110] Connick, 131 S. Ct. at 1358.

to be "so obvious" that failure to do so could properly be characterized as "deliberate indifference" to constitutional rights.

It could also be that the police, in exercising their discretion, so often violate constitutional rights that the need for further training must have been plainly obvious to the city policymakers, who, nevertheless, are "deliberately indifferent" to the need.[111]

In the *Garner* case cited above, a police officer pursued a fleeing burglar that the officer was "reasonably sure" was unarmed.[112] As the burglar scaled a fence, the officer fatally shot the burglar in the back of the head. The Court found that the shooting constituted an unreasonable seizure under the Fourth Amendment (as applied against the state via the Fourteenth Amendment) and held that "such force may not be used unless it is necessary to prevent the escape and the officer has probable cause to believe that the suspect poses a significant threat of death or serious physical injury to the officer or others."[113]

The hypothetically ill-trained police force unnecessarily shooting fleeing suspects will prove an ill fit for analyzing intentional prosecutorial misconduct in violation of a constitutional duty to disclose exculpatory evidence. First, excessive (presumably fatal) uses of force by police officers are unmistakable. A corpse or hospital report accompanies a use of force, while *Brady* violations may go undiscovered for years—as in John Thompson's case—or never come to light at all. Second, the Court focuses on failure-to-train liability, a paradigm that may have some viability when it comes to analyzing police failures, but one that does not effectively address misbehavior by attorneys.

Dead Men Tell Tales, Brady *Violations Don't*

After a recitation of the facts and relevant legal standards, Justice Thomas turns to the question of whether there was a pattern of *Brady* violations that should have prompted District Attorney Connick to institute training in *Brady* disclosure requirements. After noting that

[111] City of Canton, 489 U.S. at 390 n.10.
[112] Tennessee v. Garner, 471 U.S. 1, 3–4 (1985).
[113] *Id.* at 3.

Louisiana courts had overturned four convictions from Connick's office in a 10-year span, Thomas dismissed this as a pattern.

> None of those cases involved failure to disclose blood evidence, a crime lab report, or physical or scientific evidence of any kind. Because those incidents are not similar to the violation at issue here, they could not have put Connick on notice that specific training was necessary to avoid this constitutional violation.[114]

Using the hypothetical failure-to-train liability standard that the Court dwells on is tantamount to saying that while other officers had fatally shot four fleeing, unarmed suspects unnecessarily over the last 10 years, the officer in this instance incurs no municipal liability because he instead ran down a fleeing purse-snatcher with his police cruiser. The Court would have us believe that because the means of delivering a constitutional violation against the same essential liberty differ, the municipality is relieved of the burden of taking note of the constitutional violations and acting to prevent further missteps.

As a constitutional matter, this is nonsense. The burden that prosecutors bear under *Brady* is no lighter in the case of forensic evidence than that of eyewitness descriptions of an assailant that could prove exculpatory.[115] Indeed, it may be heavier. Eyewitness accounts and testimony often prove less reliable and more contested than a forensic test with the certainty of a blood type determination, making an exculpatory blood test a disclosure more readily identifiable as one that must be made to meet *Brady* obligations.

---

[114] Connick, 131 S. Ct. at 1360.

[115] For example, initial descriptions of the perpetrator's hairstyle in Thompson's murder trial differed greatly from Thompson's hair and tended to implicate one of the prosecution's chief witnesses instead, but the prosecution team did not release these initial police reports to the defense. See *id.* at 1374 (Ginsburg, J., dissenting). This sort of evidence, though often less accurate than blood-typing, was found to be *Brady* material by the Supreme Court in a case involving a wrongful conviction. See Kyles v. Whitley, 514 U.S. 419 (1995). The *Kyles* case also focused on conduct in the Orleans Parish District Attorney's Office, nearly contemporaneous with Thompson's trial, and involving one of Thompson's prosecutors. See Brief of Respondent at 9, Connick v. Thompson 131 S. Ct. 1350 (2011) (No. 09-571).

There is a stark mismatch between the corpse of a fleeing cat burglar and an exculpatory clue buried in the paperwork of a criminal trial concluded decades ago. Because of the very nature of *Brady* violations, the vast majority certainly go undetected. Most criminal defendants never go to trial and contest the evidence against them, and many of the defendants that go to trial do so with overworked public defenders as counsel. The requirement of a pattern of similar violations in order to put a chief prosecutor on notice that his subordinates do not know or disregard their constitutional obligations smacks of the same outcome-oriented rationalization that produced *Monell*'s "policy or custom" doctrine in the first place.

Prosecutors Are Not Police Officers

Prosecutors, Justice Thomas tells us at great length, are not police officers.[116] Thompson's case strains the application of the *Canton* police-training hypothetical beyond its point of utility. The Court plainly sees this, but fails to make the obvious conclusion: If prosecutors are expected to be more competent at the point of hiring, and without court-scrutinized training programs, then they should be held liable for all the reasons that underpin individual qualified immunity and municipal *respondeat superior* with regard to the Civil Rights Act of 1871 and the common law at the time of its framing.

"The reason why the *Canton* hypothetical is inapplicable," Justice Thomas notes, "is that attorneys, unlike police officers, are equipped with the tools to find, interpret, and apply legal principles."[117]

Further, attorneys, prosecutors included, are presumed to be competent from the moment they enter practice.

> Before they may enter the profession and receive a law license, all attorneys must graduate from law school or pass a substantive examination; attorneys in the vast majority of jurisdictions must do both. These threshold requirements are designed to ensure that all new attorneys have learned how to find, understand, and apply legal rules.[118]

[116] We should note that the comparison between prosecutors and police is not strained in one aspect. In Thompson's case, had the concealment of evidence remained hidden for a few weeks longer, Thompson's execution would have proceeded, and a corpse would have been the result, parallel to an unwarranted use of lethal force.

[117] Connick, 131 S. Ct. at 1364.

[118] *Id.* at 1361 (citations omitted).

Even with young and inexperienced lawyers in their first jury trial, the presumption remains "that the lawyer is competent to provide the guiding hand that the defendant needs."[119] The legal profession imposes other barriers to entry and self-policing mechanisms:

> [A]ttorneys in all jurisdictions must satisfy character and fitness standards to receive a law license and are personally subject to an ethical regime designed to reinforce the profession's standards. . . . Prosecutors have a special "duty to seek justice, not merely to convict." Among prosecutors' unique ethical obligations is the duty to produce Brady evidence to the defense. An attorney who violates his or her ethical obligations is subject to professional discipline, including sanctions, suspension, and disbarment.[120]

Practicing law in a district attorney's office also provides opportunities for junior attorneys to "train on the job as they learn from more experienced attorneys."[121] In the Orleans Parish District Attorney's Office, "junior prosecutors were trained by senior prosecutors who supervised them as they worked together to prepare cases for trial," and "[s]enior attorneys also circulated court decisions and instructional memoranda to keep the prosecutors abreast of relevant legal developments."[122] For all these reasons, "[f]ailure to train prosecutors in their *Brady* obligations does not fall within the narrow range of *Canton*'s hypothesized single-incident liability."[123]

Justice Thomas is correct in making all the above observations about the differences between police officers and prosecutors, but these differences do not support the Court's conclusion that Orleans Parish should be absolved of liability. Instead, John Thompson's case should have prompted a reexamination of the existing municipal and prosecutorial liability doctrines, which provide neither sufficient remedy for constitutional violations nor sufficient deterrence to prevent future prosecutorial transgressions.

---

[119] *Id.* (citing United States v. Cronic, 466 U.S. 648, 658, 664 (1984)).

[120] *Id.* at 1362–63.

[121] *Id.* at 1362.

[122] *Id.*

[123] *Id.* at 1361.

The Court's disparate treatment of prosecutors and police officers amounts to a naked exercise in judicial lawmaking.[124] The legal training that the Court uses to excuse municipalities from liability for attorneys' actions in *Connick* is the very same rationale it used in attributing liability to a municipality in *Pembaur v. City of Cincinnati*. Recall that in *Pembaur*, a prosecutor ordered sheriff's deputies to conduct a search for witnesses without arrest or search warrants specific to the premises.[125] While the Court might distinguish the two cases on the basis that the attorney in *Pembaur* was a supervisor and therefore a policymaker, this distinction is illusory.

Suppose that a police officer acting as an investigator for the Orleans Parish District Attorney's Office were inserted into the conceded *Brady* violation in John Thompson's prosecution. Suppose that this police officer was tasked with transporting evidence from the storage locker at the police station to the courthouse. What if this officer, and not "miscreant prosecutor" Gerry Deegan, had intentionally concealed the existence of the exculpatory blood-stained swatch that would have prevented Thompson's conviction from both the prosecution and the defense. There is nothing inherently prosecutorial about transporting evidence, and maintaining an unbroken evidentiary chain of custody is well within the duties of a police investigator. While the Supreme Court has never addressed Section 1983 liability for police officers who fail to turn *Brady* material over to prosecutors, the federal courts of appeal unanimously hold police officers liable for concealing exculpatory evidence.[126]

---

[124] Expectations of police behavior are eminently malleable depending on the Court's desired outcome. The Court is willing to maintain a failure-to-train theory of municipal liability that infantilizes police officers and injects federal courts into scrutiny of what constitutes adequate law enforcement training in order to raise the burden of municipal liability to the "policy or custom" standard. At the same time, the Court has no qualms about relying on "the increasing professionalism of police forces, including a new emphasis on internal police discipline," when convenient to roll back the exclusionary rule. See Hudson v. Michigan, 547 U.S. 586, 598 (2006).

[125] Pembaur, 475 U.S. at 471–73.

[126] See, e.g., Brady v. Dill, 187 F.3d 104, 114 (1st Cir. 1999); (noting that "a police officer sometimes may be liable if he fails to apprise the prosecutor or a judicial officer of known exculpatory information"); Walker v. City of New York, 974 F.2d 293, 298–99 (2d Cir. 1992) (noting that "the police satisfy their obligations under *Brady* when they turn exculpatory evidence over to the prosecutors"); Geter v. Fortenberry, 849 F.2d 1550, 1559 (5th Cir. 1988) (holding that "a police officer cannot avail himself of a qualified immunity defense if he procures false identification by unlawful means or deliberately conceals exculpatory evidence, for such activity violates clearly

Yet a prosecutor in the same situation—one who makes the blood test results unavailable to the defense while in transit to the court-house—who further consummates this omission with the constitutional sin of concealing evidence in presenting the state's case to a court, remains absolutely immune. Both *Imbler's* absolute prosecutorial immunity and *Monell's* "policy or custom" requirement bar the victim from holding the prosecutor or his employer civilly liable. The result is that attorneys who give bad advice to police can be held liable, but those willing to get their hands dirty and *personally* violate citizens' rights remain shielded from liability—as are their employers. This, we are told, is the cost of doing business with regard to criminal prosecution. We are also supposed to be comforted by the prospect of ethical sanctions and criminal prosecutions that can deter prosecutorial misconduct.

Prosecutor Discipline (In)Action

Just as the principles that animated the Declaration of Independence did not fully transfer into the Constitution, the theory that prosecutors who commit *Brady* violations will in turn be prosecuted

---

established constitutional principles''); Jean v. Collins, 221 F.3d 656, 659 (4th Cir. 2000) (en banc) (concluding that police who deliberately withhold exculpatory evidence, and thus prevent the prosecutors from complying with *Brady*, violate the due process clause); Sanders v. English, 950 F.2d 1152, 1162 (5th Cir. 1992) (holding that an officer's "deliberate failure to disclose . . . undeniably credible and patently exculpatory evidence to the prosecuting attorney's office plainly exposes him to liability under § 1983); Moldowan v. City of Warren, 578 F.3d 351, 381 (6th Cir. 2009) (holding that "there is no doubt that the police are . . . capable of depriving criminal defendants of a fundamentally fair trial by suppressing exculpatory evidence"); Jones v. Chicago, 856 F.2d 985, 994 (7th Cir. 1988) (holding that police officers who fail to disclose exculpatory evidence to prosecutors "cannot escape liability by pointing to the decisions of prosecutors"); White v. McKinley, 519 F.3d 806, 814 (8th Cir. 2008) (holding that "*Brady's* protections also extend to actions of other law enforcement officers such as investigating officers"); Tennison v. City & County of San Francisco, 570 F.3d 1078, 1088 (9th Cir.) (holding that a "deliberate indifference"or "reckless disregard" standard is appropriate for Section 1983 suits based on *Brady* violations, rejecting inspectors' request for a "bad faith" standard); Robinson v. Maruffi, 895 F.2d 649, 655–56 (10th Cir. 1990) (holding that officers' "argument that their misconduct is shielded by the acts of the prosecutor, the grand jury, and the trial and appellate courts is disingenuous . . . their actions were dependent in that they relied upon the falsified statements and testimony produced by the defendants in making their respective decisions"); McMillian v. Johnson, 88 F.3d 1554, 1566–70 (11th Cir. 1996), amended by 101 F.3d 1363 (11th Cir. 1996).

criminally has not borne out in the real world. The threat of ethical sanction has also proved to be a "paper tiger" with regard to *Brady* violations.[127] Thompson's case, tragic though it may be, is only remarkable in that it received national attention by making it all the way to the Supreme Court before the *Brady*-violation victim lost again in civil court.

As the dissent summarizes, more than one prosecutor knew of the concealed blood evidence in Thompson's case and remained silent while Thompson sat on death row.

> In 1994, nine years after Thompson's convictions, Deegan, the assistant prosecutor in the armed robbery trial, learned he was terminally ill. Soon thereafter, Deegan confessed to his friend Michael Riehlmann that he had suppressed blood evidence in the armed robbery case. Deegan did not heed Riehlmann's counsel to reveal what he had done. For five years, Riehlmann, himself a former Orleans Parish prosecutor, kept Deegan's confession to himself.[128]

Riehlmann learned of Thompson's lawyers' last-minute effort to save Thompson's life and provided an affidavit describing Deegan's admission to suppressing exculpatory evidence.[129] While it is encouraging that Riehlmann volunteered information that ultimately aided in Thompson's exoneration and a reprieve from execution, Riehlmann held this information privately for five years while Thompson sat on death row.

Riehlmann's inaction earned him professional discipline but not a penalty that would significantly deter parallel conduct in the future. Riehlmann faced ethical sanction for (1) his failure to report Deegan's professional misconduct in a timely manner[130] and (2) "engaging in conduct prejudicial to the administration of justice."[131] The initial hearing found that Riehlmann's conduct violated the latter charge, but that he did not have "knowledge of a violation" that obligated

---

[127] See, e.g., Richard A. Rosen, Disciplinary Sanctions against Prosecutors for Brady Violations: A Paper Tiger, 65 N.C. L. Rev. 693 (1987).

[128] Connick, 131 S. Ct. at 1374–75 (Ginsburg, J., dissenting).

[129] *Id.* at 1375 (Ginsburg, J., dissenting).

[130] La. Rule of Prof. Conduct 8.3(a).

[131] La. Rule of Prof. Conduct 8.4(d).

a report of Deegan's conduct.[132] On appeal, both the disciplinary board and the Louisiana Supreme Court rejected the conclusion that Riehlmann possessed anything less than "knowledge of a violation," and that he should have reported Deegan's confession of misconduct. As a skeptical Louisiana Supreme Court put it:

> The circumstances under which the conversation took place lend further support to this finding. On the same day that he learned he was dying of cancer, Mr. Deegan felt compelled to tell his best friend about something he had done in a trial that took place nine years earlier. It simply defies logic that [Riehlmann] would now argue that he could not be sure that Mr. Deegan actually withheld *Brady* evidence because his statements were vague and non-specific.[133]

Readers should temper their enthusiasm over Thompson's vindication with the sanction that Riehlmann received: a public reprimand, with one justice dissenting in favor of a harsher sanction.[134]

An ethics committee is not the only forum for providing an effective disincentive against prosecutorial misconduct. When prosecutors conceal exculpatory evidence, it moves from the merely unethical to the plainly criminal, amenable to charges of obstruction of justice and violation of rights under color of law.

The application of criminal prosecution against Thompson's prosecutors provides an answer to classic query "who watches the watchmen?" Unfortunately, the answer is "other watchmen."

The Orleans District Attorney's Office did initiate grand jury proceedings in Thompson's case, with charges possible against the prosecutors who had concealed the exculpatory blood test results. The grand jury proceedings terminated after one day, withdrawn by District Attorney Connick, the head of the very office under investigation. "He maintained that the lab report would not be *Brady* material if prosecutors did not know Thompson's blood type. And he told the investigating prosecutor that the grand jury 'w[ould] make [his] job more difficult.' In protest, that prosecutor tendered his resignation."[135]

---

[132] In re Riehlmann, 2004-B-0680 (La. 1/19/05); 891 So. 2d 1239, 1243.

[133] *Id.* at 1248.

[134] *Id.* at 1249–50.

[135] Connick, 131 S. Ct. at 1375 (Ginsburg, J., dissenting).

The lack of criminal sanction in this case is shocking, but should not be surprising. The *Imbler* Court held out the possibility that a misbehaving prosecutor could be prosecuted for violating constitutional rights, citing a single case from California discussing the subornation of perjury for this proposition.[136] Unfortunately, that case "did not involve the prosecution of a prosecutor, as the Court's citation would lead one to believe, nor did [it] suggest that a prosecutor would be subject to criminal charges, or that any prosecutor had ever been prosecuted in California for suborning perjury."[137] Indeed, the one prominent example of a prosecutor spending any time incarcerated for professional misconduct—the former Durham, North Carolina district attorney, for his actions in the aborted Duke University lacrosse team rape trial—is so exceptional that it has taken on the name of the perpetrator in academic writings: the "Mike Nifong exception."[138]

V. Conclusion: Prosecutorial and Municipal Immunity after *Connick v. Thompson*

Unwilling to reverse doctrines of prosecutorial and municipal liability that allow intentional violations of constitutional rights in clear contravention of the intent of Section 1983, the Court reversed the Fifth Circuit and practically foreclosed the prospect of any route of recovery for intentional *Brady* violations. This decision must be viewed as the convergence of two lines of bad precedent. The Court clearly erred in *Imbler* in providing absolute immunity to prosecutors, then erred again in treating public actors differently from private ones with regard to vicarious liability in *Monell*.

Hopefully, the Court will revisit both of these issues in the future and reverse its flawed liability doctrines. Members of the Court are not blind to the fact that the current treatment of official liability is not well-grounded in history or policy. Justice Scalia has noted that "prosecutorial functions, had they existed in their modern form in 1871, would have been considered quasi-judicial (wherefore they

---

[136] Imbler, 424 U.S. at 429 n. 29 (citing In re Branch, 449 P. 2d 174, 181 (1969) (en banc)).

[137] See Gershman, *supra* note 69, at 31 n.161.

[138] See Angela J. Davis, The Legal Profession's Failure to Discipline Unethical Prosecutors, 36 Hofstra L. Rev. 275, 296 (2007) (noting that "the case undoubtedly has left the public with misperceptions about prosecutorial misconduct and the extent to which it is punished").

are entitled to *qualified* immunity under § 1983)."[139] Justice Breyer has asked "for further argument that would focus upon the continued viability of *Monell*'s distinction between vicarious municipal liability and municipal liability based upon policy and custom."[140]

If the Court is not willing to reverse itself on public immunities, legislative reform may provide a route for the vindication of due process. Political leaders with law-and-order bona fides openly recognize that the American criminal justice system locks up not just too many people, but too often the wrong people.[141] A recalibration of the incentives that currently fail to deter *Brady* violations would make a worthy addition to any legislative agenda that follows from that recognition—and fulfill the intent of the Fourteenth Amendment and the Civil Rights Act of 1871 along the way.

---

[139] Burns, 500 U.S. at 500 (Scalia, J., concurring).

[140] Bryan County, 520 U.S. at 437 (Breyer, J., dissenting, joined by Stevens and Ginsburg, JJ.).

[141] See, e.g., Sen. Jim Webb, Editorial: Why We Must Fix Our Prisons, Parade, Mar. 29, 2009, available at http://www.parade.com/news/2009/03/why-we-must-fix-our-prisons.html?index = 1; David Keene, Editorial: Justice Delayed Shouldn't Be Justice Denied, Wash. Times, July 26, 2011, available at http://www.washington times.com/news/2011/jul/26/justice-delayed-shouldnt-be-justice-denied/print/.

Fourth Amendment Remedies and Development of the Law: A Comment on *Camreta v. Greene* and *Davis v. United States*

*Orin S. Kerr**

The Fourth Amendment regulates an extraordinarily wide range of government conduct. Decisions interpreting the Fourth Amendment are also notoriously fact-specific and often contingent on new technologies. As a result, most Supreme Court terms feature a handful of cases that gradually develop the direction of Fourth Amendment law. In some cases, the Court reaffirms old principles. In other cases, the Court either cuts back on preexisting protections or expands protections beyond prior law. And in some cases, the Court ventures into new territory and settles questions it has never before addressed. The course of Fourth Amendment law slowly develops through the process of case-by-case adjudication.

This method of Fourth Amendment elaboration comes with a notable cost. Fourth Amendment litigation always involves claims against government actors. Someone claims that a government actor violated his Fourth Amendment rights, the government actor denies the claim, and then a court rules. In a judicial system that requires cases and controversies, some remedy must be at stake. The litigation has to matter. As a result, development of the law requires the government to face the prospect of losing whatever remedy is at stake in the case. The potential remedy both provides an incentive to bring Fourth Amendment claims and creates the cases and controversies needed for courts to adjudicate claims and hand down rulings that develop the law.

* Professor, George Washington University Law School. The author represented the Petitioner in *Davis v. United States*, 131 S. Ct. 2419 (2011). This essay represents his personal views. Thanks to Jennifer Laurin for commenting on an earlier draft.

The potential losses of law-developing litigation involve genuine social costs because law-developing litigation typically involves facts in which the police are not acting culpably. Remedies against the police are easy to justify when officers act in flagrant violation of the law. But law-developing litigation concerns where the law should go, not where it has been. The point of the litigation is the direction of appellate case law, not the culpability of individual officers. As a result, the costs of remedies when the police lose law-developing litigation are at best a necessary evil. Those costs will be imposed either on society as a whole or else on individual officers who did not act culpably.

The difficult question for Supreme Court justices is how to distribute those costs, and how much and what kind of losses are necessary to develop the law. On one hand, the law must permit enough Fourth Amendment remedies to develop the law in the broad array of contexts in which Fourth Amendment questions arise. On the other hand, the law must limit the remedies to avoid imposing excessive costs on the police and the public in law-settling litigation. Fourth Amendment law provides for several possible remedies, ranging from exclusion of evidence in criminal cases and money damages against officers to injunctive relief. The question is, how should the remedies be designed to best develop the law at the lowest cost?

Last term, the Supreme Court decided two cases that grappled with this question: *Camreta v. Greene*[1] and *Davis v. United States*.[2] Formally speaking, the two cases addressed quite different subjects. *Camreta* involved standing and mootness issues in civil litigation, while *Davis* concerned the scope of the exclusionary rule in criminal cases. But *Camreta* and *Davis* both deal with the basic tension between the costs of Fourth Amendment remedies and the needs of law-developing litigation. Further, both cases share a common theme: *Camreta* and *Davis* suggest that today's justices are more focused on limiting short-term remedial costs than on the long-term needs of elaborating Fourth Amendment law. More specifically, both reflect an optimistic view that Fourth Amendment law development is possible in a regime of zero or very limited remedies. Given the likelihood that more cases revealing a similar optimism are on the

[1] 131 S. Ct. 2020 (2011).
[2] 131 S. Ct. 2419 (2011).

way, *Camreta* and *Davis* provide an opportune moment to explore the intersection of remedies and lawmaking in Fourth Amendment law. This essay proceeds in five parts. Part I introduces the remedies of Fourth Amendment law and their role in developing the law. Part II discusses *Camreta v. Greene*, and Part III analyzes *Davis v. United States*. Part IV offers a skeptical view of the hope underlying both cases that effective law development is possible in a zone of very limited remedies. Part V imagines what steps the Supreme Court could take to assist the goal of law development if it continues to chip away at Fourth Amendment remedies. It offers two specific proposals. First, the Court could consider a rule on the order of adjudicating claims in suppression motions. Second, the Court could adopt a more active role in adding questions presented when it grants review in Fourth Amendment cases.

I. Fourth Amendment Remedies and Development of the Law

Understanding the role of remedies in the development of Fourth Amendment law requires an understanding of existing remedies and their traditional role in developing search and seizure law. The four most important remedies are motions to suppress, civil damages actions against individual officers, suits against municipalities, and suits seeking injunctive or declaratory relief.

(1) *Motions to Suppress Evidence.* The basic idea of an exclusionary rule is that evidence obtained in violation of the Fourth Amendment often may not be admitted in criminal cases. A defendant who has been charged moves to suppress the evidence, and the court then determines whether the evidence was obtained in violation of the Fourth Amendment and therefore whether to admit or exclude the evidence. If evidence is admitted over the defendant's objection and the defendant is convicted, the defendant can appeal his conviction by challenging the trial judge's evidentiary ruling.

Exclusion of evidence is not automatic when a constitutional violation occurs. Even when a defendant convinces a court that the government violated the Fourth Amendment, doctrines such as standing,[3] inevitable discovery,[4] and attenuated basis[5] sharply limit when

---

[3] See, e.g., Rakas v. Illinois, 439 U.S. 128 (1978).

[4] See, e.g., Nix v. Williams, 467 U.S. 431 (1984).

[5] See, e.g., Wong Sun v. United States, 371 U.S. 471, 487–88 (1963).

evidence will actually be excluded. Nonetheless, the basic idea of an exclusionary rule is that a defendant can move to suppress evidence in a criminal case against him with the hopes of excluding evidence from trial.

The exclusionary rule has traditionally been the driving force of Fourth Amendment development. Before its introduction in 1914,[6] the development of Fourth Amendment law was essentially unknown. Search and seizure questions arose in litigation only very rarely, and generally in unusual contexts. The first major pronouncement on the meaning of the Fourth Amendment did not arrive until 1878, and it came as mere dicta in a case about federal power to enact postal crimes.[7] The first major Fourth Amendment holding came in an 1886 civil customs dispute,[8] and the second major holding involved a subpoena in a 1906 antitrust case.[9]

The arrival of the exclusionary rule changed everything. Criminal defendants have an obvious incentive to seek suppression because the possibility of suppression is the possibility of freedom. As a result, the exclusionary rule generally ensures significant litigation of any government practice that yields evidence or contraband. The role of the exclusionary rule in developing the law became particularly important following *Mapp v. Ohio* in 1961, which applied the exclusionary rule to the states.[10] Most police practices are state and local, not federal. *Mapp* thus triggered a flood of law-developing cases that articulated and redefined the basic rules of stops and frisks,[11] wiretapping,[12] searches incident to arrest,[13] and many other common police practices. Decades later, the exclusionary rule remains the primary means by which Fourth Amendment law develops.

---

[6] See Weeks v. United States, 232 U.S. 383 (1914) (applying the exclusionary rule to the Fourth Amendment violations).

[7] Ex Parte Jackson, 96 U. S. 727, 732–33 (1878) (articulating rules for searching and seizing postal mail).

[8] Boyd v. United States, 116 U.S. 616 (1886).

[9] Hale v. Henkel, 201 U.S. 43 (1906).

[10] 367 U.S. 643 (1961).

[11] Terry v. Ohio, 392 U.S. 1 (1968).

[12] Berger v. New York, 388 U.S. 41 (1967).

[13] Chimel v. California, 395 U. S. 752 (1969).

(2) *Damages actions Against Individual Government Agents.* Civil damages suits against government agents in their individual capacities are a second remedy for search and seizure violations. At common law, the law of unreasonable search and seizure developed in significant part as a defense to common-law tort claims against government officials.[14] The victim of a search would sue the searching officer for trespass or some other tort, and the officer would invoke the authorization of a warrant or existing search doctrine as a defense.[15]

Modern civil Fourth Amendment suits vaguely resemble common-law tort actions, but they differ in three substantial ways. First, modern Fourth Amendment litigation is based on relatively recent and mostly judge-made causes of action. In 1961, the Supreme Court invented modern Fourth Amendment civil litigation against state and local officials in *Monroe v. Pape*.[16] *Pape* adopted a highly expansive interpretation of a rarely invoked 19th-century statute, 42 U.S.C. § 1983, so as to permit federal civil cases for constitutional violations without requiring any common-law tort to be established. In 1971, the Court created a similar cause of action against federal officials in *Bivens v. Six Unknown Federal Narcotics Agents*.[17] Under these modern precedents, a person who has suffered a Fourth Amendment violation can bring a suit for damages in federal court.

Second, the doctrine of qualified immunity provides another difference between traditional tort suits and modern Fourth Amendment civil litigation. Qualified immunity dictates that government officials sued for Fourth Amendment violations in their individual capacities are liable only if their conduct violated "clearly established" rights of which a reasonable officer would be aware.[18] The plaintiff cannot recover unless the violation was flagrant. The notion of applying qualified immunity to civil Fourth Amendment claims against the police is surprisingly recent: It dates back only to 1967,[19]

---

[14] The leading case is Entick v. Carrington, (1765) 95 Eng. Rep. 807 (K.B.).

[15] See *id.*

[16] 365 U.S. 167 (1961).

[17] 403 U.S. 388 (1971).

[18] Wilson v. Layne, 526 U.S. 603, 614–15 (1999).

[19] See Pierson v. Ray, 386 U.S. 547, 555 (1967). Remarkably, the rule of qualified immunity for police in Fourth Amendment cases was introduced in a short paragraph by Chief Justice Earl Warren. It was based only on the common-law precedent that an officer was not personally liable if he arrested someone based on probable cause

shortly after the Court enabled civil suits in *Monroe v. Pape*. By the 1980s, however, the doctrine of qualified immunity had become a firmly-established defense to Fourth Amendment claims.[20]

Third, governments generally play a role in defending Fourth Amendment civil claims. Although such suits are formally filed against officers in their personal capacities, officers are typically defended either by government lawyers or by private attorneys hired pursuant to insurance arrangements, contracts, or provisions in state law. Practices vary widely. For the most part, however, federal or state attorneys defend claims asserted against federal or state officials,[21] while claims against county and local officials may be defended either by county or local attorneys, or by private attorneys.[22] In most instances, governments play a critical role in determining how the cases are defended.

Civil damages suits against government officials have traditionally played only a modest role in the development of Fourth Amendment law. This circumstance is true for two main reasons. First, relatively few people sue for Fourth Amendment violations. Innocent victims generally lack sufficient damages to make such claims worthwhile. Guilty defendants often cannot sue as a result of *Heck v. Humphrey*, which held that criminal defendants cannot bring civil claims for constitutional violations that implicitly challenge their convictions.[23] As a result, Fourth Amendment law development in civil damages actions usually involves very narrow types of facts— such as excessive force claims—that do not challenge convictions and can assert damages beyond the search or seizure.

---

who later turned out to be innocent. *Id*. The fact that an officer cannot be held liable for arresting someone with probable cause who turns out to be innocent is a curious precedent for a subsequent rule that an officer cannot be held liable for arresting someone when probable cause does not exist.

[20] See, e.g., Mitchell v. Forsyth, 472 U.S. 511 (1985); Anderson v. Creighton, 483 U.S. 635 (1987).

[21] See, e.g., United States Attorney's Manual, § 4-5.400.

[22] See, e.g., N.M. Stat. Ann. § 41-4-4(B) (providing for representation of public employees sued in the course of their official duties "[u]nless an insurance carrier provides a defense").

[23] 512 U.S. 477 (1994).

The second reason civil suits play only a modest role in law development has been the role of qualified immunity. Law-developing litigation typically involves close questions on which prior precedents are divided. In those circumstances, the illegality of police conduct will not be clearly established and officers will receive qualified immunity. Qualified immunity inhibits law-development in these circumstances in two ways. First, it discourages civil suits from being filed by making the recovery of damages much less likely. Second, it enables courts to reject claims on qualified immunity grounds without handing down a Fourth Amendment ruling that could develop the law.

Concerns with law development briefly led the Court to try a different approach. From *Saucier v. Katz*[24] in 2001 until *Pearson v. Callahan*[25] in 2009, courts had to adjudicate the merits of Fourth Amendment civil claims before turning to qualified immunity. "[T]he process for the law's elaboration from case to case" would be threatened, *Saucier* reasoned, if "a court simply . . . skip[ped] ahead to the question whether the law clearly established that the officer's conduct was unlawful in the circumstances of the case."[26] The Court reversed course in *Pearson*, however, and restored each court's discretion to decide whether to enter Fourth Amendment rulings when qualified immunity applied. Although *Saucier* had the advantage of law development, *Pearson* recognized, it often required courts to reach out to answer difficult Fourth Amendment questions that were poorly litigated and unlikely to be adjudicated effectively.

(3) *Civil Suits against Municipalities.* Fourth Amendment civil suits against governments or against officers in their official capacities are generally barred by sovereign immunity principles.[27] One narrow exception exists: City and town governments organized as municipalities can be sued for damages in some circumstances. In particular, a municipality can be sued under Section 1983 if a municipal employee conducts a search or seizure when following a policy or

---

[24] 533 U.S. 194 (2001).

[25] 555 U.S. 223 (2009).

[26] Saucier, 533 U.S. at 201.

[27] See, e.g., FDIC v. Meyer, 510 U.S. 471, 477–78 (1994) (constitutional tort suits against federal government barred by sovereign immunity); Louis Jaffe, Suits against Governments and Officers: Sovereign Immunity, 77 Harv. L. Rev. 1 (1963).

custom adopted by the municipality.[28] The basic idea is that the municipal policy means that the municipality itself is responsible for the conduct and can be sued directly for damages. Qualified immunity does not apply.[29]

Municipal liability has played only a very minor role in the growth of Fourth Amendment law because it applies only in a narrow context. For the most part, the municipality must first have a formal policy or pervasive custom concerning the relevant kind of search or seizure. But it rarely does. While city cops may conduct many kinds of searches or seizures, they do so mostly out of habit or training in the police academy rather than because the city adopted the practice as a policy. Even if the policy exists and a municipal employee follows it, finding a plaintiff to sue can be difficult thanks to the bar of *Heck v. Humphrey*.[30] And if a practice does not occur at the municipal level, such as the many high-technology surveillance methods that tend to be focused at the federal level, then municipal liability cannot reach that practice at all. For all these reasons, municipal liability has played a limited role in Fourth Amendment law development.

(4) *Injunctive and Declaratory Relief.* Civil suits brought under Section 1983 or *Bivens* seeking injunctive or declaratory relief provide another potential engine for the elaboration of Fourth Amendment law doctrine. From the standpoint of settling the law, the chief benefit of pursuing injunctive or declaratory relief is that it avoids qualified immunity. Such relief is forward-looking, not backward-looking, so no immunity applies.

Injunctive and declaratory relief have traditionally played a modest role in the establishment of Fourth Amendment doctrine, however, because a forward-looking remedy requires evidence that the plaintiff will be subject to a particular search or seizure in the future. Under *City of Los Angeles v. Lyons*,[31] a plaintiff seeking injunctive relief must show "a real and immediate threat" that he will be subject to a specific search or seizure in the future in order to establish a case or controversy. Similar standards apply when plaintiffs seek

---

[28] Monell v. Dep't of Soc. Servs., 436 U.S. 658, 691–714 (1978).

[29] Owen v. City of Independence, 445 U.S. 622, 650 (1980).

[30] 512 U.S. 477 (1994).

[31] 461 U.S. 95 (1983).

declaratory relief.[32] These requirements effectively limit injunctive and declaratory relief to cases involving ongoing programs that affect many people. This limitation has enabled law development in Fourth Amendment challenges to drug-testing schemes and road-block programs, but not the routine run of searches and seizures.

With the basic remedies of Fourth Amendment law explained, we can now turn to the Supreme Court's two new cases on Fourth Amendment remedies and development of the law. The first is *Camreta v. Greene*, and the second is *Davis v. United States*.

II. *Camreta v. Greene*

Camreta v. Greene involved a civil suit brought by the mother of a nine-year-old girl. Bob Camreta, a state child protective services worker, had reason to fear that the child's father had sexually molested her. Camreta joined a county police officer, James Alford, to investigate the allegations by interviewing the child at school.[33] Camreta conducted the interview in a private room. It lasted two hours. During the interview, the child made statements that Camreta believed implicated the child's parents. Camreta sought and obtained a court order temporarily removing the child from her parents' custody. Further investigation by the state proved inconclusive as to whether the sexual abuse had occurred, and eventually the child was returned to her mother's custody.

The child's mother, Sarah Greene, then filed suit against Camreta and Alford under Section 1983. She argued that Camreta and Alford violated the child's Fourth Amendment rights by detaining her at school for the interview without first obtaining a warrant. The district court concluded that the interview was constitutional, and further that qualified immunity attached because the interview complied with state law and no precedent had held that such interviews were unconstitutional.[34]

On appeal, the Ninth Circuit Court of Appeals took its time. Twenty-one months passed between argument and decision.[35] When

---

[32] Golden v. Zwickler, 394 U. S. 103, 109–10 (1969).

[33] 131 S. Ct. 2020 (2010).

[34] Greene v. Camreta, No. Civ. 05-6047-AA, 2006 WL 758547 (D. Or. Mar.23, 2006).

[35] The oral argument was held March 6, 2008. The decision was handed down December 10, 2009.

the decision finally came down, however, it was a doozy. On one hand, the Ninth Circuit agreed that qualified immunity attached so Camreta and Alford could not be held liable.[36] At the same time, Judge Marsha Berzon's majority opinion reasoned that the need to clarify the law justified reaching out to answer the Fourth Amendment issue. Judge Berzon then announced a new and rather remarkable Fourth Amendment rule: Once a criminal investigation has been opened into child abuse, the government must obtain a warrant to interview a child about the abuse in the presence of a police officer.[37]

In theory, the *Camreta* suit was filed against two government employees in their individual capacities, Camreta and Alford. But both employees were represented by their employers: Camreta was represented by the state of Oregon, and Alford by Deschutes County. From their perspective, the Ninth Circuit ruling surely seemed a pyrrhic victory. They won the lawsuit on immunity grounds but lost a major Fourth Amendment ruling along the way. Going forward, the broad impact of the ruling was far more significant than the outcome of one case. Even worse, the state and county had no obvious means of seeking review of the Fourth Amendment portion of the Ninth Circuit's ruling. They won the case, and winning parties generally cannot appeal. The winning officials petitioned the Supreme Court anyway, seeking a reversal of the Fourth Amendment ruling.

Once the case reached the Supreme Court, the focus shifted from the merits of the Fourth Amendment question to the procedural issue of whether government officials can obtain Supreme Court review of the merits of adverse Fourth Amendment rulings when they won below on immunity grounds. This inquiry ultimately divided into three questions: First, whether Article III standing existed to allow the Court to adjudicate the Fourth Amendment issue given that it had no impact on the lawsuit below; second, whether the Court should decline to review the claim as a matter of prudential policy; and third, whether the case was moot because several years had passed since the interview had occurred.

Justice Elena Kagan's majority opinion concluded that the Court normally can review such claims, but not in this specific case. Article

---

[36] Greene v. Camreta, 588 F.3d 1011 (9th Cir. 2009).

[37] *Id.* at 1030.

III standing existed to allow review of the Fourth Amendment ruling. According to Justice Kagan, an immunized government official has a "personal stake"[38] in the outcome that creates standing "[i]f the official regularly engages in that conduct as part of his job . . . ."[39] Because the official must "change the way he performs his duties or risk a meritorious damages action" the next time around, Kagan reasoned that the official has a personal interest in "gain[ing] clearance to engage in the conduct in the future."[40] Further, the child could be interviewed again and therefore had a stake in whether a warrant was obtained in a possible future interview.[41]

The next question was whether the Court should decline to hear such cases on prudential grounds based on the Court's usual practice of declining to review the petitions of winning parties. Justice Kagan concluded that the "special" context of qualified immunity justified "bending [the] usual rule."[42] The Court allowed lower courts to make law-developing Fourth Amendment rulings even when the courts rejected cases on qualified immunity grounds. If lower courts could hand down rulings to clarify the law even when qualified immunity existed, Justice Kagan reasoned, then surely so could the Supreme Court given its greater role in clarifying Fourth Amendment law.[43] This was necessary in part because any alternative would give the state officials an unenviable choice should they wish to challenge the lower court ruling: If they were denied an avenue of appellate review, officials would have to defy the ruling and face damages in order to try to challenge that ruling the next time around.[44] The way out was to give officials the opportunity to seek Supreme Court review.

After ruling that the Supreme Court generally could review claims from immunized state officials, the Court dismissed the case as moot because the parties were no longer in the same position as they were when the suit was filed. The child had moved to Florida and was

---

[38] Camreta v. Greene, 131 S. Ct. 2020, 2029 (2011).
[39] *Id.*
[40] *Id.*
[41] *Id.*
[42] *Id.* at 2030.
[43] *Id.* at 2032.
[44] *Id.*

now almost 18 years old. Because she was outside the Ninth Circuit and was likely about to graduate from high school, there was "not the slightest possibility of being seized in a school in the Ninth Circuit's jurisdiction as part of a child abuse investigation."[45] The intervening time and distance meant that there was no live controversy and the case was moot. The Court then opted for what it termed a "unique" disposition of the case: It tossed out the Ninth Circuit's new Fourth Amendment rule but retained its qualified immunity decision. In effect, the Supreme Court rewrote the Ninth Circuit's opinion by removing the part that had announced the new Fourth Amendment rule.[46]

In dissent, Justice Anthony Kennedy (joined by Justice Clarence Thomas) criticized the majority for departing from its usual requirements of cases and controversies in order to try to solve the difficulties created by the Court's willingness to have lower courts decide the merits of Fourth Amendment cases even when qualified immunity attached.[47] Instead of creating a new and unclear exception to the usual rule that prevailing parties cannot appeal, Kennedy suggested, the better approach might be to prohibit lower courts from settling Fourth Amendment questions when qualified immunity applied.[48] This change would eliminate the concern with "locked in" circuit precedents. While it would also inhibit law development, Kennedy acknowledged, the law could be developed in other contexts, such as motions to suppress.

III. *Davis v. United States*

The second case to consider is *Davis v. United States*, which involved the scope of the exclusionary rule when the Supreme Court adopts a new interpretation of the Fourth Amendment.[49] Willie Gene Davis was a passenger in a car that an officer stopped for a traffic violation. Davis provided the officer a false name and was arrested. The officer placed Davis in the back of his squad car and then

---

[45] *Id.* at 2034.

[46] *Id.* at 2036.

[47] *Id.* at 2042–44 (Kennedy, J., dissenting). Justice Antonin Scalia also filed a brief concurrence, and Justice Sonia Sotomayor concurred in the judgment joined by Justice Stephen Breyer.

[48] *Id.* at 2044–45.

[49] 131 S. Ct. 2419 (2011).

searched the car incident to arrest. The officer found a gun in Davis's jacket left on the front passenger seat. Davis turned out to have a felony record, and he was later charged in federal court for being a felon in possession of a gun. Shortly after Davis's indictment, the Supreme Court agreed to revisit the scope of the search-incident-to-arrest exception to the Fourth Amendment.

A bit of background is helpful. In 1981, in *New York v. Belton*,[50] the Supreme Court held that the police can routinely search the passenger compartment of a car after arresting its driver or passenger. *Belton* was widely understood to permit the police to lock an arrested driver or passenger in the back of the officer's squad car and then search the passenger compartment of the car. This holding was known as "the *Belton* rule." The Supreme Court appeared to accept that interpretation in a 2004 case, *Thornton v. United States*,[51] although separate opinions in *Thornton* suggested that the *Belton* rule was on thin ice and might be narrowed in a future decision.[52] When the Supreme Court granted certiorari to review the *Belton* rule in *Arizona v. Gant*,[53] it became clear that the rule might be overturned.

The certiorari grant in *Gant* created an opportunity for Davis. Under *Belton*, and the lower court precedent interpreting it, the officer's search of the car was constitutional. But the Supreme Court would soon consider overturning *Belton*. Under the retroactivity principle established by *Griffith v. Kentucky*,[54] whatever new decision was handed down in *Gant* would apply fully to all other cases not yet final. Because *Gant* would be handed down before Davis's case was final, Davis would receive the full benefit of whatever rule was handed down in *Gant*.

Importantly, the retroactivity rule announced in *Griffith* was established only after the Court had tried and ultimately rejected a very different approach. Starting in 1965, in *Linkletter v. Walker*,[55] the Court experimented with limited retroactivity in an attempt to cabin the

---

[50] 453 U.S. 454 (1981).

[51] 541 U.S. 615 (2004).

[52] See *id.* at 624–25 (O'Connor, J., concurring in part); *id.* at 625–32 (Scalia, J., concurring in the judgment).

[53] Arizona v. Gant, 552 U.S. 1230 (2008) (granting writ of certiorari).

[54] 479 U.S. 314 (1987).

[55] 381 U.S. 618 (1965).

exclusionary rule when criminal procedure rights expand. During the *Linkletter* era, the defendant in the actual case announcing a new criminal procedure rule received different treatment from all others in the pipeline. A decision applied retroactively to the defendant in the one case announcing the new rule to ensure that the decision was not dicta and to maintain an incentive to challenge the law.[56] The new decision did not apply retroactively to the other cases still in the pipeline, however, because such a decision would threaten many convictions and was not necessary to deter the police because they had acted in good faith.[57] But the Supreme Court had rejected that approach to retroactivity in *Griffith*, on the ground that basic principles of adjudication required treating the first case like all other cases on direct review.[58] Under *Griffith*, new criminal procedure decisions are retroactive to all cases not yet final.[59]

Soon after Davis filed his notice of appeal, the Supreme Court decided *Gant*. *Gant* rejected the *Belton* rule and announced a new and more defendant-friendly rule: Searches of cars are generally not permitted incident to arrest unless one of two exceptions applies. First, the driver or passenger must be within reaching distance of the car at the time of the search or, second, there must be reason to believe evidence relating to the crime of arrest was inside the car.[60] Because neither exception applied to the search of Davis's car, *Gant* rendered the search of Davis's car unconstitutional. And because Davis's case was not yet final, the retroactivity rule of *Griffith* ensured that Davis could benefit fully from *Gant*.

On direct appeal before the Eleventh Circuit, Judge Phyllis Kravitch agreed that Davis's Fourth Amendment rights had been violated and that *Gant* applied retroactively to Davis's case. Judge Kravitch nonetheless affirmed the conviction, ruling that the good-faith exception to the exclusionary rule applied.[61] Judge Kravitch reasoned that

---

[56] See, e.g., Stovall v. Denno, 388 U.S. 293, 301 (1967).

[57] See, e.g., Desist v. United States, 394 U.S. 244, 253 (1969).

[58] See Griffith, 479 U.S. at 320–28.

[59] *Id.* at 328.

[60] Arizona v. Gant, 129 S. Ct. 1710, 1723 (2009) ("Police may search a vehicle incident to a recent occupant's arrest only if the arrestee is within reaching distance of the passenger compartment at the time of the search or it is reasonable to believe the vehicle contains evidence of the offense of arrest.").

[61] United States v. Davis, 598 F.3d 1259 (11th Cir. 2010).

the purpose of the exclusionary rule was to deter police wrongdoing and that the police could not be deterred by a Supreme Court ruling handed down after a search. Because the officers had relied in good faith on Eleventh Circuit precedent interpreting *Belton*, the good-faith exception applied and the court affirmed the conviction.[62] Judge Kravitch recognized that such a rule could weaken defendants' incentive to argue for changes in the law, but she reasoned that the exclusionary rule was about deterrence, not "foster[ing] the development of Fourth Amendment law."[63]

The Supreme Court affirmed the Eleventh Circuit in a decision by Justice Samuel Alito. According to Justice Alito, the "bitter pill"[64] of the exclusionary rule could only be justified by wrongful police conduct. The police in *Davis* had followed then-existing law, however, and therefore had not acted wrongfully. To the contrary, the police had acted in an exemplary manner by following existing precedent "to the letter."[65] The police had done what they should have done, and therefore there was nothing to deter and the exclusionary rule had no place.

Justice Alito saw no conflict between the Court's ruling and the retroactivity principles established by *Griffith v. Kentucky*. According to him, retroactivity simply "raises the question" of whether the suppression remedy applies by allowing a defendant to "invoke" the new rule.[66] But whether a defendant can invoke the new rule is different from whether a remedy is actually available to enforce it. Justice Alito reasoned that the availability of a remedy was a question of the good-faith exception, not retroactivity. Thus there was no contradiction between concluding that *Gant* applied retroactively and concluding that Davis could not obtain a remedy because his search preceded *Gant*.

Justice Alito next considered the defendant's argument that the absence of a remedy would stunt the development of Fourth Amendment law by discouraging defense challenges to precedents. Such considerations were irrelevant, Alito concluded, because "the *sole*

---

[62] *Id.* at 1266.
[63] *Id.* at 1266 n.8.
[64] Davis, 131 S. Ct. at 2427.
[65] *Id.* at 2428.
[66] *Id.* at 2431.

purpose of the exclusionary rule is to deter misconduct by law enforcement."[67] Even assuming law development was relevant, lower court precedents could still be challenged: A good-faith exception for binding precedent permitted defendants in one circuit to challenge precedents in other circuits, which might then lead to a circuit split that could, in turn, prompt Supreme Court review. Concerns that the Court's rule would insulate Supreme Court decisions from review were overblown because defendants could still frame their arguments as efforts to distinguish binding cases rather than overturn them.

Alito did not entirely shut the door to relief when a defendant successfully persuades the Court to overturn its own precedent. In such a case, the Court would at least consider granting relief:

> Davis's argument might suggest that—to prevent Fourth Amendment law from becoming ossified—the petitioner in a case that results in the overruling of one of this Court's Fourth Amendment precedents should be given the benefit of the victory by permitting the suppression of evidence in that one case. . . . Therefore, in a future case, we could, if necessary, recognize a limited exception to the good-faith exception for a defendant who obtains a judgment overruling one of our Fourth Amendment precedents.[68]

Because the relevant change in the law had already occurred in *Gant*, relief was clearly unavailable in *Davis*.

Justice Stephen Breyer dissented, joined by Justice Ruth Bader Ginsburg.[69] The majority's attempted distinction between retroactivity and the good-faith exception was "highly artificial,"[70] Breyer contended, and amounted to overturning the rule of *Griffith* in Fourth Amendment cases. If the Court did ultimately recognize that the first case must be treated differently from later cases to ensure incentives to argue for changes in the law, then the Court had simply recreated all the problems it had faced during the *Linkletter* retroactivity era. On the other hand, if the Court rejected a remedy even in the first case, then the Court had eliminated all incentives to

---

[67] *Id.* at 2432 (emphasis in the original) (citations omitted).
[68] *Id.* at 2433–34.
[69] *Id.* at 2436–40 (Breyer, J., dissenting).
[70] *Id.* at 2437 (Breyer, J., dissenting).

challenge the law: The defendant would lose on relief even if he won on the merits, and would no longer challenge adverse precedents.[71]

IV. The Hope of Law Development without Remedies

Both *Camreta v. Greene* and *Davis v. United States* wrestle with the tension between the development of Fourth Amendment law and the availability of Fourth Amendment remedies. The case-by-case elaboration of Fourth Amendment law requires a stream of cases, and a stream of cases generally demands remedies to create cases and controversies and to encourage claims to be brought. The proper scope of those remedies raises difficult questions. Their potential costs are obvious in the short run. Criminals may go free, and police officers may be held personally liable. The long-term benefits are harder to assess. For generalist justices, the broad arc of Fourth Amendment development is at best an abstraction. And how clear is "clear enough" for Fourth Amendment law? Searches and seizures touch on so many types of government conduct, and the Supreme Court addresses so few of them, that the clarity of Fourth Amendment law may strike the justices as a difficult variable to measure and value.

Both *Camreta* and *Davis* suggest that today's justices are more focused on limiting the short-term costs of Fourth Amendment litigation than on the needs of developing Fourth Amendment law. Both cases experiment with Fourth Amendment law development in a regime of zero or extremely limited remedies. In *Davis*, the Court's wish to limit the exclusionary rule for Fourth Amendment violations triggered what amounts in practice to a Fourth Amendment exception from traditional retroactivity rules. The growth of the law was treated at most as an afterthought—something that might justify a very minor tweak down the road if necessary but was much less significant than the costs of suppression. While *Camreta* discussed the needs of law development, it did so only within the confines of the Court's embrace of qualified immunity and the recent rule of *Pearson v. Callahan*. The justices' desire to allow law development within the zone of qualified immunity pushed the Court to find a way to review lower court decisions in a remedy-free zone.

---

[71] *Id.* at 2438 (Breyer, J., dissenting).

More broadly, *Camreta* and *Davis* suggest a hope that remedies can be minimized in Fourth Amendment litigation without substantially affecting the substance of Fourth Amendment law. In civil cases, the thinking runs, state officials will want "clearance" from Fourth Amendment restrictions and civil plaintiffs will litigate because they fear being searched or seized again in the future. In criminal cases, defendants will somehow make the needed challenges even if no remedies are available. Put together, *Camreta* and *Davis* hint at a Field of Dreams-like optimism about Fourth Amendment remedies and law development. As long as the courts are open, claims will be litigated that enable law development regardless of the remedies. Build it and they will come.

This optimism isn't new. *Camreta* builds on the Court's 2009 decision in *Pearson v. Callahan*,[72] which overturned the law-developing two-step requirement of *Saucier v. Katz*.[73] *Davis* builds on the Court's 2009 decision in *Herring v. United States*,[74] which introduced the focus on culpability as a key to the application of the exclusionary rule. In each of those cases, the Court has moved toward less law development, fewer remedies, or both. Significantly, the trend is coming from all directions simultaneously. When the Court chips away at law development in civil cases, it points to the continuing availability of law development using other remedies, such as the exclusionary rule.[75] When the Court chips away at the exclusionary rule, it points to the continuing availability of law development with other remedies, including civil liability.[76] Cases in each context point to the others, but all seem to be moving in the same direction at the same time.[77]

---

[72] 555 U.S. 223 (2009).

[73] 533 U.S. 194 (2001).

[74] 555 U.S. 135 (2009).

[75] See, e.g., Pearson v. Callahan, 555 U.S. 223, 242–43 (2009) (noting that "the development of constitutional law is by no means entirely dependent on cases in which the defendant may seek qualified immunity.").

[76] Davis, 131 S. Ct. at 2433. Justice Alito authored the opinions in both *Davis* and *Pearson*.

[77] Several cases point to the continuing availability of municipal liability and injunctive or declaratory relief, although those remedies are so narrow they are almost never a significant engine of Fourth Amendment law development. See Orin S. Kerr, The Limits of Fourth Amendment Injunctions, 7 J. Telecom. & High Tech. L. 127 (2009).

How far might the justices go? The opinions leave some major hints. On its face, for example, *Davis* only concerns objectively reasonable reliance on "binding precedent."[78] If the exclusionary rule solely concerns culpability, however, its hard to see why binding precedent is required. Reliance on binding precedent seems inherently reasonable, but reliance is often reasonable without binding precedent. A local police officer who conducts a search widely upheld among the circuits but not yet addressed by the federal circuit in his jurisdiction is no more culpable than an officer who conducts a search upheld only by his regional circuit. If the former has acted reasonably, then surely so has the latter. Given that the deferential standard of qualified immunity law has been the standard of objective reasonableness in Fourth Amendment law,[79] and has been equated in some contexts with the good-faith exception to the exclusionary rule,[80] the Court may be headed toward limiting the exclusionary rule to the rare instances when police conduct is so egregious that qualified immunity does not apply.[81]

---

[78] See Davis, 131 S. Ct. at 2428 ("The question in this case is whether to apply the exclusionary rule when the police conduct a search in objectively reasonable reliance on binding judicial precedent."). Exactly what counts as "binding" precedent can be unclear. A federal circuit precedent is binding in federal court but not binding in state court. Similarly, a state supreme court case is binding in state court but not in federal court. If a federal circuit has approved a search but the state supreme court has not, does the exclusionary rule apply in state court but not in federal court? Given the concurrent jurisdiction of many criminal cases, especially drug cases, this would be a very odd result.

Similarly, the line between reliance on circuit court precedent and reliance on Supreme Court precedent remains murky. Eleventh Circuit precedent on *Belton* had simply recited the *Belton* rule in a case with facts quite similar to *Belton*. See United States v. Gonzalez, 71 F.3d 819, 822, 824–27 (11th Cir. 1996). Justice Alito announced in *Davis* that the officer had reasonably relied on circuit precedent rather than Supreme Court precedent. Davis, 131 S. Ct. at 2434 (stating that the police "reasonably relied on binding Circuit precedent"). It is difficult to know why that was true. It would be odd if mere recognition of a Supreme Court precedent by a circuit court transformed an officer's search from one made in objective reliance on Supreme Court precedent to one made in objective reliance on circuit court precedent.

[79] See Pearson, 555 U.S. at 243–44.

[80] See Malley v. Briggs, 475 U. S. 335, 344–45 (1986).

[81] Cf. Jennifer E. Laurin, Trawling for Herring: Lessons in Doctrinal Borrowing and Convergence, 111 Colum. L. Rev. 670 (2011). See also Davis, 131 S. Ct. at 2434–36 (Sotomayor, J., concurring in the judgment) (noting that the good-faith exception does not necessarily apply when the governing law is uncertain).

My own preference would be for the Court to reverse course and retain more robust remedies for Fourth Amendment violations. The importance of Fourth Amendment law development is far greater than a majority of the current Court realizes. Many of the doctrines that limit Fourth Amendment remedies do so without hindering law development, and they should be retained.[82] But the Court should be wary of adopting a remedies scheme that leaves law development to hope, or that imagines it can occur without real remedies. Governments employ about 870,000 law enforcement officers in the United States,[83] and the Fourth Amendment regulates them together with many other government actors. Effective regulation of these officers' conduct requires real stakes in litigation over a wide range of cases.

This is particularly true given the close connection between the Fourth Amendment and developing technology. The bad guys are constantly coming up with new ways to commit crimes, and the police are constantly devising new ways to catch them. The introduction of new technology in criminal investigations often raises fresh and difficult questions of Fourth Amendment law. The new technology changes the implication of the old rules, and the question is if and how the Fourth Amendment should adapt.[84] The strong Fourth Amendment remedies of the past have ensured that the law governing older technologies is largely settled and clear. Every cop knows how the law applies to the ubiquitous traffic stop that governs that

---

[82] For example, I would retain the current doctrines on standing, inevitable discovery, independent source, and the fruit of the poisonous tree. For a range of reasons beyond the scope of this essay, these doctrines limit the scope of the exclusionary rule in ways that do not substantially interfere with its role in elaborating the scope of Fourth Amendment law.

[83] As of 2008, there were 765,000 sworn law enforcement personnel with general arrest powers at the state and local levels. See Brian A. Reaves, Census of State and Local Law Enforcement Agencies, 1 (2008), available at http://bjs.ojp.usdoj.gov/content/pub/pdf/csllea08.pdf. As of 2004, there were 105,000 sworn law enforcement personnel with general arrest powers at the federal level. See Brian A. Reaves, Census of Federal, Law Enforcement Agencies, 1 (2004), available at http://bjs.ojp.usdoj.gov/content/pub/pdf/fleo04.pdf. If we assume the numbers today roughly match the numbers from 2004 and 2008, the combined total is 870,000 law enforcement officers.

[84] See Orin S. Kerr, An Equilibrium-Adjustment Theory of the Fourth Amendment, 125 Harv. L. Rev. (forthcoming 2011), available at http://papers.ssrn.com/sol3/papers.cfm?abstract;usid = 1748222.

great 20th-century technology, the automobile. But the law governing new technologies is murky, and the limited remedies of the Fourth Amendment are largely to blame.

Consider the long road to the first appellate ruling on whether the Fourth Amendment protects email. Although email has been used widely since the early 1990s, the first circuit court decision on how the Fourth Amendment applies to email was not handed down until 2007.[85] That Sixth Circuit decision was overturned on remedies grounds without reaching the merits, however: The en banc court ruled that the limits of injunctive remedies precluded relief.[86] Next, the Eleventh Circuit ruled on the subject in 2010.[87] That opinion too was overturned on remedies grounds without reaching the merits: The panel granted rehearing and issued a new opinion deciding the case on qualified immunity grounds.[88]

The first appellate ruling on the Fourth Amendment and email that has stayed on the books appeared only recently, and it required reaching out despite the prevailing remedies scheme to get there. In December 2010, the Sixth Circuit revisited Fourth Amendment protection for email in reviewing a motion to suppress.[89] The government's brief sought to have the court decide the case on remedies grounds by invoking the good-faith exception for reliance on statutory law, without reaching whether the Fourth Amendment had been violated.[90] The Sixth Circuit rebuffed the government's approach and instead handed down a ruling on the merits. According to the Sixth Circuit, deciding the case on the good-faith exception would make the limited remedies "a perpetual shield against the consequences of government violations."[91]

While a single circuit court ruling now addresses email protection, it has been a long road thanks to the Court's narrow remedies scheme. And how long would the road have been if remedies had been cut back even more?

---

[85] Warshak v. United States, 490 F.3d 455, 460 (6th Cir. 2007).

[86] Warshak v. United States, 532 F.3d 521 (6th Cir. 2008).

[87] Rehberg v. Paulk, 598 F.3d 1268 (11th Cir. 2010).

[88] Rehberg v. Paulk, 611 F.3d 828 (11th Cir. 2010) cert. granted, 131 S. Ct. 1678 (2011).

[89] United States v. Warshak, 631 F.3d 266 (6th Cir. 2010).

[90] Brief for Plaintiff-Appellee United States at 105–20, United States v. Warshak 631 F.3d 266 (6th Cir. 2010) (No. 08-3997), 2009 WL 3392997.

[91] Warshak, 631 F.3d at 282 n.13.

V. The Future of Law Development without Remedies

Whatever my own preferences, it appears likely that the Supreme Court will soon take more steps toward requiring Fourth Amendment development in a zone of limited or no remedies. Let's assume that prediction comes true. In 10 or 20 years, Fourth Amendment remedies will be more limited than they are today. The question becomes, what legal rules or procedures might enhance law development in that future? Fourth Amendment remedies are a well-covered subject in the literature, and perhaps there are no new proposals under the sun. But let me offer two ideas that may be among the more fruitful: a *Saucier*-like rule for motions to suppress and active involvement of the justices in adding questions presented in Supreme Court litigation.

If the Court eventually aligns the exclusionary rule with qualified immunity, the development of the Fourth Amendment would be sharply stunted. Because liability would attach only when the constitutional violation seemed rather obvious, law-developing claims would arise mostly when the lack of a suppression was clear. If that comes to pass, some sort of *Saucier* rule governing the reaching of merits claims may become necessary. When it remained good law, *Saucier* required courts to first evaluate the merits of Fourth Amendment claims and then to turn, if necessary, to qualified immunity. A similar rule could require courts to evaluate the merits of Fourth Amendment claims in motions to suppress before proceeding to the remedy.

At first blush, such a rule might seem quite unlikely to be adopted. The Court recently rejected *Saucier* in *Pearson*,[92] and the Court has traditionally rejected a *Saucier*-type rule in the suppression context.[93] The critical difference is the tremendous loss of law-developing litigation that would follow adoption of a qualified immunity standard. The extent of law development in Fourth Amendment damages cases is relatively modest, as is law development in the context

---

[92] 555 U.S. 223 (2009).

[93] United States v. Leon, 468 U.S. 897, 924–25 (1984) ("There is no need for courts to adopt the inflexible practice of always deciding whether the officers' conduct manifested objective good faith before turning to the question of whether the Fourth Amendment has been violated.").

of defective warrants where the good-faith exception originally arose.[94]

The exclusionary rule is different. It has served as the engine of settling Fourth Amendment law since its inception. Without an exclusionary rule, many of the basic rules of Fourth Amendment law that govern everyday interactions with the police might still be unclear.[95] The loss of clarity that would follow adopting the qualified immunity standard for all suppression claims would be dramatic. In my view, that difference could justify different treatment. If the Court insists on moving toward law development in a zone of limited remedies, it may need a *Saucier*-like rule to ensure that limited remedies don't end law development.

An alternative approach would be for the Supreme Court to take a more active role in law development by adding questions presented when it agrees to review Fourth Amendment claims. In most Supreme Court litigation, the petitioner crafts the questions the Court should answer. When the Court grants a petition for certiorari, it usually adopts the question presented by the petition in whole or in part. The Court always has the option of adding questions, however. If the remedies of Fourth Amendment law recede, the Court may need to fuel law development by adding its own questions for parties to brief that the Court can then decide.

This process already occurs occasionally in Fourth Amendment litigation, and there is some evidence of a recent uptick in its frequency. In *Pearson v. Callahan*, the Court added the question of whether to overturn *Saucier*.[96] And earlier this year, the Supreme Court added the question of whether police installation of a GPS

---

[94] See *id.*

[95] Experience with the Electronic Communications Privacy Act, the federal statute that governs email and computer network privacy, provides a helpful illustration. Congress passed the ECPA in 1986 without a statutory suppression remedy. The lack of a suppression remedy has made the statute a source of remarkable confusion: Legal challenges brought under the statute do not arise in the context in which the statute was intended to be used, meaning that there is no case law answering how the statute applies in many routine settings. See generally Orin S. Kerr, Lifting the "Fog" of Internet Surveillance: How a Suppression Remedy Would Change Computer Crime Law, 54 Hastings L.J. 805 (2003).

[96] Pearson, 555 U.S. at 227 ("In granting review, we required the parties to address the additional question whether the mandatory procedure set out in Saucier should be retained.").

device on a car is a search or seizure when it granted certiorari in *United States v. Jones*.[97] In *Pearson*, the petitioners did not think to petition for review on the issue added by the Court because it was not a question that affected the parties' rights. In *Jones*, the respondent's brief opposing certiorari suggested the addtional question,[98] and the Court added it even though it had not been decided below and there was no circuit split. The Court's decision to add the questions presented pushed the law along, facilitating new holdings that would not have occured without the Court's initiative.

This solution is admittedly imperfect. It requires the justices to know what issues need review without much guidance by the parties. Given that the justices are generalists, that sort of forethought will arise only sporadically. Plus, if the issue added does not clearly affect the rights of the parties, the parties may see little reason to litigate it fully. In *Pearson*, for example, the parties had no particular stake in the future of *Saucier*. Because *Pearson* was briefed and argued by private lawyers without government involvement, and overturning *Saucier* only concerned the order of issues rather than their resolution, the parties had little interest in litigating the question. The petitioners' brief devoted only six pages to overturning *Saucier* and the respondent's brief gave it only eight pages.[99] Substantial contributions by various amici filled the gap, to be sure, but the basic point about adding questions with no obvious stakes to the parties remains.

Despite these problems, there may be no better options if the Supreme Court substantially cuts back on Fourth Amendment remedies. If the remedies needed to drive litigation and generate cases wither away, the Court itself may be best situated to restore cases to the docket by adding questions beyond those raised in petitions for certiorari.

[97] See United States v. Jones, No. 10-1259, 2011 WL 1456728, at *1 (June 27, 2011) ("In addition to the question presented by the petition, the parties are directed to brief and argue the following question: 'Whether the government violated respondent's Fourth Amendment rights by installing the GPS tracking device on his vehicle without a valid warrant and without his consent.'").

[98] See Brief in Opposition at 33–34, United States v. Jones (No. 10-1259), available at http://sblog.s3.amazonaws.com/wp-content/uploads/2011/06/Jones-BIO.pdf.

[99] See Brief for Petitioners at 55–60, Pearson v. Callahan, 555 U.S. 223 (2009) (No. 07-751) 2008 WL 4154542 at 55–60; Brief for Respondent at 48–56, Pearson v. Callahan, 555 U.S. 223 (2009) (No. 07-751), 2008 WL 3895481 at *48–56.

Conclusion

The debate over Fourth Amendment remedies has traditionally focused on deterrence. Despite this focus, remedies such as suppression and damages have had an equally significant role over time in ensuring the case-by-case elaboration of Fourth Amendment law. This term's decisions in *Camreta v. Greene* and *Davis v. United States* suggest that today's Court is willing to limit those remedies—and to bend traditional principles of adjudication—to lessen their costs. If that trend continues, the development of Fourth Amendment law may be threatened. Whether the police are following the law may be subsumed by the more pressing question of whether anyone knows what law the police are supposed to follow. Such concerns may seem abstract to the justices today. But today's decisions on remedies will have a major impact on tomorrow's decisions about Fourth Amendment substance. A greater eye toward the law-developing function of remedies today will pay dividends in the future.

Into the Preemption Thicket Again—Five Times!

Roger Pilon*

Two years ago on these pages, I ventured into the preemption thicket in *Wyeth v. Levine*,[1] a decision noteworthy for the Supreme Court's having made a hash of things.[2] Writing in dissent, Justice Samuel Alito remarked that the majority had turned a simple medical malpractice suit "into a 'frontal assault' on the FDA's regulatory regime for drug labeling."[3] Undaunted, or perhaps spurred on, by the frequent criticisms of its long string of "difficult-to-reconcile preemption rulings,"[4] the Court this term decided no fewer than five preemption cases,[5] almost equaling the six it decided in its 2007 term.[6] And once again it has produced a mixed record, getting it right in three of the cases, not in the other two—or so I shall argue.

Although each of the cases decided this term turns on statutory interpretation, preemption itself takes us to basic constitutional principles. To place the discussion in a constitutional context, therefore,

---

* Roger Pilon is vice president for legal affairs at the Cato Institute, director of Cato's Center for Constitutional Studies, and publisher of the *Cato Supreme Court Review*.

[1] 555 U.S. 555; 129 S. Ct. 1187 (2009).

[2] Roger Pilon, Into the Pre-emption Thicket: *Wyeth v. Levine*, 2008–2009 Cato Sup. Ct. Rev. 85 (2009).

[3] Wyeth, 129 S. Ct. at 1218 (Alito, J., dissenting).

[4] See, e.g., Eric G. Lasker, U.S. Supreme Court Preemption Trilogy: The Sequel, 26 Wash. Legal Found. Backgrounder 7, Mar. 25, 2011, available at http://www.wlf.org/publishing/publication;usdetail.asp?id=2236.

[5] Six, if you count *Am. Elec. Power Co. v. Connecticut*, 131 S. Ct. 2527 (2011), where the Court simply noted at the end that "[i]n light of our holding that the Clean Air Act displaces federal common law, the availability *vel non* of a state lawsuit depends, *inter alia*, on the preemptive effect of the federal Act," suggesting that the Act preempts any such state law remedy. *Id.* at 2540.

[6] See Daniel E. Troy & Rebecca K. Wood, Federal Preemption at the Supreme Court, 2007–2008 Cato Sup. Ct. Rev. 257 (2008).

and for the benefit of readers unfamiliar with this complex area of our law, I will begin with a brief outline of those principles.

Preemption as Federal Supremacy

To better protect liberty, the Constitution institutes federalism, a system of dual sovereignty between the federal and state governments, sometimes pitting power against power, other times allowing overlapping power.[7] Although the Tenth Amendment makes it clear that the federal government's powers are delegated and hence limited, the balance of power being reserved to the states or the people,[8] the Supremacy Clause of Article VI resolves conflicts between federal and state law by providing that federal law "shall be the supreme Law of the Land, . . . any Thing in the Constitution or Laws of any State to the Contrary notwithstanding." Thus, although the Tenth Amendment establishes a fairly clear presumption in favor of the states, when state law conflicts with—is "to the Contrary" of— federal law, the presumption, by virtue of the Supremacy Clause, is on the other side, with federal law.

In any preemption case, therefore, the crucial question is whether the relevant federal and state laws do in fact conflict—oftentimes not an easy question to answer. In some cases, federal law *expressly* preempts state law, yet even there the statutory terms may be ambiguous or subject to manipulation.[9] Moreover, as in three of the cases

---

[7] See The Federalist No. 51 (James Madison).

[8] "The powers not delegated to the United States by the Constitution, nor prohibited by it to the States, are reserved to the States respectively, or to the people." U.S. Const. amend. X.

[9] See, e.g., Michael Greve, Preemption Strike, Nat'l Review Online, Mar. 23, 2009, http://www.nationalreview.com/articles/227135/preemption-strike/michael-greve:

> Because Congress cannot possibly foresee [all state] stratagems, it cannot "clearly" preempt them. For example, the clearest federal preemption provision of all prohibits states from administering "a law or regulation related to fuel economy standards." California's proposed greenhouse-gas standards do not simply "relate to" fuel economy; they *are* fuel-economy standards. Even so, federal courts have upheld them against preemption challenges because California describes them as emission standards instead. (original emphasis)

For examples of courts rejecting preemption challenges of this type, see, e.g., Cent. Valley Chrysler-Jeep v. Goldstene, 529 F. Supp. 2d 1151 (E.D. Cal. 2007) and Green Mountain Chrysler-Plymouth-Dodge v. Crombie, 508 F. Supp. 2d 295 (D. Vt. 2007).

this term, a federal statute that expressly preempts state law may contain a "saving clause" that preserves at least some of the state law over the matter at issue. Quite often, however, courts face only *implied* preemption, of which there are two kinds. Field preemption concerns limited but exclusive areas of federal authority, even without any express congressional statement to that effect. More common, and more difficult, are cases in which preemption is implicit insofar as a party finds it impossible to comply with both federal and state law, or, more difficult still, insofar as state law stands as an obstacle to the accomplishment and execution of the full "purposes and objectives" of the federal law.

Finally, as Justice Clarence Thomas notes in one of this term's cases, *PLIVA v. Mensing*,[10] the *non obstante* ("notwithstanding") provision of the Supremacy Clause "suggests that federal law should be understood to impliedly repeal conflicting state law, . . . that courts should not strain to find ways to reconcile federal law with seemingly conflicting state law," and "that pre-emption analysis should not involve speculation about ways in which federal agency and third-party actions could potentially reconcile federal duties with conflicting state duties."[11] In a word, a statute's "ordinary meaning" should speak for itself. And even if the Court does "get it right" in a preemption case by reading the law correctly, that does not mean, of course, that the decision necessarily secures or advances the liberty the Constitution was written, at bottom, to secure. That will be a function, rather, of whether Congress and federal agencies, on one hand, or states, on the other, have done a better job of regulating toward that end.

Before turning to the cases, a note on the "politics" of preemption is in order, not least because it can be confusing. As I wrote two years ago:

> One ordinarily thinks of conservatives and libertarians as supporting limited federal power, especially police power over health and safety matters, a power that belongs mainly with the states. Yet here, for constitutional reasons just discussed, most such people believe that in many if not most cases federal power should trump state power. By contrast,

[10] 131 S. Ct. 2567 (2011).

[11] *Id.* at 2580.

modern liberals are ordinarily thought to favor federal power, especially federal regulatory power over economic affairs under Congress's power to regulate interstate commerce. Yet many of those liberals, in the tort bar and among consumer advocates and state officials, will be found arguing for the supremacy of state law as providing more protection for individual "rights" than federal law may provide. [12]

Those political tendencies can be seen, in part, in the five preemption cases the Court decided this term. Federal preemption was found in three of the five, and in all three the Court's conservatives were in the majority; two were decided 5-4, the other was decided 6-2, with Justice Stephen Breyer joining the conservatives, but writing separately. Of the two decisions that went for the states, one was unanimous; the other was decided 5-3, but here again it was the Court's conservatives who were in the majority. Yet this case, *Chamber of Commerce v. Whiting,*[13] upheld the Legal Arizona Workers Act against a challenge by business interests, so one could read the decision "politically" as saying that, for the conservatives, immigration trumped business, and for the liberals, the other way around. Or one could say, more charitably, that the two sides simply read the law differently.

In any case, my concern here is less with politics than with what the Constitution requires, and so I turn now to the cases, starting with *Whiting.*

Chamber of Commerce v. Whiting

Whiting is a fairly straightforward case. Again, the U.S. Chamber of Commerce and various business and civil rights organizations brought a pre-enforcement suit against state officials charged with administering Arizona's Legal Arizona Workers Act, which provides that the licenses of state employers who knowingly or intentionally employ unauthorized aliens may be, and in certain circumstances must be, suspended or revoked. Arizona's law also requires that all Arizona employers use the federal E-Verify system to determine the immigration status of their employees.

---

[12] Pilon, *supra* note 2, at 87 (internal citations omitted).
[13] 131 S. Ct. 1968 (2011).

In its suit, the Chamber argued that the provisions of Arizona's law "allowing the suspension and revocation of business licenses for employing unauthorized aliens were both expressly and impliedly preempted by federal immigration law, and that the mandatory use of E-Verify was impliedly preempted"[14]—citing the federal Immigration Reform and Control Act, which expressly preempts "any State or local law imposing civil or criminal sanctions (*other than through licensing and similar laws*) upon those who employ . . . unauthorized aliens."[15] Clearly, however, a saving clause is embedded within the express preemption provision. Accordingly, Chief Justice John Roberts, writing for the Court in the 5-3 decision (Justice Elena Kagan took no part in the decision), held that because "the State's licensing provisions fall squarely within the federal statute's savings clause and . . . the Arizona regulation does not otherwise conflict with federal law, . . . the Arizona law is not preempted."[16] He thus affirmed both the district court and the Ninth Circuit panel that had previously ruled in the case.

Given IRCA's plain text, a brief summary of Roberts's opinion will suffice here. He makes three main points. First, because "Arizona's licensing law falls well within the confines of the authority Congress chose to leave to the States,"[17] it is not expressly preempted—a conclusion he buttresses by showing, in excruciating detail, how the state's definition of "license" largely "parrots" the definition that Congress codified in the Administrative Procedure Act.[18] Second, he responds to the Chamber's contention that the state's law is impliedly preempted because it conflicts with federal law by showing, again in painstaking detail, that there is no conflict and that "Arizona's procedures simply implement the sanctions that Congress expressly allowed Arizona to pursue through licensing laws."[19] Here, he notes in particular that "Arizona went the extra mile in ensuring that its law closely tracks IRCA's provisions in all material

---

[14] *Id.* at 1977.
[15] *Id.* at 1973 (quoting 8 U.S.C. § 1324a(h)(2)) (emphasis added).
[16] *Id.*
[17] *Id.* at 1981.
[18] *Id.* at 1978.
[19] *Id.* at 1981.

respects."[20] Finally, he shows that Arizona's E-Verify mandate neither conflicts with the federal scheme nor obstructs federal objectives. "In fact," he points out, "the Federal Government has consistently expanded and encouraged the use of E-Verify" and, indeed, recently referenced Arizona's mandate as a permissible use of the system.[21] Thus, the mandate cannot be shown to be impliedly preempted.

In their dissents, Justice Breyer, writing for himself and for Justice Ruth Bader Ginsburg, and Justice Sonia Sotomayer, writing for herself, rely heavily on legislative history. But as Roberts notes, "It is not surprising that the two dissents have sharply different views on how to read the statute. That is the sort of thing that can happen when statutory analysis is so untethered from the text."[22] In sum, quite apart from the merits or demerits of our current immigration law, policy, and practices, given the text and the facts, this was not a difficult case, as three courts found.

AT&T v. Concepcion

Concepcion[23] is rather more complicated. Here too a saving clause was at issue, but here—where AT&T argued that the Federal Arbitration Act preempted state law, not expressly but by implication, due to a conflict between the two—the clause did not save state law. In brief, the Court held, 5-4, that the FAA preempted a California state court ruling that standard-form ("adhesion") consumer arbitration contracts that prohibit class arbitration are unconscionable and hence unenforceable. But a core purpose of the FAA, the Supreme Court said, was to allow and encourage companies to use arbitration as a fast and efficient way to resolve consumer disputes, which class arbitration would only frustrate. Thus, California's law was in direct conflict with the federal law.

The case arose when the Concepcions charged AT&T with false advertising and fraud after they were charged a $30.22 sales tax on the retail value of a "free" phone under a standard-form service contract with AT&T. The contract provided for arbitration of all

---

[20] *Id.*

[21] *Id.* at 1986.

[22] *Id.* at 1980 n.6.

[23] AT&T Mobility LLC. v. Concepcion, 131 S. Ct. 1740 (2011).

disputes, but required plaintiffs to arbitrate as individuals, not as members of a class. In defense, AT&T invoked the FAA, which makes agreements to arbitrate "valid, irrevocable, and enforceable, *save upon such grounds as exist at law or in equity for the revocation of any contract.*"[24] To try to revoke the contract as provided for in that saving clause, the Concepcions cited the California Supreme Court's *Discover Bank* decision, which held that class waivers in consumer arbitration agreements are unconscionable if the agreement is in an adhesion contract, the damages are small, and the party with inferior bargaining power alleges a deliberate scheme of fraud.[25] The courts below found for the Concepcions: the FAA's saving clause was satisfied by the *Discover Bank* rule, they held; thus, the FAA did not preempt the state law. The Supreme Court reversed, finding that the state law "stands as an obstacle to the accomplishment and execution of the full purposes and objectives of Congress."[26] Thus, the FAA does indeed preempt the state law.

Writing for the Court, Justice Antonin Scalia begins by noting that the FAA was enacted in 1925 in response to widespread judicial hostility to arbitration agreements, that it reflects both a federal policy favoring arbitration and the "fundamental principle that arbitration is a matter of contract,"[27] and that "courts must place arbitration agreements on an equal footing with other contracts and enforce them according to their terms."[28] Turning then to the central question, the force and effect of the FAA's saving clause, he writes that it "permits agreements to arbitrate to be invalidated by '*generally applicable contract defenses, such as fraud, duress, or unconscionability,*' but not by defenses that apply only to arbitration or that derive their meaning from the fact that an agreement to arbitrate is at issue."[29] Thus, he concludes, the question is whether the FAA "preempts California's rule classifying most collective-arbitration waivers in consumer contracts as unconscionable," or, one could

---

[24] *Id.* at 1744 (citing 9 U.S.C. § 2) (emphasis added).

[25] Discover Bank v. Superior Court, 113 P.3d 1100 (Cal. 2005).

[26] Concepcion, 131 S. Ct. at 1753 (citing Hines v. Davidowitz, 312 U.S. 52, 67 (1941)).

[27] *Id.* at 1745 (citing Rent-A-Center, West, Inc. v. Jackson, 130 S. Ct. 2772, 2776 (2010)).

[28] *Id.* at 1745 (citations omitted).

[29] *Id.* at 1748 (citing Doctor's Associates, Inc. v. Casarotto, 517 U.S. 681, 687 (1996)) (emphasis added).

add, whether the *Discover Bank* rule satisfies the brake imposed on preemption by the FAA's saving clause.

The issue here, Scalia argues, goes back to the long-standing hostility of courts to arbitration agreements, especially in California,[30] and to the tendency of courts to expand the body of "generally applicable contract defenses" to include ever narrower grounds for contract revocation. Thus, he writes that although the FAA's saving clause

> preserves generally applicable contract defenses, nothing in it suggests an intent to preserve state-law rules that stand as an obstacle to the accomplishment of the FAA's objectives. As we have said, a federal statute's saving clause "cannot in reason be construed as [allowing] a common law right, the continued existence of which would be absolutely inconsistent with the provisions of the act. In other words, the act cannot be held to destroy itself."[31]

Yet that is what allowing the *Discover Bank* rule as a ground for revoking the arbitration agreement at issue here would do, Scalia continues. Requiring class-wide arbitration to be available if a party requests it, notwithstanding the terms of the arbitral agreement, not only fails to enforce those terms but "interferes with fundamental attributes of arbitration and thus creates a scheme inconsistent with the FAA," the "principal purpose" of which is "to 'ensure that private arbitration agreements are enforced according to their terms.'"[32]

Scalia then goes on to show, first, how allowing parties discretion in designing arbitral agreements allows for efficient dispute resolution tailored to their circumstances and, second, how allowing parties to opt out of their agreements regarding class-wide arbitration would utterly frustrate the purposes of arbitration. Indeed, the Court had previously held that the "changes brought about by the shift

---

[30] *Id.* at 1747 ("it is worth noting that California's courts have been more likely to hold contracts to arbitrate unconscionable than other contracts") (citing Stephen A. Broome, An Unconscionable Applicable of the Unconscionability Doctrine: How the California Courts are Circumventing the Federal Arbitration Act, 3 Hastings Bus. L. J. 39, 54, 66 (2006)); Susan Randall, Judicial Attitudes toward Arbitration and the Resurgence of Unconscionability, 52 Buffalo L. Rev. 185, 186–87 (2004).

[31] Concepcion, 131 S. Ct. at 1748 (citations omitted).

[32] *Id.*

from bilateral arbitration to class-action arbitration" are "fundamental."[33] Class-action arbitration, for example, sacrifices informality—in fact, requires *procedural* formality—"and makes the process slower, more costly, and more likely to generate procedural morass than final judgment," as the evidence clearly shows.[34] Moreover, the formality that class arbitration requires in turn imposes duties on arbitrators that are inconsistent with quick and efficient arbitration. And with limited judicial review, class arbitration greatly increases the risks for defendants, especially when the stakes are high from aggregation, pressuring them to settle questionable claims. Those are just a few of the ways class arbitration shifts the balance and conflicts with the FAA's purposes.

In his dissent for himself and Justices Ginsburg, Sotomayor, and Kagan, ending in a stern plea for honoring federalist principles, Justice Breyer never really addresses the importance of honoring contracts. His focus instead is on the power of the California court to say what contracts it will and will not enforce. Thus, he writes that "California is free to define unconscionability as it sees fit, and its common law is of no federal concern so long as the State does not adopt a special rule that disfavors arbitration."[35] That, of course, is just what the California court did, as Scalia details—adding that "[w]e find it hard to believe that defendants would bet the company with no effective means of review, and even harder to believe that Congress would have intended to allow state courts to force such a decision."[36]

But Breyer continues:

> Because California applies the same legal principles to address the unconscionability of class arbitration waivers as it does to address the unconscionability of any other contractual provision, the merits of class proceedings should not factor into our decision. If California had applied its law of duress to void an arbitration agreement, would it matter if the procedures in the coerced agreement were efficient?[37]

---

[33] Stolt-Nielsen S.A. v. AnimalFeeds Int'l Corp., 130 S. Ct. 1758, 1776 (2010).

[34] Concepcion, 131 S. Ct. at 1751.

[35] *Id.* at 1760 (Breyer, J., dissenting).

[36] *Id.* at 1752 (majority opinion).

[37] *Id.* at 1760 (Breyer, J., dissenting).

Here, of course, the merits matter, because the question is whether the class proceedings conflict with the purposes of the federal law. Indeed, here we have a "special rule that disfavors arbitration," the very subject of that law. Unlike the law of duress, that special rule does not apply to "any" contract, just to those that prohibit class-wide arbitration. Moreover, with duress there is no contract in the first place. Here there is a contract, enforceable in other states if not in California—the kind of contract the California court has singled out and made unenforceable, for *policy* reasons. As Scalia points out, of the two main purposes of the federal statute—enforcement of private agreements and encouragement of efficient and speedy dispute resolution—both are frustrated by the California court's rule and the dissent's view.

That brings us to one of the more interesting aspects of *Concepcion*, which is found in Justice Thomas's concurrence. Describing himself as reluctant to join the Court's opinion because of his (well-known) views on purposes-and-objectives preemption—the Court's approach here—Thomas writes separately to say that he would read the FAA's text as requiring

> that an agreement to arbitrate be enforced unless a party successfully challenges the *formation* of the arbitration agreement, such as by proving fraud or duress. Under this reading, I would reverse the Court of Appeals because a district court cannot follow both the FAA and the *Discover Bank* rule, which does not relate to defects in the *making* of an agreement.[38]

Thus, rather than resting preemption on the Court's discernment of the FAA's purposes, a methodology he has long criticized as fraught with subjectivity, Thomas would rest it on a kind of "impossibility" principle—not the impossibility of parties to comply with both federal and state law, which often justifies conflict preemption, but the impossibility of a *court's* following both laws.

Thomas supports his narrowing of the reach of the FAA's saving clause with a close analysis of the FAA's text. He first notes that the statute requires courts to enforce arbitration agreements as written, and that an arbitration provision "shall be valid, irrevocable, and enforceable, save upon such grounds as exist at law or in equity for

---

[38] *Id.* at 1753 (Thomas, J., concurring) (emphasis added).

the revocation of any contract." But, second, he points out that only "revocation" is used in the saving clause: "the conspicuous omission of 'invalidation' and 'nonenforcement' suggest[s] that the exception does not include all defenses applicable to any contract but rather some subset of those defenses."[39]

Conceding that the ordinary meanings of the terms at issue overlap, and that the Court has referred to them interchangeably, Thomas adds that this alone cannot justify ignoring Congress's clear decision to repeat only one of the three terms. Moreover, he continues, when read in light of the broader statutory scheme, which says that when a party seeks to enforce an arbitration agreement, the court, "upon being satisfied that the *making* of the agreement for arbitration or the failure to comply therewith is not in issue," must order arbitration "in accordance with the terms of the agreement."[40] Thomas concludes, therefore, that "[t]his would require enforcement of an agreement to arbitrate unless a party successfully asserts a defense concerning the formation of the agreement to arbitrate, such as fraud, duress, or mutual mistake. Contract defenses unrelated to the making of the agreement—such as public policy—could not be the basis for declining to enforce an arbitration clause."[41] Thus, as he reads the federal statute, California's *Discovery Bank* rule "is not a 'groun[d] . . . for the revocation of any contract.'"[42] It is, accordingly, preempted.

In sum, it takes no leap to discern in Thomas's concurrence a certain unease with modern doctrines of substantive unconscionability, an uneasiness that one senses, though less surely, in the Court's opinion as well. *Concepcion* may have been argued and decided as a preemption case, but at bottom it's a contracts case.

*   *   *

We turn now to the three other preemption cases the Court decided this term, all concerning torts, and all raising the question,

---

[39] *Id.* at 1754.

[40] *Id.* (quoting 9 U.S.C. § 4) (emphasis added).

[41] *Id.* (citations omitted).

[42] *Id.* at 1756 (citations omitted).

in particular, of how best to handle risk. Two involve pharmaceuticals, the other automobile safety—staples in the preemption corpus. The policy questions are thus never far below the surface: whether the risks at issue are better handled through state police power—*ex ante* through regulation or *ex post* through adjudication—or through federal legislation and executive branch regulation and adjudication. Here again, however, our main concern will not be with such questions but rather with the constitutional question of whether federal or state power should prevail.

PLIVA v. Mensing

With *PLIVA*[43] we have a case that looks simple on the surface, but in the end it is not, and the dissent has the better of it. The question was whether individuals injured by generic drugs they claimed had inadequate warning labels could sue the manufacturers for damages under state law, or whether federal Food and Drug Administration regulations for drug labeling preempted such suits. The Court ruled 5-4 that the manufacturers could not be sued because it was impossible for them to comply with both federal and state law. Thus, the majority saw *PLIVA* as a straightforward case of conflict preemption.

This case was brought by plaintiffs who suffered from stomach ailments for which they had taken the generic drug metoclopramide—sold under the brand name Reglan—for an extended period of time, after which they developed tardive dyskinesia, a serious neurological disorder. Because evidence had accumulated that long-term use can result in the condition, warning labels have been strengthened and clarified several times over the years. Nevertheless, the plaintiffs charged that the warnings were inadequate. The manufacturers responded that federal statutes and FDA regulations required them to use the same safety and efficacy labeling as brand-name manufacturers. Thus, it was impossible for them to comply with both federal law and state tort law that required, by implication, different or stronger labeling. The Fifth and Eighth Circuits rejected the manufacturer's claims. The Supreme Court reversed, Justice Thomas writing for the majority.

---

[43] PLIVA, Inc. v. Mensing, 131 S. Ct. 2567 (2011).

Thomas begins his opinion by comparing federal and state law on the subject. State tort law, he says, requires a drug manufacturer "that is or should be aware of its product's danger to label that product in a way that renders it reasonably safe."[44] By contrast, federal drug labeling law is far more complex. Manufacturers of new drugs must first conduct lengthy and expensive testing to satisfy the FDA that the drug is safe and effective and that the labeling is accurate and adequate, all of which must be approved by the FDA before the drug can be marketed. To better enable manufacturers to develop inexpensive *generic* drugs, however, which usually appear on the market several years after brand-name drugs are approved, Congress in 1984 passed the Hatch-Waxman Amendments, which allow generic drugs to gain FDA approval simply by showing equivalence to the brand-name drug and, important here, by having the same labeling, which the FDA had already approved for the brand-name drug.[45] Thus, "[a] brand-name manufacturer seeking new drug approval is responsible for the accuracy and adequacy of its label," Thomas notes. "A manufacturer seeking generic drug approval, on the other hand, is responsible for ensuring that its warning label is the same as the brand name's."[46]

None of which the parties dispute, Thomas continues, "What is in dispute is whether, and to what extent, generic manufacturers

---

[44] *Id.* at 2573. In truth, a label cannot, of course, render a drug safe; it can only render the risk associated with its use *known*, after which the user can decide whether to assume that risk. Noticing that, however, helps explain why we have relied mainly on *ex ante* federal regulation of drug labeling. An *ex post* state tort decision for a plaintiff can imply only that the labeling was "inadequate," not what it should have been to be "adequate." And more often than not the decision is circular: if the injury occurred, then *ipso facto* the warning was inadequate. (In *Wyeth*, the label had no fewer than six warnings **in bold**, prompting Justice Alito to ask whether a seventh warning would have made any difference.) After each adverse decision, the manufacturer can strengthen its warning, of course, and raise the price of the drug to cover its losses—or, ultimately, remove the drug from the market. But since the jury sees only the injured plaintiff, not those costs, including the costs of the drug's ultimate unavailability, we rarely if ever get a rational assessment of risk and adequate labeling from the tort system. The system serves instead simply to compensate plaintiffs for their losses, regardless of whether the labeling may in fact have been adequate to warn a rational user or whether plaintiffs or their health care providers may have ignored the warnings, as happened in *Wyeth*. I have discussed this issue more fully in Pilon, *supra* note 2, at 101–07.

[45] 21 U.S.C § 355 (2006).

[46] PLIVA, 131 S. Ct. at 2574.

may change their labels *after* initial FDA approval." The plaintiffs claimed that several avenues were open to manufacturers to change their labels. The FDA disagreed, saying the labeling must be the same "because the [brand-name] drug product is the basis for the [generic drug] approval."[47] Thus were the issues joined.

Thomas turns then to the plaintiffs' claim that manufacturers have "several avenues" to make changes. The FDA's "changes-being-effected" (CBE) process is one: it allows brand-name manufacturers to change their labels if evidence warrants it and then to seek FDA approval afterward; but that process, the FDA said, allows changes to generic drug labels only when the brand-name label is changed. Were the generic manufacturer to change its label unilaterally, it would violate the statute and regulations. Again, plaintiffs claimed that manufacturers could have sent "Dear Doctor" letters indicating additional warnings. But the FDA counts such letters as "labeling," which if sent would inaccurately imply a therapeutic difference between brand-name and generic drugs and thus be misleading. Finally, the FDA itself points to a "duty" *all* manufacturers have to propose stronger labels if evidence warrants it, after which the FDA, if it agreed, would work with brand-name manufacturers to change the labels of both brand-name and generic drugs. But there is disagreement over whether any such "duty" exists, Thomas says: there is no evidence of a generic drug manufacturer ever acting pursuant to it; and even if it did exist, performing it, he concludes, would not have satisfied the state-law duty to provide adequate warning. "State law demanded a safer label; it did not instruct the Manufacturers to communicate with the FDA about the possibility of a safer label."[48]

With that, Thomas turns to the preemption question. Here, he notes, we have no express preemption—nor any saving clause preserving state law.[49] But that does not mean that conflict preemption principles do not apply. And here they apply straightforwardly, he believes: "state law imposed a duty on the Manufacturers to take a certain action, and federal law barred them from taking that action."[50] This is a case of simple impossibility preemption.

[47] *Id.* at 2575 (quoting Abbreviated New Drug Application Regulations, 57 Fed. Reg. 17961 (Apr. 28, 1992)).

[48] *Id.* at 2578.

[49] *Id.* at 2577 n.5.

[50] *Id.* at 2581.

Writing a lengthy dissent for herself and Justices Ginsburg, Breyer, and Kagan, Justice Sotomayor challenges the manufacturers' and the majority's impossibility thesis, arguing that it is not impossible for manufacturers to satisfy both state and federal law. All they need do is persuade the FDA to change the label, which is entirely possible.

She begins by observing, first, that the purpose of Congress is the touchstone of every preemption case and, second, that particularly when Congress legislates in such traditional areas of state authority as the police power, aimed at protecting the rights of a state's citizens, the presumption is against preemption, absent an express congressional indication to the contrary. And here, when Congress amended FDA's generic statute in 1962, it expressly preserved a role for state law that did not conflict. Under state law, manufacturers have a duty to provide adequate drug labeling. And under federal law, especially given FDA's limited resources and the superior knowledge manufacturers have about their drugs, both brand-name and generic manufacturers are obliged to monitor the safety of their products.

Thus, Sotomayor continues, she does not need to decide whether the uncertain "duty" Thomas considered

> in fact obliges generic manufacturers to approach the FDA to propose a label change. The majority assumes that it does. And even if generic manufacturers do not have a duty to propose label changes, two points remain undisputed. First, they do have a duty under federal law to monitor the safety of their products. And, second, they *may* approach the FDA to propose a label change when they believe a change is required.[51]

Turning to the manufacturer's basic claim, Sotomayor notes that the sole ground on which the manufacturers rest their argument, impossibility, is an affirmative defense, and a demanding one: "the mere possibility of impossibility is not enough."[52] She continues:

> The Manufacturers had available to them a mechanism for attempting to comply with their state law duty to warn. . . . [H]ad they approached the FDA, the FDA may well have

[51] *Id.* at 2586 (Sotomayor, J., dissenting) (emphasis added).
[52] *Id.* at 2587.

agreed that a label change was necessary. Accordingly, . . .
I would require the Manufacturers to show that the FDA
would not have approved a proposed label change. They
have not made such a showing: They do "not argue that
[they] attempted to give the kind of warning required by
[state law] but [were] prohibited from doing so by the
FDA."[53]

Nor would it be impossible or even difficult for a generic manufacturer to show impossibility. Sotomayor homes in on the heart of
the matter:

If a generic-manufacturer defendant proposed a label change
to the FDA but the FDA rejected the proposal, it would be
impossible for that defendant to comply with a state-law
duty to warn. Likewise, impossibility would be established
if the FDA had not yet responded to a generic manufacturer's
request for a label change at the time a plaintiff's injuries
arose. A generic manufacturer might also show that the FDA
had itself considered whether to request enhanced warnings
in light of the evidence on which a plaintiff's claim rests but
had decided to leave the warnings as is. (The Manufacturers
make just such an argument in these cases.) *But these are
questions of fact to be established through discovery.* Because the
burden of proving impossibility falls on the defendant, I
would hold that federal law does not render it impossible
for generic manufacturers to comply with a state-law duty
to warn as a categorical matter.[54]

Thomas has two main responses, by implication. (He offers very
little in the way of a direct response to the dissent's arguments.)
First, he claims that the proper test for impossibility is whether the
defendant could have *independently* satisfied both federal and state
law; generic manufacturers could not, he argues, because not only
is the CBE process not available to them, but they require the cooper-
ation of both the FDA and the brand-name manufacturer before
they can make a label change. Sotomayor answers that there is no
precedent for such a rule and, moreover, only two years earlier, in
Wyeth, the Court had held that *brand-name* manufacturers could be

---

[53] *Id.* at 2588 (quoting Wyeth, 129 S. Ct. at 1198).

[54] *Id.* at 2589 (emphasis added).

held liable under state law for not changing their labels even though they too require FDA approval after they've made such a change. Thus, they too, at least other than temporarily, cannot "independently" satisfy their state-law duty—and Sotomayor would hold them to the same impossibility test as generic manufacturers.

Second, following on his first point, Thomas argues that "[t]he only action the Manufacturers could independently take—asking for the FDA's help—is not a matter of state-law concern."[55] Sotomayor never really addresses that point, likely because to make her argument she did not need to assume that that action was a "duty" under federal law. In any event, assuming, as the FDA claims, that there is a "duty" *all* manufacturers have to propose stronger labels if evidence warrants it, Thomas is right: that is not a matter of state-law concern. *But that is irrelevant to the issue before the Court,* which is whether the *state-law* duty to provide adequate labeling is preempted by federal law. (This is truly a case of overlapping jurisdictions.) As the dissent makes clear, nothing in federal law *prevents* generic manufacturers from taking steps that *might* enable them to satisfy their state-law duties. And if in fact there is this federal-law "duty"—albeit not a matter of *state-law* concern—all the more reason there is to take such steps when the evidence warrants it. None of which is to say, of course, that the evidence warranted it here: that is yet another matter to be determined at trial. The point here, however, is that the manufacturer's duty, under state law, is to its customers. Insofar as federal law does not frustrate but rather facilitates that duty with one of its own, however uncertain, all the better. And that, I submit, is what the Court should have found here.

As *PLIVA* was coming up, the question was how the Court would distinguish it from *Wyeth,* where the Court found for the plaintiff. That was a brand-name case, finding no preemption because Wyeth's state-law duty to strengthen its labeling was held not to conflict with the "purposes and objectives" of federal law. Again, the decision was in error, I believe, because the case involved simple medical malpractice, not a failure to warn: unlike what the evidence suggests here, in *Wyeth* the physician's assistant ignored six warnings in bold and administered a double dose of the medication in the one place most likely to produce the injury, all the while ignoring

---

[55] *Id.* at 2581 (majority opinion).

the complaints of pain from the patient plaintiff, all of which was clearly addressed by the several warnings. As the dissent said, no additional warnings would likely have made a bit of difference.

More to the point, however, *Wyeth*'s holding clearly conflicted with the purposes and objectives of federal drug law, which are to ensure the availability of both safe *and effective* drugs. The plaintiffs claim in *Wyeth*, which the Court implicitly sanctioned, was that the more risky *but more effective* IV-push method of administering the drug at issue "was not reasonably safe" and therefore, impliedly, should be banned. But the FDA had already determined, through its testing and labeling requirements, the proper balance between safety and efficacy. After *Wyeth*, however, that determination was turned over to state juries, who of course have no expertise in such matters, but do have an injured plaintiff before them. After *PLIVA*, the error goes the other way, with manufacturers being shielded from their failure to take the steps that may be necessary to provide us with an adequate measure of safety. None of which is to say, again, that a jury would have done any better here than it did in *Wyeth*. But if Congress and the FDA want to shield such determinations from juries, they have the power to do so. Here, they have not done so. Thus, the question should have remained one of state law.

Bruesewitz v. Wyeth

Bruesewitz[56] is another complex drug decision. Here, however, the Court decided for the defendant, ruling 6-2, with Justice Kagan again recusing herself, that plaintiffs injured by vaccines they claim were improperly designed cannot sue vaccine manufacturers but must seek remedies instead from the no-fault compensation system Congress created in 1986 to address the problem that manufacturers, fearful of such suits, would simply not produce vaccines. Thus, the Court held that the federal law creating that system expressly preempted state tort liability "for a vaccine's unavoidable, adverse side effects."[57]

Although compensation for vaccine-related injuries had been left for years to state tort law, by the mid-1980s suits for such injuries had increased to such an extent that many manufacturers, including

---

[56] Bruesewitz v. Wyeth, 131 S. Ct. 1068 (2011).

[57] *Id.* at 1074.

those producing vaccines against diphtheria, tetanus, and pertussis (DTP), had left the market, while others were threatening to leave.[58] Into the breach stepped Congress with the National Vaccine Injury Compensation Act of 1986. The Act was designed to handle the risks inherent in vaccinations through a federal no-fault system rather than through the vagaries of state tort law. No liability without fault is a principle that works well in a great range of tort claims. But here the inability to make vaccines entirely safe, plus uncertainty surrounding causation, coupled with the penchant of state juries to discount those issues in favor of sympathetic plaintiffs, had rendered most manufacturers unwilling to produce essential vaccines at reasonable costs.

The Act created a mandatory federal vaccine court—a less adversarial no-fault forum designed to enable alleged victims to be compensated quickly from federal funds drawn from surcharges on vaccines. With "table injuries," found to result from particular vaccines, the system seems to have worked well.[59] If victims suffer a non-table injury, however, they can still prevail, but they must prove that the vaccine caused the injury. Nonetheless, critics claim that the court has not worked as intended, with unconscionable delays, among much else, and victims are wrongly being denied relief.[60]

One such case was that of Hannah Bruesewitz, who was administered her third dose of DTP vaccine on schedule, just short of her six-month birthday. She then suffered a series of seizures, later diagnosed as residual seizure disorder and developmental delay. Now a teenager, she'll likely require medical care related to her condition for the rest of her life.

---

[58] "Whereas between 1978 and 1981 only nine product-liability suits were filed against DTP manufacturers, by the mid-1980s the suits numbered more than 200 each year. This destabilized the DTP vaccine market, causing two of the three domestic manufacturers to withdraw; and the remaining manufacturer, Lederle Laboratories, estimated that its potential tort liability exceeded its annual sales by a factor of 200." *Id.* at 1072–73.

[59] This refers to the Vaccine Injury Table, which delineates common injuries resulting from vaccinations. The table can be found at http://www.hrsa.gov/vaccinecompensation/table.htm.

[60] See Brief of Vaccine Injured Petitioners Bar Association, the George Washington Univ. Law School Vaccine Injury Clinic, et al. as Amici Curiae Supporting Petitioners at 9-18, Bruesewitz v. Wyeth, 131 S. Ct. 1068 (2011) (No. 09-152).

Hannah's parents filed a petition with the vaccine court when she was three, one month after new regulations deleted her disorder as a DTP table injury. Nearly eight years later, the court ruled that they had not proved causation, dismissing the claim with prejudice. The parents then filed a federal suit against Wyeth, which manufactured the vaccine, claiming, among other things, that Wyeth was strictly liable for a design defect. Again they lost in both the district and appellate courts.[61]

Hard cases make bad law, but bad law also makes hard cases. And the law in this case has taxed the interpretive skills of more than one court. The narrow question before the Supreme Court was whether a unanimous Third Circuit panel had correctly applied the Act's preemption language—made more pressing because only five months before the panel ruled, a unanimous Georgia Supreme Court, facing a similar case, read the same language as *not* preempting design defect suits.[62] In relevant part, that language reads:

> No vaccine manufacturer shall be liable in a civil action for damages arising from a vaccine-related injury or death associated with the administration of a vaccine . . . if the injury or death resulted from side effects that were unavoidable even though the vaccine was properly prepared and was accompanied by proper directions and warnings.[63]

Although the Act allows victims to sue over manufacturing defects, conduct that would subject a manufacturer to punitive damages, and a manufacturer's failure to provide a proper warning or exercise due care, nowhere does it define "unavoidable"—and there is the nub of the matter. The fact that Congress included that term implies, the Georgia court argued, that at least some vaccine-related injuries could be avoided, and so in those cases federal law did not preempt state civil suits to determine whether the injury was in fact "avoidable." Indeed, preempting all design-defect suits would render the text superfluous, the Georgia court added, contrary to a

---

[61] Bruesewitz v. Wyeth, 508 F. Supp. 2d 430 (E.D. Pa. 2007), aff'd 561 F.3d 233 (3d Cir. 2009).

[62] Am. Home Prod. Corp. v. Ferrari, 668 S.E.2d 236 (2008).

[63] 42 U.S.C. § 300aa-22(b)(1) (2006).

cardinal principle of statutory construction that text is there for a reason.[64]

But the Third Circuit countered that if that reading were correct, statutory construction rules aside, the Act would not bar *any* design-defect claims, because *every* such claim would be subject to case-by-case determination by a court—precisely what Congress sought to avoid.[65]

Sound as that rejoinder may have been, based on the Act's purpose as seen in its structure and, mostly, its legislative history, it hardly helped that that history included two inconsistent committee reports following the Act's passage.[66] Thus, the report of the House Energy and Commerce Committee, which had jurisdiction over the matter, focused on the core problem of state-imposed strict liability without fault, the implications for vaccine manufacturing, and the need for a no-fault victim compensation system—which would be undermined, the Third Circuit argued, if state courts were permitted to determine case-by-case whether a manufacturer might have created a safer vaccine.[67]

But a year later, when Congress finally provided funding for the program, the House Budget Committee's report claimed that Congress never undertook "to decide as a matter of law whether vaccines were unavoidably unsafe."[68] It left that decision instead to the courts, the report said, prompting this from the Third Circuit: "The views of a subsequent Congress form a hazardous basis for inferring the intent of an earlier one."[69]

In his concurrence, Justice Breyer found the textual question a close call, although the majority, he thought, had the better argument. Thus, like the dissent, he looks to legislative history, statutory purpose, agency views, and medical opinion to conclude, unlike the dissent, that each reinforces the Court's conclusion. His principal concern, however, seems to be that allowing design-defect suits would upset the Act's central purposes: to provide the safest possible

---

[64] Am. Home Prod., 668 S.E.2d at 238, 240, 242.

[65] Bruesewitz, 561 F.3d at 246.

[66] *Id.* at 249.

[67] *Id.*

[68] Bruesewitz, 131 S. Ct. at 1092 (Sotomayor, J., dissenting) (citation omitted).

[69] *Id.* at 250 (quoting United States v. Price, 361 U.S. 304 (1960)).

vaccines plus a compensation system for those who may be injured.[70] And in that connection, he is particularly concerned that to allow juries to decide complex design-defect and causal questions "is to substitute less expert for more expert judgment,"[71] thereby threatening to undermine the entire system.

Justice Scalia, writing for the Court, devotes the better part of his opinion to answering the lengthy dissent of Justice Sotomayor, joined by Justice Ginsburg, so we can weigh the two opinions together. He begins by analyzing the crucial text, which I repeat:

> No vaccine manufacturer shall be liable in a civil action for damages arising from a vaccine-related injury or death associated with the administration of a vaccine ... if the injury or death resulted from side effects that were unavoidable even though the vaccine was properly prepared and was accompanied by proper directions and warnings.[72]

Again, "unavoidable" is the problematic term. The "even though" clause clarifies it, Scalia says: it tells us what preventative measures a manufacturer *must* have taken—proper manufacture, proper warning—for the side effects to be considered "unavoidable" under the statute. Given that those measures were taken, "any remaining side effects, including those resulting from design defects, are deemed to have been unavoidable."[73] Those side effects are "unavoidable," one might add, because there will always be *some* risk of injury, which is avoidable only by avoiding the vaccine—thereby, as a practical matter, making *other* risks unavoidable.

Continuing with his textual analysis, Scalia points out that "[i]f a manufacturer could be held liable for failure to use a different design, the word 'unavoidable' would do no work."[74] The work it does, he seems to say next (the argument is abstruse), is to focus on *this* design, not some other *possible* design that *might* have been used: "The language of the provision thus suggests that the *design* of the vaccine is a given, not subject to question in a tort action."[75] And

---

[70] Bruesewitz, 131 S. Ct. at 1084 (Breyer, J., concurring).

[71] *Id.* at 1085.

[72] 42 U.S.C. § 300aa-22(b)(1) (2006).

[73] Bruesewitz, 131 S. Ct. at 1075 (majority opinion).

[74] *Id.*

[75] *Id.* (emphasis in original).

he elaborates in a footnote: "The dissent advocates for another possibility: '[A] side effect is 'unavoidable' . . . where there is no feasible alternative design that would eliminate the side effect of the vaccine without compromising its cost and utility.'"[76] But the dissent makes no effort to ground that reading in the text, Scalia notes, nor are "cost" and "utility" judicially administrable factors. Notice too that if a manufacturer must demonstrate unavoidability by showing that there was no other "feasible" vaccine, proving that negative is impossible. Unlike in *PLIVA*, where proving impossibility *within a finite regulatory system* was possible, here the domain is open-ended. One can always *imagine* a safer, more effective vaccine.

Scalia's textual analysis turns next to the well-known triumvirate of grounds for products liability: design defects, manufacturing defects, and inadequate directions and warnings. "If all three were intended to be preserved," he writes, "it would be strange to mention specifically only two, and leave the third to implication."[77] He then launches into a textual and structural exegesis that in places is all but inscrutable—and will not be examined here—observing in the process, in response to the dissent, that "the rule against giving a portion of text an interpretation which renders it superfluous does not prescribe that a passage which could have been more terse does not mean what it says."[78] To be sure, Congress here could have made its intent more clear, but working with what it gave him, he has made far more sense out of its language than has the dissent.

Scalia concludes by making short work of the dissent's attempt to muddy the waters of congressional intent. Assuming that legislative history is even needed here, not only does the dissent quote incompletely from a report by a committee of the Congress that enacted the vaccine statute, but it relies on a committee report from a *later* Congress that it believes "authoritative[ly]" vindicates its interpretation. Echoing the Third Circuit, Scalia notes that "[t]his is a courageous adverb since we have previously held that the only authoritative source of statutory meaning is the text that has passed through

---

[76] *Id.* at 1076 n.35.

[77] *Id.*

[78] *Id.* at 1078.

the Article I process,"[79] adding that post-enactment legislative history is "a contradiction in terms."[80]

Based, then, on text, structure, and legislative history, the Court was right to hold that "the National Childhood Vaccine Injury Act preempts all design-defect claims against vaccine manufacturers brought by plaintiffs who seek compensation for injury or death caused by vaccine side effects."[81] Were it otherwise, as the Third Circuit said, the Act would not bar *any* design-defect claims, because *every* such claim would be subject to case-by-case determination by a court—precisely what Congress sought to avoid in order to enable a viable vaccine market to exist.

Williamson v. Mazda

Williamson,[82] our final case, takes us from drugs to automobiles, but the basic policy question remains the same: whether risk is best regulated at the federal or state level. Here, the Court ruled unanimously, with Justice Kagan recusing herself, that the family of a woman killed in an auto accident may sue the manufacturer of the minivan in which she was riding for its failure to install a lap-and-shoulder belt in the rear middle seat rather than simply a lap belt. Although the decision was unanimous—Justice Breyer writing for the Court, with concurrences by Justices Sotomayor and Thomas—it raises some of the most interesting and perplexing questions about our current preemption law, and was wrongly decided, I believe.

The Court reversed two lower state courts that had ruled, along with several other courts in recent years, that Federal Motor Vehicle Safety Standard 208, written pursuant to the National Traffic and Motor Vehicle Safety Act of 1966, preempted the plaintiffs' suit in light of the Court's 2000 decision in *Geier v. Honda American Motor Co.*[83] *Geier* concerned passive restraint systems: it held that the regulation preempted a suit based on the manufacturer's failure to install airbags instead of automatic seatbelts. There, the Court found that

---

[79] *Id.* at 1081 n.72.

[80] *Id.* at 1081.

[81] *Id.* at 1082.

[82] Williamson v. Mazda Motor of Am., Inc., 131 S. Ct. 1131 (2011).

[83] Geier v. Am. Honda Motor Co., 529 U.S. 861 (2000).

regulators intended to assure manufacturers a choice between several different systems, a choice the state suits would deny them. Here, the Court held that assuring manufacturers a choice of seat-belt types was not, as with the choice in *Geier*, "a significant regulatory objective,"[84] and so the Williamsons' suit was not preempted.

To understand those disparate rulings in seemingly similar cases we need to look first at the Court's 5-4 decision in *Geier*, where Breyer also authored the majority opinion. The question before the Court there, as here, was whether the regulation preempted a state tort suit that would have held manufacturers liable and effectively denied them the choice the regulation seemed to give them. Breyer divided that inquiry into three steps.

First, he noted that the statute expressly preempted state law: "no State" may "establish, or . . . continue in effect . . . *any safety standard* applicable to the same aspect of performance" of a motor vehicle or item of equipment "which is not identical to the Federal standard."[85] But he added, "We had previously held that a word somewhat similar to 'standard,' namely, 'requirements' (found in a similar statute) included within its scope state 'common-law duties,' such as duties created by state tort law."[86] That interpretation raises a problem, which Thomas brings out in his concurrence: "standard," especially as used in the statute here, ordinarily denotes a *regulatory* standard, not a tort judgment. The two are different, and they function differently. Eliding that difference, Breyer wrote next, "But we nonetheless held that the state tort suit in question fell *outside* the scope of this particular pre-emption clause. That is primarily because the statute also contains a saving clause, which says that '[c]ompliance with' a federal safety standard 'does not exempt any person *from any liability under common law*.'"[87] Thus, state tort suits, he concluded, fall outside the statute's express preemption clause.

Second—and at this point in *Geier*, Breyer's argument took an interesting turn, as Thomas will discuss in his concurrence:

> We asked the converse question: The saving clause *at least* removes tort actions from the scope of the express pre-emption clause. But does it do more? Does it foreclose or limit

---

[84] Williamson, 131 S. Ct. at 1137.

[85] *Id.* at 1135 (quoting 15 U.S.C. § 1392(d)) (emphasis in the original).

[86] *Id.* (citing Medtronic, Inc. v. Lohr, 518 U.S. 470, 502 (1996) (plurality opinion)).

[87] *Id.* at 1135 (quoting 15 U.S.C. § 1397(k)) (emphasis in original).

> 'the operation of ordinary pre-emption principles insofar as those principles instruct us to read' federal statutes as pre-empting state laws (including state common-law standards) that 'actually conflict' with the federal statutes (or related regulations)? We concluded that the saving clause does not foreclose or limit the operation of 'ordinary pre-emption principles, grounded in longstanding precedent.'[88]

Thus, he concluded that "the statute's express pre-emption clause cannot pre-empt the common-law tort action; but neither can the statute's saving clause foreclose or limit the operation of ordinary *conflict* pre-emption principles."[89] Accordingly, third, the question there, as here, was "whether, in fact, the state tort action conflicts with the federal regulation."[90]

In *Geier*, Breyer answered that question in the affirmative, unlike here. He did so because the *Geier* tort action conflicted with—stood as an obstacle to—the federal agency's accomplishment and execution of its full "purposes and objectives." Turning to numerous sources concerning everything from the state of airbag technology to ignition interlocks to public backlash and more, Breyer concluded that giving manufacturers a choice among passive restraint systems was "an important regulatory objective" that, as the solicitor general told the Court, a tort suit would stand in the way of accomplishing. Examining similar sources here, however, concerning consumer acceptance, safety, child car seats, ingress and egress concerns, cost, and more—including the solicitor general's representation of the agency's views—Breyer concludes that allowing manufacturers a choice between seat-belt types was *not* "a significant regulatory objective."[91]

In her concurrence, Justice Sotomayor only reinforces Breyer's "rejection of an overreading of *Geier*.'"[92] For Justice Thomas, however, Breyer's conflict analysis is, of course, fodder for his long-standing antipathy to the Court's "purposes and objectives" preemption jurisprudence. Thomas would reach the same result the Court does, but

---

[88] *Id.* at 1135–36 (quoting Geier, 529 U.S. at 874).
[89] *Id.* at 1136 (emphasis added).
[90] *Id.*
[91] *Id.* at 1137.
[92] *Id.* at 1140 (Sotomayor, J., concurring).

"by a more direct route: the Safety Act's saving clause, which speaks directly to this question and answers it."[93] The Court does not rely on the saving clause, Thomas says, "because [it] read it out of the statute in *Geier*. . . . That left the Court free to consider the effect of conflict preemption principles on such tort actions."[94]

Thomas then draws the distinction noted above between state *regulatory* law and state *tort* actions, which Breyer elided:

> The [statute's] express pre-emption clause bars States from having any safety "standard applicable to the same aspect of performance" as a federal standard unless it is "identical" to the federal one. That clause pre-empts States from establishing "objective rule[s] prescribed by a legislature or an administrative agency" in competition with the federal standards; it says nothing about the tort lawsuits that are the focus of the saving clause. Read independently of the express pre-emption clause, the saving clause simply means what it says: [the federal regulation] does not pre-empt state common-law actions.[95]

Having elided that distinction, however, rather than take the text at face value, the Court tries to determine "whether the regulators *really* wanted manufacturers to have a choice,"[96] Thomas continues. And it does so by "engag[ing] in a freewheeling, extratextual, and broad evaluation of the 'purposes and objectives'" of the regulation, "wad[ing] into a sea of agency musings and Government litigating positions [to] fish[] for what the agency may have been thinking 20 years ago when it drafted the relevant provision."[97] In fact, "[t]he dispositive difference between this case and *Geier*—indeed, the only difference—is the majority's 'psychoanalysis' of the regulators," he concludes.[98]

Thomas is certainly right to flag the problems inherent in the Court's "purposes and objectives" jurisprudence. But insofar as he

---

[93] *Id.* at 1141 (Thomas, J., concurring in the judgment).

[94] *Id.*

[95] *Id.* at 1141–42.

[96] *Id.* at 1142 (emphasis in original).

[97] *Id.* (citation and some internal quotation marks omitted).

[98] *Id.* at 1143 (citing Public Util. Comm'n of Cal. v. United States, 345 U.S. 295, 319 (1953) (Jackson, J., concurring) (describing reliance on legislative history)).

attempts here to preserve the saving clause through a textual reading, plus the distinction he draws just above, his argument is problematic. The statute's preemption clause states, again, that "no State" may "establish, or . . . continue in effect . . . *any safety standard* applicable to the same aspect of performance" of a motor vehicle or item of equipment "which is not identical to the Federal standard."[99] Thomas reads that, along with the saving clause, as distinguishing state *regulatory* standards (preempted) from state *tort* actions (allowed, due to the saving clause). But a successful state tort suit concerning "the same aspect of performance"—say, seatbelts: finding lapbelts "unsafe"—would imply a state safety standard that is *not* "identical to the Federal standard," which means that state tort suits *too* should be preempted, by operation of the preemption clause—save for the flat-out contradictory saving clause. (But see below for a reading that reconciles the two clauses.)

Thus, the "floor and ceiling" metaphor common in preemption cases does not work here, not if we take the preemption clause at face value. If no state may establish any safety standard that is not *identical to the federal standard*, then that "floor" is in fact a "ceiling" too, which means that a state tort suit that implies otherwise is barred—unless we read the saving clause, again, as undercutting the plain text of the preemption clause. And notice: the saving clause doesn't simply *qualify* the preemption clause, as Thomas seems to be arguing; again, it flat-out *undercuts* it. There is either one (federal) standard—to which state standards, if there are such, must be "identical"—or there is not.

Neither Breyer nor Thomas addresses that point, although Breyer, toward the end of his opinion and in a different context, merely mentions, implying the contrary, that he "cannot reconcile" the idea that the federal agency intended to set a "maximum" standard "with a statutory saving clause that foresees the likelihood of a continued meaningful role for state tort law."[100] Neither can I; but, unlike Breyer, for textual reasons: there is no reconciling a contradictory statute. Not noticing the contradiction, Breyer moves ahead, with his "converse question," whether an express preemption clause, followed by a saving clause, leaves us still with the need to ask

[99] 15 U.S.C. § 1392(d) (2006) (emphasis added).
[100] Williamson, 131 S. Ct. at 1139 (majority opinion).

about "ordinary conflict preemption"—which takes us, of necessity, to the purposes-and-objectives preemption that Thomas dismisses, not without reason.

Sharing no such reservations, Breyer wades right into the job of discerning the purposes and objectives not only of the Congress that wrote the statute but of the regulators who wrote the regulations under it and of the lawyers who litigated the cases to which the statute and regulations gave rise. Thus, he writes that here, unlike in *Geier*, the Department of Transportation "was not concerned about consumer acceptance; it was convinced that lap-and-shoulder belts would increase safety; it did not fear additional safety risks arising from use of those belts; it had no interest in assuring a mix of devices; and, though it was concerned about additional costs, that concern was diminishing."[101] In sum, and again, providing manufacturers with a seatbelt choice was not a "significant objective" of the regulation, so unlike in *Geier*, allowing state tort actions here would not conflict with the purposes and objectives of the federal statute.

But we are still left with the question: to what end were tort actions left available, pursuant to the saving clause, especially given the plain text of the preemption clause, which clearly requires a single standard, even if that "standard" gives manufacturers options? The Court upheld that standard in *Geier*, but not here, where it allowed the state to impose a *different* standard, one "not identical to the *Federal* [seatbelt] standard" that allowed manufacturers a choice. A better reading of the statute, I submit, would make state tort actions available *not* against manufacturers who made "the wrong choice" among federally *approved* options but against manufacturers *who failed to choose one of those federally approved options—manufacturers who ignored federal law.* That may be the null set, given the sanctions for regulatory noncompliance. And that reading of the saving clause may not conform to what we ordinarily think of when we think of state tort actions. But at least it renders the statute coherent—and avoids the often incoherent and conclusory "purposes and objectives" methodology that Breyer is so fond of.

What then is the result of the Court's decision? The Williamsons, of course, will now go back to court to make out their case. But what is their case? That Mazda was negligent in installing lap belts

---

[101] *Id.* at 1138.

rather than lap-and-shoulder belts in their minivan inner seats? Where is the negligence in that? That Mazda could have made the vehicle safer? Yes, it could have, at a higher cost, as DOT recognized, which is one of the more important reasons it allowed Mazda the choice. But we are not talking here about some hidden risk, known only to the manufacturer. The risk was "open and obvious," in the nomenclature of the old, more rational, common law—not the tort law that today presumes that for every loss a deep pocket must be found, a system that socializes losses not simply through strict but through what amounts to absolute liability.

And so we come to what is so often at issue in this preemption debate, namely, that manufacturers favor preemption because, first, as a matter of simple efficiency they want a single standard, not 50 ever-changing standards; and because, second, they want some relief from a state tort system that, as Justice Alito said in *Wyeth*, turns an ordinary medical malpractice case into a frontal assault on the FDA's arguably rational regulation of risk, thereby rendering the regulation pointless if it cannot function to determine who assumes the risk and hence who suffers the loss if it materializes.

When *Williamson* is reargued below, Mazda should be able, of course, to raise DOT's regulation as an affirmative defense, because the regulation implied that *either* choice—either lap belts or lap-and-shoulder belts—was "safe enough" in a context in which it is impossible to eliminate *all* risk. That is, Mazda should be held liable only if it was "at fault." But again, where is the fault here? DOT was right to raise the cost issue, but it cuts in favor of the assumption-of-risk principle and hence in favor of choice and liberty. The Williamsons could have chosen a vehicle with lap-and-shoulder belts on the inner rear seats. Likely it would have been a bit more expensive. They chose instead the less expensive model, and paid the price—unless they can prevail upon the court below to shift at least some of their tragic losses to Mazda, which is likely, given our current tort system. And so Mazda, like most manufacturers, was hoping that preemption, together with the modern regulatory state, operating here in a domain that is perfectly legitimate under our Constitution,[102] would do the job that modern tort law fails to do, namely, police risk rationally.

---

[102] I discussed that issue more fully in Pilon, *supra* note 2, at 95–107.

Conclusion

Five more preemption decisions, but not much more clarity. Perhaps we are expecting too much from the Court. After all, it often is no easy matter to determine just whether state law is "to the Contrary" of federal law. The Court made short work of it this term in *Whiting*, where the text was fairly clear. But in *Concepcion*, Justice Scalia had to employ the often-difficult purposes-and-objectives approach, which was fairly straightforward there, to uphold the federal arbitration statute. In *PLIVA*, however, it fell to Justice Sotomayor to show the majority that the case was not one of straightforward impossibility and that federal law did not trump state law. *Bruesewitz* was an equally hard case, thanks to Congress's drafting, but Justice Scalia again cut to the quick, parsing the text in a way not only to make the most sense of it but to ensure, as a policy matter, the survival of a federal scheme designed itself to ensure the survival of the vaccine industry. But perhaps the hardest case of all was *Williamson*, despite the Court's unanimous ruling, because here the statute, if read in an ordinary way, was internally inconsistent when its full implications were drawn out—which neither Justice Breyer's opinion for the Court nor the concurrences of Justices Sotomayor or Thomas did. Instead, Breyer's wide-ranging purposes-and-objectives analysis led him, and the Court, to find that federal law written to set auto safety standards could be undermined simply by the Court's "psychoanalysis" of the regulators, as Thomas colorfully put it. As in so many of these cases, that leaves the law uncertain for plaintiffs and defendants alike, in this most uncertain area of our law of dual sovereignty.

The Supreme Court Disposes of a Nuisance Suit: *American Electric Power v. Connecticut*

*Jonathan H. Adler**

In *American Electric Power v. Connecticut*,[1] the Supreme Court confronted climate change litigation for the second time in five years. The Court's previous foray into this terrain yielded 2007's *Massachusetts v. EPA*, easily one of the most consequential decisions of the Roberts Court. In *Massachusetts*, a closely divided Court rebuked the Environmental Protection Agency for denying it had the authority to regulate greenhouse gas emissions and propped open the courthouse doors to future climate litigation.[2] In the wake of *Massachusetts*, EPA regulation of greenhouse gases proliferated,[3] and warming-based litigation blossomed.[4]

The Court was cooler to global warming claims the second time around. In *AEP*, a unanimous Court hewed closely to well-settled precedent, turning down an ambitious effort to turn the federal

* Professor of Law and Director, Center for Business Law and Regulation, Case Western Reserve University School of Law; 2011 Lone Mountain Fellow, Property & Environment Research Center.

[1] 131 S.Ct. 2527 (2011).

[2] 549 U.S. 497 (2007). For a discussion of this decision, see Andrew P. Morriss, Litigating to Regulate: *Massachusetts v. EPA*, 2006–07 Cato Sup. Ct. Rev. 193 (2007); Jonathan H. Adler, Warming Up to Climate Change Litigation, 3 Va. L. Rev. In Brief 61 (2007), available at http://www.virginialawreview.org/inbrief/2007/05/21/adler.pdf.

[3] For an overview of federal regulatory initiatives governing greenhouse gases, many of which were triggered by *Massachusetts v. EPA*, see Jonathan H. Adler, Heat Expands All Things: The Proliferation of Greenhouse Gas Regulation under the Obama Administration, 34 Harv. J. L. & Pub. Pol'y 421 (2011).

[4] As of December 31, 2009, over 130 climate change cases had been filed, a majority of them in federal court. See David Markell and J. B. Ruhl, An Empirical Survey of Climate Change Litigation in the United States, 40 Envtl. L. Rep. 10644 (2010). Only 18 climate cases were filed before 2006. *Id.* at 10650.

common law of nuisance into a judicially administered environmental regulatory regime. The Court avoided thorny jurisdictional questions and refused to open new avenues of litigation for climate plaintiffs. At the same time, the Court's narrow opinion did not retreat from its prior holdings in *Massachusetts*. It also refrained from erecting new obstacles to future suits, thus ensuring that climate litigation will continue. Yet in explaining its decision, the Court raised cautions about trying to make climate change policy through the judiciary. That climate change is a serious concern does not mean it is a matter for the courts.

I. A Nuisance Suit

In July 2004, eight states,[5] the City of New York, and three conservation organizations[6] filed suit in federal district court against several of the nation's largest electric power producers.[7] The plaintiffs alleged that the power companies' greenhouse gas (GHG) emissions contributed to the public nuisance of global warming under federal common law.[8] According to the complaints, the defendant companies were "the five largest emitters of carbon dioxide in the United States." Each company owned dozens of power plants throughout the United States that, taken together, were responsible for an estimated 650 million tons of carbon dioxide emissions each year. These emissions constitute approximately 10 percent of U.S. emissions and 2.5 percent of all anthropogenic GHG emissions worldwide.[9]

The complaints charged that global warming, and its consequent effects, constitute an interstate public nuisance subject to redress

---

[5] The states that initially filed suit were California, Connecticut, Iowa, New Jersey, New York, Rhode Island, Vermont, and Wisconsin. New Jersey and Wisconsin subsequently withdrew from the suit. See AEP, 180 L. Ed. 2d at 443 n.3.

[6] The three conservation groups were the Open Space Institute, Inc., Open Space Conservancy, Inc., and the Audubon Society of New Hampshire. See *id.* at 443 n.4.

[7] The companies named in the suit were American Electric Power Company, Inc. (and American Electric Power Service Corporation, a wholly owned subsidiary), Southern Company, Xcel Energy, Inc., Cinergy Corporation, and the Tennessee Valley Authority. See AEP, 180 L. Ed. 2d at 443–44 n.5.

[8] Although the cases were combined, they were initially filed as two separate lawsuits, one by the states and New York City, the other by the three conservation groups. See No. 04 Civ. 5669, 2004 WL 1685122 (S.D.N.Y. filed July 21, 2004); No. 04 Civ. 5670, 2004 WL 5614409 (S.D.N.Y., filed July 21, 2004).

[9] AEP, 180 L. Ed. 2d at 444.

under federal common law.[10] Among other things, plaintiffs cited concerns that average warmer temperatures would increase sea levels, reduce mountain snowpack, increase urban smog formation, and disrupt local ecosystems.[11]

Relying on a series of cases beginning around the turn of the last century, the plaintiffs argued that federal courts had the power to enjoin activities that contribute to interstate pollution that could constitute a public nuisance.[12] As the plaintiffs noted, such equitable power had been invoked many times to control interstate pollution. As a remedy, the plaintiffs sought an injunction requiring each of the defendant power companies "to cap its carbon dioxide emissions and then reduce them by a specified percentage each year for at least a decade."[13]

Nuisance law traces its roots to the English law of the mid-13th century. Henry of Bracton, a prominent jurist of the time, wrote that "no one may do in his own estate any thing whereby damage or nuisance may happen to his neighbor."[14] So, for example, it was not permissible for one landowner to emit noxious odors or fumes onto the land of another or cause a neighbor's land to be flooded. This principle became embodied in the Latin maxim *Sic utere tuo ut alienum non laedas*, or "Use your own property so as not to harm another's."[15]

While the law of private nuisance focused on those activities that interfered in the use or enjoyment of private land, the doctrine of public nuisance developed to address those activities that interfered with the rights of the public at large, such as obstructing a highway,

---

[10] The plaintiffs' complaints also alleged, in the alternative, that the defendants' emissions would constitute a nuisance under applicable state law.

[11] See Connecticut v. Am. Elec. Power, 582 F.3d 309, 317–18 (2nd Cir. 2009).

[12] See, e.g., Missouri v. Illinois, 180 U.S. 208 (1901) (Missouri I); Missouri v. Illinois, 200 U.S. 496 (1906) (Missouri II); Georgia v. Tenn. Copper Co., 206 U.S. 230 (1907); New York v. New Jersey, 256 U.S. 296 (1921); New Jersey v. New York, 283 U.S. 473 (1931).

[13] 180 L. Ed. 2d. at 444.

[14] See Elizabeth Brubaker, The Common Law and the Environment: The Canadian Experience, in Who Owns the Environment? 88–89 (Peter J. Hill and Roger E. Meiners eds., 1997).

[15] See Aldred's Case, 9 Co. Rep. 57b, 77 Eng. Rep. 816 (1610). This case, involving a dispute between a landowner and the owner of a neighboring pigsty, is the first known reported case to expressly rely upon this rule for its decision.

disrupting a public market, or fouling the air of the town square.[16] Because public nuisance actions are intended to protect rights common to the public, they are most often filed by public authorities, acting on behalf of the state in its sovereign capacity. Those activities subject to suit as public nuisances are those also subject to regulation under the sovereign police power. Private parties may also file suits alleging public nuisances, but only if they are able to demonstrate that they have suffered a "special injury" to distinguish their interest from that of the public at large.[17]

The Restatement (Second) of Torts defines a public nuisance as "an unreasonable interference with a right common to the general public."[18] Though it does not provide a precise definition of what would constitute an "unreasonable" interference, the Restatement notes public nuisances are typically characterized by one or more of the following characteristics: (1) the offending conduct creates a "significant interference with the public health, the public safety, the public peace, the public comfort or the public convenience"; (2) the conduct is "proscribed by statute, ordinance or administrative regulation"; and (3) the conduct is "of a continuing nature or has produced a permanent or long-lasting effect, and, as the actor knows or has reason to know, has a significant effect upon the public right."[19] As Professor Thomas Merrill observes, this only provides the most general guidance for resolving nuisance claims as it does not, for instance, make clear whether courts should balance the degree of harm against the utility of the defendant's conduct or adopt something closer to a strict liability rule.[20]

---

[16] See William L. Prosser, Private Action for Public Nuisance, 52 Va. L. Rev. 997, 998–99 (1966).

[17] See Robert Abrams & Val Washington, The Misunderstood Law of Public Nuisance: A Comparison with Private Nuisance Twenty Years after *Boomer*, 54 Alb. L. Rev. 359, 364 (1990).

[18] Restatement (Second) of Torts § 821B (1977).

[19] *Id.*

[20] Thomas W. Merrill, Global Warming as a Public Nuisance, 30 Colum. J. Envtl. L. 293, 329 (2005). See also Int'l Paper Co. v. Ouellette, 479 U.S. 481, 496 (1987) ("nuisance standards often are vague and indeterminate"); North Carolina v. Tenn. Valley Auth., 615 F.3d 291, 302 (4th Cir. 2010) ("while public nuisance law doubtless encompasses environmental concerns, it does so at such a level of generality as to provide almost no standard of application.").

Although public nuisance claims in federal court are not particularly common, states have repaired to the federal common law of interstate nuisance in seeking to reduce or eliminate pollution emanating from other jurisdictions. In the noted case of *Georgia v. Tennessee Copper Company*, for example, the state of Georgia sought relief from the "noxious gas" emitted by copper companies in an adjoining state.[21] These emissions, Georgia claimed, caused the "wholesale destruction of forests, orchards, and crops" within its territory.[22] In an opinion by Justice Oliver Wendell Holmes, the Supreme Court agreed that Georgia was entitled to relief, explaining:

> It is a fair and reasonable demand on the part of a sovereign that the air over its territory should not be polluted on a great scale by sulphurous acid gas, that the forests on its mountains, be they better or worse, and whatever domestic destruction they have suffered, should not be further destroyed or threatened by the act of persons beyond its control, that the crops and orchards on its hills should not be endangered from the same source.[23]

In other cases, the Supreme Court recognized public nuisance claims against upstream discharges of untreated sewage and ocean dumping of waste, among other things.[24]

The plaintiffs in *AEP* sought to claim that theirs was a straightforward nuisance suit of the sort federal courts had long accepted. Yet there are many ways in which global climate change is anything but an ordinary public nuisance. Among other things, the causal link between any one facility's or industry's emissions and the alleged interference in public rights is fairly attenuated. All of the defendant power companies' facilities combined are responsible for less than three percent of the relevant GHG emissions. Any interference in public or other rights caused by the GHG emissions is indirect and only results from the aggregate accumulation of such emissions from all sources over time.

Past interstate nuisance actions have typically involved binary pollution problems in which pollution from State A is causing harms

---

[21] Georgia, 206 U.S. at 236.

[22] *Id.*

[23] *Id.* at 238.

[24] See, e.g., Missouri I, 180 U.S. at 208; New Jersey, 283 U.S. at 473.

in State B, or in which the parties can be identified as those causing and those being harmed by the allegedly polluting behavior. Yet with climate change, all states are both the sources of emissions and "victims" of the consequences, including states not party to any suit. While some facilities or some jurisdictions are responsible for more emissions than others any harms are ultimately the result of global atmospheric concentrations. Had the plaintiffs in *AEP* sued all domestic power producers—or even all GHG emitters within the nation—they still would not have reached all significant contributors to the alleged nuisance. For these reasons, some commentators suggest global warming is better conceptualized as a large-scale common-pool management problem than as an interstate pollution dispute.[25]

Given the scale and complexity of climate change, it should be no surprise that judges have been reluctant to green-light nuisance suits against GHG emissions. In several cases, federal district court judges have dismissed climate-based nuisance suits filed against automakers and oil companies on the grounds that global warming is not suitable for resolution in the context of a common nuisance suit.[26] Although the potential consequences of global climate change can be characterized in nuisance-like terms, applying the law of public nuisance to GHG emissions would require stretching the bounds of the traditional nuisance action.

In *AEP*, the district court dismissed the complaints on the grounds that the plaintiffs' "unprecedented 'nuisance' action" raised a "nonjusticiable political question."[27] Determining whether defendants' emissions constituted or contributed to an actionable public nuisance and, if so, what relief to award were matters beyond judicial purview, the court concluded. The court explained that it lacked any discernible basis on which to balance the competing environmental and economic interests implicated by the suit. Unlike "simple nuisance

[25] See, e.g., David A. Dana, The Mismatch between Public Nuisance Law and Global Warming, 18 Sup. Ct. Econ. Rev. 9 (2010).
[26] See California v. Gen. Motors Corp., No. C06-05755, 2007 WL 2726871 (N.D. Cal. Sept. 17, 2007); Comer v. Murphy Oil USA, No. 05-436, 2007 WL 6942285 (S.D. Miss. Aug. 30, 2007) (unpublished ruling), rev'd, 585 F.3d 855, 880 (2009), vacated 589 F.3d 208 (2010), appeal dismissed 607 F.3d 1049 (2010); Native Vill. of Kivalina v. Exxon Mobil Corp., 663 F. Supp. 2d 863 (N.D. Cal. 2009).
[27] Connecticut v. Am. Elec. Power, 406 F. Supp. 2d 265, 271 (S.D.N.Y. 2005).

claim[s] of the kind courts have adjudicated in the past," plaintiffs' claims were of a "transcendently legislative nature."[28] Insofar as climate change was an important matter of national—if not international—policy, the court concluded, it was a question best left to the political branches. The plaintiffs appealed.

II. A Tale of Two Climate Cases

At the same time as the states and conservation groups were bringing their nuisance action against American Electric Power and other major electricity producers, several of the same states were suing the EPA alleging that GHG emissions constituted "pollutants" subject to regulation under the Clean Air Act.[29] Environmentalist groups had petitioned the EPA to regulate automotive GHG emissions several years earlier. After the Clinton administration demurred and the Bush administration denied their request, they filed suit.

Both cases sought the imposition of GHG emission controls, one through administrative regulation, the other through judicial fiat. Both were a reaction to the federal government's steadfast refusal to adopt such policies on its own. If politicians in Washington, D.C., would not regulate GHGs, state attorneys general and environmentalist groups reasoned, perhaps litigation could force their hand. And if either case produced an unwieldy legal settlement, perhaps that would spur legislative action on Capitol Hill.[30]

Although the cases raised different legal arguments, and followed different courses, their fates were intertwined. It was well understood that prevailing in one case would likely preclude victory in the other. Indeed, that was the point. The arguments used by the EPA and industry to defend against GHG emission controls in one case would undercut their arguments in the other. The EPA had determined GHGs were not subject to regulation under the CAA.[31]

[28] *Id.* at 272.

[29] See Massachusetts v. EPA, 415 F.3d 50 (D.C. Cir. 2005), rev'd 549 U.S. 497 (2007). A large number of nonprofit advocacy organizations were also involved in this suit.

[30] See John Schwartz, Courts as Battlefields in Climate Fights, N.Y. Times, Jan. 26, 2010, at A1 (noting legal cases were increasing pressure on Congress to enact climate change legislation).

[31] See Control of Emissions from New Highway Vehicles and Engines, 68 Fed. Reg. 52922 (Sept. 8, 2003).

If that were so, the states argued, the CAA could not preclude common-law-based claims against GHG emissions.[32] The aim was to place the EPA and those industry groups opposing regulation in a no-win situation, further enhancing the pressure for climate legislation.[33]

The states eventually prevailed in *Massachusetts*. The Court held, among other things, that GHG emissions "fit well within the Clean Air Act's capacious definition of 'air pollutant,'" and could be regulated by the EPA.[34] Indeed, given the agency's repeated statements over many years about the dangers posed by greenhouse warming, the *Massachusetts* decision ensured that GHGs would be regulated by the EPA. This disposition all but ensured the outcome of *AEP*— it just took a while for this message to be heard.

III. *AEP*'s Stop in the Second Circuit

Massachusetts was decided in April 2007. By that point, *AEP* had already been before the U.S. Court of Appeals for the Second Circuit for over a year,[35] where it would continue to sit. The three-judge panel assigned to the case requested supplemental briefing on the effect of *Massachusetts* on the parties' arguments, but that did not accelerate the case's disposition. An opinion would not issue for over two more years, by which time one of the panel's judges, Sonia Sotomayor, had been nominated and confirmed to the Supreme Court.[36]

---

[32] See, e.g., Brief for Respondents Connecticut, et al. at 1–2, Am. Elec. Power v. Connecticut (2011) (No. 10-174) (noting state suit was filed in response to the EPA's taking the position that it lacked the authority to regulate greenhouse gases under the Clean Air Act.).

[33] Not all of those involved in the suits would accept this characterization, however. See Schwartz, *supra* note 30, at A1 (quoting attorney Matthew F. Pawa denying that the cases were brought to influence federal policy).

[34] Massachusetts, 549 U.S. at 532.

[35] The appeal was filed in September 2005. The plaintiff-appellants' initial briefs were filed in December 2005 and the Second Circuit heard oral argument in *AEP* in June 2006. See Marcia Coyle, Questions Arise about Long Delay by Sotomayor-Led Panel in Climate Case, Nat'l. L.J., May 29, 2009, available at http://www.law.com/jsp/article.jsp?id=1202431051311&slreturn=1&hbxlogin=1.

[36] Then-Judge Sotomayor had been on the original three-judge panel that heard the case and called for supplemental briefing. She was confirmed as an associate justice to the U.S. Supreme Court on August 6, 2009; the Second Circuit released its opinion on September 21, 2009.

When the Second Circuit finally issued its decision in September 2009, four years after the case was docketed, it handed the plaintiffs a resounding (if short-lived) victory. The panel found that the district court had erred in dismissing the complaint on political question grounds, concluding that *all* the plaintiffs had standing and that they had properly stated claims under the federal common law of nuisance that were not displaced by the CAA.[37] This last conclusion was easily the weakest and least convincing portion of the panel's lengthy opinion. The Second Circuit accurately cited the Supreme Court's relevant precedents on displacement of federal common law, and quoted the appropriate test, but then proceeded to disregard them in resolving the case.

Whether federal common-law actions for interstate pollution are displaced turns on *legislative* action. As the Second Circuit explained, citing *Milwaukee v. Illinois* (*Milwaukee II*), "Because 'federal common-law is subject to the paramount authority of Congress,' federal courts may resort to it only 'in absence of an applicable Act of Congress.'"[38] For this reason, it was generally presumed that federal common-law public nuisance actions against interstate air pollution were displaced by the CAA.[39] If the CAA's expansive statutory scheme

---

[37] AEP, 582 F.3d at 315.

[38] *Id.* at 371 (quoting Milwaukee II, 451 U.S. 304, 313 (1981)). The Second Circuit also cited *Milwaukee II*'s instructions that: "when Congress addresses a question previously governed by a decision rested on federal common law the need for . . . lawmaking by federal courts disappears" and "the question [of] whether a previously available federal common-law action has been displaced by federal statutory law involves an assessment of the scope of the legislation and whether the scheme established by Congress addresses the problem formerly governed by federal common law." *Id.* (quoting Milwaukee II, 451 U.S. at 314, 315 n.8).

[39] See, e.g., Robert V. Percival, The Clean Water Act and the Demise of the Federal Common Law of Interstate Nuisance, 55 Ala. L. Rev. 717, 768 n.476 (2004) ("Although the Supreme Court has not directly addressed the question of whether the federal Clean Air Act preempts federal common law in disputes over transboundary air pollution, it is widely assumed to do so, particularly in light of the Clean Air Act Amendments of 1990, which created a comprehensive federal permit scheme similar to that established by the Clean Water Act."); see also Gerald Torres, Who Owns the Sky? 19 Pace Envtl. L. Rev. 515, 555 (2002) ("Since 1981, federal courts have recognized that the regulatory framework of the Clean Air Act has replaced the federal common law cause of action in nuisance."); James A. Sevinsky, Public Nuisance: A Common-Law Remedy Among the Statutes, 5 Nat. Res. & Env't. 29, 30 (1990) (noting as "various comprehensive environmental statutes were put in place, the Supreme Court virtually gutted the federal common law of nuisance as an environmental remedy").

were to apply to GHGs, it would follow that federal common-law nuisance claims would be displaced as well.[40]

Despite the clear language of *Milwaukee II*, the Second Circuit rejected the defendants' displacement claim. It focused not on the CAA itself, but on its implementation by the EPA. Since the EPA had not yet begun to exercise its authority to regulate GHGs, the Second Circuit reasoned, the states' nuisance claims had yet to be displaced. Whether or not such claims would be displaced in the future, the court added, would depend upon the precise contours of future EPA regulations governing GHGs.[41] The Second Circuit's approach may have been reasonable had it been a question of first impression, but it was not. Further, by shifting the locus of displacement authority from Congress to the EPA, it made displacement hinge on particular policy choices that could change from one presidential administration to the next.

While the Second Circuit's failure to follow applicable Supreme Court precedents on the displacement of federal common law was the court's most conspicuous error, it was not the only questionable element of its opinion. On the question of standing, the Court concluded that all the plaintiffs—states and conservation groups alike—had standing. Yet it is only necessary for one plaintiff to demonstrate standing to maintain a federal court's jurisdiction. Once the Second Circuit had concluded that one or more of the states satisfied the constitutional standing requirements, it should have stopped.[42] By stretching to consider the private conservation groups' standing, it also stretched the relevant standing precedents by, among other things, holding that the conservation groups could satisfy the injury-in-fact requirement without asserting any present harms. Not only did the conservation groups "not allege any current injury,"[43] those

---

[40] Before *Massachusetts v. EPA* was decided, I had heard more than one attorney involved in both cases concede this point. Strangely, once *Massachusetts* had been decided, this concession was forgotten.

[41] AEP, 582 F.3d at 380 ("Until EPA completes the rulemaking process, we cannot speculate as to whether the hypothetical regulation of greenhouse gases under the Clean Air Act would in fact 'spea[k] directly' to the 'particular issue' raised here by Plaintiffs.").

[42] Consideration of the other plaintiffs' standing would only have been necessary insofar as the other plaintiffs were asserting different claims or seeking different relief.

[43] AEP, 582 F.3d at 341.

injuries they did allege would only manifest themselves over a period of many years and were based on predictions of the future. Nonetheless, the Second Circuit found that the private plaintiffs satisfied the requirement of an "actual or imminent" injury.

The Second Circuit also concluded that nonstate actors, including the private conservation groups, could sue under the federal common law of nuisance, despite the lack of meaningful precedent supporting this result.[44] In every case in which the Supreme Court has sustained suits alleging public nuisances under federal common law, the plaintiffs were states. Indeed, the Supreme Court often characterized such suits as analogous to disputes between sovereigns.[45] The Court was presented with the question of whether private parties could maintain a suit under the federal common law of nuisance in *National Sea Clammers Association v. City of New York*, but did not reach the question after it concluded federal common-law nuisance actions for interstate water pollution were displaced by federal law.[46] But the Second Circuit was undaunted, relying on the since-vacated opinion of the U.S. Court of Appeals for the Third Circuit in *National Sea Clammers*.[47] Yet, as with standing, this foray into the outer regions of federal common law was unnecessary once the Second Circuit concluded that the state parties could maintain the suit.

IV. Before the High Court

With several climate-based nuisance claims in federal court, it was likely one such case would be granted review. The odds of *AEP* being that case increased dramatically after the solicitor general submitted a brief supporting the power companies' petition for certiorari. Whatever ideological sympathy the Obama administration may have had for the plaintiffs and their claims, the Department of

---

[44] See *id.* at 361 (noting "cases addressing the issue of whether private parties may sue under the federal common law of nuisance have been sparse"). "Sparse" may be something of an overstatement, however, as the Supreme Court noted in *AEP* that it has never "decided whether private citizens . . . may invoke the federal common law of nuisance to abate out-of-state pollution." 131 S.Ct. at 2536.

[45] See, e.g., Missouri I, 180 U.S. at 241. See also Merrill, *supra* note 20, at 303.

[46] 453 U.S. 1, 11 n.17 (1981).

[47] AEP, 582 F.3d at 363.

Justice recognized the tenuous nature of the Second Circuit's opinion, particularly its untethered conclusion regarding the displacement of federal common-law claims. Given the positions traditionally espoused by the Justice Department, however—on standing in particular—the solicitor general's merits brief was quite restrained. It urged the Supreme Court to reverse the standing holding on prudential, rather than constitutional, grounds, and recommended remand so the Second Circuit could reconsider its displacement holding in light of subsequent regulatory events.[48] In the months following the circuit court's decision, the EPA had proceeded to propose and adopt expansive regulations of GHG emissions under the CAA. The SG's arguments provided a way for the Court to reverse the Second Circuit without necessarily precluding the continued use of public nuisance suits for other environmental purposes. Environmentalist groups were nonetheless dismayed.[49]

Given the number of issues in the case, there was substantial speculation as to what the Court might do with *AEP*. After oral argument in April 2011, however, the ultimate outcome was no longer in doubt. The justices exhibited deep skepticism about using federal courts to drive climate policy across the board. Even the more liberal justices seemed uneasy with allowing federal judges a hand in balancing the equities involved with climate change. More than one justice suggested the plaintiffs were seeking to have federal judges perform the EPA's job. It was fairly clear the petitioners would prevail. The only question was on what grounds they would win, and whether the SG's modest arguments would carry the day.

V. Obvious Displacement

On June 20, 2011, the Supreme Court announced its opinion in *AEP*, unanimously reversing the Second Circuit.[50] Although many

[48] Brief for the Tenn. Valley Auth. as Respondent Supporting Petitioners, AEP v. Connecticut, 131 S.Ct. 2527 (2011) (10-174).

[49] See Steven Mufson, Obama Administration Sides with Utilities in Supreme Court Case about Climate Change, Wash. Post, Aug. 26, 2010, available at http://www.washingtonpost.com/wp-dyn/content/article/2010/08/26/AR2010082606632.html.

[50] 131 S.Ct. 2527 (2011) (8-0). Justice Sotomayor was recused due to her participation in the case as a judge on the Second Circuit. Justice Samuel Alito wrote an opinion concurring in part and concurring in the judgment, joined by Justice Clarence Thomas, "on the assumption (which I make for the sake of argument because no party contends otherwise)" that the Supreme Court's interpretation of the CAA in *Massachusetts* was correct. *Id.* at 2540–41 (Alito, J., concurring).

issues were on the table, the Court confined its consideration to the question of displacement, because that was enough to decide the case. The Second Circuit's failure to follow the very precedents on which it purported to rely made it easy for the Court to coalesce in what could otherwise have been a divisive case. As Justice Ruth Bader Ginsburg explained for a unanimous Court, whether a federal regulatory program displaces preexisting federal common-law claims is dependent on what legislation Congress has enacted, not how such legislation has or will be implemented by federal regulatory agencies: "The test for whether congressional legislation excludes the declaration of federal common law is simply whether the statute 'speak[s] directly to [the] question at issue.'"[51] If Congress adopted a statute governing GHG emissions, federal common-law actions concerning GHG emissions would be displaced without regard to the nature of the resulting regulatory regime. "As *Milwaukee II* made clear," Justice Ginsburg wrote, "the relevant question for purposes of displacement is 'whether the field has been occupied, not whether it has been occupied in a particular manner.'"[52]

Given the Supreme Court's prior holding that GHGs were subject to regulation under the CAA, displacement follows. As Justice Ginsburg explained,

> the Clean Air Act and the EPA actions it authorizes displace any federal common law right to seek abatement of carbon-dioxide emissions from fossil-fuel fired power plants. *Massachusetts* made plain that emissions of carbon dioxide qualify as air pollution subject to regulation under the Act. . . . And we think it equally plain that the Act 'speaks directly' to emissions of carbon dioxide from the defendants' plants.[53]

The "critical point," Justice Ginsburg explained, was that "Congress delegated to EPA the decision whether and how to regulate carbon-dioxide emissions from power plants,"[54] not whether the

---

[51] *Id.* at 2537 (citation omitted) (Ginsburg, J., for the unanimous Court).

[52] *Id.* at 2538 (quoting Milwaukee II, 451 U.S. at 324).

[53] *Id.* at 2537.

[54] *Id.* at 2538. To this, Justice Ginsburg added, somewhat cheekily, "Congress could hardly preemptively prohibit every discharge of carbon dioxide unless covered by a permit. After all, we each emit carbon dioxide merely by breathing." *Id.*

resulting regulations were effective or desirable.[55] Indeed, Justice Ginsburg noted, were the EPA to adopt inadequate regulations, or even to "decline to regulate carbon-dioxide emissions altogether," it would be immaterial to the question of displacement.[56] Even if the Clean Water Act could be said to impose a more comprehensive system of effluent controls than the CAA, this was irrelevant, for "[o]f necessity, Congress selects different regulatory regimes to address different problems."[57]

In enacting the CAA, as interpreted in *Massachusetts*, Congress made the scope and stringency of federal GHG emissions something for the EPA to determine in the first instance. Should states or private groups disagree with the EPA's policy conclusions, or believe that the EPA's regulations are insufficiently stringent, they retain the ability to petition the agency or file suit in federal court, much as the states and environmentalist groups did in *Massachusetts*. What they cannot do is seek to transfer authority over emission controls from the political branches to the courts through the use of federal common law.

The Court's opinion emphasized that federal common law is a disfavored remedy. "There is no federal general common law," the opinion noted, quoting *Erie Railroad v. Tompkins*.[58] Instead, most questions governed by the common law are left to the states. Federal common law is reserved for "'subjects within national legislative power where Congress has so directed,'" such as in the case of antitrust law, or "where the basic scheme of the Constitution so demands," such as where it is necessary to resolve interstate disputes.[59] In the absence of federal environmental statutes, interstate air and water pollution would be governed by federal common law, but only in the absence of relevant federal legislation. The federal common law of interstate nuisance is thus a backstop—a means of filling interstices insofar as is necessary to enable states to safeguard

---

[55] There are plenty of reasons to believe EPA regulation of greenhouse gases under the Clean Air Act is not desirable. See Adler, *supra* note 3.

[56] AEP, 131 S.Ct. at 2539. ("As *Milwaukee II* made clear, however, the relevant question for purposes of displacement is 'whether the field has been occupied, not whether it has been occupied in a particular manner.'" (citation omitted)).

[57] *Id*. at 2538.

[58] *Id*. at 2535 (quoting Erie R.R. Co. v. Tompkins, 304 U.S. 64, 78 (1938)).

[59] *Id*. (citation omitted).

their sovereign interests in their own territory. Yet as the Court had held in *Milwaukee II*, "when Congress addresses a question previously governed by a decision rested on federal common law, the need for such an unusual exercise of law-making by federal courts disappears."[60]

Whereas the Court has adopted (though not always applied) a presumption against the preemption of state law, no such presumption applies with displacement. If anything, the constitutional structure would warrant a "special presumption" *against* the use of federal common law.[61] Preemption of state law must be clearly shown so as to protect states' sovereign interests within the federal system of dual sovereignty. No such interest protects the policymaking power of the federal courts. Justice Ginsburg explained that "it is primarily for the office of Congress, not the federal courts, to prescribe national policies in areas of special federal interest."[62] Thus, whereas the justices routinely disagree and divide over the *preemptive* effect of various federal laws, they were of one mind on the question of *displacement* and unanimously rejected the use of federal common law to control emissions already subject to administrative control under federal law.

Sidestepping Standing

In a typical case, a federal court must assure itself of jurisdiction before reaching the merits of the case. Article III of the Constitution restricts federal court jurisdiction to "Cases" and "Controversies," and one requirement of Article III, as interpreted by the Supreme Court, is that the party seeking to invoke federal jurisdiction have standing. Not only was standing a threshold issue in *AEP*, but the question also presented the Court with an opportunity to clarify the implications of its decision to recognize the Commonwealth of Massachusetts's standing to sue the EPA in *Massachusetts*. It was not to be. With Justice Sotomayor recused, the participating justices split evenly on the matter.[63] Four of the justices concluded that "at least some plaintiffs," most likely the states, could establish standing

---

[60] 451 U.S. at 314.

[61] See Merrill, *supra* note 20, at 314.

[62] *AEP*, 131 S.Ct. at 2537.

[63] *Id.* at 2535.

under the Court's holding in *Massachusetts*.[64] Four others would have denied standing, as they either adhered to Chief Justice John Roberts's standing dissent in *Massachusetts* or found the case distinguishable.[65] Therefore, under longstanding Court practice, the Court affirmed the Second Circuit's exercise of jurisdiction without deciding that question, missing an opportunity to clarify the law of standing.[66]

Climate change presents a particularly difficult standing challenge. Global warming is just that—a *global* phenomenon. GHG emissions, whether from motor vehicles, coal-fired power plants, or any other source, contribute to *global* GHG concentrations in the atmosphere that affect the *global* climate. As a consequence, concerns about global warming would appear to represent the sort of "generalized grievance" that is "common to all members of the public,"[67] and is therefore beyond the scope of Article III. Invoking the power of federal courts requires something more than an abstract legal wrong or a harm that is visited on the entire body politic.

Under *Lujan v. Defenders of Wildlife*, there are three necessary components to Article III standing.[68] First, the "plaintiff must have suffered an 'injury in fact,'" that is both "actual or imminent" and "concrete and particularized."[69] Second, there must be a "causal connection between the injury and the conduct complained of."[70] Third, there must be a sufficient likelihood that "the injury will be 'redressed by a favorable decision.'"[71] Strictly applied, *Lujan*'s requirements would seem to create a problem for plaintiffs seeking to litigate warming-based claims. "The very concept of global warming

---

[64] *Id.*

[65] *Id.*

[66] The defendant-petitioners and some *amici curiae* also maintained that plaintiffs' claims presented a nonjusticiable political question, as the district court had concluded. See, e.g., Brief Amicus Curiae of Cato Institute in Support of Petitioners, Am. Elec. Power v. Connecticut, 131 S.Ct. 2527 (2011) (No. 10-174). At least four justices rejected this claim, but it was not resolved by the Court. AEP, 131 S.Ct. at 2535.

[67] United States v. Richardson, 418 U.S. 166, 176–77 (1974) (quoting Ex parte Levitt, 302 U.S. 633, 634 (1937) (per curiam); Laird v. Tatum, 408 U.S. 1, 13 (1972)).

[68] 504 U.S. 555 (1992).

[69] *Id.* at 560.

[70] *Id.*

[71] *Id.* at 561 (quoting Simon v. E. Ky. Welfare Rights Org., 426 U.S. 38, 43 (1976)).

seems inconsistent with [the] particularization requirement," observed Chief Justice Roberts in his *Massachusetts* dissent.[72]

The Commonwealth of Massachusetts addressed this difficulty by focusing on a specific, concrete harm that would result from climatic warming: sea-level rise and the consequent flooding of Massachusetts's coast.[73] It submitted affidavits alleging that present and continuing anthropogenic GHG emissions would lead to increased sea-level rise that would, in turn, produce coastal flooding.[74] By focusing on sea-level rise, Massachusetts sought to satisfy the particularization requirement by demonstrating how global warming would affect it in a distinct and identifiable way.

The focus on sea-level rise eased the standing inquiry, but it did not make the problems go away. Under *Lujan*, an "injury in fact" must be *both* actual or imminent *and* concrete and particularized. Satisfying both of these requirements simultaneously remained a challenge, for insofar as Massachusetts sought to argue that its injury was occurring in the here and now, it became more difficult for it to identify the specific harms that were caused by anthropogenic contributions to climate change, as opposed to other factors (for example, subsidence, natural variation, and non-anthropogenic warming). In order to identify any particular quantum of its coastline under threat from global warming, Massachusetts had to rely on computer model projections far into the future. Specifically, Massachusetts cited estimates of projected sea-level rise due to global warming "by 2100."[75] Such harm may have been particular to the Commonwealth of Massachusetts—even if the amount attributable to anthropogenic emissions would still be measured in centimeters—but sea-level rise over the course of a century would not seem to be an "imminent" harm.

The Court further assisted the standing claim by announcing a "special solicitude" for state litigants.[76] Justice Stevens's opinion noted it was "of considerable relevance" that the petitioner was "a

---

[72] 549 U.S. at 541 (Roberts, C.J., dissenting).

[73] *Id.* at 522 (majority opinion).

[74] *Id.* at 521–22.

[75] *Id.* at 523 n.20 (discussing "possible" effects of rising sea levels over the next century).

[76] *Id.* at 520.

sovereign State and not, as it was in *Lujan*, a private individual."[77] Because states had ceded a portion of their sovereignty to the federal government, they were entitled to this "special solicitude" when seeking to invoke the authority of federal courts. With this clarification "in mind," the Court concluded that the loss of even small portions of Massachusetts's coastline would be a sufficient injury under Article III.[78] This aspect of the *Massachusetts* holding would certainly seem to establish that the state plaintiffs in *AEP* had suffered an equivalent injury, and the Second Circuit held as much.[79] But injury-in-fact is only one component on the inquiry and is not, by itself, sufficient to establish standing.

Even if a climate-related harm satisfies the injury-in-fact requirement, a plaintiff must still demonstrate that the injury is fairly traceable to the conduct complained of and that any such injury would be redressed by a victory in court. Here again, strict application of traditional standing requirements would appear to be fatal, as it would be nearly impossible to attribute any degree of warming-induced harm to a subset of domestic GHG emissions, or to identify with any degree of precision the extent to which such harms could be avoided by a reduction in emissions on the margin.

In *Massachusetts*, the Court eased these difficulties by noting that Massachusetts was seeking to vindicate a "procedural right" to challenge unlawful agency action (or inaction) sanctioned by Congress. According to the Court, it was "of critical importance" that Congress had "authorized this type of challenge to EPA action."[80] This authorization made the difference because, as the Court had held in *Lujan*,

---

[77] *Id.* at 518.

[78] The majority based Massachusetts's injury on the fact that "global seal levels rose somewhere between 10 and 20 centimeters over the 20th century as a result of global warming," *id.* at 522, even though plaintiff's affidavit did not attribute all, or even any specific portion, of this sea-level rise to anthropogenic GHG emissions. See MacCracken Decl. ¶5(c), Stdg. App. at 225, Massachusetts, 549 U.S. 497 (No. 05-1120).

[79] 582 F.3d at 344. The Second Circuit also inexplicably went on to hold that the City of New York and the private litigants had Article III standing even though the private litigants did "not allege any current injury." *Id.* at 341. This holding was inexplicable because it was completely unnecessary to the disposition of the case as it is only necessary for one plaintiff to possess standing for the Court to have jurisdiction. See Massachusetts, 541 U.S. at 518 (quoting Rumsfeld v. Forum for Academic & Institutional Rights, Inc., 547 U.S. 47, 52 n.2 (2006) .

[80] Massachusetts, 549 U.S. at 516.

the "normal standards for redressability and immediacy" required for Article III jurisdiction are relaxed when a litigant is seeking to vindicate procedural rights created by Congress.[81] This relaxation was certainly useful to the petitioners in *Massachusetts*, but it could not help the plaintiffs in *AEP*. Even assuming that the Court properly recognized a procedural right in *Massachusetts*,[82] the *AEP* plaintiffs claimed no such right—nor could they as their claim rested on the federal common law of nuisance. Thus, insofar as the existence of a procedural right was necessary to establish the requisite degree of traceability and redressability for purposes of standing in *Massachusetts*, there was ample basis to distinguish the standing claim in *AEP*. Nonetheless, it appears no justice who had been in the *Massachusetts* majority was interested in distinguishing the cases on that basis.

Although the Court did not resolve the standing claim, one might surmise that a majority of the current justices would have found for the plaintiffs on this issue. In her relatively brief time on the Court, Justice Sotomayor, who sat on the Second Circuit panel below through oral argument and supplemental briefing, has indicated that she is likely to side with those justices urging a more permissive approach to standing.[83] If that is so, she would have joined Justice Anthony Kennedy and the "liberal" justices to find that at least one state plaintiff satisfied Article III's standing requirements. The only question is whether the resulting majority would have rested squarely on *Massachusetts* or, recognizing the distinctions between the cases, would have lowered the standing hurdle even further.

VII. The Future of Climate Litigation

The Supreme Court's holding that the CAA displaces public nuisance suits under federal common law does not mean the states and conservation groups are left without legal remedy. As initially filed, the suits also asserted state-law-based claims alleging a public nuisance under the law of the 20 states in which defendants' power

---

[81] Lujan, 504 U.S. at 572 n.7.

[82] This is a nontrivial assumption. See Jonathan H. Adler, Standing Still in the Roberts Court, 59 Case W. Res. L. Rev. 1061, 1076–77 (2009); Ronald A. Cass, Massachusetts v. EPA: The Inconvenient Truth about Precedent, 93 Va. L. Rev. In Brief 75, 80 (2007), available at http://www.virginialawreview.org/inbrief/2007/05/21/cass.pdf.

[83] See, e.g., Ariz. Christian Sch. Tuition Org. v. Winn, 131 S. Ct. 1436 (2011)

facilities are located. The Second Circuit did not reach this issue, as it concluded plaintiffs had viable federal common-law claims.[84] As a consequence, the Supreme Court did not consider whether the CAA preempts public nuisance suits under state law or even whether such claims are viable. This subject was not briefed, and the Court expressly left the matter "open for consideration on remand."[85]

The displacement of federal common law implicates a different legal standard than does the preemption of state-law-based claims.[86] Whereas the invocation of federal common law is generally disfavored, so too is the federal preemption of state law. As noted above, if a federal statute "speaks directly" to a given question, that is sufficient to displace federal common-law claims—even if the federal legislation does not resolve the problem at hand. More is required, however, to preempt state-law-based claims. As a general matter, preemption will not be found unless the Court concludes preemption "was the clear and manifest purpose of Congress"[87] or that "a scheme of federal regulation . . . [is] so pervasive as to make reasonable the inference that Congress left no room for the states to supplement it."[88] This more stringent standard protects the states' sovereign interests in maintaining their police powers free of federal interference.[89]

In the case of interstate water pollution, the Court's prior holdings that the federal Clean Water Act displaces federal common-law public nuisance suits have not preempted state-law-based claims against interstate water pollution. Under *International Paper Co. v. Ouellette*, states may file public nuisance suits against sources of interstate pollution so long as such claims are brought under the

---

[84] Milwaukee II, 451 U.S. at 314 n.7 ("If state law can be applied, there is no need for federal common law; if federal common law exists, it is because state law cannot be used."). See also Merrill, *supra* note 20, at 306 ("Federal common law and state common law are not cumulative causes of action . . . They are mutually exclusive.").

[85] AEP, 131 S.Ct. at 2540.

[86] See Merrill, *supra* note 20, at 314.

[87] Rice v. Santa Fe Elevator Corp., 331 U.S. 218, 230 (1947).

[88] Pacific Gas & Elec. Co. v. State Energy Res. Conservation & Dev. Comm'n, 461 U.S. 190, 204 (1983).

[89] See, e.g., Jones v. Rath Packing Co., 430 U.S. 519, 525 (1977) ("This assumption provides assurance that 'the federal-state balance' will not be disturbed unintentionally by Congress or unnecessarily by the courts.").

common law of the *source* state.[90] There is no *a priori* reason why a similar standard would not apply in the context of interstate air pollution. Among other things, the CAA contains a savings clause that is quite similar to that contained in the Clean Water Act.[91]

While *AEP* does not preclude state-law-based nuisance actions, Justice Ginsburg's opinion offered cautionary notes about the potential consequences of allowing such suits to proceed. Whatever the value of public nuisance claims generally, she explained why courts are particularly ill-suited to address climate change claims. Identifying and setting appropriate GHG emission targets requires the consideration of numerous tradeoffs—economic, environmental, and otherwise. Considering how to balance such competing considerations is typically the sort of legislative policy judgment Congress either delegates to an administrative agency or reserves for itself. In *AEP*, Justice Ginsburg noted, it was "altogether fitting" that Congress concluded that "an expert agency" was "best suited to serve as primary regulator of greenhouse gases."[92] As she explained:

> The expert agency is surely better equipped to do the job than individual district judges issuing ad hoc, case-by-case injunctions. Federal judges lack the scientific, economic, and technological resources an agency can utilize in coping with issues of this order. . . . Judges may not commission scientific studies or convene groups of experts for advice, or issue rules under notice-and-comment procedures inviting input by any interested person, or seek the counsel of regulators in the States where the defendants are located. Rather, judges are confined by a record comprising the evidence the parties present.[93]

Whatever the limitations of agency rulemaking, there is no reason to think state judges, or even federal judges applying state law, would fare any better. If anything, the application of variable state standards to a global, interjurisdictional concern could further frustrate the development of a coherent climate change policy. As Justice Ginsburg noted, allowing these lawsuits to proceed could open the

---

[90] 479 U.S. at 481.
[91] Compare 33 U.S.C. § 1365(e) (2011) and 42 U.S.C. § 7604(a)(1) (2011).
[92] 131 S.Ct. at 2539.
[93] *Id.* at 2539–40.

door to lawsuits against "'thousands or hundreds or tens' of other defendants" deemed to be "large contributors" to GHG emissions.[94] Yet displacement alone is not sufficient to prevent the proliferation of climate lawsuits. State-law nuisance claims could just as easily thrust climate policy into the hands of the judiciary.

Conclusion

AEP was undoubtedly a victory for the corporate defendants, but it was quite a limited one. Existing precedent clearly called for displacement, so such a holding does not, in itself, prevent further climate-based nuisance litigation in either federal or state court. The displacement holding could also complicate industry efforts to limit federal regulatory authority over GHG emissions. Should Congress enact legislation withdrawing EPA authority over GHGs under the CAA, for example, public nuisance suits under federal common law could be revived.[95]

More broadly, recognizing the impracticability of adjudicating climate policy in the context of individual nuisance suits in federal court does not in any way minimize the seriousness of global climate change, nor does it necessarily cast doubt on the potential value of common-law litigation to address conventional pollution. Libertarians and others have argued that using the common law to address environmental pollution concerns is better than resorting to decision-making by centralized administrative agencies.[96] While global climate change is anything but a typical environmental pollution concern, even a modest warming could produce the sorts of harms

[94] *Id.* at 2540 (quoting Transcript of Oral Argument at 57, AEP, 131 S.Ct. 2527 (No. 10-174)).

[95] See Douglas Kysar, Supreme Court Ruling Is Good, Bad and Ugly, 474 Nature 421 (2011).

[96] See, e.g., Terry Anderson & Donald Leal, Free Market Environmentalism 132 (rev. ed. 2001) ("The free market environmental approach to pollution is to establish property rights to the pollution disposal medium and allow owners of those rights to bargain over how the resource will be used."); see also Jonathan H. Adler & Andrew P. Morriss, Introduction: Common Law Environmental Protection, 58 Case W. Res. L. Rev. 575 (2008); Roger Meiners & Bruce Yandle, Common Law and the Conceit of Modern Environmental Policy, 7 Geo. Mason L. Rev. 923 (1999); Elizabeth Brubaker, Property Rights in the Defence of Nature (1995); Bruce Yandle, Common Sense and Common Law for the Environment: Creating Wealth in Hummingbird Economies (1997); Fred L. Smith Jr., A Free-Market Environmental Program, 11 Cato J. 457 (1992).

common-law nuisance actions have addressed.[97] The common law has long recognized actions that cause the flooding of a neighbor's land as a trespass or nuisance, and even so-called skeptics recognize global warming could produce a measurable increase in sea level.[98]

Yet opening the door to climate-based nuisance suits could unleash a torrent of litigation. Given the ubiquity of GHG emissions, allowing suits against one set of firms inevitably opens the door to suits against others—without any prospect of addressing the underlying concern. Given the global nature of the problem, climate change can only be mitigated or averted on a global scale. Reducing emissions from the 5, 50, or 500 largest GHG emitters within the United States will have no appreciable effect on the accumulation of GHGs in the broader atmosphere.

The global nature of climate change also counsels against trying to fit it within the contours of common-law nuisance claims. In many respects, climate change presents a common-pool resource management problem in which the challenge is not simply to prevent one group from polluting another, but also how to manage the aggregate effects of human activity on a given resource that is shared by all.[99] And whether or not there is a scientific consensus about the scope and scale of human influence on the global climate, addressing climate change requires confronting fundamental tradeoffs among economic, environmental, and ethical concerns. Some degree of human influence on the climate is inevitable, so the question becomes what degree of interference is desirable or acceptable—and what ameliorative or adaptive measures are warranted.

Such questions lie far beyond the capability of common-law courts. For better or worse, then, we have to leave climate change in the hands of the political process, to be addressed—if at all—by legislative and (duly authorized) administrative action.

[97] See, e.g., Jonathan H. Adler, Taking Property Rights Seriously: The Case of Climate Change, 26 Soc. Phil. & Pol'y 296 (2009).

[98] See, e.g., Patrick J. Michaels and Robert C. Balling, Jr., The Satanic Gases: Clearing the Air about Global Warming 162 (2000) (predicting a warming-induced sea-level rise of 5 to 11 inches over the next century).

[99] See Dana, *supra* note 25, at 12 ("Global warming, however, is not best conceived as a binary pollution dispute between producers and recipients of 'pollution'; rather, global warming is an issue of how to manage a common natural resource (the atmosphere) so that the human 'load' on the resource will not push the resource beyond a 'tipping point' it is generally understood we (human kind) should not want to reach.").

Wal-Mart v. Dukes: Class Actions and Legal Strategy

*Andrew J. Trask**

> Cutty: The game done changed...
> Slim: Game's the same, just got more fierce.[1]

I. The Role of Legal Strategy

Despite the dire warnings of its staunchest advocates and the occasional frustrated wishes of its critics, the class action has proved extremely hard to kill.[2] Notwithstanding the Private Securities Litigation Reform Act, which curbed some of the worst abuses by plaintiffs' lawyers in securities cases, securities class actions are still thriving. Similarly, the Class Action Fairness Act, which ensured that plaintiffs had to bring nationwide class actions in federal court rather than more sympathetic state courts, has simply created a booming business in federal class actions.

The truth is, class actions are big business for lawyers on both sides. Plaintiffs' lawyers can win multi-million dollar paydays from settling just a single case. Elite defense firms can earn millions more slowly by defending a steady stream of class actions against their clients. And that makes class-action practice the subject of a game of legal strategy all its own.

---

* Andrew J. Trask is counsel at McGuireWoods LLP and co-chair of its Securities Class Action Group. He is the coauthor (with Brian Anderson) of *The Class Action Playbook* (2010), and maintains the Class Action Countermeasures blog at http://www.classactioncountermeasures.com.

[1] The Wire, episode 3.4, "Hamsterdam," written by George Pelecanos, directed by Ernest Dickerson (HBO 2004).

[2] See, e.g., Myriam Gilles, Opting Out of Liability: The Forthcoming, Near-Total Demise of the Modern Class Action, 104 Mich. L. Rev. 373 (2005); Benjamin Sachs-Michaels, The Demise of Class Actions Will Not Be Televised, 12 Cardozo J. Conflict Resol. 665 (2011).

What do I mean by legal strategy? Strategy is

> (1) a plan for action toward a goal;
> (2) that comprises a series of actions over time; and
> (3) that assumes other parties will oppose (or otherwise inter-
> fere with) the plan.[3]

In litigation, a party is concerned with at least two possible other parties—its opponents and the court. Courts are made up of judges, and judges—even the most conscientious ones—have innate biases and agendas of their own,[4] even the Supreme Court (which is largely assumed, rightly or not, to be pro-business).[5]

Strategy extends beyond simply winning the immediate case, however. For repeat litigants, securing favorable developments in legal doctrine for future cases can be more important than a single victory or loss. And legal doctrine emerges from the way in which courts are presented with cases, which in turn reflects strategic choices made by litigators. In the United States, federal courts limit themselves to deciding live controversies. And the selection of live controversies that arrive in court is the product of strategic choices that both the plaintiff and defendant have made—from which claims

---

[3] Brian Anderson & Andrew Trask, The Class Action Playbook xiv (2010).

[4] Chief Judge Dennis Jacobs of the Court of Appeals for the Second Circuit, for example, has said that judges have an "inbred preference for . . . all things that need and use lawyers, enrich them, and empower them vis-à-vis other sources of power and wisdom." Dennis Jacobs, The Secret Life of Judges, 75 Fordham L. Rev. 2855, 2855 (2007). And Judge Richard Posner of the Court of Appeals for the Seventh Circuit has pointed out that judges cannot escape the life experience they bring to each case, no matter how conscientious they are. Richard A. Posner, How Judges Think 68–69 (2008).

[5] See, e.g., Robert Barnes and Carrie Johnson, Pro-Business Decision Hews to Pattern of Roberts Court, Wash. Post, Jun. 22, 2007, available at http://www.washington post.com/wp-dyn/content/article/2007/06/21/AR2007062100803.html (last viewed Jul. 30, 2011); Associated Press, Is the Roberts Court Pro-Business? Aug. 5, 2010, available at http://www.cbsnews.com/stories/2010/06/10/politics/main6568825. shtml (last viewed Jul. 30, 2011). But see, e.g., David G. Savage, Justices Have Been Siding with Workers, Underdogs, L.A. Times, Mar. 13, 2011, available at http:// articles.latimes.com/2011/mar/13/nation/la-na-court-unanimous-20110313 (last viewed Aug. 8, 2011); Hans Bader, *Free Enterprise Fund v. PCAOB*: Narrow Separation-of-Powers Ruling Illustrates That the Supreme Court Is Not "Pro-Business," 2009–10 Cato S. Ct. Rev. 269, 283 (2010) (noting that "business has lost ground repeatedly" before the Supreme Court).

to bring to which cases to settle.[6] Given the high stakes involved in class actions, both sides invest heavily in strategic efforts to shape legal doctrine and, as a result, class action law around the trial and appellate federal judiciary is constantly pushed in divergent and inconsistent directions, the result of particular battles in front of particular courts.

About once a decade, the Supreme Court steps squarely into the middle of this fray like a referee at a heated homecoming game and rules certain tactics off-limits. The last time it did so was in 1997 in *Amchem Products, Inc. v. Windsor*, when it held that courts could not use class action settlements to sidestep the formidable problems of administering mass tort litigation.[7] This term it did so again, sweeping away a number of tactics both plaintiffs and defendants had developed in the years since *Amchem*. And it did so, at least in part, because of the way those issues were presented by the time they reached the Court. Of the several class action cases it decided, the centerpiece was *Wal-Mart v Dukes*. As we will see, for those interested in the debate over class actions, *Dukes* provides an excellent view of the strategic maneuvering that goes on, both between plaintiffs and defendants and among courts.

The *Dukes* decision provoked a loud outcry in the popular press, which for the most part reflected opinions about social politics rather than legal policy. Yet the decision is fairly straightforward doctrinally. And one of the Court's two holdings—a holding sufficient to reverse the lower court's opinion—was unanimous.

II. Creative Certification Strategies

Rule 23 of the Federal Rules of Civil Procedure authorizes the class action, a method of aggregating a large number of claims into a single lawsuit. Under Rule 23, the lawsuit begins with an individual plaintiff. If that plaintiff can convince the court that her claim is enough like those of the people she seeks to represent, the court certifies the case as a class action. Once the class is certified, the plaintiff offers proof of her individual claim at trial. If she wins, the whole class wins; if she loses, the whole class loses with her.

---

[6] See Oona A. Hathaway, Path Dependence in the Law: The Course and Pattern of Legal Change in a Common Law System, 86 Iowa L. Rev. 601, 603–05 (2001).

[7] Amchem Prods. Inc. v. Windsor, 521 U.S. 591, 619 (1997).

What makes class action strategy so interesting (and so complex) is that few class actions ever go to trial.[8] Instead, the real battle is over class certification itself. If the court certifies the class, then the plaintiffs have effectively won. If it does not, the defendants have. (Rule 23 recognizes this effect by allowing interlocutory appeals of the certification decision, because it usually sounds the "death knell" for one side or the other in the litigation.[9])

As a result, in the high-stakes game of class action litigation, plaintiffs will try any number of inventive tactics to get class actions certified. In its last major class action opinion, the Court remarked on the "adventuresome" tactics lawyers used in conjunction with Rule 23.[10] Similarly, defendants will get as creative as they can in opposing certification.

How does a plaintiff get a class certified? She must demonstrate that she meets a number of minimum prerequisites (described in Rule 23(a)) and that she meets one of three additional categories of lawsuit (described in Rule 23(b)).

Rule 23(a) lists four requirements, each of which is designed to test whether a proposed class is cohesive enough to justify a massive trial culminating in a one-size-fits-all verdict. Those requirements are: (1) numerosity (are there enough members to justify a class?); (2) commonality (is there a common issue that unites the class?); (3) typicality (is the named plaintiff typical of the class?); and (4) adequacy (will the named plaintiff protect the interests of the class above her own or her attorney's?).

Rule 23(b) lays out three additional categories for class actions. A plaintiff may bring a class action under Rule 23(b)(1) if she can show that winning her lawsuit would necessarily mean that some other potential plaintiff would have to lose an identical lawsuit. This happens in one of two circumstances: either the rights the plaintiff seeks

---

[8] Anderson & Trask, *supra* note 3, at 192 (2010).

[9] Fed. R. Civ. P. 23(f); see also Blair v. Equifax Check Serv., 181 F.3d 832, 834 (7th Cir. 1999) ("just as a denial of class status can doom the plaintiff, so a grant of class status can put considerable pressure on the defendant to settle, even when the plaintiff's probability of success on the merits is slight"). For more on the "death knell" doctrine, see Anderson & Trask, *supra* note 3, at 170–72 (2010).

[10] Amchem, 521 U.S. at 617–18 ("In the decades since the 1966 revision of Rule 23, class-action practice has become ever more 'adventuresome' as a means of coping with claims too numerous to secure their 'just, speedy, and inexpensive determination' one by one.").

to enforce would require not enforcing someone else's rights or the plaintiff seeks a money award from a limited fund, so paying one plaintiff the full amount she deserves necessarily means not paying others. Rule 23(b)(2) covers cases where a plaintiff seeks some form of declaratory or injunctive relief. And Rule 23(b)(3) addresses cases in which a plaintiff seeks monetary relief; it requires a plaintiff to show that (1) common issues do not just exist but predominate over more individual issues and (2) the class action is superior to other methods of resolving the controversy. Rule 23(b)(1) and (b)(2) classes are known as "mandatory" classes: if a court certifies them, all class members are involved whether they like it or not. Rule 23(b)(3) classes are known as "opt-out" classes because individual class members may choose not to participate in the lawsuit and not to be bound by its verdict.

So the game for plaintiffs in class action litigation is to demonstrate that their lawsuit is full of common issues that can be tried with classwide evidence, so that an aggregated trial will not compromise the due process rights of either the defendant or the absent class members. The game for the defendants is to show that plaintiffs' proposed lawsuit is full of lurking individual issues, each of which must be given its proper due.

This past term, the Court largely addressed (and rejected) some of the more creative approaches to litigating class actions. In *AT&T Mobility, LLC v. Concepcion*, it held that, because there is no inherent right to try a case as a class action, arbitration clauses that waived the right to prosecute a class action were not per se unconscionable.[11] In *Morrison v. Australia National Bank*, the Court held that a securities class action with no connection to the United States (sometimes called a "foreign-cubed" class action because it involves foreign plaintiffs, foreign defendants, and foreign conduct) cannot be brought in a U.S. court under U.S. securities laws.[12]

The Court's class action rulings were not solely pro-defendant. In *Erica John Fund v. Halliburton*, it held that Rule 23 does not require a court to take the additional step of determining whether a securities fraud actually caused an individual investor's loss when certifying

---

[11] 131 S. Ct. 1740 (2011).

[12] 130 S. Ct. 2869 (2010).

a securities class action.[13] And in *Smith v. Bayer Corp.*, the Court held that if an earlier court has refused to certify a proposed class, the members of the proposed class are not barred from bringing another class action based on the same facts.[14]

Each of these rulings declined to read either extra powers (such as the implicit ability to trump an arbitration clause) or extra requirements (such as loss causation) into Rule 23. Instead, the Court has made clear that Rule 23 is a straightforward procedural device. That device allows a plaintiff to represent others who have been similarly wronged in an all-or-nothing trial, but it does not confer separate substantive rights of any kind. *Dukes* fits squarely into this way of looking at the Court's class action term. In *Dukes*, the Court took on several tactics that class action plaintiffs had been trying for some time. Those tactics included the following:

Seeking certification for money damages under Rule 23(b)(2) rather than Rule 23(b)(3). Rule 23(b)(2) has a storied history as a civil rights tool. It was specifically designed to mimic the civil rights class actions that had helped achieve desegregation.[15] As a result, Rule 23(b)(2) is far more concerned with injunctive or declaratory relief than it is with money damages. Rule 23(b)(3) is better designed to address claims for money damages. It has more thorough notice requirements, an opt-out procedure, and methods of ensuring that the litigation is actually a good idea. Plaintiffs developed the tactic of seeking monetary damages under Rule 23(b)(2) rather than Rule 23(b)(3) on the theory that the money they requested was not the primary relief they sought.[16] Were a case to go to trial, the poor fit of Rule 23(b)(2) for monetary class actions would be harder to ignore. But in most cases the plaintiffs' goal is to certify the class and then

---

[13] 131 S. Ct. 2179 (2011).

[14] 131 S. Ct. 2368 (2011).

[15] David Marcus, Flawed but Noble: Desegregation Litigation and Its Implications for the Modern Class Action, 63 Fla. L. Rev. 657, 660 (2011). For a contemporaneous account of how civil rights advocates used the class action device, see Comment, The Class Action Device in Antisegregation Cases, 20 U. Chi. L. Rev. 577 (1953).

[16] Sarah Dale, Reconsidering the Approach to 23(b)(2) Employment Discrimination Class Actions in Light of *Dukes v. Wal-Mart*, 38 Conn. L. Rev. 967, 979–88 (2006) (discussing cases in which plaintiffs sought certification of classes for money damages under Rule 23(b)(2)).

settle the case, rather than to try it in front of a jury.[17] And while courts in the 1990s and 2000s enforced Rule 23(b)(3) stringently, they were less rigorous about enforcing Rule 23(b)(2).[18]

Hybrid certification. If the two subsections offer differing advantages, why not invoke both? Also known as "divided" or "composite" classes, hybrid class actions, where the plaintiff seeks certification under both Rule 23(b)(2) and 23(b)(3), have long been a method for plaintiffs to avoid the problems with meeting the requirements of Rule 23(b)(3).[19]

Claim-splitting. Claim-splitting involves the strategic shaving of causes of action away from a complaint until only those that stand the best chance of certification remain. For example, in a case involving an alleged fraud, a plaintiff might forgo her fraud claim itself (because fraud claims are notoriously difficult to certify) but assert a breach-of-warranty claim invoking the same facts.[20] From the plaintiff's point of view, claim-splitting can be an extremely effective tool for turning an unwieldy individual case into something streamlined enough to try on a classwide basis.

Offering statistical proof to minimize individual issues. Often, a case may involve issues that would ordinarily require individualized proof, in particular, issues that involve causation of some kind, such as whether a particular worker's failure to obtain promotion was due to her gender (as she might claim) or her poor performance (as

---

[17] Mark A. Perry & Rachel S. Brass, Rule 23(b)(2) Certification of Employment Class Actions: A Return to First Principles, 65 N.Y.U. Ann. Surv. Am. L. 681, 681 (2010).

[18] For more on hybrid certification under Rule 23(b)(2), see Anderson & Trask, *supra* note 3, at 38.

[19] See Fisher v. Va. Elec. & Power Co., 217 F.R.D. 201, 214 (E.D. Va. 2003) ("Instead of divided certification, a district judge may grant composite certification. Composite certification allows a court to certify the class under Rule 23(b)(2) for both monetary and equitable remedies and exercise its plenary authority under Rules 23(d)(2) and 23(d)(5) to provide all class members with personal notice and the opportunity to opt out, as if the class were certified under Rule 23(b)(3)."); Jefferson v. Ingersoll Int'l, Inc., 195 F.3d 894, 898 (7th Cir. 1999). For more on hybrid certification, see Anderson & Trask, *supra* note 3, § 2.6.1 (2010).

[20] For more on claim-splitting generally, see Edward F. Sherman, "Abandoned Claims" in Class Actions: Implications for Preclusion and Adequacy of Counsel, 79 Geo. Wash. L. Rev. 483 (2011). For some recent examples of claim-splitting, see Mays v. Tenn. Valley Auth., 2011 U.S. Dist. LEXIS 50225, *28–29 (E.D. Tenn. May 10, 2011); Gates v. Rohm & Hass Co., 265 F.R.D. 208, 218 n.15 (E.D. Pa. 2010); Kelecseny v. Chevron USA, Inc., 262 F.R.D. 660, 673 (S.D. Fla. 2009).

the company might). As a result, plaintiffs' lawyers will often attempt to develop statistical proof that they argue can substitute for the individual proof required in individual actions.[21] While that proof might not be enough to establish the elements of an individual claim, the plaintiffs will argue that the class action device somehow changes the nature of the proof required.

Asking courts to decide certification without facts. For more than a decade, plaintiffs have asked courts to take their factual allegations as true when deciding certification motions. Their ground for doing so was language in a 1974 Supreme Court case, *Eisen v. Carlisle & Jacquelin,* that stated "nothing in either the language or history of Rule 23 . . . gives a court any authority to conduct a preliminary inquiry into the merits of a suit in order to determine whether it may be maintained as a class action."[22] Plaintiffs have argued (and a number of courts have agreed) that that language actively prohibited any inquiry into the merits of a class action claim.[23]

One of the places this tactic has been employed most aggressively is in the use of expert testimony. Plaintiffs often use expert testimony to support motions for certification.[24] If the defendants counter with expert testimony of their own,[25] or argue that the plaintiff's expert has not used a reliable or acceptable method to reach his conclusions

---

[21] Richard A. Nagareda, Class Certification in the Age of Aggregate Proof, 84 N.Y.U. L. Rev. 97, 101 (2009) ("the flashpoints today over class certification concern the role of aggregate proof of a statistical or economic nature."). For examples of this tactic, see McReynolds v. Merrill Lynch, Pierce, Fenner & Smith, Inc., 2010 U.S. Dist. LEXIS 80002, *16 (N.D. Ill. Aug. 9, 2010) (plaintiffs offered statistical proof to demonstrate common employment-discrimination issues among African-American financial advisers in discrimination class action); In re Neurontin Mktg. & Sales Practice Litig., 244 F.R.D. 89, 111 (D. Mass. 2009) (plaintiffs offered statistical evidence to show that marketing campaign caused increase in off-label drug prescriptions in pharmaceutical marketing class action); In re Ford Motor Co. Ignition Switch Prods. Liab. Litig., 194 F.R.D. 484, 488 (D. N.J. 2000) (plaintiffs offered statistical proof of tendency for cars to catch fire as evidence of common causation in products liability class action).

[22] Eisen v. Carlisle & Jacquelin, 417 U.S. 156, 177 (1974).

[23] See, most recently, DG v. Devaughn, 594 F.3d 1188, 1197 (10th Cir. 2010) ("Despite Defendants' repeated suggestions otherwise, at the class certification stage Named Plaintiffs do not bear the burden of proving the veracity of their complaint's allegations.").

[24] Nagareda, *supra* note 21, at 102–03.

[25] *Id.*

(often called "invoking *Daubert*"),[26] the plaintiffs will then argue that ruling on the admissibility of the expert's testimony—or, alternatively, choosing between the experts—is a merits inquiry better left to trial.[27] The result of this tactic is that the plaintiffs' expert testimony becomes unassailable at class certification. At its worst, it means that so long as a plaintiff can find an expert, any expert, to testify that classwide evidence exists, she can meet her Rule 23 burden.

Each of these tactics came into play at some point in the *Dukes* litigation. And each had a role in shaping the final opinion by the Supreme Court. In short, the *Dukes* certification debate was less a sweeping statement on due process than it was a high-profile housecleaning.

III. The *Dukes* Certification Debate

Few would question that ending—or at least reducing—sex discrimination where possible is an admirable, even compelling goal. As a result, courts face a strong temptation to bypass some of the procedural hurdles that Rule 23 imposes in order to gain some kind of "rough justice" for victims of discrimination.

In the popular press, the debate over certifying the *Dukes* class was framed almost solely as a women's rights issue. Advocates sought to cast the Court's decision as one on whether women could enforce the right to equal treatment on the job. But there is a very real question as to whether the best means to combat sex discrimination is through class actions. This question is not just a matter of technical interest to lawyers. If a class representative loses at trial, she can doom the hopes of those absent class members with stronger, valid claims. This outcome will not be a problem if she is typical of the class and shares common issues with these class members. But if she is not, she may also doom the hopes of women with stronger—or just different—claims.

---

[26] Daubert v. Merrell Dow Pharm., 509 U.S. 579 (1993), identified the factors a court must consider when deciding whether to admit expert testimony at trial. Among those factors are (1) whether the expert's methodology can be proved wrong (its falsifiability); (2) whether the method has undergone publication and peer review; (3) the method's known or potential rate of error; and (4) whether the method enjoys general acceptance in the relevant expert community. *Id.* at 592–95.

[27] See, e.g., Brown v. Nucor Corp., 576 F.3d 149, 156 (4th Cir. 2009) (probing into basis of statistics plaintiffs offered to support commonality was impermissible merits inquiry).

327

Because the Supreme Court's rulings address the various strategic choices that each party makes along the way to class certification, it is worth rehearsing some of the procedural moves made throughout the *Dukes* litigation. Rehearsing the tactical moves each side made shows (1) the kind of inventive arguments made in high-stakes procedural battles and (2) how the issues were presented by the time they reached the Court.

The *Dukes* trial court opinion showcases a number of typical strategies used by each side in arguing for or against certification.[28] Since I have no special access to the plaintiff or defense attorneys in this case, the account I give is a reconstructed one. It identifies each party's strategy from the arguments they actually advanced. While this may lack the "inside baseball" quality of insider accounts, it has the advantage of a "play at home" version; this is the kind of strategic analysis most lawyers can (and should) employ when they read cases.

The case as certified involved seven plaintiffs, each of whom alleged that members of Wal-Mart's management had discriminated against her:[29]

- *Betty Dukes* is an African-American woman who was promoted to manager but then demoted allegedly after she complained about discrimination at Wal-Mart. She decided against applying for other management positions because she was "discouraged" by the discrimination she experienced; some of those positions were eventually filled by African-American women and a Hispanic woman.

---

[28] A trial court opinion is not a perfect source for determining plaintiffs' or defendants' strategies. Courts, like parties, characterize the facts of a given case to support their holdings. (For an excellent example, see Judge Posner's dissection of an opinion by Judge Patricia Wald in Richard A. Posner, Judges' Writing Styles, 62 U. Chi. L. Rev. 1421, 1436–43 (1995).) Nonetheless, assuming that most judges are conscientious despite their innate biases, one can treat a judicial opinion as an important and usually accurate secondary source for the arguments and strategies each side employs.

[29] Description of individual plaintiffs taken from Dukes v. Wal-Mart Stores, Inc., 474 F.3d 1214, 1246–47 (9th Cir. 2007) (Kleinfeld, J., dissenting). It is interesting that, of the various opinions published in the *Dukes* litigation, the only one to describe the plaintiffs' claims is Judge Kleinfeld's dissent from the original appellate opinion. That fact is hardly surprising. Courts, like individual litigants, tend to pay more attention to the facts that favor their arguments; focusing on the plaintiffs' actual experiences tends to support arguments against certifying a class.

- *Patricia Surgeson* alleged that she was sexually harassed and then replaced by a man who got both a better title and a larger paycheck.
- *Cleo Page* was promoted to manager but alleged that she was denied a further promotion after being told "it's a man's world." The position she sought went to another woman instead. While Page was later promoted to department manager, she had been passed over for other positions in favor of a white male, a Latina, and a white woman. She also claimed that she was paid less than a less experienced white man.
- *Chris Kwapnoski* alleged that her manager made sexist remarks. She also alleged that she had been passed over for various management positions in favor of less qualified men.
- *Deborah Gunter* also claimed that she was passed over in favor of less qualified men, some of whom she had trained. When she complained about the discrimination, she was fired.
- *Karen Williamson* alleged that, while she was qualified for—and actively sought out—management positions, she was never promoted. Meanwhile, she watched men receive promotions that were not posted.
- *Edith Arana* was an African-American woman who alleged that she was passed over for promotion to management because her store manager had said he "did not want women." She was later fired. Wal-Mart claimed she was stealing time, while she claimed it was in retaliation for her discrimination complaints.

Wal-Mart, meanwhile, "is the largest private employer in the world."[30] At the time the class was originally certified, Wal-Mart had more than a million employees across 3,400 stores.[31]

The plaintiffs faced a number of difficulties in employing these individual accounts as reason to certify their proposed class. First, the individual facts of each plaintiffs' case varied significantly. Ms. Dukes, for example, had what was in essence a retaliation claim based on both racial and gender discrimination. Ms. Surgeson had a sexual harassment claim. And Ms. Kwapnoski had a straightforward discrimination-in-promotion claim. Given the sheer number of

---

[30] Dukes v. Wal-Mart Stores, Inc., 222 F.R.D. 137, 141 (N.D. Cal. 2004).
[31] *Id.*

women the plaintiffs sought to represent—who spanned the entire country and years of employment—it was likely these variations would only multiply. If the plaintiffs wanted to maximize their chances of certification, they would have to gloss over these variations and find a common issue that could unite disparate claims.

Second, while the plaintiffs stood the best chance of certification if they argued that there was a pattern and practice of sex discrimination at Wal-Mart,[32] they faced the problem that Wal-Mart had a strong central anti-discrimination policy in place—and in fact had won several diversity awards.[33] So if they tried to argue some kind of generalized practice, Wal-Mart's stated policies would undercut them.

The plaintiffs' solution to these problems was a three-part strategy: (1) they would argue an amorphous version of "commonality," (2) they would seek certification under Rule 23(b)(2) instead of Rule 23(b)(3) (thus avoiding the predominance analysis that might have highlighted the variations among their claims), and (3) they would convince the court to use statistical evidence of widespread discrimination instead of looking at the facts of each individual case.

In defending the case, Wal-Mart argued that plaintiffs' proposed class was "too large" to certify—a phrase that deserves closer examination. As the trial court described its argument:

> [Wal-Mart] emphasizes that the proposed class covers at least 1.5 million women who have been employed over the past five years at roughly 3,400 stores, thus dwarfing other employment discrimination cases that have come before. In its view, these numbers alone make this case impossible.[34]

Wal-Mart argued that the size of the proposed class made the case "historic in nature," and presumably without exact precedent.[35] It seems clear from the court's characterization that Wal-Mart was using size as a proxy for diversity: the larger and more sweeping the class in this case, the more variations in claims the court would have to address.

---

[32] *Id.* at 151.

[33] *Id.* at 154.

[34] *Id.* at 142.

[35] *Id.*

Nonetheless, the emphasis on sheer size was risky. The largest risk was that, by emphasizing size, Wal-Mart was in fact venturing into rhetorical terrain that was much friendlier to plaintiffs. Rule 23 specifically contemplates that a class may be too *small* to certify—that is the whole point of the numerosity requirement in Rule 23(a)(1). However, few (if any) cases hold that a given class is too *large* to certify. In fact, the stated purpose of Rule 23 is to aggregate small claims into large cases. Moreover, courts have traditionally viewed class actions as a way of balancing the scales between the "little guy" (a consumer or victim of discrimination) and a faceless corporation. That view is why advocates of class certification have long invoked David-versus-Goliath imagery.[36]

As it turned out, Wal-Mart's central theme was unfortunately chosen for another reason. When Wal-Mart first chose to emphasize size as a shorthand for diversity, the phrase "too big to fail" had not yet taken on the connotations that it would after the financial crisis of 2008.[37] But by the time the Ninth Circuit decided the case *en banc*, advocates of certification had summarized Wal-Mart's argument as "too big to sue,"[38] echoing the now-disreputable "too big to fail."[39]

It is hard to say exactly how risky the "huge and historic" theme was. It was a clear goad to any trial court. This trial court, for

[36] See Katz v. Blanche Corp., 496 F.2d 747, 772 (3d. Cir. 1974) ("the social desirability of consumer class actions was to insure that a David plaintiff has a Goliath capability against the Goliath propensities of his adversary . . ."); Broussard v. Meineke Discount Muffler Shops, Inc., 155 F.3d 331, 348 (4th Cir. 1998) ("plaintiffs and some *amici* would portray franchisees as helpless Davids to the franchisor's Goliath,"); Arch v. Am. Tobacco Co., Inc., 175 F.R.D. 469, 496 n.28 (E.D. Pa. 1997) ("Plaintiffs claim that [their case] is 'David versus Goliath.'").

[37] See Andrew Ross Sorkin, Too Big to Fail: The Inside Story of How Wall Street and Washington Fought to Save the Financial System–and Themselves (2009).

[38] Ariane de Vogue, Supreme Court Justices Seem Leery of Walmart Plaintiffs, http://abcnews.go.com/m/story?id = 13248119&sid = 77 (Mar. 29, 2011) (quoting Catholic University law professor Suzette Malveaux: "'If you are going to employ so many employees and be a worldwide player, [then] you assume the risk that you might be liable for billions of dollars of back pay. It's a function of the size of the company, it shouldn't immunize them from the law simply because they are big.'").

[39] See Alexandra D. Lahav, The Curse of Bigness and the Optimal Size of Class Actions, 63 Vand. L. Rev. En Banc 117, 118 (2010) ("[A]re some class actions 'too big to fail?' The slogan might mean that the class must be certified because the alternative is that the defendant who has broken the law on a large scale will be more likely to avoid legal responsibility for the full extent of its wrongdoing.").

example, wound up taking the "huge and historic" theme as a challenge, holding that "[i]nsulating our nation's largest employers from allegations that they have engaged in a pattern and practice of gender or racial discrimination—*simply because they are large*—would seriously undermine these imperatives."[40] But "huge" and "historic" also raised red flags to the Supreme Court. And if one believes one will be railroaded by an unsympathetic trial or appeals court, why wouldn't one use the entire briefing process as a long certiorari petition? As it turned out, Justice Antonin Scalia began his opinion by calling the *Dukes* class action the "most expansive" the Supreme Court had ever faced.[41] So it appears Wal-Mart's rhetorical strategy ultimately succeeded.

The trial court heard seven hours of oral argument before certifying a class of "[a]ll women employed at any Wal-Mart domestic retail store at any time since December 26, 1998, who have been or may be subjected to Wal-Mart's challenged pay and management track promotions policies and practices."[42]

The court appeared more concerned with remedying possible discrimination than it did with the manageability of the proposed class. In fact, it went so far as to note that it was issuing its opinion on the 50th anniversary of *Brown v. Board of Education*, an anniversary it claimed "serves as a reminder of the importance of the courts in addressing the denial of equal treatment under the law wherever and by whomever it occurs."[43]

The trial court's analysis of commonality did not consider whether the common issues would advance the litigation. Instead, it called the burden of establishing commonality "permissive and minimal."[44] It specifically said that a plaintiff could demonstrate commonality by

---

[40] Dukes v. Wal-Mart Stores, Inc., 222 F.R.D. 137, 142 (N.D. Cal. 2004) (emphasis added).

[41] Wal-Mart Stores, Inc. v. Dukes, 131 S. Ct. 2541, 2547 (2011).

[42] Dukes, 222 F.R.D. at 142.

[43] *Id.*

[44] *Id.* at 166. This was not a baseless opinion. Many courts had decided that commonality was a minimal standard. See 7A Charles Alan Wright, et al., Federal Practice & Procedure § 1763, at 218 (3d ed. 2005) ("In other [cases], the court simply has stated that 'clearly' or 'certainly' common questions exist, without indicating the basis for that conclusion or shedding any light on the way Rule 23(a)(2) might be applied in other cases.").

showing that class members shared either "legal issues but divergent facts" or "a common core of facts but base their claims for relief on different legal theories."[45]

The trial court identified two "common issues" in *Dukes*: (1) whether women, all other things being equal, were paid less than men in comparable positions and (2) whether women received fewer promotions to management than men, after longer waiting periods.[46]

The court found that the plaintiffs had presented evidence showing that each of these issues was common, including evidence of common compensation and promotion policies, a "strong corporate culture which includes gender stereotyping," and, most importantly, "a common feature of excessive subjectivity which provides a conduit for gender bias that affects all class members in a similar fashion."[47]

The court acknowledged that proving Wal-Mart discriminated against women by granting its store managers too much leeway would be difficult to establish with classwide proof.[48] But it maintained that that leeway—combined with its expert's conclusion that Wal-Mart's corporate culture was vulnerable to sex discrimination and plaintiffs' statistical evidence of disparities in pay and promotion—was enough to create an issue common to the class.[49] In other words, while the court acknowledged that subjective decisionmaking would likely lead to variations in how those decisions were made, it adopted plaintiffs' argument that Wal-Mart's "strong corporate culture" would ensure that those subjective decisions discriminated against women in a common fashion.[50]

The plaintiffs also presented statistical evidence that Wal-Mart's managers discriminated against women. Their expert, statistician Richard Drogin, had concluded that there were significant disparities between men's and women's compensation and promotion rates,

[45] Dukes, 222 F.R.D. at 145 (internal citations omitted).

[46] *Id.* at 141.

[47] *Id.* at 145.

[48] *Id.* at 149–50.

[49] *Id.* at 149–50.

[50] *Id.* at 153 ("Plaintiffs also rely on the expert testimony of Dr. Bielby to support their contention that gender stereotyping is likely to exist at Wal-Mart, and that it persists to the present day.").

disparities that remained consistent across regions, and could only be explained by gender discrimination.[51]

Wal-Mart did not let this argument go unchallenged. It pointed out that if subjective decisionmaking might lead to stereotyping, its admittedly "strong corporate culture" coupled with its anti-discrimination record should pull managers back from the brink. Among other things, Wal-Mart promoted diversity in its company handbooks and training sessions, established explicit diversity goals, incorporated diversity into its performance assessments of management, and imposed penalties for any violations of its policy.[52] It contested the statistical evidence as well, both by highlighting the methodological flaws in the plaintiffs' analysis (having to do with the scope of the statistics) and by providing an alternative expert analysis of its own.[53]

The court admitted that the experts' opinions contained "a built-in degree of conjecture," in particular because plaintiffs' sociological expert could not "definitively state how regularly stereotypes play a meaningful role in employment decisions at Wal-Mart."[54] But faced with a dispute between dueling statisticians and social scientists, it put off deciding whether any of their methods were sound. Instead, it claimed that deciding between the two experts' conflicting accounts would impermissibly decide the merits of the case.[55]

In other words, there was a vigorous dispute over whether the alleged "common issue" the plaintiffs identified was common at all. If the experts' methods were sound, then the plaintiffs could prove their allegations with classwide evidence. But if either's methods were flawed, there would be no common proof of discrimination. That would suggest that, if one wanted to show that the plaintiffs had met their burden of demonstrating commonality, one would have to make the factual finding that they had demonstrated the link between the two. Nonetheless, the trial court refused to explicitly find that final link, claiming that inquiry was best left until trial.[56]

---

[51] *Id.* at 154.

[52] *Id.*

[53] *Id.* at 154–55.

[54] *Id.* at 154.

[55] *Id.* at 155.

[56] *Id.* at 151.

The court certified the class under Rule 23(b)(2). At the trial level, Wal-Mart did not challenge certification of back-pay claims under Rule 23(b)(2).[57] Instead, it argued that the inclusion of punitive damages meant that monetary damages would predominate over any injunctive relief plaintiffs sought.[58] The trial court disagreed, stating that "focusing on the potential size of a punitive damage award would have the perverse effect of making it more difficult to certify a class the more egregious the defendant's conduct or the larger the defendant."[59] This reasoning, of course, assumes that one could not certify a class under Rule 23(b)(3), only under Rule 23(b)(2).

According to the trial court, the proposed class would be manageable at trial because the liability phase of the trial could focus solely on "statistical analysis and evidence of system-wide policies and practices."[60]

The trial court recognized that holding individual hearings to determine back pay was "impractical on its face."[61] Instead, it accepted plaintiffs' proposal to use a statistical formula to determine back pay.[62] The trial court conceded that "a formula approach is certainly not the norm,"[63] but it decided that determining back pay by formula "is a potential option where the employer uses largely subjective criteria for hiring or promotion decisions, objective requirements are minimal, and many more class members qualified for the positions than would have been hired or promoted even absent discrimination."[64] The court also favored the formula approach because it would be "virtually impossible" to determine which class members would actually have been hired or promoted had there been no discrimination.[65] As a result, it decided that there was "little point in going through the exercise of individual hearings."[66]

---

[57] *Id.* at 170.
[58] *Id.*
[59] *Id.* at 171.
[60] *Id.* at 174.
[61] *Id.* at 176.
[62] *Id.*
[63] *Id.*
[64] *Id.*
[65] *Id.*
[66] *Id.* at 176–77.

When working out how to identify potentially victimized class members, the court concluded that it could "safely assume that all employees uniformly desire equal pay for equal work."[67] This assumption is not consistent with the idea that Wal-Mart's policy of "excessive subjectivity" resulted in discrimination. If all employees want equal pay for equal work, and Wal-Mart largely promotes from within, then management should want equal pay for equal work as well. This logic directly contradicted the trial court's *other* finding that Wal-Mart's corporate culture was discriminatory.

The court admitted that its formula-based approach would result in a windfall for those who would have lost promotions to other class members.[68] But it decided that "rough justice" was better than no justice at all.[69] There is no question this was results-oriented reasoning. Rather than look at whether the proposed class met the requirements of Rule 23, it looked at what it considered to be the proper result, and reverse-engineered a holding that would enable that result. Indeed, given its references to *Brown v. Board of Education*, it appears that the trial court was aware that its opinion would be results-oriented.[70]

IV. The Appellate Opinions

Both parties appealed the ruling. Wal-Mart appealed because it believed that *any* certification of plaintiffs' proposed class was error. The plaintiffs appealed because the trial court had limited back pay to those class members still employed at Wal-Mart. The Ninth Circuit would not be a receptive audience for Wal-Mart. It has an established reputation for pushing legal boundaries to achieve results it deems just, even at the risk of reversal by the Supreme Court.[71]

---

[67] *Id.* at 184.

[68] *Id.* at 177.

[69] *Id.*

[70] It is no secret that *Brown v. Board of Education* was a results-oriented opinion. In fact, it has prompted a subgenre of scholarship (familiar to first-year law students everywhere) about when it is appropriate to depart from established legal principles to achieve a result most would consider an unqualified good. See Herbert Wechsler, Towards Neutral Principles of Constitutional Law, 73 Harv. L. Rev. 1, 1–10 (1959).

[71] See Kevin M. Scott, Supreme Court Reversals of the Ninth Circuit, 48 Ariz. L. Rev. 341, (2006) (finding for the Ninth Circuit a reversal rate over the past 21 years of almost three times that of the next-highest federal circuit court).

In 2007, a three-judge panel of the Ninth Circuit affirmed the trial court's certification order in a 2-1 opinion. Like the trial court, it was not overly concerned about commonality.[72] It conceded that plaintiffs' theory of subjective decisionmaking, by itself, could not establish discrimination. But it found that the plaintiffs' evidence of corporate culture provided a "nexus" between the subjective decisionmaking and the evidence of pay and promotion disparities.[73] (It did not explain why that same corporate culture would not transmit Wal-Mart's express anti-discrimination policies.)

The panel explicitly held that merits inquiries were not appropriate at the certification stage, claiming that "it has long been recognized that arguments evaluating the weight of evidence or the merits of a case are improper at the class certification stage."[74] Building on that holding, the panel also held that a *Daubert* inquiry at the class certification stage was premature, and therefore it could "avoid resolving 'the battle of the experts'"[75] by employing "a lower *Daubert* standard ... at this class certification stage of the proceedings."[76] (It justified this departure in part by claiming that it was "well-established" that plaintiffs could use statistics to demonstrate class-wide discrimination.)[77] The Ninth Circuit also considered Wal-Mart's concerns about its right to raise individualized affirmative defenses to be merits-oriented.[78] And it held that neither Title VII nor any subsequent case law required individualized hearings to establish liability in discrimination suits, just that those were the usual methods employed for determining individual liability.[79]

Turning to Rule 23(b)(2), the panel conceded that "Rule 23(b)(2) is not appropriate for all classes" but decided that the trial court retained the discretion to decide *when* Rule 23(b)(2) certification was

---

[72] Dukes v. Wal-Mart Stores, Inc., 474 F.3d 1214, 1225 (9th Cir. 2007) ("The commonality test is qualitative rather than quantitative—one significant issue common to the class may be sufficient to warrant certification.").

[73] *Id.* at 1231.

[74] *Id.* at 1227.

[75] *Id.* at 1229.

[76] *Id.* at 1227 (internal quotation omitted).

[77] *Id.* at 1228.

[78] *Id.* at 1238.

[79] *Id.* at 1238–39.

appropriate.[80] It also held that plaintiffs' intent—rather than the award's size—determined whether monetary relief predominated. And it called the size of the monetary award (potentially billions) "principally a function of Wal-Mart's size."[81]

The Ninth Circuit appeared unconcerned by the fact that much of the class seeking injunctive relief could not in fact benefit from the injunction. Instead, it contented itself with the idea that former-employee class members would benefit from knowing that others would not suffer from discrimination "as they once did."[82] It also affirmed the district court's holding that back pay was equitable in nature and therefore appropriate for Rule 23(b)(2). "[I]t is well-established that backpay is an equitable, make-whole remedy under Title VII that is fully consistent with Rule 23(b)(2), notwithstanding its monetary nature."[83]

The decision was not unanimous. Judge Andrew Kleinfeld dissented. Noting that "[w]hile a class action can have the virtue of assuring equal justice to all class members, it can also have the vice of binding them to something less than justice,"[84] he raised particular problems with the majority's findings on commonality, typicality, and the use of Rule 23(b)(2). He was particularly concerned about the possibility that the class would endanger the rights of women who had actually suffered discrimination in order to benefit women who had not.[85] Noting that each of these protections existed to prevent a court's riding roughshod over a litigant's due process rights, he asked, "Since when were the district courts converted into administrative agencies and empowered to ignore individual justice?"[86]

The En Banc *Opinion*

Wal-Mart appealed the opinion to an *en banc* panel of the Ninth Circuit—which in that sprawling circuit does not comprise the entire court—but it fared no better than it had with the three-judge panel.

---

[80] *Id.* at 1234 (internal quotations omitted).

[81] *Id.* at 1235 (emphasis in original).

[82] *Id.*

[83] *Id.* at 1237.

[84] *Id.* at 1244 (Kleinfeld, J., dissenting).

[85] *Id.* at 1249.

[86] *Id.*

The *en banc* panel admitted that the class was "broad and diverse."[87] It decided, however, that Rule 23(a) requires different analysis from Rule 23(b). "The lesson for future district courts is that, in a given case, the text of Rule 23(a), as compared to Rule 23(b), may require them to determine more or different facts (typically more under Rule 23(b)(3)) to determine whether the plaintiffs have met their Rule 23 burden."[88] Despite its analysis of commonality, the *en banc* panel either would not or could not articulate the specific common issue. Instead, it held "that the large class is united by a complex array of company-wide practices, which Plaintiffs contend discriminate against women."[89]

Like the original Ninth Circuit panel, the *en banc* panel found that the plaintiffs had provided enough evidence of commonality to meet the requirements of Rule 23(a)(2). In particular, it found that they had presented evidence that there was a common pattern of discrimination because there were (1) a uniform management structure, (2) a strong, centralized corporate culture, and (3) gender disparities in every domestic region of the country.[90]

Like the lower courts, the *en banc* panel saw no contradiction between a strong, central corporate culture and a policy of excessive subjectivity in decisionmaking. "Wal-Mart is incorrect, however, that decentralized, subjective decisionmaking cannot *contribute* to a common question of fact regarding the existence of discrimination."[91] And, adopting the original panel's reasoning, it held that Wal-Mart's "corporate culture" created a nexus between the alleged discriminatory conduct and the statistical pattern the plaintiffs had identified.[92] That said, the panel found only that plaintiffs had established that Wal-Mart's culture was "vulnerable" to discrimination, not that discrimination actually existed.[93]

The *en banc* panel did announce that there *must* be a "rigorous analysis" of Rule 23's requirements, one that could delve into the

---

[87] Dukes v. Wal-Mart Stores, Inc., 603 F.3d 571, 598 (9th Cir. 2010) (en banc).

[88] *Id.* at 594.

[89] *Id.* at 598.

[90] *Id.* at 600.

[91] *Id.* at 612 (emphasis in original).

[92] *Id.* (internal citation omitted).

[93] *Id.* at 601.

merits.[94] It also spent a great deal of time correcting the original panel (and the trial court) about whether a court could engage in merits inquiries in order to do so.[95] That said, it tried to carve out an exception by saying that a court could cut short that merits inquiry under certain circumstances like those currently before it "because the statistical disputes typical to Title VII cases often encompass the basic merits inquiry and need not be proved to raise common questions."[96]

More curiously, the *en banc* panel decided that the trial court had not refrained from looking at merits issues.[97] Instead, it claimed that by listening to (and rejecting) Wal-Mart's arguments about Rule 23(a), the "district court actually weighed evidence and made findings sufficient under the standard we have described above."[98]

Rather than confront the question of whether to allow a *Daubert* challenge at certification, the *en banc* panel simply denied one had taken place. Instead, it claimed that Wal-Mart had challenged the "persuasiveness" of—rather than the methodology underlying—the conclusions of Wal-Mart's expert witness.[99] That said, the *en banc* panel did hint that it disagreed with applying a full *Daubert* analysis at the certification stage.[100] Nonetheless, it found that the statistical evidence would have passed *Daubert* muster.[101]

The *en banc* panel also held that, while "Rule 23(b)(2) is not appropriate for all classes," it was appropriate where monetary relief was not the primary relief sought.[102] It based this holding on a sentence

[94] *Id.* at 581.

[95] See *id.* at 581–90. The *en banc* panel argued that the error in the trial court arose from a misreading of its earlier case *Blackie v. Barrack*, 524 F.2d 891 (9th Cir. 1975). Dukes, 603 F.3d at 589.

[96] *Id.* at 594

[97] *Id.*

[98] *Id.*

[99] *Id.* at 602. This account does not match the trial court's, which reported that Wal-Mart attacked the statistical evidence as "substantially flawed." Dukes, 222 F.R.D. at 152.

[100] Dukes, 603 F.3d at 602 n.22 ("We are not convinced by the dissent's argument that *Daubert* has exactly the same application at the class certification stage as it does to expert testimony relevant at trial. However, even assuming it did, the district court here was not in error.") (internal citation omitted).

[101] *Id.* at 604.

[102] *Id.* at 615.

in the notes of the advisory committee on the 1966 amendments to the federal rules of civil procedure that mentioned Rule 23(b)(2) was not available where plaintiffs sought monetary relief "exclusively" or "predominantly," reasoning that to hold otherwise would render the note redundant.[103]

So what standard would the *en banc* panel use for certifying a monetary damages class under Rule 23(b)(2)? "Rule 23(b)(2) certification is not appropriate where monetary relief is 'predominant' over injunctive relief or declaratory relief."[104] The panel was less sure what that meant in practice. It recommended a "case-by-case" analysis of the "objective effect" of the relief plaintiffs sought, in which the court could consider "key procedures that will be used," and whether deciding on the relief would introduce "new and significant legal and factual issues."[105] The *en banc* panel also pointed out that "even ... circuits that are generally restrictive in certifying classes seeking monetary damages under Rule 23(b)(2)" treated back pay as compatible with Rule 23(b)(2) certification.[106]

Finally, addressing Wal-Mart's objections to the fact that certifying the class would mean denying it the right to present individualized defenses at trial, the *en banc* panel called the trial plan "tentative" and noted that there was a "range of possibilities" that would allow a manageable trial consistent with due process.[107]

What possibilities were in that range? The *en banc* panel did not specify. But it did point to *Hilao v. Estate of Marcos*, one of the few class actions in the Ninth Circuit ever to go to trial, as an example of a workable class trial.[108] *Hilao* was a human-rights class action, brought under the Alien Tort Claims Act, that alleged that the late dictator Ferdinand Marcos had illegally tortured a number of Filipino citizens.[109] The class trial was divided into different phases.

[103] *Id.* at 615–16.

[104] *Id.* at 617.

[105] *Id.*

[106] *Id.* at 618.

[107] *Id.* at 625.

[108] Dukes, 603 F.3d at 625 (citing Hilao v. Estate of Marcos, 103 F.3d 767, 772 (9th Cir. 1996)).

[109] The Alien Tort Claims Act, 28 U.S.C. § 1350 (2006), allows foreign nationals to bring tort claims in U.S. courts.

After the parties had tried the issue of liability, the plaintiffs presented the damages sustained by a random sample of the class as representative of the entire class.[110] The trial court assigned a special master to review the testimony of 137 class members.[111] The special master then presented a report to the jury recommending the damages for these class members, which would provide a statistically valid basis for determining damages for the rest of the class.[112] The defendants challenged the procedure, arguing that due process required each claim to be individually tried.[113] The trial court rejected the challenge, holding that "[t]he use of aggregate procedures, with the help of an expert in the field of inferential statistics, for the purpose of determining class compensatory damages is proper."[114] The Ninth Circuit affirmed the holding on appeal.[115]

The *en banc* panel in *Dukes* presumably believed that the trial court could adopt a similar method for resolving class members' claims. It is telling, however, that the panel did not offer any further guidance on how that trial could proceed.

There were two dissents from the *en banc* decision, one by Judge Sandra Ikuta (joined by four other judges) and one by Chief Judge Alex Kozinski. Judge Ikuta, in a long and measured dissent, pointed out a number of factors that would make trying a class action in this case more difficult, including the complexity of Wal-Mart's corporate structure, the varied ways in which the discretion Wal-Mart granted its managers played out in practice, and the different kinds of discrimination claimed by different class members who had submitted affidavits.[116] Judge Kozinski's separate dissent was shorter and more incendiary, concluding that the more than a million class members "have little in common but their sex and this lawsuit."[117]

So, by the time the case had made it through the lower courts, they had effectively ruled that:

[110] Hilao, 103 F.3d at 772.

[111] *Id.* at 782.

[112] *Id.* at 783.

[113] *Id.* at 785.

[114] In re Estate of Marcos Human Rights Litigation, 910 F. Supp. 1460, 1464 (D. Haw. 1995).

[115] Hilao, 103 F.3d at 786.

[116] Dukes, 603 F.3d at 628–52 (Ikuta, J., dissenting).

[117] *Id.* at 652 (Kozinski, C.J., dissenting).

- under the right circumstances, a plaintiff could certify a class for monetary damages under Rule 23(b)(2), even though the text of that subsection only provided for "injunctive" or "declaratory" relief;
- either a full *Daubert* inquiry was not necessary at the certification stage or a challenge to whether an expert's conclusions properly arose from his methods was not itself a *Daubert* challenge;
- the plaintiffs could satisfy Rule 23(a)(2)'s commonality requirement by alleging that managerial discretion resulted in pervasive discrimination; and
- trial by statistics did not violate due process, even if it precluded defenses that due process would require in an individual trial on the same subject.

Against the backdrop of these sweeping holdings, Wal-Mart appealed the case to the Supreme Court.

V. The Supreme Court

The Supreme Court granted certiorari to review two questions: (1) when plaintiffs can seek Rule 23(b)(2) certification for a class that seeks money damages and (2) *sua sponte*, "[w]hether the class certification ordered under Rule 23(b)(2) was consistent with Rule 23(a)."[118] (Rule 23(a) applies to *all* class actions, regardless of the kind of relief the plaintiff seeks.)

The oral argument focused on two issues in particular. A number of justices, including Justice Ruth Bader Ginsburg, expressed concern about certifying a class seeking monetary damages under Rule 23(b)(2).[119] In addition, several justices, including Justices Scalia and Anthony Kennedy, probed at plaintiffs' theory of commonality. Justice Kennedy spotted what he called an "inconsistency" in the plaintiffs' position on commonality; namely, that Wal-Mart's corporate culture could transmit the informal stereotyping plaintiffs alleged,

---

[118] Wal-Mart Stores, Inc. v. Dukes, 131 S. Ct. 795 (Mem).

[119] Tr. of Oral Arg. at 50, Wal-Mart Stores, Inc. v. Dukes, 131 S. Ct. 2541 (2011) (No. 10-277).

but not the anti-discrimination policy that actually existed.[120] Justice Scalia complained that he felt "whipsawed" by that same inconsistency.[121]

As a result, the Court's final decision should have come as no surprise to either party. The court held, 9-0, that Rule 23(b)(2) could not be used to certify a class seeking primarily money damages. It also held, 5-4, that the commonality requirement mandated identifying an issue whose resolution would be common to the entire class. And, in the course of reaching that holding, it also ruled on the extent to which a court could inquire into the merits of a class action at the certification stage, and the degree to which a court could rely on statistics as classwide proof of common issues.

A. The Applicability of Rule 23(b)(2)

The Court unanimously held that plaintiffs could not use Rule 23(b)(2) as an alternative means of certifying a difficult monetary-damages class. It stopped short of declaring that one could *never* certify a claim for monetary relief under Rule 23(b)(2) because the back pay that plaintiffs sought was too individualized to allow for certification under the rule.[122]

While the Court claimed not to address the "broader question" of whether Rule 23(b)(2) extended beyond injunctive and declaratory relief, its holding certainly limits the kinds of relief plaintiffs can seek under the section. A number of plaintiffs (and scholars sympathetic to them) had argued that if *any* form of relief bridged the gap between monetary and injunctive relief, it was back pay under Title VII.[123] (In fact, the *en banc* panel had adopted exactly that reasoning.)[124]

The Court's primary concern was that Rule 23(b)(2) does not allow class members to opt out of the litigation. Because classwide declaratory or injunctive relief is indivisible—that is, it applies to all class

---

[120] *Id.* at 28 ("Number one, you said this is a culture where Arkansas knows, the headquarters knows, everything that's going on. Then in the next breath, you say, well, now these supervisors have too much discretion. It seems to me there's an inconsistency there, and I'm just not sure what the unlawful policy is.").

[121] *Id.* at 29.

[122] Dukes, 131 S. Ct. at 2558–59.

[123] See, e.g., Suzette Malveaux, Class Actions at the Crossroads: An Answer to *Wal-Mart v. Dukes*, 5 Harv. L. & Pol'y Rev. (forthcoming 2011).

[124] Dukes, 603 F.3d at 618.

members equally or not at all—there is no need for an opt-out mechanism.[125] Nor is there any need for notice; in fact, neither Rule 23(b)(1) nor (b)(2) requires the court to provide anything other than "reasonable" notice to the class.[126] As the Court pointed out, Rule 23(b)(2) would not apply to a class seeking individualized injunctive relief.[127] So there would be no reason to use it where class members sought individualized monetary relief, either.[128]

The Court also pointed out that the structure of Rule 23(b) made it clear that Rule 23(b)(3) was the best mechanism for certifying a class for monetary damages.[129] Specifically, the additional protections Rule 23(b)(3) imposed (requiring findings that common issues predominated and that a class action was superior to other methods of resolving the dispute, and requiring class members to receive notice and an opportunity to opt out) served the purpose of protecting the due process rights of class members who did not want to forfeit their individual claims.[130] As the Court put it, they were "missing from (b)(2) not because the Rule considers them unnecessary, but because it considers them unnecessary to a (b)(2) class."[131]

This was not the first time in the term that the Court had expressed a concern that there was a reason for the protections afforded to a class action. It did the same in *Concepcion* (another 5-4 majority opinion authored by Justice Scalia), when it decided that classwide arbitration was not a realistic alternative to individualized arbitration.[132] There, the Court reasoned that because classwide arbitration lacked the protections of a Rule 23 class action, it could violate the due process rights of the absent class members.[133]

Finally, the Court was unconvinced by the plaintiffs' argument that the history of the class action as a civil rights device required a

---

[125] Dukes, 131 S. Ct. at 2557 (citing Nagareda, *supra* note 21, at 132). The majority opinion relied heavily on the work of the late Professor Nagareda.

[126] *Id.* at 2558.

[127] *Id.* at 2557.

[128] *Id.*

[129] *Id.* at 2558.

[130] *Id.* at 2559.

[131] *Id.* at 2558.

[132] AT&T Mobility LLC, v. Concepcion, 131 S. Ct. 1740 (2011).

[133] *Id.* at 1752.

more permissive reading of Rule 23(b)(2) in a Title VII discrimination case.[134] As the Court pointed out, the plaintiffs in those historical desegregation cases sought only injunctive relief, not monetary damages.[135] As a result, there was no compelling reason to extend Rule 23(b)(2) certification to non-injunctive "equitable" relief, even in service of civil rights cases.

B. Commonality

When it granted certiorari, the Court *sua sponte* (without being asked) requested that the parties brief the question of whether the various parts of Rule 23(a) had been fulfilled in certifying the class. (In retrospect, it would appear that the conservative wing of the Court may have been looking at this issue from the time it received the briefs.)

Strictly speaking, it probably was not necessary for the Court to decide whether the plaintiffs had demonstrated commonality. The unanimous decision on the scope of Rule 23(b)(2) was enough to vacate the certification, and it was unlikely that the trial court would have certified the same class under Rule 23(b)(3). But the Court's decision did resolve several other debates that had raged in the lower-court proceedings (and elsewhere): specifically, the question of how much a court may look at the merits of a case and the implicit debate over whether a plaintiff's theory of commonality must be internally consistent. Given the Ninth Circuit's maneuverings during the course of the *Dukes* appeals, the majority may have believed that ruling on commonality would prevent another certification on shaky grounds that might evade higher-court review.

The gist of the opinion is as follows: commonality requires identifying questions that can yield common answers, not just questions that are common to the entire class. (What's the difference? The question "Has Wal-Mart discriminated against women?" is a common question, but it may not yield common answers: Wal-Mart may

---

[134] Dukes, 131 S. Ct. at 2557–58.

[135] *Id.* at 2558. This conclusion stood on firm historical ground. See The Class Action Device in Antisegregation Cases, *supra* note 15, at 578 ("One reason that the class action appears to be an advantageous method of securing relief for the group is that a favorable decree will in its terms apply to all class members.").

have discriminated against some women under some circumstances but not against others under different circumstances.)[136]

Instead, the Court held that any common element "must depend upon a common contention."[137] For example, if the plaintiffs had all shared the same supervisor, they could argue that common evidence of his particular management practices would be common to all of them.[138] (The Court found it far less likely that, in a company as broad and diverse as Wal-Mart, all managers would discriminate against women if left to their own devices.) What was important to the Court was that the common issue be "capable of classwide resolution—which means that determination of its truth or falsity will resolve an issue that is central to the validity of each one of the claims in one stroke."[139]

C. Inquiries into the Merits

While the Court did not treat it as a separate issue, it did squarely address whether a trial court could engage in merits inquiries in deciding class certification. And it did so in strong words:

> Rule 23 does not set forth a mere pleading standard. A party seeking class certification must affirmatively demonstrate his compliance with the Rule—that is, he must be prepared to prove that there are in fact sufficiently numerous parties, common questions of law or fact, etc.[140]

The Court attributed the continued confusion over the propriety of inquiries into the merits to a statement in *Eisen v. Carlisle & Jacquelin*.[141] In *Eisen*, the Court had held that a trial court could not shift the costs of class notice based on its opinion of which side would most likely prevail in the underlying litigation.[142] In *Dukes*,

---

[136] See Gaston v. Exelon Corp., 247 F.R.D. 75, 82 (E.D. Pa. 2007) ("Plaintiffs could simply propose the question 'has employer discriminated against class members' and always meet the commonality requirement. Obviously, something more is necessary.").

[137] Dukes, 131 S. Ct. at 2551.

[138] *Id.*

[139] *Id.*

[140] *Id.*

[141] *Id.* at 2552 n.6 (discussing Eisen v. Carlsle & Jacquelin, 417 U.S. 156 (1974)).

[142] 417 U.S. at 177.

the Court dismissed any further applications of that narrow holding as "the purest dictum."[143] In other words, the Court definitively settled the question of whether a court may inquire into the merits of a claim in deciding certification—if doing so will help it determine whether the plaintiffs have met their Rule 23 burdens, then it not only *can* inquire into the merits, it *must* do so.

The majority did not decide the question of when expert testimony could support a certification decision. But it did hint—in strong terms—that expert testimony supporting a motion to certify a class should pass the *Daubert* requirements.[144]

D. Trial by Formula

Finally, Justice Scalia's opinion addressed the various courts' reliance on statistical methods to avoid potential manageability and due process concerns. Justice Scalia referred to this tactic as "Trial by Formula." As he described the tactic:

> A sample set of the class members would be selected, as to whom liability for sex discrimination and the back[ ]pay owing as a result would be determined in depositions supervised by a master. The percentage of claims determined to be valid would then be applied to the entire remaining class, and the number of (presumptively) valid claims thus derived would be multiplied by the average back[ ]pay award in the sample set to arrive at the entire class recovery—without further individualized proceedings.[145]

The Court held that "Trial by Formula" would violate the Rules Enabling Act. The Rules Enabling Act—which gave legal force to the Federal Rules of Civil Procedure—forbids interpreting any rule to "abridge, enlarge or modify any substantive right."[146] Since the proposed trial by formula would not allow Wal-Mart to assert valid defenses, it was (at best) modifying its substantive due process rights.[147]

---

[143] Dukes, 131 S. Ct. at 2552 n.6.

[144] *Id.* at 2553–54 ("The District Court concluded that *Daubert* did not apply to expert testimony at the certification stage of class-action proceedings. We doubt that this is so.") (citations omitted).

[145] *Id.* at 2561.

[146] *Id.* (citing 28 U.S.C. § 2072 (b) (1934)).

[147] *Id.*

E. *Justice Ginsburg's Dissent*

Justice Ginsburg's dissent (which was joined by Justices Stephen Breyer, Sonia Sotomayor, and Elena Kagan)[148] focused solely on the issue of commonality. It expressed concern that "the Court imports into the Rule 23(a) determination concerns properly addressed in a Rule 23(b)(3) assessment."[149] According to the dissent, a common question need only be a "dispute, either of fact or of law, the resolution of which will advance the determination of the class members' claims."[150] While the standard sounds similar to the one announced by the majority, the dissent believed that this standard was not demanding and could be met by a "global" issue that had some loose connection to the plaintiff's case.[151]

In this case, Justice Ginsburg believed that plaintiffs had met this less demanding standard. According to her, "Wal-Mart's supervisors do not make their discretionary decisions in a vacuum."[152] She was more convinced that the plaintiffs' evidence (including anecdotes from class members) "suggests that gender bias suffused Wal-Mart's company culture."[153]

Like the lower courts before her, Justice Ginsburg's dissent assumes the existence of pervasive sex discrimination, and then tries to reverse-engineer the mechanism that would explain that bias as the result of discrimination. If there are (1) discrepancies in pay and promotion at Wal-Mart, (2) a strong corporate culture, and (3) anecdotal evidence of bias among some supervisors, then there

---

[148] A number of commentators have argued that the fact that all three female justices were in the minority in this case may indicate that the majority is biased against women. It is hard to say whether this is the case, although Judge Ikuta's dissent from the *en banc* panel plainly shows that not all women share the same view of the case. On the one hand, as those judges candid enough to write about judging have noted, no one can escape his own prior experiences. Richard A. Posner, How Judges Think 68–69 (2008). On the other, the same minority dissented in *Concepcion*, joining an opinion by Justice Breyer. 131 S. Ct. at 1756 (Breyer, J., dissenting). Under these circumstances, it is just as likely that these justices share a common set of beliefs about how class actions should be tried.

[149] Dukes, 131 S. Ct. at 2562 (Ginsburg, J., dissenting).

[150] *Id.*

[151] *Id.* at 2565.

[152] *Id.* at 2563.

[153] *Id.*

must be (4) a strong corporate culture that encourages sex discrimination. In fact, the dissent was noticeably deferential to the trial court's findings. It made no attempt to resolve the tension identified between "excessive subjectivity" and "strong corporate culture," most specifically why the "strong corporate culture" could not in fact have transmitted Wal-Mart's express policies *against* sex discrimination. It also did not address, let alone resolve, the *Daubert* issue.

By itself, Justice Ginsburg's dissent is not likely to have a large effect on class action practice going forward. If anything, it solidifies the reading that the majority's commonality analysis has real teeth, as opposed to being a minimal, easily met standard.

It is worth noting that not a single opinion in the *Dukes* litigation (save one section in the Supreme Court's opinion) was unanimous. Instead, at each stage, the issues were hotly contested even by the judges. At each stage, the contested issues relied largely on judges' preconceptions about the case, and on their inclinations to either promote or restrain the use of class actions in litigation generally. What these differences of judicial opinion mean in the long term is that the class action is far from dead. Instead, the debates over when class actions are appropriate and how they should be conducted will shift to other venues.

VI. The New Strategic Landscape

There is no question that, like *Amchem* before it, *Dukes* has changed some of the rules for class action attorneys. In particular, it has made it far more difficult to enjoy the benefit of certain tactics that had been in common use. But because lower courts rely on a mix of precedent, and have their own agendas, the *Dukes* opinion will not eliminate those tactics completely. So what will the strategic landscape look like over the next decade? While it is difficult to out-invent a group as collectively creative as class action lawyers, we can at least identify some of the immediate effects of the *Dukes* opinion.

Fewer hybrid classes. Now that the Court has rejected certifying class actions that seek individualized monetary damages under Rule 23(b)(2), plaintiffs should find hybrid classes significantly more difficult to certify. This difficulty is compounded by the Court's ruling limiting the kind of case in which a plaintiff could seek Rule 23(b)(2) certification by explicitly stating that Rule 23(b)(2) is not available for all "equitable" relief.[154]

Dukes does not eliminate the hybrid class action completely. For those cases asserting some claims that are independently entitled to certification under different subsections, hybrid certification is still possible. However, this discussion effectively kills the tactic of asking courts to certify a money-oriented class under Rule 23(b)(2) rather than Rule 23(b)(3) and then fix the procedural deficiencies of the former by other means, such an order requiring separate notice.

More rigorous merits inquiries. For years, plaintiffs have invoked *Eisen* to dodge merits examination at the certification stage. Over the last decade, most appellate courts had chipped away at the mistaken reading that *Eisen* prohibited *any* merits inquiry during certification.[155] The *Dukes* ruling lays that mistaken reading to final rest.

But greater rigor in certification decisions is not necessarily an unqualified victory for defendants. One additional consequence is that it may become more difficult to prevail in certain early challenges to class actions that are flawed on their face. In the last few years, an increasing number of defendants have begun filing facial challenges to class actions, such as motions to strike class allegations.[156] The attraction is clear: if a defendant can rid itself of facially defective class allegations at the beginning of a case, it will not have to engage in the costly discovery that comes with a class certification battle.

A number of courts, however, have refused to hear such motions to strike on the ground that they are "premature."[157] These courts

[154] Dukes, 131 S. Ct. at 2560.

[155] See, e.g., Szabo v. Bridgeport Machs., Inc., 249 F.3d 672, 677 (7th Cir. 2001); Gariety v. Grant Thornton LLP, 368 F.3d 356, 365–66 (4th Cir. 2004); In re Hydrogen Peroxide Antitrust Litigation, 552 F.3d 305, 316–17 (3d Cir. 2008). Nonetheless, as late as 2009, the Tenth Circuit was still holding that a trial court should accept a plaintiff's allegations as true at the certification stage. DG v. Devaughn, 594 F.3d 1188, 1197 (10th Cir. 2010).

[156] See, e.g., Bradley v. Mason, 2011 U.S. Dist. LEXIS 64877, *10 (N.D. Ohio Jun. 20, 2011); Adamson v. United States, 2011 U.S. Dist. LEXIS 62243, *5 *(D. Nev. Jun. 10, 2011). Motions to strike are often heard under the same standard as a motion to dismiss.

[157] See, e.g., Martin v. Ford Motor Co., 765 F. Supp. 2d 673, 680 (E.D. Pa. 2011); 2011 U.S. Dist. LEXIS 67718, *34 (D.N.J. Jun. 20, 2011).

have largely based their decisions on the plaintiffs' need to conduct discovery before testing the merits of their proposed class action.[158] To the extent that *Dukes* may be read as placing greater emphasis on the merits inquiries in a "rigorous analysis," these courts have additional reasons to deny motions to strike without reaching their merits.

Another consequence may be more demanding requests for discovery from plaintiffs. If plaintiffs cannot fall back on their allegations, or on loosely defined common issues, they will need more facts demonstrating that their common issues can be resolved with classwide proof. This dynamic provides plaintiffs with additional justifications for seeking comprehensive—and expensive—discovery from defendants.[159]

Fiercer battles of the experts. In the course of deciding most class actions, the court must evaluate expert testimony. The Supreme Court declined to decide explicitly whether *Daubert* applies at the class certification stage. It did, however, hint that it would apply *Daubert* standards if necessary. Nonetheless, subsequent courts have already declined to take that hint to heart. For example, since the Court announced the *Dukes* opinion, the Eighth Circuit has already ruled that a trial court need not conduct a full *Daubert* inquiry when deciding whether to certify a class, distinguishing the Supreme Court's strong hint as "dicta."[160]

---

[158] Korman v. The Walking Co., 503 F. Supp. 2d 755, 762–63 (E.D. Pa. 2007) (calling motion to strike "improper" because it challenges merits of class proposal before plaintiff has benefit of discovery).

[159] See Thorogood v. Sears Roebuck & Co., 624 F.3d 842, 849 (7th Cir. 2010) (noting asymmetry in costs between plaintiff and defendant in class actions).

[160] See In re Zurn Pex Plumbing Prods. Liab. Litig., No. 10–2267, 2011 U.S. App. LEXIS 13663, *17 (8th Cir. Jul. 6, 2011) (*Daubert* inquiry "cannot be reconciled with the inherently preliminary nature of pretrial evidentiary and class certification rulings"). The Eighth Circuit did not describe what the "targeted *Daubert* inquiry" it allowed would look like. *Zurn Pex* keeps alive a circuit split over whether a court should rule on the admissibility of expert testimony at the class certification stage. On one side are the Second, Third, and Seventh Circuits, each of which holds that a court should engage in a full inquiry into expert qualifications before deciding class certification. See In re Initial Public Offering Secs. Litig., 471 F.3d 24, 36 (2d Cir. 2006); In re Hydrogen Peroxide Antitrust Litig., 552 F.3d 305, 323 (3d Cir. 2008); Am. Honda Motor Co., Inc. v. Allen, 600 F.3d 813, 819 (7th Cir. 2010). On the other are the Fourth, Eighth, and Ninth Circuits, each of which holds that the expert inquiry can be put off until trial. Brown v. Nucor Corp., 576 F.3d 149, 156 (4th Cir. 2009); Dukes v. Wal-Mart Stores, Inc. 603 F.3d 571, 602 n.22 (9th Cir. 2010). (Since the Supreme Court

The result is that, for now, plaintiffs in these jurisdictions have a strong incentive to hire experts—no matter what their qualifications or methodology—to support motions for class certification. Since certification in many cases ends any real debate of the merits of the case, courts' continued refusal to engage in a full *Daubert* inquiry at certification means that even questionable expert testimony will sometimes be enough to meet Rule 23's requirements.

Less claim-splitting. In individual litigation, claim-splitting is hardly a concern: after all, the plaintiff is the master of her complaint, and if she wants to forgo asserting certain claims because others fit her strategy better, that's her prerogative.

Class actions, though, are different. The named plaintiff seeks to represent hundreds (or, in the case of *Dukes*, hundreds of thousands) of people who will never see the inside of the courtroom and will never talk to a lawyer about legal strategy. If she wins, so do they. But if she loses, so do they, and because they could have litigated those claims in the class action, they will be precluded from bringing a new case based on the same subject matter. So if a named plaintiff strategically decides to drop certain claims that are strong on the merits but likely to interfere with her chances of certification, then she has placed the interests of her burgeoning class action against those of the members who have strong other claims on the merits. (Since it is an open secret among judges that class actions are run not by the named plaintiffs but by their lawyers, it really is a case of the lawyers putting their interests ahead of class members'.[161])

The Court's decision supports the argument (often advanced by defendants) that claim-splitting is bad for absent class members. In rejecting plaintiffs' attempt to certify their class under Rule 23(b)(2) (which would mean that absent class members could not opt out), it worried that if the jury decided back pay were not available to the named plaintiffs, class members with stronger pay or promotion claims would be precluded from raising them in later litigation.[162] That discussion is the strongest statement out of the Supreme Court

did not decide the expert question, that portion of the Ninth Circuit's opinion was not overturned.)

[161] See Culver v. City of Milwaukee, 277 F.3d 908, 913 (7th Cir. 2002) ("Realistically, functionally, practically, [the lawyer] is the class representative, not [the plaintiff].").

[162] Dukes, 131 S. Ct. at 2559.

yet that claim-splitting is a problem worth a court's attention. (Plaintiffs' lawyers seeking certification have tended to argue that claim-splitting is a phantom issue.)[163]

More challenges to commonality. Defendants have not traditionally challenged commonality because they have viewed those challenges as losing battles.[164] The *Dukes* opinion changes that strategic terrain. The Supreme Court has announced a test for commonality that is both easy to understand and has teeth. As a result, defendants can be expected to challenge commonality in more cases—and are in fact already doing so.[165]

In the longer term, the *Dukes* decision may also prompt class action complaints with better-articulated common issues because plaintiffs now have less to gain from keeping the nature of any common issues vague. To that extent, *Dukes* favors larger, more established plaintiffs' firms, which have the resources to thoroughly research and test a case before filing a complaint.

VII. Conclusion

The Court's decision in *Wal-Mart v. Dukes*, like its other class action rulings in the 2010–11 term, reflects an effort to "reset" class certification strategies. By passing judgment on the propriety of a number of the more strategic innovations in class action practice, the Court has cleared away doctrinal developments that did not necessarily reflect the intent of Rule 23.

In doing so, the Court did not put an end to the class action, or even just the Title VII class action. Instead, it recognized that certain

---

[163] See, e.g., Mays v. Tenn. Valley Auth., 2011 U.S. Dist. LEXIS 50225, *24 (E.D. Tenn. May 10, 2011); Bentley v. Honeywell, 223 F.R.D. 471, 483 (S.D. Ohio 2004).

[164] Anderson & Trask, *supra* note 3, at 154 ("At first blush, commonality appears difficult for a defendant to challenge.").

[165] See United States v. Vulcan Soc'y, Inc., 2011 U.S. Dist. LEXIS 73660, *3 (E.D.N.Y. Jul. 8, 2011) (defendants moved for decertification of class in light of *Dukes* commonality ruling); MacGregor v. Farmers Ins. Exch., 2011 U.S. Dist. LEXIS 80361, *13–14 (D.S.C. Jul. 22, 2011) (refusing to certify collective action because of lack of common issues); Creely v. HCR ManorCare, Inc., 2011 U.S. Dist. LEXIS 77170, *3 (N.D. Ohio Jul. 1, 2011) (defendants requested reconsideration of certification in light of *Dukes*); In re Bisphenol-A Polycarbonate Plastic Prods. Liab. Litig., MDL No. 1967, 2011 U.S. Dist. LEXIS 73375, *19 (W.D. Mo. Jul. 5, 2011) (refusing to certify products-liability class because of lack of common issues).

tactics—such as identifying amorphous common issues and allowing plaintiffs to seek monetary relief while evading the strictures of Rule 23(b)(3)—did not comport with the requirements of due process. Nor did they serve the goals of the federal rules of civil procedure generally, which, as expressed in Rule 1, are supposed to "secure the just, speedy, and inexpensive determination of every action."

Dukes is hardly a revolutionary decision. While it discourages some procedural shortcuts, parties on both sides of class action litigation will still face strong incentives to develop adventuresome new tactics. *Dukes* is an important opinion, but it has not doomed the class action, nor even changed it much. All it has done is make the game of certification a little fiercer.

Looking Ahead: October Term 2011

*Gregory G. Garre and Roman Martinez**

After a fairly low-key 2010 term and the first June in three years with no retirement on the Supreme Court, the signs point to an interesting and potentially momentous year ahead for the Court. Already on tap are a host of important issues, including those involving individual rights, criminal law and procedure, separation of powers, and intellectual property rights. And several potential blockbuster cases, including constitutional challenges to the Patient Protection and Affordable Care Act, have either arrived at the Court in the form of certiorari petitions or will reach the Court in coming months.

This article previews some of the key cases that the Court has already agreed to hear and flags a few of the more interesting cases that could reach the Court this term. Especially in the wake of the Eleventh Circuit's recent decision holding that the Affordable Care Act's individual mandate is unconstitutional, much of the focus on the coming term is likely to center on whether—or when—the Court will step into the healthcare debate. But even putting that proverbial "elephant in the room" to one side, the Justices will have their hands

* Gregory Garre is a partner in the Washington, D.C., office of Latham & Watkins LLP and head of the firm's Supreme Court and Appellate Practice. In 2008–2009, he served as the 44th Solicitor General of the United States. He previously served as Principal Deputy Solicitor General (2005–2008) and Assistant to the Solicitor General (2000–2004). He has argued 30 cases before the Supreme Court and is counsel of record in several cases pending before the Court this term. Roman Martinez is an associate in the Supreme Court and Appellate Practice at Latham & Watkins LLP. In 2009–2010, he served as a law clerk to Chief Justice John G. Roberts Jr. The authors wish to thank Jennifer Halbleib, Michael Drezner, and Thomas Yeh for their contributions to this article.

full with an array of intriguing and challenging cases when they return to the bench on October 3, 2011.

Individual Rights

Broadcast Indecency

Once again, the First Amendment will play a marquee role at the Court. In recent years, the Court has considered the application of the First Amendment to violent video games,[1] depictions of animal cruelty,[2] and incendiary hate speech at military funerals.[3] Next term, the Court adds "the F-word" to the list, taking up the constitutionality of the FCC's so-called "fleeting-expletives" policy in *Federal Communications Commission v. Fox*.[4]

Since 1927, federal law has made it unlawful to utter "indecent" language by means of radio communications.[5] The FCC defines "indecency" as communications that "describe or depict sexual or excretory organs or activities" in terms that are "patently offensive as measured by contemporary community standards for the broadcast medium."[6] The determination of whether a communication is "patently offensive" turns on its explicit or graphic nature; whether the material "dwells on or repeats at length" the description or depiction; and whether it "appears to pander," "is used to titillate," or has been presented for "shock value."[7]

For many years, the FCC did not enforce the indecency restrictions against "fleeting expletives"—the isolated utterance of indecent words. Then along came Bono. His use of the F-word during an acceptance speech at the 2003 Golden Globe Awards prompted the FCC to announce that it would begin enforcing its indecency policies even against fleeting expletives. The FCC later enforced the new

---

[1] Brown v. Entm't Merchs. Ass'n, 131 S. Ct. 2729 (2011).

[2] United States v. Stevens, 130 S. Ct. 1577 (2010).

[3] Snyder v. Phelps, 131 S. Ct. 1207 (2011).

[4] Fed. Comm'cns Comm'n v. Fox, 2011 U.S. LEXIS 4926 (2011) (No. 10-1293).

[5] 18 U.S.C. § 1464 (2006); see Fed. Commc'ns Comm'n v. Pacifica Found., 438 U.S. 726, 735–38 (1978).

[6] Industry Guidance on the Comm'n's Case Law Interpreting 18 U.S.C. § 1464 and Enforcement Policies Regarding Broad. Indecency, 16 F.C.C. Rcd. 7999, 8002 at ¶¶ 7–8 (2001).

[7] *Id.* at 8002 ¶ 10.

interpretation of its policy against various TV networks for the use of the F-word by Cher and Nicole Richie at back-to-back Billboard Music Awards.

The TV networks challenged the FCC's indecency policy, alleging violations of the First Amendment and the Administrative Procedure Act. In 2007, the Second Circuit struck down the policy as arbitrary and capricious under the APA based on the FCC's purported failure to adequately explain its adoption of a fleeting-expletives policy, but the Supreme Court reversed that ruling and remanded for consideration of the networks' First Amendment claim.[8]

On remand, the Second Circuit again invalidated the FCC policy, this time on the ground that the commission's definition of indecency is unconstitutionally vague and thereby promotes self-censorship.[9] Because the court decided the case on vagueness grounds, it did not reach the networks' broad-scale attack on the continuing validity of the Supreme Court's decision in *Federal Communications Commission v. Pacifica Foundation*—the "seven dirty words" case—which had upheld the FCC's prior indecency restrictions under a form of intermediate First Amendment scrutiny.[10]

The government asked the Supreme Court to once again review the Second Circuit's invalidation of the FCC's fleeting-expletives policy, and the Court obliged. The *Fox* case provides an opportunity for the Court not only to resolve the constitutionality of the FCC's fleeting-expletives policy once and for all but also to clarify the nature of the First Amendment inquiry in the broadcast media context. The Court will likely proceed without Justice Sonia Sotomayor, who recused herself from consideration of the certiorari petition. But the case will be "Must See TV" for Court watchers, especially if the Justices choose to revisit *Pacifica*.[11]

---

[8] Fox Television Stations, Inc. v. Fed. Commc'ns Comm'n, 489 F.3d 444 (2d Cir. 2007), rev'd, 129 S. Ct. 1800 (2009).

[9] Fox Television Stations, Inc. v. Fed. Commc'ns Comm'n, 613 F. 3d 317 (2d Cir. 2010).

[10] 438 U.S. at 777.

[11] In a related action, the government also sought review of a separate Second Circuit decision invalidating the FCC's enforcement of its indecency policy against the broadcast of fleeting nudity on the TV series *NYPD Blue*. See ABC, Inc. v. Fed. Commc'ns Comm'n, 2011 WL 9307 (2d Cir. 2011). The Court granted certiorari in that case as well, adding "fleeting nudity" to the issues that will be before the Court alongside *Fox*.

Mandatory Union Fees

The Court will address another recurring First Amendment question in *Knox v. SEIU*—the right of non-unionized state employees to avoid mandatory assessment of union fees for expenditure on political activities.[12] The Court has held that state employees who choose not to join unions that serve as their exclusive collective-bargaining representative can still be forced to pay their fair share of the union's expenses associated with collective bargaining, but cannot be forced to pay for the union's political activities.[13]

The plaintiffs in *Knox* are California state employees who argue that the union forced them to support political activities by garnishing their wages as an "emergency" fee for political purposes—to build a campaign fund for use on advertising, direct mail, voter registration and education, and get-out-the-vote activities—without giving them sufficient notice or opportunity to object. The activities funded by the fee included efforts to defeat a proposition that would have further restricted the use of union dues for political purposes. The union counters that its annual notice was sufficient to pass First Amendment muster. The Court has not been friendly to union claims involving fees for political activities in recent years.[14] Now the Court will decide if a union unconstitutionally compels nonmembers' political speech by coercing the payment of fees in this context.

Ministerial Exception

This fall the Court will also reconsider the scope of the First Amendment-based "ministerial exception," which has been applied by the courts to insulate certain employment decisions made by religious institutions from challenge under labor and anti-discrimination laws. In *Hosanna-Tabor Evangelical Lutheran Church and School v. EEOC*, a fourth-grade teacher at a Lutheran school sought to return to her job after a prolonged medical leave of absence for narcolepsy.[15] When the school did not take her back, she brought suit under the Americans with Disabilities Act. The school invoked the ministerial

---

[12] Knox v. Serv. Employees Int'l Union, Local 1000, 2011 U.S. LEXIS 4827 (2011) (No. 10-1121).

[13] Chicago Teachers Union v. Hudson, 475 U.S. 292 (1986).

[14] See, e.g., Ysursa v. Pocatello Educ. Ass'n, 555 U.S. 353 (2009).

[15] Hosanna-Tabor Evangelical Lutheran Church & Sch. v. EEOC, 131 S. Ct. 1783 (2011) (No. 10-553).

exception to challenge the court's subject-matter jurisdiction. The district court granted summary judgment for the school. But the Sixth Circuit reversed, holding that the exception applies only to ministerial employees—and that the teacher, whose primary duties involved teaching *secular* subjects, did not qualify as such. *Hosanna-Tabor* provides the Court with an opportunity to clarify the contours of the ministerial exception and its intersection with anti-discrimination laws.

Property Rights

The Court will also have an opportunity to expound on the procedural protections that individuals enjoy from the government's encroachment on asserted property rights. In *Sackett v. EPA*, the Court will consider the rights of landowners to challenge mandatory compliance orders issued by the Environmental Protection Agency under the Clean Water Act.[16] As a first step in building a new home, the Sacketts filled a portion of their property with dirt and rock. Six months later, they received a house-warming present from the EPA in the form of an administrative compliance order. The order charged them with violating the Clean Water Act by filling a wetland on their property without a federal permit and directed them to restore the wetland immediately. The Sacketts challenged the EPA's conclusion that their property was a wetland subject to the act. When the EPA refused their request for a hearing, they challenged the compliance order in federal court, asserting a due-process right to pre-enforcement judicial review of the order.

Both the district court and the Ninth Circuit denied their claims, demonstrating little sympathy for the homeowners' predicament.[17] The courts reasoned that, to obtain review, the Sacketts were required either to wait for the EPA to enforce the order against them (and thereby to expose themselves to millions of dollars in potential penalties) or to seek a permit and then appeal any denial of the permit (despite the significant expense and delays associated with the permitting process). The Sacketts sought certiorari, arguing that the government had impermissibly intruded on their property rights without sufficient process. On the last day that the Court sat together

---

[16] Sackett v. EPA, 2011 U.S. LEXIS 5010 (2011) (No. 10-1062).

[17] Sackett v. EPA, 2008 WL 3286801 (D. Idaho), aff'd, 622 F.3d 1139 (9th Cir. 2010).

in June, the Court agreed to hear the case and address a property owner's right to pre-enforcement judicial review of the order under the Administrative Procedure Act and, alternatively, the Due Process Clause.

Federal-State Balance

Preemption

The relationship between federal and state power is familiar and important territory for the Supreme Court, especially in the preemption context. Last term, the Court decided several preemption cases, spanning a wide array of subject areas including immigration, automobiles, arbitration, and pharmaceuticals.[18] Not missing a beat, this term the Court will consider in *National Meat Association v. Harris* whether a California criminal statute mandating the immediate, humane euthanasia of nonambulatory livestock—animals that become unable to stand or walk on their own—is preempted by the Federal Meat Inspection Act.[19]

The regulation of livestock and general animal cruelty laws falls within the traditional purview of the states, but for decades Congress has mandated an inspection process to ensure that meat destined for human consumption is safe and unadulterated. The FMIA contains an express preemption clause barring states from imposing "[r]equirements within the scope of this Act with respect to premises, facilities and operations [of slaughterhouses], which are in addition to, or different than those made under this Act."[20] But the act also has a savings clause stating that it "shall not preclude any State . . . from making requirement[s] or taking other action, consistent with this Act, with respect to any other matters regulated under this Act."[21] The California law at issue prohibits anyone from buying,

---

[18] PLIVA, Inc. v. Mensing, 131 S. Ct. 2567 (2011) (pharmaceuticals); Bruesewitz v. Wyeth, 131 S. Ct. 1068 (2011) (vaccines); Chamber of Commerce of the United States v. Whiting, 131 S. Ct. 1968 (2011) (immigration); AT&T Mobility L.L.C. v. Concepcion, 131 S. Ct. 1740 (2011) (arbitration); Williamson v. Mazda Motor of America, Inc., 131 S. Ct. 1131 (2011) (automobiles).

[19] Nat'l Meat Ass'n v. Harris, 2011 U.S. LEXIS 4961 (2011) (No. 10-224). Latham & Watkins LLP represents several of the respondents in this case.

[20] 21 U.S.C. § 678 (2006).

[21] *Id.*

selling, or receiving nonambulatory animals and requires slaughter-houses to immediately euthanize such animals.

A national organization representing the meatpacking industry sued for an injunction to block enforcement of the California law, claiming it was preempted by the FMIA. The district court agreed that the provisions at issue were preempted and granted the injunction.[22] The Ninth Circuit reversed.[23] The Court granted certiorari over the solicitor general's opposition and will once again venture into the preemption thicket.

Sovereign Immunity

Next term, the Court will also revisit the scope of states' sovereign immunity from suit. In *Coleman v. Maryland Court of Appeals*, the Court will decide whether Congress validly abrogated state sovereign immunity in the self-care provision of the Family and Medical Leave Act.[24] Daniel Coleman alleges that he was fired from his job at a state court after taking sick leave for a documented medical condition. He sued under the FMLA, which has several provisions guaranteeing medical leave for an employee who is sick or has an ill relative. The district court dismissed his claim based on Maryland's sovereign immunity from suit,[25] and the Fourth Circuit affirmed.[26] The Supreme Court granted certiorari.

To subject a nonconsenting state to suit, Congress must abrogate state sovereign immunity through a clear legislative statement and pursuant to a valid exercise of its power. In the landmark case of *Seminole Tribe v. Florida*, the Court held that Congress could not use its Commerce Clause authority to abrogate such immunity.[27] In *Nevada Department of Human Resources v. Hibbs*, however, the Court held that the FMLA's *family-care* provision guaranteeing leave to take care of an ill family member was a valid exercise of Congress's authority to enforce the Fourteenth Amendment—there, to address state-fostered stereotypes found by Congress that caring for family

---

[22] National Meat Ass'n v. Brown, 2009 WL 426213 (E.D. Cal. 2009).

[23] National Meat Ass'n v. Brown, 599 F.3d 1093 (9th Cir. 2010).

[24] Coleman v. Md. Court of Appeals, 2011 U.S. LEXIS 4972 (2011) (No. 10-1016).

[25] Coleman v. Md. Court of Appeals, No. 1:08-cv-02464-BEL (D. Md. 2009).

[26] Coleman v. Md. Court of Appeals, 626 F.3d 187 (4th Cir. 2010).

[27] 517 U.S. 44 (1996).

members is "women's work."[28] The Court will now decide whether the FMLA's *self-care* provision is sustainable under the same line of analysis.

Arbitration

In recent years, the Court has shown great interest in the law of arbitration.[29] It appears that 2011 will be no different. In *CompuCredit Corp. v. Greenwood*, the Court will consider the relationship between a contract provision mandating arbitration and the private "right to sue" established in the Credit Repair Organizations Act.[30]

The CROA requires credit-repair organizations—that is, organizations that provide services aimed to "improv[e] any consumer's credit record, credit history, or credit rating"—to inform their customers that they have the "right to sue" the organizations for violating the CROA.[31] The CROA also contains a provision invalidating "[a]ny waiver by any consumer of any protection provided by or any right of the consumer" under the statute.[32]

The plaintiffs in *CompuCredit* are consumers who applied for a subprime credit card marketed by a credit-repair organization, CompuCredit, which they alleged violated the CROA by failing to give them proper notice of the fees. In particular, they argued that the company was liable because it had purportedly buried the fees in fine print while misleadingly highlighting the card's credit limit and lack of deposit.

CompuCredit moved to compel arbitration based on the arbitration clause contained in the parties' contracts. The district court concluded that the CROA's nonwaiver provision voided the arbitration clause, and the Ninth Circuit affirmed.[33] It now falls to the Supreme Court to decide whether a contractual arbitration clause may be given effect in these circumstances.

---

[28] 538 U.S. 721, 731 (2003).

[29] See AT&T Mobility, L.L.C., 131 S. Ct. 1740 (2011); Rent-A-Center, West, Inc. v. Jackson, 130 S. Ct. 2772 (2010); Stolt-Nielsen S.A. v. AnimalFeeds Int'l Corp., 130 S. Ct. 1758 (2010); 14 Penn Plaza L.L.C. v. Pyett, 129 S. Ct. 1456 (2009).

[30] CompuCredit Corp. v. Greenwood, 131 S. Ct. 2874 (2011) (No. 10-948).

[31] 15 U.S.C. § 1679c(a) (2006).

[32] 15 U.S.C. § 1679f(a) (2006).

[33] Greenwood v. CompuCredit Corp., 617 F. Supp. 2d 980 (N.D. Cal. 2009), aff'd, 615 F.3d 1204 (9th Cir. 2010).

Intellectual Property

The Supreme Court has also shown an increasing appetite for intellectual property cases in recent terms, particularly in the area of patents. Since 2005, the number of patent cases that the Court has taken has nearly doubled compared to the previous decade. The 2011 term is shaping up to be another big one in this important area of law.

Subject-Matter Eligibility for Patents

Section 101 of the Patent Act establishes patent eligibility for "any new and useful process, machine, manufacture, or composition of matter, or any new and useful improvement thereof."[34] The Supreme Court has long held that this language does not allow patents for "laws of nature, physical phenomena, and abstract ideas."[35] In *Mayo Laboratories v. Prometheus*, the Court will address whether a medical diagnostic method of calibrating the proper dose of drugs to give a patient is patent-eligible subject matter under Section 101.[36]

Prometheus's patented method claims a test that measures a patient's individual metabolism of a drug. The test is effective against certain chronic gastrointestinal disorders that are treated with drugs that can become toxic if they build up in a patient's body. Because the rate at which the human body metabolizes the drug varies greatly from person to person, doctors have a difficult time determining a standard dose that is both safe and effective. Prometheus's method measures each patient's metabolism of the drug by determining blood metabolite levels, so the doctor knows whether to increase or decrease the drug dosage for that individual patient. Mayo challenged the patent on the grounds that it improperly claimed ownership of a natural phenomenon—the correlation between metabolite levels and the efficacy and toxicity of the dose.

The district court held that Prometheus's patent was ineligible under Section 101.[37] But the Federal Circuit reversed, applying the so-called machine-or-transformation test for patent eligibility.[38] Mayo

---

[34] 35 U.S.C. § 101 (2006).

[35] See, e.g., Diamond v. Chakrabarty, 447 U.S. 303, 309 (1980).

[36] Mayo Collaborative Servs. v. Prometheus Labs., 2011 U.S. LEXIS 4764 (2011) (No. 10-1150). Latham & Watkins LLP represents the respondent in this case.

[37] Prometheus Labs., Inc. v. Mayo Collaborative Servs., 2008 WL 878910 (S.D. Cal. 2008).

[38] Prometheus Labs., Inc. v. Mayo Collaborative Servs., 581 F.3d 1336 (Fed. Cir. 2009).

sought certiorari, but while its petition was pending, the Supreme Court decided *Bilski v. Kappos*.[39] In *Bilski* the Court held that the machine-or-transformation test was not the exclusive test of patentability, but still serves as a "useful and important clue" and "an investigative tool."[40] The Supreme Court then remanded *Prometheus* to the Federal Circuit for reconsideration in light of *Bilski*.

On remand, the Federal Circuit reaffirmed its original conclusion that Prometheus's medical diagnostic method was indeed patentable.[41] It explained that Prometheus's patent involved one application of certain natural phenomena, but did not preempt *all* applications of those phenomena.[42] It also found that the patent satisfied the "transformation" prong of the machine-or-transformation test, insofar as it involved transformations of the human body when the drugs were administered and the blood was tested.[43] Mayo again sought certiorari. And this time the Court agreed to hear the case on the merits.

Prometheus provides the Supreme Court with another opportunity to clarify Section 101's gateway eligibility standard for patentability—this time in the area of biotechnology and medical diagnostic testing, a rapidly growing and critical economic sector.

Copyright Law and Public Domain

A crucial aspect of copyright law is the concept of the "public domain." Works in the public domain are available to all, without payment to the creator of the work. Although copyrights reward authors for the development of creative works, the ultimate goal is to "allow the public access to the products of their genius after the limited period of exclusive control has expired."[44] *Golan v. Holder* presents the question of whether Congress may lawfully remove works from the public domain and whether such a removal infringes

---

[39] Bilski v. Kappos, 130 S. Ct. 3218 (2010).

[40] *Id.* at 3227.

[41] Prometheus Labs., Inc. v. Mayo Collaborative Servs., 628 F.3d 1347 (Fed. Cir. 2010).

[42] *Id.* at 1355.

[43] *Id.* at 1356.

[44] Eldred v. Ashcroft, 537 U.S. 186, 227 (2003) (quoting Sony Corp. of Am. v. Universal City Studios, Inc., 464 U.S. 417, 429 (1984)).

the First Amendment rights of those using the works previously in the public domain.[45]

The Supreme Court addressed a similar issue several years ago in *Eldred v. Ashcroft*.[46] There, the Court held that Congress has the power to extend the duration of copyrights on works about to enter the public domain.[47] But the Court's decision in *Eldred* relied on the fact that the affected works were *"not yet* in the public domain."[48] *Golan* presents a new wrinkle: What happens when Congress seeks to impose copyright protection on works *already* in the public domain?

Golan's roots lie in the United States' 1989 decision to join the Berne Convention for the Protection of Literary and Artistic Works, an international treaty that sets minimum standards of copyright protection and gives authors automatic protection in each member nation. The United States implemented its obligations under the convention in part by passing the Uruguay Round Agreements Act. Section 514 of the URAA grants copyright protection to millions of foreign works that were previously in the public domain.[49] The United States enacted Section 514 in order to strengthen the reciprocal copyright protections extended to American authors and artists by the other countries that are party to the convention.

The *Golan* plaintiffs include a variety of orchestra conductors, educators, and performers who claim that Section 514 curtails their ability to perform, distribute, or sell foreign-authored works that the statute removes from the public domain—and literally stops the orchestra from playing certain songs. They challenged Section 514's constitutionality on the grounds that it violates both the Copyright Clause and First Amendment. The Tenth Circuit rejected both arguments.[50] The Supreme Court, with Justice Elena Kagan recused, granted certiorari.

The case provides the Court with an opportunity to address the novel and important question whether or to what extent the Constitution limits Congress's right to grant new copyright protection to

---

[45] Golan v. Holder, 131 S. Ct. 1600 (2011) (No. 10-545).

[46] See Eldred, 537 U.S. 186.

[47] *Id.* at 199–222.

[48] *Id.* at 213 (emphasis added).

[49] 17 U.S.C. § 104 (2006).

[50] See Golan v. Holder, 609 F.3d 1076 (10th Cir. 2010); Golan v. Holder, 501 F.3d 1179 (2007).

works that have traditionally been part of the public domain. Plaintiffs and amici—including the Cato Institute—have also asked the Court to clarify whether, in the absence of Copyright Clause authority, Congress is authorized to enact Section 514 as a necessary and proper means of executing the treaty power.

Patent Litigation

In the last week of June, the Supreme Court agreed to hear two additional patent cases. In *Kappos v. Hyatt*, the Court will address the rules that govern the introduction of new evidence in a civil action challenging the rejection of a patent by the Board of Patent Appeals and Interferences pursuant to 35 U.S.C. § 145.[51] And in *Caraco Pharmaceuticals v. Novo Nordisk*, the Court will address the circumstances under which generic-drug manufacturers may challenge, under the "counterclaim" provision of the Hatch-Waxman Act, the accuracy of patent descriptions submitted by name-brand manufacturers to the Food and Drug Administration.[52] In both cases, the government sought or recommended review—a request the Court almost always heeds in patent cases. Together, the cases will shape the nature of patent litigation in the federal courts. In addition, *Caraco* will likely have a significant impact on the streamlined generic-drug approval process.

Criminal Law and Procedure

GPS Surveillance

As always, there is no shortage of criminal law and procedure cases on the Court's docket. In *United States v. Jones*, the Court will decide the interesting and important question of whether police use of a GPS tracking device to conduct long-term surveillance constitutes a "search" that is subject to the Fourth Amendment's warrant requirement.[53]

The Court has never addressed the use of GPS technology in police investigations. But in *United States v. Knotts*, the Court held that police officers had conducted a Fourth Amendment "search" when they placed a "beeper" inside a chemical drum purchased by

---

[51] Kappos v. Hyatt, 2011 U.S. LEXIS 4908 (2011) (No. 10-1219).

[52] Caraco Pharm. Labs. Int'l v. Novo Nordisk, 2011 U.S. LEXIS 4901 (2011) (No. 10-844).

[53] United States v. Jones, 2011 U.S. LEXIS 4956 (2011) (No. 10-1259).

a suspect.[54] The beeper emitted radio signals that enabled police to track the drum to the defendant's cabin. Employing the "reasonable expectation of privacy" framework established by Justice John Marshall Harlan II in *United States v. Katz*, the Court concluded that "[a] person traveling in an automobile on public thoroughfares has no reasonable expectation of privacy in his movement from one place to another."[55] Shortly thereafter, however, the Court held that *Knotts* does not allow police to use tracking devices to monitor "property that has been withdrawn from public view."[56]

Jones arose out of a police investigation of Antoine Jones, the owner of a local nightclub, for potential drug violations. The police obtained a warrant allowing them to place a GPS tracking device on Jones's Jeep Grand Cherokee.[57] But while the warrant required the device to be installed within 10 days, the police inexplicably waited until the 11th day to attach it to Jones's vehicle. Then they monitored the Jeep's movements 24/7 for close to a month. The investigation was a success. The police eventually raided Jones's car and various other locations, seizing hundreds of thousands of dollars in cash and wholesale quantities of drugs.[58]

Jones was convicted on drug charges, in part because of the GPS evidence of his movements. But the D.C. Circuit threw out that conviction after concluding that the GPS tracking had violated the Fourth Amendment.[59] The court distinguished *Knotts* on the ground that it applied only to the limited use of electronic signals to track a discrete journey—and not to the sort of longer-term, continuous monitoring to which the police subjected Jones.[60] And the court concluded that Jones had a reasonable expectation of privacy that his particular movements would remain discrete, disconnected, and disaggregated from the others.

The government sought certiorari, claiming that the D.C. Circuit's decision would "stifle the ability of law enforcement agents to follow

---

[54] United States v. Knotts, 460 U.S. 276 (1983).

[55] *Id.* at 281 (relying on Katz v. United States, 389 U.S. 347, 361 (1967) (Harlan, J., concurring)).

[56] United States v. Karo, 468 U.S. 705, 716 (1984).

[57] Petition for Writ of Certiorari at 3, United States v. Jones, No. 10-1259 (Apr. 15, 2011).

[58] *Id.* at 4.

[59] United States v. Maynard, 615 F.3d 544 (D.C. Cir. 2010).

[60] *Id.* at 556–63.

leads at the beginning stages of an investigation, provide no guidance to law enforcement officers about when a warrant is required before placing a GPS device on a vehicle, and call into question the legality of various investigative techniques used to gather public information."[61] The Court granted review and will now decide how the Fourth Amendment applies to GPS tracking.

Jailhouse Strip Searches

In *Florence v. Chosen Board of Freeholders*, the Court will consider whether the Fourth Amendment prevents a jail from adopting a blanket policy of strip-searching individuals arrested and admitted for entry without any particularized suspicion of danger.[62]

The police arrested Albert Florence during a traffic stop based on an erroneous bench warrant for a civil contempt violation. Florence was strip-searched several times before eventually being released. He then filed a civil rights lawsuit under 28 U.S.C. § 1983 charging the local government and officials with violating his Fourth Amendment rights. The district court granted summary judgment for Florence,[63] but the Third Circuit reversed, holding that the Fourth Amendment permitted a blanket policy of strip-searching *all* arrestees.[64]

In *Bell v. Wolfish*, the Supreme Court upheld strip searches of all inmates returning to their cells from loosely supervised "contact" meetings with outside visitors.[65] Explaining that the Fourth Amendment "requires a balancing of the need for the particular search against the invasion of personal rights that the search entails," the Court rejected any blanket requirement of probable cause.[66] Instead, the Court held that the proper inquiry required consideration of four factors: "the scope of the particular intrusion, the manner in which it is conducted, the justification for initiating it, and the place in which it is conducted."[67]

[61] Petition for Writ of Certiorari at 24, United States v. Jones, No. 10-1259 (Apr. 15, 2011).

[62] Florence v. Chosen Bd. of Freeholders, 131 S. Ct. 1816 (2011) (No. 10-945).

[63] Florence v. Bd. of Chosen Freeholders of Burlington, 595 F. Supp. 2d 492, 519 (D. N.J. 2009).

[64] Florence v. Bd. of Chosen Freeholders of Burlington, 621 F.3d 296 (3d Cir. 2010).

[65] Bell v. Wolfish, 441 U.S. 520 (1979).

[66] *Id.* at 559.

[67] *Id.*

In *Florence*, the Court will clarify the application of the Fourth Amendment to strip searches in the jailhouse context in the absence of individualized suspicion.

Miranda *Warnings*

Miranda is a frequent presence at the Court. In *Howes v. Fields*, the Court will consider when police must give an incarcerated inmate a *Miranda* warning in order to interrogate him about a different crime.[68] The general rule is that *Miranda* warnings are necessary when a suspect is in police custody, unable to leave, and subject to coercive pressures that might compel him to speak when otherwise he might remain silent.[69] *Howes* tests whether these conditions are necessarily met when a suspect is isolated from the general prison population for interrogation.

Randall Lee Fields was incarcerated in a Michigan jail on a charge of disorderly conduct. Police then sought to interview him concerning different allegations of sexual misconduct with an underage boy. Fields was taken to a conference room at the jail and interrogated for five to seven hours. The officials in the room informed Fields that he could leave and return to his cell whenever he wished. While Fields reportedly stated multiple times that he did not wish to speak any further, he was never taken back to his cell. Fields eventually confessed, and he was later convicted in Michigan court of two counts of third-degree criminal sexual conduct. His conviction was upheld on appeal.[70]

Fields then filed a federal habeas petition. The district court granted the petition and the Sixth Circuit affirmed, reasoning that the Supreme Court's precedents establish a bright-line rule that a *Miranda* warning is required whenever a prisoner is isolated from the general population and questioned regarding conduct outside of prison.[71]

---

[68] Howes v. Fields, 131 S. Ct. 1047 (2011) (No. 10-680).

[69] See Maryland v. Shatzer, 130 S. Ct. 1213, 1224 (2010).

[70] People v. Fields, No. 249137, 2004 Mich. App. LEXIS 2524 (Mich. Ct. App. Sept. 28, 2004), appeal denied, 698 N.W.2d 394 (Mich. 2005).

[71] Fields v. Howes, 2009 WL 304751, *6 (E.D. Mich. 2009); Fields v. Howes, 617 F.3d 813, 818 (6th Cir. 2010).

The Supreme Court has been closely divided on *Miranda* issues over the past few terms.[72] One different wrinkle here is that *Howes* arises on federal habeas review. It is therefore possible that the Court could decide the case on narrower statutory grounds under the Anti-Terrorism and Effective Death Penalty Act—which would bar habeas relief unless the Michigan court's application of federal law in granting Fields's habeas petition was not merely wrong, but *unreasonable*.[73]

Ineffective Assistance of Counsel

The Court has granted review in several cases involving Sixth Amendment claims of ineffective assistance of counsel, including two raising these claims in the context of plea bargaining (circumstances in which the jurisprudence is relatively undeveloped). In both of these cases, *Missouri v. Frye* and *Lafler v. Cooper*, defendants rejected plea deals and ended up with longer sentences as a result—one following a later guilty plea, the other after a trial.[74]

The Court has applied *Strickland v. Washington*[75] to pretrial errors, but only in cases where the error affected the trial process itself or led to a waiver of the defendant's trial rights altogether. *Frye* and *Cooper* provide an opportunity for the Court to address whether the Sixth Amendment right to counsel applies to the plea-bargaining process. Because the vast majority of criminal cases are resolved by guilty pleas, the Court's decisions here could potentially have significant consequences for criminal defendants.

In a separate case, *Martinez v. Ryan*, the Court will consider whether the Sixth Amendment guarantees a convicted inmate the effective assistance of counsel in a state postconviction proceeding that represents the inmate's first opportunity to seek relief based on the allegedly ineffective assistance of his trial counsel.[76]

---

[72] See, e.g., J.D.B. v. North Carolina, 131 S. Ct. 2394 (2011); Berghuis v. Thompkins, 130 S. Ct. 2250 (2010).

[73] 28 U.S.C. § 2254(d)(1) (2006).

[74] Missouri v. Frye, 131 S. Ct. 856 (2011) (No. 10-444); Lafler v. Cooper, 131 S. Ct. 856 (2011) (No. 10-209).

[75] Strickland v. Washington, 466 U.S. 668 (1984).

[76] Martinez v. Ryan, 2011 U.S. LEXIS 4217 (2011) (No. 10-1001).

Foreign Affairs

In *Zivotofsky v. Clinton*, the Court will address whether the political-question doctrine bars the judiciary from considering whether the State Department is violating a federal statute addressing the status of Jerusalem on federal passports and identity documents.[77]

For decades, U.S. foreign policy has declined to recognize any state as having sovereignty over Jerusalem. The State Department has therefore historically refused requests by U.S. citizens born in Jerusalem to have their place of birth listed as "Israel" on their passports and other official documents. Congress sought to change this policy in 2002, when it passed a bill directing the secretary of state to identify such citizens, at their request, as having been born in "Israel." President Bush signed the bill into law but simultaneously issued a statement announcing that he would construe the statutory provision as "advisory" in light of "the President's constitutional authority to conduct the Nation's foreign affairs and to supervise the unitary executive branch."[78] The State Department subsequently declined to enforce the provision.

Menachem Binyamin Zivotofsky was born in Jerusalem to parents who are U.S. citizens.[79] Zivotofsky's mother requested that the U.S. Embassy list her son's birthplace as "Jerusalem, Israel" on his U.S. passport.[80] The embassy refused; it simply listed Zivotofsky's birthplace as "Jerusalem."[81] Zivotofsky's parents sued, challenging the secretary's violation of the 2002 statute's plain terms.

The district court dismissed the case under the political question doctrine.[82] The D.C. Circuit affirmed, explaining that the doctrine prevents courts from considering "claims that raise issues whose resolution has been committed to the political branches by the text of the Constitution."[83] The court concluded that Article II of the

---

[77] Zivotofsky v. Clinton, 131 S. Ct. 2897 (2011) (No. 10-699).

[78] Zivotofsky v. Sec'y of State, 571 F.3d 1227, 1229 (D.C. Cir. 2009); President George W. Bush, Statement on Signing the Foreign Relations Authorization Act, 38 Weekly Comp. Pres. Doc. 1659 (Sept. 30, 2002).

[79] Zivotofsky, 571 F.3d at 1229

[80] *Id.*

[81] *Id.*

[82] Zivotofsky v. Sec'y of State, 511 F. Supp. 2d 97, 107 (D.D.C. 2007) (citing Baker v. Carr, 369 U.S. 186 (1962)).

[83] Zivotofsky, 571 F.3d at 1230 (citing Baker v. Carr, 369 U.S. at 217.).

Constitution grants the president the authority to recognize foreign governments—and that any decision directing the State Department to list "Israel" on Zivotofsky's documents would conflict with that recognition power.[84]

Zivotofsky provides the Court with an opportunity to address a number of interesting and important separation-of-powers issues, including the scope of the political-question doctrine and the president's power to recognize foreign sovereigns.

Certiorari Pipeline

At this point, nearly half of the Court's docket for the 2011 term remains unfilled and thus unknown. While the Court has already taken a number of interesting cases, much of the focus for the upcoming term is centered on a question that the Court has not yet even agreed to hear—the constitutionality of the Affordable Care Act and its individual mandate provision requiring Americans to purchase qualifying health insurance policies.

A number of cases presenting constitutional challenges to the ACA are currently pending before the federal courts of appeals, and a petition for certiorari has just reached the Court from a divided Sixth Circuit.[85] The odds that the Court will grant certiorari to address the constitutionality of ACA during the 2011 term jumped considerably on August 12, 2011, when a divided panel of the Eleventh Circuit held that the individual mandate exceeded Congress's power under the Commerce Clause.[86] The plaintiffs in that case include 26 states, two private individuals, and the National Federation of Independent Business. The Eleventh Circuit's decision creates a direct circuit split on the constitutionality of the individual mandate. It is now up to the government to decide whether to seek rehearing en banc in the Eleventh Circuit or go directly to the Supreme Court. The Fourth Circuit has yet to issue a decision in an ACA case that was argued in May, while the D.C. Circuit will hear argument in

---

[84] Id. at 1231.

[85] Thomas More Law Ctr. v. Obama, No. 10-2388, 2011 U.S. App. LEXIS 13265 (6th Cir. June 29, 2011); Petition for Writ of Certiorari, Thomas More Law Ctr. v. Obama, No. 11-117 (July 26, 2011), available at http://aca-litigation.wikispaces.com/file/view/Petition + for + cert + %2807.27.11%29.pdf.

[86] Florida v. U.S. Dep't of Health & Human Servs., Nos. 11-11021 & 11-11067, 2011 WL 3519178, (11th Cir. Aug. 12, 2011).

yet another ACA case this coming September.[87] But neither of these cases can undo the conflict that now exists between the Sixth and Eleventh Circuits.

Perhaps the biggest question hanging over the upcoming term as of this writing is whether it will grant certiorari in one of these cases—and when. But, even if the Court grants certiorari in one of the healthcare cases, it is unclear whether the case would be argued and decided during the 2011 term or carried over to the next term. Usually only those cases in which certiorari is granted by early January are argued and decided the same term. But the Court makes exceptions from time to time for especially important or time-sensitive cases. So while it is fair to say that ACA has officially arrived at the Court, it is unclear whether the Court will actually decide its fate this term.

Healthcare is just one of the blockbuster issues that could reach the Court this term. Last April, the Ninth Circuit upheld a preliminary injunction barring Arizona from enforcing components of its initiative to address unauthorized immigration (S.B. 1070).[88] The court concluded that four different provisions of the law—including its requirement that state officials check the immigration status of those being released after any arrest, its prohibition on any effort by illegal immigrants to seek or obtain work, and its authorization of state police to arrest individuals without a warrant when there is probable cause to suspect they have committed an offense that would render them removable from the United States—are preempted by the text and purpose of federal immigration laws. Arizona has recently filed a petition for certiorari seeking review of the Ninth Circuit's decision.[89]

There is also an array of other high-profile issues that could reach the Court this term in some form, including in the areas of affirmative

---

[87] Virginia v. Sebelius, 728 F. Supp. 2d 768 (E.D. Va., 2010), argued, No. 11-1057 (4th Cir. May 10, 2011); Mead v. Holder, 766 F. Supp. 2d 16 (D.D.C. 2011) appeal docketed sub nom., Seven-Sky v. Holder, No. 11-5047 (D.C. Cir. Mar. 17, 2011); see generally, http://www.acalitigationblog.blogspot.com.

[88] See United States v. Arizona, 641 F.3d 339 (9th Cir. 2011).

[89] Petition for Writ of Certiorari, Arizona v. United States, No. 11-____ (Aug. 10, 2011), available at http://sblog.s3.amazonaws.com/wp-content/uploads/2011/08/AZ-petition-on-SB-2070.pdf.

action,[90] Second Amendment rights,[91] campaign finance,[92] gay rights,[93] and the Alien Tort Statute.[94] The Court's decision to grant certiorari in one or more of these cases could have a major impact on the 2011 term.

*   *   *

If history is any guide, the Court will hear argument and issue signed opinions in somewhere between 70 and 80 cases this term. That means that the Court still has much to say about what October Term 2011 will look like. But the 43 cases granted thus far—along with the healthcare cases and others in the certiorari pipeline—have the potential to make it an extremely interesting and perhaps even a blockbuster term. And no matter how the Court fills out its docket, the Justices will have their hands full starting the first Monday in October.

---

[90] See Coal. to Defend Affirmative Action v. Regents of the Univ. of Mich., Nos. 08-1387, 08-1389, 08-1534, 09-1111, 2011 WL 2600665 (6th Cir. July 1, 2011) (affirmative action in public institutions of higher education); Fisher v. Univ. of Tex., 631 F.3d 213 (5th Cir. 2011) (same).

[91] See, e.g., Williams v. Maryland, 10 A.3d 1167 (Md. 2011) (right to carry); Nordyke v. King, No. 07-15763, 2011 WL 1632063 (9th Cir. May 2, 2011) (gun shows on county property); Heller v. District of Columbia, 698 F. Supp. 2d 179 (D.D.C. 2010) (registration requirements) (now pending in D.C. Cir.).

[92] See, e.g., Bluman v. FEC, No. 10-1766, 2011 U.S. Dist. LEXIS 86971 (D.C. Cir. Aug. 8, 2011) (right of foreign nationals to make campaign contributions and expenditures).

[93] See, e.g., Perry v. Schwarzenegger, 704 F. Supp. 2d 921 (N.D. Cal. 2010) (same-sex marriage referendum), question certified, 628 F.3d 1191 (9th Cir. 2011); Gill v. Office of Personnel Management, 699 F. Supp. 2d 374 (D. Mass. 2010) (Defense of Marriage Act) (now pending in 1st Cir.); Massachusetts v. U.S. Dep't of Health & Human Servs., 698 F. Supp. 2d 234 (D. Mass. 2010) (same).

[94] See, e.g., Kiobel v. Royal Dutch Petroleum, 621 F.3d 111 (2d Cir. 2010) (corporate liability under Alien Tort Statute); Doe v. Exxon Mobil Corp., No. 09-7125, 2011 WL 2652384 (D.C. Cir. July 8, 2011) (same).

Contributors

Jonathan H. Adler is professor of law and director of the Center for Business Law & Regulation at the Case Western Reserve University School of Law, where he teaches courses in environmental, administrative, and constitutional law. Adler is the author or editor of four books on environmental policy and over a dozen book chapters. His articles have appeared in publications ranging from the *Harvard Environmental Law Review* and *Supreme Court Economic Review* to the *Wall Street Journal* and the *Washington Post*. He is a contributing editor to *National Review Online* and a regular contributor to the popular legal blog, *The Volokh Conspiracy*. A 2007 study identified Adler as the most cited legal academic in environmental law under age 40, and his *Boston College Law Review* article, "Money or Nothing: The Adverse Environmental Consequences of Uncompensated Law Use Controls," was selected as one of the ten best articles in land use and environmental law in 2008. In 2004, Adler received the Paul M. Bator Award, given annually by the Federalist Society to an academic under 40 for excellence in teaching, scholarship, and commitment to students. In 2007, the Case Western Reserve University Law Alumni Association awarded Adler their annual "Distinguished Teacher Award." Adler serves on the academic advisory board of the *Cato Supreme Court Review*, and the *Environmental Law Reporter* and ELI Press Advisory Board of the Environmental Law Institute. A regular commentator on environmental and legal issues, he has appeared on numerous media programs, ranging from *NewsHour with Jim Lehrer* and NPR's *Talk of the Nation* to the *O'Reilly Factor* and *Entertainment Tonight*. Before joining the faculty at Case Western, Adler clerked for the Honorable David B. Sentelle on the U.S. Court of Appeals for the D.C. Circuit. From 1991 to 2000, Adler worked at the Competitive Enterprise Institute, where he directed CEI's environmental studies program. He holds a B.A. *magna cum laude* from Yale University and a J.D. *summa cum laude* from the George Mason University School of Law.

John C. Eastman is the Henry Salvatori Professor of Law and Community Service at Chapman University School of Law, specializing in constitutional law and legal history. He also served as dean from 2007 until 2010, when he stepped down to pursue a campaign for California attorney general. Eastman is also the founding director of the Center for Constitutional Jurisprudence, a public interest law firm affiliated with the Claremont Institute for the Study of Statesmanship and Political Philosophy. He has a Ph.D. in Government from the Claremont Graduate School and a J.D. from the University of Chicago Law School. Before joining the Chapman law faculty, Eastman served as a law clerk to the Honorable Clarence Thomas, Associate Justice, U.S. Supreme Court, and to the Honorable J. Michael Luttig of the U.S. Court of Appeals for the Fourth Circuit. He also practiced law with Kirkland & Ellis, representing major corporate clients in federal and state courts and with respect to state attorneys general investigations, in complex commercial contract litigation, and in consumer litigation. Eastman has also represented various pro bono clients in matters involving property rights, economic opportunity, and First Amendment freedom of speech, freedom of association, and freedom of religion issues. He has a weekly segment on the nationally syndicated Hugh Hewitt Show and has appeared as an expert legal commentator on numerous television and radio programs, including C-SPAN, Fox News, NPR, WABC in New York, the *Michael Reagan Show*, the *O'Reilly Factor*, and the *NewsHour with Jim Lehrer*. Eastman publishes a periodic column entitled "First Principles" in the Los Angeles and San Francisco *Daily Journals*, and has published numerous op-eds in newspapers, including the *Washington Post* and the *Wall Street Journal*.

Gregory G. Garre is a partner in the Washington, D.C. office of Latham & Watkins and global chair of the firm's Supreme Court and appellate practice group. In 2008-2009, he served as the 44th Solicitor General of the United States. Before his nomination by the president and unanimous confirmation by the Senate, he served as principal deputy solicitor general from 2005 to 2008, and then as acting solicitor general. In addition, he served as an assistant to the solicitor general from 2000 to 2004. Garre has argued 30 cases before the Supreme Court, including cases in each of the past 11 terms and more cases since 2000 than all but three lawyers in private practice.

He has successfully argued numerous high-profile cases before the Court in recent years, including *Ashcroft v. Iqbal*; *Monsanto v. Geerston Seed Farm*; *Christian Legal Society v. Martinez*; and *FCC v. Fox Television Stations, Inc.* Garre has argued and briefed cases involving a wide array of other nationally important matters, including in the areas of administrative law, alien tort statute, antitrust, bankruptcy, business and employment law, contract law, civil rights, education, environmental law, family law, First Amendment, Fifth Amendment, food and drug, intellectual property, international law, labor, media, telecommunications, preemption, separation of powers, torts, and voting rights. In 2009, Garre was named to *Washingtonian Magazine*'s list of top Supreme Court lawyers. In 2006, he was named to *The American Lawyer*'s "Fab 50" list of top litigators under the age of 45 expected to be "leading the field for years to come." Garre has received numerous awards for his public service, including the Attorney General's Medallion for his service as solicitor general and the Navy's Distinguished Public Service Award—the Navy's highest civilian honor—for his successful argument in *Winter v. NRDC*, which secured a major Supreme Court victory for the Navy on its ability to conduct critically important exercises. Garre received his J.D. with high honors from the George Washington University Law School, where he served as editor-in-chief of the law review and was selected to Order of the Coif, and his B.A. degree *cum laude* from Dartmouth College, where he was a Rufus Choate Scholar. Following law school, he served as a law clerk to Chief Justice William H. Rehnquist and to Judge Anthony J. Scirica of the U.S. Court of Appeals for the Third Circuit. Garre is a member of the advisory board of the Georgetown University Law Center Supreme Court Institute and of the Edward Coke Appellate Inn of Court. He has taught constitutional law and Supreme Court practice for many years at the George Washington University Law School, has testified before Congress, and speaks frequently on issues related to the Supreme Court and appellate practice. He has also published articles in the *Wall Street Journal*, *Legal Times/National Law Journal*, and other national publications.

Joel M. Gora is a professor of law at Brooklyn Law School and a nationally known expert in the area of campaign finance law. He has been a member of the faculty since 1978, teaching constitutional law, civil procedure and a number of other related courses. He also served as associate dean for academic affairs from 1993 to 1997 and again from 2002 to 2006. He is the author of a number of books and articles dealing with First Amendment and other constitutional law issues. His most recent book is *Better Parties, Better Government: A Realistic Program for Campaign Finance Reform*, which he co-authored with financial market expert Peter J. Wallison. Gora continues to be active in campaign finance policy issues, including filing briefs in the Supreme Court, advising various organizations, and publishing articles in the news media. An honors graduate of Pomona College and Columbia Law School, he served for two years after law school as the pro se law clerk for the U.S. Court of Appeals for the Second Circuit. After that, he became a full-time lawyer for the ACLU, first as national staff counsel, then as acting legal director and associate legal director. During his ACLU career, he worked on dozens of Supreme Court cases, including many landmark rulings. Chief among them was *Buckley v. Valeo*, the Court's historic 1976 decision on the relationship between campaign finance restrictions and First Amendment rights. He has worked, on behalf of the ACLU, on most of the important campaign finance cases to come before the high court. He also served for more than 25 years on the board of directors of the New York Civil Liberties Union, and as one of its general counsel. He has served on a number of policy committees of the New York City Bar Association, and is on the Board of Directors of the Federal Bar Council and the Board of Academic Advisers of the Center for Competitive Politics.

Tim Keller is the Institute for Justice Arizona Chapter's executive director. He joined IJ as a staff attorney in August 2001 and litigates school choice, economic liberty, and other constitutional cases in state and federal court. Keller currently serves on the board of the Phoenix Lawyers' Chapter of the Federalist Society, and is a volunteer lawyer with the Arizona Center for Disability Law. He received his law degree from Arizona State University, where he was the president of the Arizona State Federalist Society chapter and a member of the National Moot Court team. Before that, he earned his bachelor's degree in economics from Arizona State University, graduating *magna cum laude*. Before law school, Tim worked as a research assistant at the Goldwater Institute. Upon graduation from law school, Mr. Keller clerked for the then-Presiding Judge of the Maricopa County Superior Court, Robert D. Myers. After leaving the Superior Court, he clerked for the Honorable Ann A. Scott Timmer on the Arizona Court of Appeals.

Orin S. Kerr is professor of law at George Washington University Law School. He teaches criminal law, criminal procedure, and computer crime law. His articles have appeared in the *Harvard Law Review, Yale Law Journal, Stanford Law Review, Columbia Law Review, University of Chicago Law Review*, and many other journals. His scholarly articles have been cited by all of the regional U.S. Courts of Appeals and many federal district courts. Before joining the GW faculty in 2001, Kerr was an honors program trial attorney in the Computer Crime and Intellectual Property Section of the Criminal Division at the U.S. Department of Justice, as well as a special assistant U.S. attorney for the Eastern District of Virginia. He is a former law clerk of Justice Anthony M. Kennedy of the U.S. Supreme Court and Judge Leonard I. Garth of the U.S. Court of Appeals for the Third Circuit. In the summers of 2009 and 2010, he served as special counsel for Supreme Court nominations to Senator John Cornyn on the Senate Judiciary Committee. He has also been a visiting professor at the University of Chicago Law School and the University of Pennsylvania Law School. Kerr is co-author of the leading casebook in criminal procedure with Yale Kamisar, Wayne LaFave, Jerold Israel, and Nancy King (now in its 12th edition). He is also co-author of the leading treatise in criminal procedure (with LaFave, Israel, and King) and is the author of a casebook on computer crime law. Kerr is frequently interviewed by major media outlets and his scholarship and advocacy have been profiled in the *New York Times* and NPR. The GW Law Class of 2009 awarded Kerr the Distinguished Faculty Service Award, the Law School's teaching award. In April 2011, he argued a *pro bono* case before the U.S. Supreme Court, *Davis v. United States*. He also recently argued a criminal appeal in the Sixth Circuit and successfully represented Lori Drew in a widely publicized criminal case in Los Angeles. Before law school, he earned undergraduate and graduate degrees in mechanical engineering. Kerr posts regularly at the *Volokh Conspiracy* law blog and is a member of the American Law Institute.

Roman Martinez is an associate in the Washington, D.C., office of Latham & Watkins. He is a member of the firm's Supreme Court and appellate practice group. Before joining Latham, Martinez served as a clerk to Chief Justice John G. Roberts of the U.S. Supreme Court and Judge Brett M. Kavanaugh of the U.S. Court of Appeals for the D.C. Circuit. He earned his J.D. from Yale Law School, his M. Phil. in International Relations from Cambridge University, and his A.B. *summa cum laude* from Harvard College. He also served as advisor on the Iraqi Constitutional Process to the U.S. ambassador to Iraq in 2005, director for Iraq at the National Security Council staff from 2004 to 2005, and advisor on Iraq's postwar political transition at the Coalition Provisional Authority in Baghdad from 2003 to 2004. He received the U.S. Department of Defense Distinguished Public Service Award for his service in Iraq. His work has appeared in the *Washington Post* and the *Wall Street Journal*, among other national publications.

Roger Pilon is the vice president for legal affairs at the Cato Institute. He holds Cato's B. Kenneth Simon Chair in Constitutional Studies and is the founder and director of Cato's Center for Constitutional Studies. Established in 1989 to encourage limited constitutional government at home and abroad, the Center has become an important force in the national debate over constitutional interpretation and judicial philosophy. Pilon's work has appeared in the *Wall Street Journal, New York Times, Washington Post, Los Angeles Times, Legal Times, National Law Journal, Harvard Journal of Law & Public Policy, Notre Dame Law Review, Stanford Law & Policy Review, Texas Review of Law and Politics* and elsewhere. He has appeared, among other places, on ABC's *Nightline*, CBS's *60 Minutes II*, NPR, Fox News, CNN, MSNBC, CNBC. He lectures and debates at universities and law schools across the country and testifies often before Congress. Before joining Cato, Pilon held five senior posts in the Reagan administration, including at State and Justice. He has taught philosophy and law and was a national fellow at Stanford's Hoover Institution. Pilon holds a B.A. from Columbia University, an M.A. and a Ph.D. from the University of Chicago, and a J.D. from the George Washington University School of Law. In 1989, the Bicentennial Commission presented him with the Benjamin Franklin Award for excellence in writing on the U.S. Constitution. In 2001, Columbia University's

School of General Studies awarded him its Alumni Medal of Distinction.

David G. Post is the I. Herman Stern Professor of Law at the Beasley School of Law at Temple University, where he teaches intellectual property law and the law of cyberspace. He is also a fellow at the Center for Democracy and Technology, a fellow of the Institute for Information Law and Policy at New York Law School, an adjunct scholar at the Cato Institute, and a contributor to the *Volokh Conspiracy* law blog. Post is the author of *In Search of Jefferson's Moose: Notes on the State of Cyberspace*, a Jeffersonian view of Internet law and policy. He is also coauthor, with Paul Schiff Berman and Patricia Bellia, of *Cyberlaw: Problems of Policy and Jurisprudence in the Information Age*, as well as numerous scholarly articles on intellectual property, the law of cyberspace, and complexity theory. He has been a regular columnist for the *American Lawyer* and *InformationWeek*, a commentator on the *NewsHour with Jim Lehrer*, Court TV's *Supreme Court Preview*, NPR's *All Things Considered*, BBC's *World*, and recently was featured in the PBS documentary *The Supreme Court*. After receiving a Ph.D. in physical anthropology, he taught in the anthropology department at Columbia University before attending Georgetown University Law Center, from which he graduated *summa cum laude* in 1986. After clerking with then-Judge Ruth Bader Ginsburg on the U.S. Court of Appeals for the D.C. Circuit, he spent six years at the law firm of Wilmer, Cutler & Pickering, after which he clerked again for Justice Ginsburg during her first term at the Supreme Court. He then joined the faculty of the Georgetown University Law Center and later Temple University Law School.

David H. Rittgers is a legal policy analyst at the Cato Institute, where he concentrates on civil liberties, counterterrorism, and criminal justice. Before joining Cato, Rittgers served in the United States Army as an Infantry and Special Forces officer, including three tours in Afghanistan. He has been awarded an Army Commendation Medal with a "V" Device for valorous action and two Bronze Star Medals, and continues to serve as a reserve Judge Advocate. Rittgers has published articles in the *Wall Street Journal*, the *Christian Science Monitor*, *National Review (Online)*, *Findlaw*, and *The First Amendment Law Review*. He has appeared on Fox's *The O'Reilly Factor*, CNN's

Lou Dobbs Tonight, the BBC, and NPR's *Talk of the Nation*. In 2009, Rittgers was selected for the Center for a New American Security's Next Generation National Security Leaders Program. Rittgers earned his J.D. from the University of North Carolina and is a member of the Virginia bar.

Paul E. Salamanca is the Wyatt, Tarrant, and Combs Professor of Law at the University of Kentucky College of Law. He graduated from Dartmouth College in 1983 and Boston College Law School in 1989, where he was a note editor for the *Boston College Law Review*. Salamanca served as a law clerk to then-Judge David H. Souter of the U.S. Court of Appeals for the First Circuit, and later clerked for Justice Souter on the U.S. Supreme Court. He practiced law with Debevoise & Plimpton in New York from 1991 to 1994 and was a visiting assistant professor at Loyola University School of Law in New Orleans before joining the faculty at UK in June 1995. Salamanca writes in the areas of separation of powers, freedom of speech, freedom of religion, and privacy. He has published articles in the *University of Cincinnati Law Review*, the *Missouri Law Review*, the *Georgia Law Review*, and the *Kentucky Law Journal*, among other publications. He has also written numerous briefs and pleadings in the areas of free speech and separation of powers.

Richard A. Samp is chief counsel of the Washington Legal Foundation, a nonprofit public interest law firm located in Washington, D.C. WLF litigates in support of individual rights and the free-enterprise system and against excessive government regulation. Samp has been with WLF since 1989. He practices regularly before the U.S. Supreme Court and other federal courts, with a specialty in health care law. He regularly represents patients seeking to obtain health care without undue interference from the federal government. He successfully argued before the Supreme Court in *Phillips v. Washington Legal Foundation* (1998) in support of Fifth Amendment property rights. Samp is a graduate of Harvard College and the University of Michigan Law School. Before joining WLF, he clerked in Detroit for federal district court judge Robert DeMascio and was a litigator at the Washington, D.C., law firm of Shaw Pittman.

Ilya Shapiro is a senior fellow in constitutional studies at the Cato Institute and editor-in-chief of the *Cato Supreme Court Review*. Before joining Cato, he was a special assistant/advisor to the Multi-National Force in Iraq on rule of law issues and practiced international, political, commercial, and antitrust litigation at Patton Boggs and Cleary Gottlieb. Shapiro has contributed to a variety of academic, popular, and professional publications, including the *Harvard Journal of Law & Public Policy, L.A. Times, Washington Times, Legal Times, Weekly Standard, Roll Call,* and *National Review Online,* and from 2004 to 2007 wrote the "Dispatches from Purple America" column for *TCS Daily.com.* He also regularly provides commentary on a host of legal and political issues for various TV and radio outlets, including CNN, Fox News, ABC, CBS, NBC, Univision, *The Colbert Report,* and American Public Media's *Marketplace.* He lectures regularly on behalf of the Federalist Society and other educational and professional groups, is a member of the board of visitors of the Legal Studies Institute at The Fund for American Studies, was an inaugural Washington Fellow at the National Review Institute, and has been an adjunct professor at the George Washington University Law School. Before entering private practice, Shapiro clerked for Judge E. Grady Jolly of the U.S. Court of Appeals for the Fifth Circuit, while living in Mississippi and traveling around the Deep South. He holds an A.B. from Princeton University, an M.Sc. from the London School of Economics, and a J.D. from the University of Chicago Law School (where he became a Tony Patiño Fellow). Shapiro is a member of the bars of New York, D.C., and the U.S. Supreme Court. He is a native speaker of English and Russian, is fluent in Spanish and French, and is proficient in Italian and Portuguese.

Andrew J. Trask is co-chair of the securities class action litigation group at McGuire Woods LLP. Mr. Trask has participated in the defense of more than 100 class actions, involving all stages of the litigation process. While his work has concentrated on securities, products liability, and consumer fraud cases, Trask has also defended class actions involving telecommunications products, business contracts, ERISA, the U.S. antitrust laws, and environmental claims, among others. In addition to his class action practice, Trask has defended mass tort cases involving financial regulations. He is the co-author, with Brian Anderson of *The Class Action Playbook* (2010), and maintains the Class Action Countermeasures blog, where he discusses the strategic considerations involved in class action defense. He received his B.A. and J.D., both with honors, from the University of Chicago.

William Van Alstyne was appointed Lee Professor of Law at the Marshall-Wythe Law School at the College of William and Mary in 2004. He is a graduate of the University of Southern California and Stanford University Law School. Following his admission to the California bar and brief service as deputy attorney general of California, he joined the Civil Rights Division of the U.S. Department of Justice, handling voting rights cases in the South. After active duty with the U.S. Air Force, he was appointed to the law faculty of the Ohio State University, advancing to full professor in three years. Appointed to the Duke law faculty shortly thereafter, he was named to the William R. & Thomas S. Perkins Chair of Law in 1974. Van Alstyne's professional writings have appeared in the principal law journals in the United States, with frequent republication in foreign journals. They address virtually every major subject in the field of constitutional law. His work has been cited in a large number of judicial opinions, including those of the Supreme Court. *The Journal of Legal Studies* for January 2000, named Van Alstyne in the top 40 most frequently cited U.S. legal scholars of the preceding half-century. Van Alstyne has also taught and given professional papers internationally, in Germany, Austria, Denmark, Chile, the former Soviet Union, China, Japan, Canada, and Australia. He has been a visiting faculty member on the law faculties of the University of Chicago, Stanford, California (Berkeley and UCLA), Pennsylvania, Michigan, and Illinois, a Fulbright Lecturer in Chile, a senior fellow at the Yale Law School, and a faculty fellow at the Hague International Court of Justice. He has appeared as counsel and as amicus curiae in constitutional litigation in the federal courts, including the Supreme Court. He has also appeared in numerous hearings before congressional committees, on legislation affecting the separation of powers, war powers, constitutional amendments, impeachments, legislation affecting civil rights and civil liberties, and nominations to the Supreme Court. In 1987, Van Alstyne was selected in a poll of federal judges, lawyers, and academics by the *New York Law Journal* as one of three academics among "the ten most qualified" persons in the country for appointment to the Supreme Court, a distinction repeated in a similar poll by *The American Lawyer*, in

1991. Van Alstyne is a past national president of the American Association of University Professors, and former member of the National Board of Directors of the ACLU. He was elected into the American Academy of Arts and Sciences in 1994.

ABOUT THE CATO INSTITUTE

The Cato Institute is a public policy research foundation dedicated to the principles of limited government, individual liberty, free markets, and private property. It takes its name from *Cato's Letters,* popular libertarian pamphlets that helped to lay the philosophical foundation for the American Revolution.

Despite the Founders' libertarian values, today virtually no aspect of life is free from government encroachment. A pervasive intolerance for individual rights is shown by government's arbitrary intrusions into private economic transactions and its disregard for civil liberties.

To counter that trend, the Cato Institute undertakes an extensive publications program that addresses the complete spectrum of policy issues. It holds major conferences throughout the year, from which papers are published thrice yearly in the *Cato Journal,* and also publishes the quarterly magazine *Regulation* and the annual *Cato Supreme Court Review.*

The Cato Institute accepts no government funding. It relies instead on contributions from foundations, corporations, and individuals and revenue generated from the sale of publications. The Institute is a nonprofit, tax-exempt educational foundation under Section 501(c)(3) of the Internal Revenue Code.

ABOUT THE CENTER FOR CONSTITUTIONAL STUDIES

Cato's Center for Constitutional Studies and its scholars take their inspiration from the struggle of America's founding generation to secure liberty through limited government and the rule of law. Under the direction of Roger Pilon, the center was established in 1989 to help revive the idea that the Constitution authorizes a government of delegated, enumerated, and thus limited powers, the exercise of which must be further restrained by our rights, both enumerated and unenumerated. Through books, monographs, conferences, forums, op-eds, speeches, congressional testimony, and TV and radio appearances, the center's scholars address a wide range of constitutional and legal issues—from judicial review to federalism, economic liberty, property rights, civil rights, criminal law and procedure, asset forfeiture, tort law, and term limits, to name just a few. The center is especially concerned to encourage the judiciary to be "the bulwark of our liberties," as James Madison put it, neither making nor ignoring the law but interpreting and applying it through the natural rights tradition we inherited from the founding generation.

CATO INSTITUTE
1000 Massachusetts Ave., N.W.
Washington, D.C. 20001